MEXICO BEFORE CORTEZ

Photograph by courtesy of Gordon C. Abbott

FEATHERED SERPENT DECORATION, TEMPLE OF QUETZALCOATL, TEOTIHUACAN

MEXICO BEFORE CORTEZ

AN ACCOUNT OF THE DAILY LIFE, RELIGION, AND RITUAL OF THE AZTECS AND KINDRED PEOPLES

BY

J. ERIC THOMPSON

IN CHARGE OF CENTRAL AND SOUTH AMERICAN ARCHÆOLOGY
FIELD MUSEUM, CHICAGO
CO-AUTHOR WITH THOMAS GANN OF "THE HISTORY OF THE MAYAS"

CHARLES SCRIBNER'S SONS
NEW YORK · LONDON
1933

PREFACE

IN this short account of daily life, religion, and ritual as it existed in Mexico before the Spanish conquest I have tried, as far as possible, to avoid technical terms, lists of tribal designations, and detailed descriptions of archæological work. In this connection the term *Mexican*, as used in this book, should be defined. It is here used to describe the Aztecs, the Texcocans, and other tribes of the Valley of Mexico and adjacent regions who possessed the same general culture with minor local variations. It does not cover Oaxaca, Vera Cruz, Michoacan, and other regions where local culture varied to a greater degree from that of the Aztecs. Less attention is paid to these areas in this book, partly from lack of information from early sources, partly from lack of space.

T. A. Joyce's excellent book *Mexican Archæology* is now out of print, but for the benefit of those who have had the fortune of reading or possessing a copy, I have tried to make this book to a certain extent complementary to his. This has been achieved by outlining in detail certain ethnological customs to which he paid little attention, and, on the other hand, stressing little the archæological aspects fully developed in his book. Naturally, a considerable amount of duplication cannot be avoided, for we have both, perforce, syphoned off much literary wine from casks of the same sixteenth- and seventeenth-century vintages.

Aztec names have a somewhat terrifying aspect, but are actually easy to pronounce. X has a Sh sound; Qu, following Spanish custom, has a K sound; Hu and Gu before a vowel have a W sound; while all vowels are pronounced as in Spanish. For example, Xochicalco (Shochecalco); Quetzalcoatl (Kaytzalcoatl); Huehue-teotl (Waywaytayotl).

I am greatly indebted to Field Museum of Natural History, Chicago, for generous permission to illustrate this book with many pieces from the museum's Mexican collections. Through the courtesy of the trustees of the British Museum and Captain T. A. Joyce, deputy keeper of Ceramics and Ethnography of that museum, I am able to reproduce the mosaic mask shown on Plate X. Doctor Robert Redfield, of the University of Chicago, kindly supplied the print of Xochicalco pyramid, while I owe thanks to the Mexican Ministry of Education for the use of the photograph of the pyramid at Tajin.

Mr. Gordon C. Abbott and Professor Charles J. Chamberlain, both of Chicago, placed at my disposal their wonderful collections of photographs of Teoti-huacan and Mitla. I owe a deep debt of gratitude to both of them for their kind co-operation. Finally, without the tedious tracings from codices made by my wife this book would have been impossible.

J. ERIC THOMPSON.

CONTENTS

LIST OF PLATES

ix

LIST OF PLATES

MEXICO BEFORE CORTEZ

CHAPTER I

A HISTORICAL OUTLINE

Man Did Not Originate in the New World. Early Man Associated with Extinct Fauna. First Immigrants via the Behring Straits. Physical Appearance. Mexico as a Cradle of Civilization. Agricultures and Invention. The "Archaic" Cultures. Teotihuacan Period. The Toltecs. Fresh Immigrants. Aztec Migrations and Early History. Foundation of Mexico City. Independence. Imperial Expansion under Various Rulers. The Autocracy of Montezuma. Coming of Cortez and the Fall of the Aztec Confederation.

LITTLE is known about the earliest man in America, but at least it is certain that man did not originate in the New World. There are no anthropoid apes on this continent from which he could have developed. Furthermore, no primitive types, such as Neanderthal or earlier races, have ever been found on American soil. All human remains so far found in the New World clearly belong to *Homo sapiens*, and in addition can be placed without any serious question in the specialized American-Indian race.

Until a few years ago archæologists were of the opinion that the first immigrants had reached the shores of America some ten or fifteen thousand years ago. It was generally held that these first inhabitants had crossed over into Alaska from Asia via the Behring Straits during and subsequent to the glacial periods.

In the last four or five years important discoveries

3

have been made that may lead to an upward revision of this estimate. The most important of these was made by Mr. M. R. Harrington of the Southwest Museum of Los Angeles. At Gypsum Cave in southern Nevada he has recently discovered remarkable associations of man with supposedly Tertiary fauna. The upper deposits revealed remains of modern Indians, while below were found typical remains of the Pueblo peoples of a thousand years ago and traces of the basket-makers, who preceded them. Below these were thick deposits carrying no human remains. Under these again were two thick bands of sloth dung, and below this the remains of two camp fires, in one of which sloth dung had been used as fuel. Other chambers of the cave revealed bones of the sloth, an extinct species, as well as remains of extinct horses and the American camel, a llama-like animal, but not directly associated with human remains. Nevertheless spear-thrower shafts painted green and red were found far below the sloth-dung levels. With the remains of this extinct fauna, however, were found the bones of mountain sheep and other animals still in existence.

Additional evidence from other localities would seem to confirm the Gypsum Cave finds. At Folsom in New Mexico bison of an extinct species have been found with peculiar points of stone mixed with the bones, and even imbedded in the bones in one case. Few tail bones were found among the forty skeletons, suggesting that the skins were removed with the tails attached after the slaughter of the herd. The soil above the remains is believed to have been deposited near the close of the Pleistocene period. The peculiar grooved well-made points are different from anything else previously reported from America.

Spear-points of the Folsom type have even been found in apparent association with mastodon bones in Illinois, but the most sensational discoveries of this nature were made a few years ago in Ecuador. There a well-preserved mastodon was found in apparently clear association with man. Several fires had been lighted around where he lay, for the soil showed clear marks of having been burned at the edge of where the body lay. Furthermore, some of the mastodon's bones were also partly burned. Close at hand were sherds of polychrome pottery, which the discoverers believed belonged to the slayers of the mastodon. Doctor Max Uhle, the first man to carry out scientific excavations in Peru, was present during part of the excavations, and has expressed his conviction of the correctness of the deductions.

Doctor Duncan Strong of the Bureau of American Ethnology reports folk-lore and legends among the Naskapi Indians of Labrador that seem to be memories of the time when man hunted the mastodon in America.

The evidence indicates either that man has lived longer in the New World than was previously supposed, or that various animals, such as the giant sloth, American camel, and mastodon, which were believed to have become extinct in Tertiary times, actually lingered on in favorable parts of the New World until quite recent times. Perhaps it would be best to accept a compromise between these two possibilities until further evidence is available. On this assumption the arrival of man in the New World should be pushed back to, say, twenty thousand years ago.

Of the physical appearance of these first Americans we have little or no knowledge. Actually all human remains found in the New World belong to the same general American Indian group, although certain skulls from eastern Brazil and other parts of South America represent a primitive proto-American Indian group. The American Indians form part of the Mongoloid race, of which the Chinese are another division. The American Indians are not of Chinese descent, but both races originally came of the same stock, and this is evidence that the American Indian is descended from immigrants who crossed from Asia. We are probably correct in assuming a constant dribble of immigrants passing over the Behring Straits from Asia for many centuries.

In the course of centuries the new arrivals spread over North America, seeped down into Mexico, and even passed into South America, populating the whole continent in the course of centuries. America's first inhabitants were on a low plane of culture, possessing no knowledge of agriculture, weaving, pottery making or metals. Their food they obtained by hunting, collecting wild roots, berries and clams, and by fishing. For hunt-ing they employed the spear-thrower, a very ancient weapon, which still survives in two or three parts of Mexico, but later immigrants probably introduced the bow and arrow. Half-tamed dogs, also of Old World origin, were man's companions and helped him in his hunting.

Clothing consisted of skins in the colder climates, and simple necklaces of shells or seeds were almost certainly worn for adornment. Baskets, too, were in all probability woven from the earliest times, but the polishing of stone axes was due to later immigrants from Asia. Fire was made with a wooden drill of the same type as that used by the Aztecs until the arrival of the Spaniards. (Plate XVI.)

Organized religion was still in the future, but there was probably a well-developed magic competing with animism for supremacy. We can deduce the existence of men who practised as shamans or sorcerers in their spare time, gradually developing a reputation for the cure of sickness by magical methods.

We can be certain that life wasn't so free and easy as that of the caveman is popularly supposed to have been. Family life was probably fairly well developed with descent through the father. Monogamy was probably the rule with occasional communal promiscuity during special ceremonies or moments of tribal crisis. It is to be doubted if ladies were clubbed and dragged off by the dominant male to any greater extent than women are abducted in automobiles at the present time, since communal discipline was possibly stricter then than it is to-day, and all the members of a family would have been held responsible for the crime of one of their number. Nevertheless, life must have been harsh owing to man's precarious domination of nature. In the course of many centuries the scattered groups undoubtedly diverged linguistically. The number of languages would also have been increased by the later immigrants from Asia.

In the course of centuries the descendants of the first groups, who had drifted down to Mexico, increased in numbers to a certain point, but the population could never have become dense under such conditions, since hunting communities require a much greater area for their support than equally numerous agricultural peoples would find necessary.

In Mexico or Guatemala the first discovery of agriculture in North America was made. One might ask as to whether there were any reasons why this should have taken place in this area rather than in any other locality?

A cross-section of central or south Mexico is like the layout of a giant coaster track. One starts on the west coast at sea level, and climbs steeply into the mountains after a short run along the narrow coastal plains. After laboriously climbing to the greatest height, one sweeps down in a short rush into the plateau country of central Mexico. A series of short ups and downs follows for some time until one is nearing the eastern coast. Suddenly the plateau ends, the giant coaster drops from under your feet, your heart jumps into your mouth, and before you know what has happened you are running along on the low level of the Atlantic plains, and the ride is over.

Actually the real journey is much better than a ride in a giant coaster, for you have kaleidoscopic changes of scenery and climate. You start in the hot humid lands of the *tierra caliente*—a wonderful climate for all kinds of tropical produce. You climb up into an area of snow-clad peaks. Then there is a short drop into the plateau country, a land suitable for every kind of subtropical produce. It is cold enough to make you wrap a blanket round yourself in the early morning, but pleasantly warm during practically the whole year. In short, it is the ideal summer resort of that favorite character of fiction—the tired business man. There is another short climb at the edge of the plateau followed by one great swoop down into the climate you started with. The coast is very unpleasant in summer, but an ideal place to bask in during the winter months.

We have no reason to believe that the ancient Mexican of some 10,000 years ago had different tastes in climate from those of our hypothetical business man. He probably enjoyed basking in the heat of the lowlands during winter, and relaxing in the coolness of the plateau country in summer just as much as we do. Probably more so, since his clothing and shelters were inferior to ours.

9

With such ideal conditions within a small area it would not have been strange if central and southern Mexico became overcrowded for hunting peoples, who required a great deal of territory to live in comparative ease. Such was probably the situation in this area between five and ten thousand years ago. The original population had increased until living conditions were becoming uncomfortable despite the richness of the country. The invention of agriculture eased the pressure.

On the plateau country grew a wild grass known to the Aztecs as Teocentli, or "food of the gods." This was an apt name, for from it either by chance, or, more probably, by deliberate effort, maize was produced.

Probably this came about through the germination of seed accidentally spilt out of the baskets of its gatherers, or by faulty winnowing. Once the idea of planting seeds, instead of making long journeys in search of places where the plants grew wild, was taken up, selection of seeds would soon follow. This was the greatest stride ever made by man along the path of progress, for the cultivators were practically freed from the menace of starvation. The danger of overpopulation had practically disappeared, as now a much greater population could be maintained in the same extent of territory. By communal labor in the fields and the need for communal protection of the crops, the individual lost much of his independence and was welded more firmly into the community. This meant the emergence of civic organization.

Finally leisure was born. With the eternal struggle for food in the hand-to-mouth existence of a hunting and seed-gathering community this had been impossible. With the introduction of agriculture it became possible to raise enough food by the labor of a few months to last the whole year, and while some of the group were raising food others were set free for other pursuits. In the train of leisure came numerous inventions. The old tag that necessity is the mother of invention is not strictly true. One invention leads to another, and in a comparatively short time other plants, such as beans and squashes, were domesticated. The art of pottery-making was learned, and out of basket-making developed weaving. The materials for weaving were at first coarse fibres such as those of plants of the agave family, but later cotton was developed in the lowlands.

To this cultural horizon belong the basket-makers of our own Southwest and the cultures that immediately followed. A similar culture doubtlessly existed all through middle America at about the time pottery was being invented. No definite trace of it has been found in this region owing to the damp climate which militates against the survival of such perishable objects as baskets, woodwork or woven materials, whether of cotton or yucca fibres. Nevertheless excavations in the drier climate of northern Mexico have revealed its existence.

From this culture doubtlessly developed the civilizations known in middle America as "Archaic." This is a misnomer, since the cultures were well developed and show every evidence of sophistication. A very long interval must have elapsed between this basket-maker horizon and the earliest division of the "Archaic" so far reported.

Some twenty years ago excavations in the Valley of Mexico revealed, below deposits many feet deep, objects which were of considerably more primitive technique than the Aztec and Teotihuacan-Toltec pieces found in the overlying strata. This early culture was misnamed "Archaic" because of its crudeness in comparison with the objects of the later periods. In some cases deposits of the "Archaic" were buried under lava flows, which effectively sealed them off from the other periods. The discovery of pottery and small pottery figurines of the Teotihuacan-Toltec and Aztec periods above the lava clinched the argument. Such conditions are to be seen at Copilco, a suburb of Mexico City, where, owing to the careful work of Mexican archæologists, visitors may pass through electrically lit tunnels below the lava. There they can see the skeletons of these people lying just as they were buried. This lava flow can not be dated with any certainty, but it would appear to be quite late—perhaps not over 1500 years old.

The "Archaic" actually embraces a number of different cultures that followed each other in succession, some of them widely distributed, others, apparently, confined to small areas. Some of the successive phases show a complete break with the past, representing invasions of new cultures, and possibly culture bearers.

PLATE I.   CARVED STONE "PALMA," VERA CRUZ

Doctor George Vaillant, of the American Museum of Natural History, has during the past three or four years carried out very thorough excavations at two sites in the Valley of Mexico. He suggests five divisions in the pre-Teotihuacan culture in the Valley of Mexico as the result of his work at two sites. Work at other sites, which he is now undertaking, may well cause him to increase this number, since he is still at an early stage of his investigations, and his conclusions are, perforce, tentative.

Even now the earliest recognized stage, which Doctor Vaillant calls Early Zacatenco from the place where he first established its position in the sequence, shows every sign of being a culture already well developed. It is far removed from the basket-maker horizon—the earliest known in the United States outside of the scant finds of the Folsom and Gypsum Cave horizons. Doubtless other finds will reveal cultures earlier than the Early Zacatenco.

A detailed discussion of archæological finds is outside the scope of this book, nevertheless a short description of the Early Zacatenco culture as reconstructed by Doctor Vaillant from his finds is not out of place in giving us an insight into the earliest civilization yet recognized in Mexico.

The Early Zacatencans made good pottery of a variety of shapes. Although most of the vessels were of simple red, black, or white, decoration in more than one color is met with, as well as occasional incised designs. Simple geometric designs in white on red are fairly common, and pleasant shallow white bowls supported on small teat-like feet are also represented with fair frequency.

Small pottery figurines hand-modelled, often with considerable feeling and skill, are found on this horizon. They differ in style from those of later periods. Much may be learned from their examination. Many of them, for instance, wear very complicated turbans. The way these are arranged strongly suggests that they were of cotton, since they appear to show more pliability than maguey fibre possesses. The wearing of earplugs, necklaces, bracelets, and anklets is shown by their occurrence on figurines of this period.

One tiny fragment of textile was found inside a skull. This appears to have been of henequen, but traces of a white substance found around corpses may have been a bark bast or a maguey fibre. The burials were found in shallow graves about four or five feet below the surface; the bodies had been buried in all kinds of positions, but the legs were usually extended.

Tools were made of bone, antler, obsidian, and probably quartz. Obsidian arrow-heads, probably refined by the technique known as pressure flaking, indicate that the bow and arrow were in use, but occasional lance points suggest that spears, probably propelled by spearthrowers, were also used. Obsidian was also used to make knife flakes of the type shown on Plate XI. Spindle-whorls of pottery bear out the evidence for the use of textiles at this time, and pottery whistles show that music had probably advanced almost as far as it had at the time of the conquest, so far as the range of instruments was concerned. Numerous grinding stones of lava indicate the cultivation of maize.

Houses were probably made of adobe, and settlements were located on high ground close to the shores of the lake. Occasional pottery vessels of non-local ware and decoration show that trade existed. Naturally, little can be gathered about the religious beliefs of the Early Zacatencans. The fact that all the pottery figurines are female would suggest that they were used in some fertility rites in connection with the crops, possibly representing a goddess of the earth and vegetation, some kind of a progenitress of the goddesses of the soil, crops, and rain to be described in Chapter V. The lack of any other objects that seem to point to religious observances would suggest that organized religion was not very advanced. Later we shall see that Mexican religion in the fifteenth century was an amalgamation of a simple agricultural cult with concepts derived from sacerdotalism and the imposition of a warrior class.

Such in brief is the culture of the Early Zacatencans. It was succeeded by others, displaying a somewhat higher level of attainment. In the succeeding period trade had developed to a marked extent. Imports included shells from the Pacific Ocean, jade, presumably from the Guerrero-Oaxaca region, and painted pottery, apparently from the east coast regions. Metals were unknown.

The fifth period, called by Doctor Vaillant Late Ticoman, shows many new features not met with in the
earliest period. Stone sculpture occurs and pottery incense burners are used. Pottery vessels and figurines
are more elaborate, and beautifully carved pottery ear-
plugs with their surfaces painted red, appear during
this last period. Pottery seals are also occasionally found,
and cinnabar is in use, either as a paint or as the source
of quicksilver.

Indicative of the advance in organized religion is a
well-made pyramid discovered some years ago at Cuicuilco, near Mexico City. This also had been covered by
the lava flow, only the upper half projecting above the
sea of rock. Excavation of this pyramid below the lava
level revealed only figurines of this Late Ticoman
period, thereby tying it in with this horizon. Furthermore excavation revealed that the pyramid had already
been abandoned and was crumbling away when it was
partly sealed in by the flow, suggesting that the flow is
not of great age.

The presence of a pyramidal structure of considerable
size indicates that the communities were already well
organized with a centralized worship and a well developed system of communal labor. It is, of course,
absurd to label such a culture as archaic, but the word
serves in a book of this nature, where the average reader
would be little interested in the more elaborate nomen-
clature of archæologists.

The next culture to appear in the Valley of Mexico

is the Teotihuacan-Toltec, named from the site of San Juan Teotihuacan where it is particularly richly represented. The early and middle stages of this civilization were contemporaneous with the later phases of the "Archaic," such as the Cuicuilco pyramid, but it did not appear in the Valley of Mexico until after the close of Late Ticoman, although, possibly, it flourished for a long time before its appearance in the valley.

With Teotihuacan-Toltec straight archæology makes its first tentative contacts with the shadowy outlines of early Mexican history, as its name implies. The Teotihuacan represents the archæology, Toltec is a concession to nebulous tradition. The word *Toltec* was used by the Aztecs and other late inhabitants of the plateau land to describe their predecessors, the supposed builders of a high civilization—Mexico's golden age. The word itself means skilled worker, and was applied by the Aztecs to their predecessors because of their legendary skill as workers of turquoise and jade mosaics and decorated featherwork.

The traditional capital of the Toltecs was Tula or Tollan, a ruin in the state of Hidalgo north of the Valley of Mexico. Here are to be found extensive archæological remains of a high order. Unfortunately, practically no excavation has been carried out here, and there is no information as to whether the pottery and artifacts there resemble those of Teotihuacan. The architecture of the two sites is very distinct, but it is possible that this is so because only late buildings are known

17

at Tula. Surface finds there have revealed columns in the shape of feathered serpents and Atlantean figures, the upraised hands of which supported altars or roofs. Nothing comparable has been found at Teotihuacan.

This, by itself, would suggest that there was originally little or no connection between the peoples of Tula and Teotihuacan. History records that the Toltecs spoke a Nahua (Mexican language of the Aztec group), but in contradictory statements it is also claimed that the inhabitants of Teotihuacan were non-Nahua speaking Otomies.

It is possible that the so-called Toltec Empire was a federation of a number of communities of diverse race and speech, such as formed the Aztec confederation at a later date. In that case Tula may have been the civil capital with Teotihuacan as the principal religious centre and cultural head of the Valley of Mexico section of the federation. Teotihuacan culture, as represented by pottery and mold-made figurines, covered practically the whole Federal District with extensions in the directions of Puebla and southern Hidalgo.

Much in Teotihuacan civilization suggests that it was to a considerable extent molded by influences from the south. This is in accordance with tradition, if one accepts Teotihuacan as a part of the Toltec federation. Tradition relates that the Toltecs were responsible for the introduction of the working of metals, mosaics and precious feathers.

There is no doubt that metallurgy spread up from

southern Central America into the Maya-Mexican area. Mosaic working, too, was probably of southern origin, since the jade employed came from the Oaxaca-Guerrero region, while the turquoise, an object of special veneration, was probably first mined in the Vera Cruz region. By precious feathers are usually understood those of the quetzal bird, which is only found in the western Maya country. The names of several of the day signs, also, are those of animals that are found only in the hot lowlands of the south.

Metal working certainly did not reach Mexico before the close of the ninth century of our era. The twelfth century is a more likely date for its introduction. A very fine Maya jade plaque found at Teotihuacan helps a little to date this culture. It was probably manufactured in the eighth or ninth century, and a second Maya trade piece found at Tula is of about the same date, or slightly earlier, to judge by the head-dress. This piece is carved on mother of pearl, and is now in Field Museum. These lines of evidence check in well with the traditional dates of Toltec influence, for its fall is generally placed in the twelfth century, and its rise some four hundred years earlier.

Peculiarly enough no hieroglyphic inscriptions have as yet been reported from Teotihuacan, but there is little doubt that the Toltec horizon possessed the calendar. It is possible that dates were modelled in stucco, which has crumbled away.

Early Spanish historians give lists of Toltec "kings,"

but these are unreliable, the names of the rulers, the length of their reigns and their sequence varying from one account to another.

There is one man who stands out against this background of confusion, although he, too, emerges a shadowy character in floodlights fogged by contradiction. This was Quetzalcoatl, possibly the last Toltec ruler. Quetzalcoatl, which means Quetzal bird-serpent, was also the name of an important Mexican deity (p. 157), whose name was borne by the Toltec high priests, who were in turn temporal rulers.

Great confusion has naturally ensued, for the acts of god and individual are inextricably confused. Finally, it is quite possible that the actions of other Toltec rulers also bearing the name of the feathered serpent god have been transferred to the last ruler.

Quetzalcoatl was supposed to have introduced culture to the pre-Aztec peoples, and he is credited with a great number of inventions, which certainly were not made at the same time. He was said to have been white-skinned and bearded. A bearded white culture bearer figures in the legendary history of many peoples of the New World outside of the Toltecs, and it does not seem unlikely that this concept is of considerable antiquity, antedating by a very long period the rise of the Toltecs. At the same time there is usually a fire to account for the smoke clouds of history.

Toltec civilization was doubtlessly at its height during Quetzalcoatl's rulership. The possible introduction

PLATE II. AZTEC POTTERY FIGURINES, VALLEY OF MEXICO

Top, left to right: God Xipe; model of a temple; God Quetzalcoatl as Eecatl. *Below,* left to right: Goddess Xochiquetzal; Eecatl on a pyramid; Goddess Ciuacouatl with child

of metals and growing imports at about this time may have been an added cause for attributing the prowess of the legendary leader to the actual ruler.

The wide commerce carried on at this time with distant peoples is typified by the account of Quetzalcoatl's residence at Tula. This, legend relates, consisted of four rooms. One was decorated with gold, the second had walls covered with jade and turquoise mosaics, the third was enhanced with motifs worked in sea shells, while the fourth had walls of red sandstone inlaid with shells. Sea shells, one must remember, were highly prized by all primitive inland peoples, and furthermore a conch shell in cross-section was the special symbol of Quetzalcoatl himself. Hence the decoration was very appropriate. Doubtlessly this account has not lost in the telling. It reflects the attitude of the later inhabitants of the Mexican plateau toward the earlier civilization.

Over and over again the world's history has recorded the destruction of great civilizations at the hands of more virile invaders. The Mexican plateau was no exception to the rule. The Toltecs with centuries of settled existence, devoted to the accumulation of wealth with its consequential introduction of softness, were no match for the new arrivals hardened by wandering through the barren wastes of northern Mexico. The Toltec federation fell as Rome had fallen, but like Rome succeeded in passing on much of her culture to her conquerors.

Legend typifies the overthrow of the older civilization as a series of struggles between Tezcatlipoca, chief god of the invading peoples, and Quetzalcoatl, patron deity of the Toltecs. By means of sorcery and general trickery Tezcatlipoca overthrows Quetzalcoatl, and the Toltecs like helpless sheep were herded to their death. History relates that these invaders from the north were next door to barbarians, but modern opinion grants the new arrivals a fair degree of culture. It is practically certain that the newcomers were Nahua-speaking.

With the destruction of the Toltec federation, the component peoples relapsed into independence. The remnants of the Nahua-speaking Toltecs appear to have gathered at Cholula and in the territory of Tlaxcala with other settlements in the direction of the east side of Lake Texcoco, probably amalgamating with the original inhabitants. If the Toltecs were, indeed, Otomi-speaking, the change to the Nahua language probably took place at this time in the south, while in the general direction of Tula they would seem to have retained their own language. This theory, however, conflicts with the statement of early Spanish chroniclers that the Otomies were not on a particularly high cultural level.

The new arrivals, known as Chichimecs, or Acolhua, settled in various parts of the Valley of Mexico and surrounding country, doubtlessly mingling with the earlier inhabitants of the late "Archaic" horizon, whose distinctive culture lingered on well into the Teotihuacan horizon.

A number of important city states rose to prominence.

Of these Azcapotzalco, Colhuacan, Texcoco and Tlacopan were to play an important part in Aztec affairs.
Probably all of these sites had been already occupied
for many centuries before the arrival of the Chichimec
invaders. The next arrivals were the Aztecs.

There are fairly detailed accounts of Aztec history
starting from a legendary emergence from underground
at a place called Seven Caves up to the Spanish conquest.
Naturally the later events chronicled are closer to actual
history than are those of the early stages. The starting
point of Aztec migration is said to have been the north.
This agrees well with linguistic evidence, for the Nahua
tongue, spoken by both Chichimecs and Aztecs, belongs
to the Shoshonean linguistic group still spoken by Indian groups as far north as Montana and Oregon.

Aztec tradition is also correct in recording the Aztecs
as having migrated from their original habitat in the
company of other Nahua-speaking tribes. Perhaps a
thousand years elapsed between the departure of the
tribe from the northern regions, and its arrival in the
Valley of Mexico. Apparently the migration passed
down the west coast of Mexico, for the Aztecs were reported to have passed through Michoacan. The inhabitants of this area are also Nahua-speaking, and Aztec
tradition supplies an amusing explanation of the origin
of this Nahua group.

During their wanderings the Aztecs arrived at the
shores of Lake Patzcuaro. Some of the tribe thought
this was a suitable place where they should settle, but

the oracle of Huitzilopochtli, the tribal god, ordered them to continue the journey. The members of the party opposed to the continuance of the march happened to be bathing in the lake. The oracle told the rest of the tribe to steal the clothes of the bathers and to continue on their way without more delay. When the bathers left the water they were unable to find their clothing. Ashamed to pursue their fellow tribesmen in the garb of nature, they decided to remain where they were. From these nudists, tradition relates, are descended the Nahua-speaking Tarascans, who still live in the vicinity of Lake Patzcuaro.

The lot of the faint-hearted was hard. Later the Aztecs are said to have resided for some time at Coatepec near Tula. Again some of the tribe wished to disobey Huitzilopochtli's orders to continue the march. One morning these persons were found with their breasts cut open and their hearts plucked out. From this, legend relates, originated the custom of human sacrifice in the peculiar Mexican method of removing the heart.

About the beginning of the thirteenth century the Aztecs settled at Chapultepec, where the modern Mexican presidential palace is situated. Apparently they intended to settle permanently at this spot, but the Tepanecs of Azcapotzalco and the Chalcans attacked them. The Aztecs were disastrously defeated. Their leader Huitzilihuitl was taken prisoner, and subsequently put to death at Colhuacan, probably as a sacrificial victim. After more wanderings, the defeated Aztecs petitioned the ruler of Colhuacan for land on which to make a permanent settlement. They were granted land at Tizapan. This was a barren rattlesnake-infested area, where the Colhuacan leader believed they could not prosper, but were apparently out of harm's way. In the ensuing years they lived on friendly terms with the Colhuacans, trading and intermarrying with them.

The settlement advanced. Tradition relates that the Aztecs petitioned the Colhuacan leader for one of his daughters to become their ruler and goddess. The ruler consented, but the Aztecs slew the girl, and flaying her, dressed one of their warriors in her skin. The Colhuacan ruler, unaware of this outrage, visited the Aztec settlement, taking offerings to the temple. On realizing that in the darkness of the temple he had made his offerings to a warrior clad in his daughter's skin, he collected his followers to avenge the wrong. In the ensuing battle the Aztecs were again defeated, but were able to retire in good order to Acatzintlan, where they reformed their ranks and settled down once more. Later they moved to Tenochtitlan, the present Mexico City. The glyph for this town was a cactus plant (*nochtli*) growing from a rock (*tetl*), the last syllable *tlan* having the meaning of "The place of."

The settlement of Tenochtitlan took place in the year 1 Tecpatl, corresponding to A.D. 1324 in our calendar. The land was little suitable for settlement, being mostly swamp, and the original settlement, apparently, consisted of pile buildings standing in the water. The Aztecs were still a weak tribe in comparison with their neighbors, and doubtlessly they were forced to make the best of land their neighbors wouldn't trouble to occupy. Tenochtitlan, or Mexico City as it will be called in this book, was situated between the territories of Azcapotzalco and Texcoco, but tribute was paid to the former city.

One of the first tasks that faced the settlers was the erection of a suitable temple to house their tribal god, Huitzilopochtli. Suitable building materials did not exist in their swampy territory. They surmounted this difficulty by trading the products of the lake, such as fish, water fowl, frogs and aquatic beetles for stone, lime and hard wood. With the aid of these materials they were able to erect a fairly presentable pyramid crowned with the temple of their deity.

In the year A.D. 1375, that is fifty-one years after the foundation of their new city, the Aztecs decided to elect a chief ruler. The choice fell on Acamapichtli, whose mother was a daughter of the Colhuacan ruler, but whose father was Aztec.

This was a good move since the alliance with the Colhuacans was thereby strengthened to offset dangers from Azcapotzalco and Texcoco. At the same time it gave the Aztec rulers a pedigree, for the Colhuacan rulers claimed descent from the old Toltec rulers. Probably this pedigree was not of such great importance at that time as it subsequently assumed, but all the political *nouveaux riches* appear to have been desirous of a Toltec

PLATE III. QUETZALCOATL PYRAMID AT TEOTIHUACAN SHOWING FEATHERED
SERPENTS, RAIN GOD MASKS AND SHELL DECORATIVE ELEMENTS

ancestry. This could be obtained by marriage or a judicially falsified pedigree.

Acamapichtli served as ruler until his death twenty-one years later. During this period the Aztecs seem to have successfully kept out of wars. Two decades of peace must have permitted a considerable increase of population and an added feeling of security. Although the Aztecs did not apparently start any wars of their own, there is some reason to believe that they aided the Colhuacans in one or two campaigns. Xochimilco was attacked and destroyed as a result of this aid from the Aztecs. An alliance of kinds was also made with the Chalcans, it would seem, since one of Acamapichtli's daughters was married to the ruler of Chalco. Nevertheless the Aztecs were still very weak, and found themselves forced to pay greater tribute to Azcapotzalco than formerly.

In 1396 on the death of Acamapichtli, his son Huitzilhuitl was chosen by the council of elders to succeed to the rulership. According to one account he was the fourth son of Acamapichtli. Huitzilhuitl married a daughter of the ruler of Azcapotzalco, as a result of which the tribute formerly paid by the Aztecs was reduced to a nominal payment of two ducks and a few fish and frogs each year. An alliance seems to have been concluded with the people of Azcapotzalco, and in the second decade of the fifteenth century the Aztecs took part in the overthrow of Texcoco by their new allies.

Huitzilhuitl died in 1417. His son, Chimalpopoca,

was elected to succeed him. Chimalpopoca was at this time a mere boy of ten or eleven years of age. One imagines that this election must have been the result of pressure from Azcapotzalco, or a desire on the part of the Aztecs to keep in with a city state of such importance. Otherwise it is not conceivable that the Aztec council of elders would have chosen a mere boy as their leader, since it was not necessary that a son should succeed his father. Probably the election of Huitzilhuitl to cement the alliance with the Colhuacans, and the subsequent election of Chimalpopoca, because he was the grandson of the ruler of Azcapotzalco, set the custom of electing the ruler from one particular family. It is more than probable that had no political reasons existed for the election of these two rulers, the subsequent Aztec rulers would have been drawn from any family, their election depending entirely on ability, instead of ability within one family. According to one account, however, Chimalpopoca was the brother, not the son, of Huitzilhuitl.

It was during his rule that the successful campaign was waged against Texcoco. It is also stated that at this time water was first brought from Chapultepec by means of an aqueduct. The first aqueduct was made of pottery. This proved useless, whereupon the Aztecs requested stone and lime from the people of Azcapotzalco. The request was refused, and relations between the Aztecs and the Azcapotzalcans became very strained. Finally a party of the latter either assassinated Chimalpopoca, or arranged for a group of disaffected Aztecs to commit the murder. This occurred in the year 1427.

Itzcoatl, a son of Acamapichtli by a slave woman, was elected to the rulership to succeed Chimalpopoca. War was pending with Azcapotzalco, and many of the Aztecs were in favor of making peace on any conditions with their powerful neighbors. However, Azcapotzalco was engaged at this time in a life-and-death struggle with Texcoco. The Aztecs, under Itzcoatl, wisely threw in their lot with the Texcocans. In the subsequent fighting Texcoco with Aztec aid destroyed the power of Azcapotzalco once and for all, crushing also Colhuacan, the second great Tecpanec centre. Another campaign by the Texcocans and their allies the Aztecs led to the conquest of Xochimilco for the second time. Tlacopan, a smaller city apparently peopled by Chichimecs, was admitted to the Texcoco-Aztec alliance at about this time.

The three city states were to remain in alliance from this time until the Spanish conquest. Spoils of war were divided between the three tribes, two-fifths going to Texcoco, two-fifths to the Aztecs, and the last fifth falling to Tlacopan. Gradually the Aztecs ousted Texcoco from the leadership of the federation, probably because of their greater skill as fighters.

On the death of Itzcoatl in 1440 Montezuma the elder was elected ruler. He was the son of Huitzilhuitl, the second ruler, and a nephew of Itzcoatl. Like his predecessor, Montezuma I was an aggressive fighter.

29

Under his leadership the federation carried on war for the first time outside the Valley of Mexico. Cuernavaca was subdued in the course of one of these campaigns. An attempt was even made to reduce the Mixtecs and Zapotecs of Oaxaca, but this was a difficult proposition. The allies were, apparently, successful in their efforts to conquer these peoples, but their permanent subjection was more difficult. After the withdrawal of the invading armies, the distant towns promptly revolted, refusing to continue the payments of tribute.

The rule of Montezuma the elder was a turning point in Aztec history. His predecessor had thrown off the yoke of Azcapotzalco, but now the Aztecs were embarked on a period of imperialistic expansion, which only the coming of the Spaniards stopped. Other expeditions invaded the territory of the Huaxtecs in the direction of the Panuco River, the Totonac territory of Vera Cruz, and the southern part of Guerrero, where the Cohuixca were supreme.

Axayacatl, apparently Montezuma's son, succeeded him in 1471. He also was an energetic and warlike ruler. The campaigns against the Totonacs were continued, and the Tarascan territory of Michoacan was invaded. The Tarascans were an extremely warlike people, and, repulsing the invasion, inflicted a very severe defeat on the Aztecs. Prior to this Axayacatl had waged a successful campaign against the Tehuantepecs, obtaining prisoners for his induction ceremony, and penetrating as far as Guatusco, a town on the Pacific coast not far from the present Guatemalan frontier. At about the same time the people of Tlatilolco, Aztecs who had broken away from Tenochtitlan during its early history, were reduced to submission.

In 1481 Axayacatl died, and his brother Tizoc was elected to succeed him. His first campaign to obtain prisoners for the inauguration ceremonies was a failure, since he and his forces were unable to defeat the people of Metztitlan in Hidalgo and their Huaxtec allies. The Huaxtecs were considered to be very poor fighters, and the capture of a Huaxtec prisoner was not reckoned a particularly brave feat. Hence a repulse at their hands was a poor start for Tizoc. Two years after his election he started to enlarge the great pyramid and temple of Huitzilopochtli, which had already been enlarged under Montezuma the First. A campaign against the Matlat-zincas of the Toluca Valley supplied a large number of prisoners to be sacrificed in connection with this pious work. Tizoc appears to have been more interested in such matters than fighting, with the result that he has been dubbed a coward. This is probably an unjust accusation. After having enjoyed the post of ruler for only five years Tizoc died a victim of poison. His death was said to have been plotted by certain nobles who either resented his inactivity, or had some personal grudge against him. Saville is of the opinion that he was poisoned by eating noxious mushrooms which had been substituted for those usually eaten at certain ceremonies to produce hallucinations (p. 74). Ahuitzol, his brother, was elected in his place in the same year of 1486. He has been described as one of the most virile figures in Aztec history. One Aztec codex states that at the dedication of the enlarged temple structure, which was completed in 1487, no less than 20,000 prisoners of war were sacrificed. This number is probably an exaggeration, nevertheless a series of brilliant campaigns would be necessary to reach a quarter of this number. By a series of well-executed campaigns Ahuitzol consolidated the Aztec federation, forcing the outlying peoples, on whom the Aztec yoke had sat lightly, to pay regular tribute. Aztec rule in such far-away regions as Oaxaca was effectually consolidated, for in the past tribute had usually ceased soon after the withdrawal of the Aztec and allied armies.

Michoacan and Tlaxcala were the two provinces that retained their complete independence. In the case of the latter, the Aztecs claimed that they did not want to subdue its inhabitants entirely. The Tlaxcalans were a small and warlike people, and the Aztecs waged frequent wars against them to obtain prisoners for sacrifice and to train the young braves, and for that reason did not desire their submission. This, at least, was their version, but it may have been a case of sour grapes.

In 1502 Ahuitzol died. His son, Montezuma the Second, was elected to be chief ruler. The choice of the council of elders and electors was unfortunate. He was imbued with ideas of class distinction more in line with those of an absolute monarch than with the social usages

32

PLATE IV. POTTERY FIGURINES OF WEST COAST TYPE

They resemble somewhat those of the "Archaic" periods in the Valley of Mexico, but date from shortly before the Spanish conquest.

of the Aztecs during the first century of their occupation of Mexico City. He appears to have wished to rid himself of the control of the council of old men and clan chiefs, administering the empire without their advice or consent. All persons who were not of the ruling caste were dismissed from positions of importance, and replaced, apparently, by sycophants.

Had Montezuma been a man of more resolution, all might have been well. Unfortunately he was the victim of a more than usually superstitious complex combined with a tendency to procrastination. When Cortez appeared in Mexico, he might have been overwhelmingly defeated at the start of the campaign. Montezuma, swayed by irresolution and superstitious fear, allowed him to gain allies through his delay in attacking him. Later vacillating between policies of conciliation or open war Montezuma disheartened his own followers by half-hearted defense, eventually allowing himself to become Cortez' prisoner. Had he followed the example of his predecessors and subordinated Aztec policy to the advice of the council of leaders and elders, a resolute resistance would probably have staved off the Spanish conquest for some years.

Eventually he was deposed, but by then the damage had been done. Aztec prestige had suffered so many blows, that many of the peoples composing the empire revolted or refused to fight the Spaniards. What might have been done at the beginning was demonstrated by the resolution with which the Spaniards were attacked

34

during their retreat from Mexico City, but then it was too late. Spanish reinforcements had arrived, and the Tlaxcalan alliance was firmly cemented. The fall of the Aztec confederation was pitiable.

CHAPTER II

THE CYCLE OF LIFE

Birth. Ceremonious Customs. Lucky and Unlucky Days. Natal Feast. Naming. Weaning. Punishments. Education. Boys' Colleges. Novices. Warrior Rank. Marriages by Arrangement. Marriage Ceremonies. Girls' Colleges. Polygamy Among the Nobility. Divorce. Death. Future Life. Journey to Underworld. Funerary Ceremonies. Cremation. Slaying of Widows and Slaves. Succession. Guardians for Orphans.

THE ancient Mexicans, like all peoples whose life centred round agriculture, were desirous of having large families to help them with their farm work. The birth of a child, particularly if it was a son, was the occasion of many ceremonies to propitiate the deities and assure a happy future for the new arrival.

For the accouchement a bed of straw was prepared in front of the hearth, where a special fire was lit. Under no circumstance was this fire allowed to go out until four days after the birth, and no visitor was allowed to remove any of its embers from the house. However, it was customary for friends to rub their knees with ashes from this fire, for it was believed that the infant's bones would thereby be strengthened. If the mother had difficulty in giving birth, she was given a decoction of opossum tails to drink, possibly because of the ease with which this animal raises its young—an interesting case of sympathetic magic.

Immediately after birth the child was washed by the midwife, who prayed to Chalchihuitlicue, goddess of water, for its happiness. After swaddling the child, the midwife addressed it in the following pessimistic terms: "Child, more precious than anything, Ometecuhtli and Omecihuatl created you in the twelfth heaven to come to this world and be born here. Know then that this world, which you have entered, is sad, doleful and full of hard toil and unhappiness. It is a valley of tears, and as you grow up in it you must earn your sustenance with your own hands and at the cost of much sorrow."

After this cheerful welcome, the baby was placed in its mother's arms with a few words of praise to her for her fortitude. Soon after this a priest-astrologer was summoned to declare the child's fortune. This depended on the day in the sacred calendar on which it had been born. Some days were lucky, some unlucky, and yet others indifferent. The day 1 Cipactli, for instance, was very lucky. Boys born on this day had a prosperous future in front of them. If of noble family they would prove to be great leaders and the owners of much property. If of humble birth they would be honest, brave and never in want. Similarly children born on 1 Acatl, or the following twelve days, would be traitorous or given to the practice of witchcraft. Unhappy was the fate of those born on one of the thirteen days starting at 1 Calli. If they did not die a violent death in battle or as sacrificial victims, they stood a good chance of being caught in adultery, and suffering death as a punishment. About the best they could hope for was to be forced by want to sell themselves into slavery.

Actually it was possible to avert impending ill-fate of this nature by a little manipulation. The most usual method of doing this was to postpone the ceremony held four days after birth to some later date when the fates were more auspicious.

Four days after birth the bed in front of the sacred fire was removed, and that night a great feast was held. Before the guests sat down to eat, the baby was passed over the sacred fire, and then its head was washed four times, four being the sacred number especially associated with men. Food and pulque wine were also sprinkled over the fire as an offering to the fire god, whose name meant "The old, old god." If the baby was a boy, toy weapons and implements of the kind he would use when he reached manhood were placed in his hands, and he was guided so as to go through the motions of using them in combat and work. In the same way miniature weaving and spinning implements were placed in the hands of a baby girl, and she was also made to go through the motions of grinding maize for tortillas. Similar ceremonies are still practised among the Mayas of Yucatan with the object of insuring that the children

38

will grow up into competent and hard-working members of the community.

The feast held in connection with these ceremonies was attended by all the friends and relations of the parents, both adults and children. The Mexicans, apparently, could never refrain from long speeches and platitudinizing, and an event, such as a birth, gave them a wonderful opportunity for long-winded discourses. The baby was again informed that he had entered a vale of tears, and sorrow would be his destiny. The other children present also addressed the baby, telling him, if he were a boy, to become a warrior so that he might die a soldier's death, thereby qualifying for the warrior's paradise. One would imagine that at celebrations of a birth so many references to death would be out of order, but the mortality of man seems never to have been far from the thoughts of the Aztecs, although death was not much feared. In modern Mexico one sees this same intimacy with death displayed in a hundred different aspects from the cemetery picnics on All Souls day to the innumerable folk drawings of dancing death.

Parents belonging to the nobility gave more elaborate feasts to celebrate the child's birth. Costly presents, such as embroidered cotton cloaks, were given to the guests, who topped off a great banquet of turkey by smoking tobacco in cane pipes.

Children were often named from the day on which they were born, especially if the birthday chanced to be of good augury. Frequently, too, a child was named for some event that took place at the time of his birth. One of the leaders of Tlaxcala, for instance, was called "Smoking Star" because a large comet was prominent in the sky at the time of his birth. Boys were sometimes named after animals, or took the name of some ancestor; girls frequently bore the name of some flower.

Children were not usually weaned until they were almost three years old, but in this connection it must be remembered that the ancient Mexicans had no milk-giving domestic animal. From a very early age the training of the child was very strict. A common punishment consisted in thrashing the disobedient child with a species of stinging nettle. (Plate V.) Sometimes a refractory child was hung head downwards over a fire on which peppers had been lain, so that the acrid smoke went up his nostrils.

Incorrigible children might be sold into slavery as a last resort. Children, who were too prone to lie, were punished by having a piece cut out of one of their lips. With such strict training it is not strange that the Spaniards were astonished at the high moral tone of the natives, and their reluctance to tell a lie. Unfortunately contact between the two civilizations soon led to a rapid moral degeneration of the native code.

Boys of what might be termed the middle class, such as sons of merchants and small local chiefs, and the sons of the agricultural masses were handed over to special priests for education at about the age of six, or even earlier. They were lodged in special boys' houses in an organization which might be compared to a modern boarding school, save that the discipline in the Mexican schools was much stricter. Each geographical group, called a calpulli, had its own college, for these groups were clans which, in the course of centuries, had largely lost their bonds of consanguinity. The college was attached to the calpulli temple, and the instruction was in the hands of priests.

In addition to receiving an education, the boys were responsible for the maintenance of the temple and its services. Their duties included the sweeping of the temples, the care of the sacred fires and incense braziers, the beating of drums to summon the people to the temple services, the hewing of wood and drawing of water required in the religious exercises, the preparation of the paint with which the priests adorned themselves, and the cutting of the maguey thorns used in drawing blood in sacrifice.

Education included a very strict moral training, lessons in history and traditions, religious instruction, and a practical course in arts and crafts. There were twenty of these colleges, one for each of the calpullis. Their purpose was to turn out good citizens and good military material.

Another college existed for the education of the sons of the nobility. This was known as the Calmecac. Here the education was even stricter, and the discipline more rigid. The college was attached to the main temple group of Mexico City (Tenochtitlan), and its principal was accorded very high rank. The boys were instructed with a view to their future positions as religious and military leaders of the community. They performed the same duties for the great temple of Huitzilopochtli (p. 225) as were performed by the youths of the other colleges in the temples of their respective calpullis.

Much more attention, however, was paid to their instruction in history and tradition, and physical training. During the whole period of the training, which varied from about six to eight years, the boys were under a very strict supervision. They slept in the college building, and, apparently, seldom saw their parents. They made frequent sacrifices of blood by piercing their ears, tongues and arms with maguey thorns, and at appropriate times fasted and kept vigil. A ceremony, in which they participated, is described elsewhere. Religion and warfare were so closely connected in ancient Mexico, that it is not strange to find young men to be dedicated to these two professions undergoing the same preliminary education.

Sometimes parents of rank would make a vow that if a sick child recovered from his illness, they would dedicate him to the priesthood. In that case a big banquet was held in honor of the priests, when the boy reached the age of ten. After this the parents took the child to the Calmecac, where he was presented to the god Quetzalcoatl, patron of the college. As part of the presentation, he was forced to listen to a moral discourse as long-winded as a Scott novel.

The achievement of warrior rank was the ambition of most members of the Calmecac. A young man might be said to have graduated when he was granted warrior's rank. Training in warfare began when the boy attained the age of fifteen, but concurrently with his general education. He continued to live in the training school, which served as a kind of bachelors' club. On reaching the age of twenty the initiate was considered fit to fight, but under the watchful eye of an old soldier, whose supervision had previously been obtained by presents from the boy's father. The objective of a Mexican warrior was not to kill as many of the enemy as possible, but to take captives, who would serve later as sacrificial victims, and this was the young soldier's ambition. Young boys wore a lock of hair down the back of the head, and the young soldier continued to do so until he had taken a prisoner in combat, either single-handed or with the aid of comrades. The cutting off of the pig-tail was, like the winning of his spurs by a knight, the occasion of great rejoicing and feasting among the young man's kith and kin.

A novice, who took a prisoner single-handed, was received by the Aztec ruler, and permitted to paint his body yellow and his face red with yellow markings on the temples. On the other hand a young man, who failed to take a captive single-handed in the course of several battles, was ignominiously returned to civil life, and branded as a coward. His disgrace followed him for the rest of his life, for he was marked off from the war-

43

riors by not being permitted to wear cotton clothing or embroidered garments.

Once a young man had won glory in battle he was admitted into the ranks of adult society, and was free to marry. Among the masses an ability to earn his living was required of a young man before he could contemplate matrimony. There was little courting among the ancient Mexicans, marriages being arranged between the parents. Among the masses ability to cook and weave was considered of more importance than beauty. Frequently the young man indicated to his parents the girl he would like to marry.

The first task was to call a priest astrologer to decide whether such a marriage would prove felicitous. This he did by ascertaining the days on which both the young man and the girl were born, and computing whether such a combination was auspicious. If such were the case, the boy's parents sent certain old women as negotiators. These go-betweens visited the girl's parents or guardians, always arriving on their mission after midnight. Armed with a present, they made speeches, urging the desirability of the marriage. The girl's parents invariably replied that they could not then agree to the marriage, upon which the intermediaries departed, returning, however, a few days later to renew the suit. On this occasion they stated what property the young man possessed and what presents he was prepared to give the girl's parents. The girl was consulted by her parents, but, apparently, she was not expected to object unless

PLATE V. ADOLESCENCE

a, Teaching young girl to weave; *b*, Marriage ceremony; *c*, Punishing boy by pricking him with thorns. Mendoza Codex.

she had conceived a very strong dislike to her suitor. The final consent of the girl's parents was carried to the boy's family by other old women related to the girl's family.

The actual marriage ceremony took place at the bridegroom's house, the bride being brought there in a special litter with great pomp. The first ceremony consisted of the groom censing the bride with copal incense and vice versa. After that the pair sat down on a reed mat, and exchanged garments, the groom giving the bride a woman's dress, and the bride giving him in return a man's clothing. Next the points of their cloaks were knotted together, and this symbolized the union. Food was served to the couple, and the new state was symbolized by the pair feeding each other. All the guests ate and drank, dancing after the feast. (Plate V.)

The newly married couple were expected to sit on the mat for four days. During this time they retained a grave mien, for this period was considered to be a vigil and time of repentance, during which they were forbidden to bathe or wash themselves. Maguey thorns were given them to draw blood from their tongues and ears, and at midnight they made offerings to the gods. At the end of this period the marriage was consummated, new clothes were given them, and they were ceremonially bathed by a priest. While the groom censed the household gods, the bride was decked in feather garments, white plumes being placed on her head and around her ankles and wrists. After this there was a fresh feast and

46

more dancing to bring the ceremonies to a final conclusion. Different parts of Mexico had different marriage customs. Among the Mixtecs of Oaxaca, for instance, the groom carried the bride to his house on his back. Among the Huaxtecs the husband did not speak to his wife's parents during the first year of married life.

Girls of the nobility and middle classes were prepared for married life by instruction in girls' schools patterned after those of the boys. They entered these at about the age of five, learning there to spin and weave, to prepare and cook meals, and to master other domestic arts. (Plate V.) Discipline, as among the boys, was very strict, and long periods of silence were imposed upon them. They were never allowed to leave the college precincts unless accompanied by an old woman, who served as chaperon. This rule was not relaxed even when exercising in the school gardens. Should they meet any one not connected with the school, they were forbidden to speak or even raise their eyes from the ground.

Punishment for infractions of these rules was severe. As in the case of their brothers, beatings with nettles were inflicted. For some offences the soles of their feet were pricked with maguey thorns, for others the ears were pricked in the same manner. Even daughters of the rulers were subjected to the same discipline.

These girls, too, served in the temples, one of their most important duties being to guard the sacred fires so that they were never extinguished and to make a daily food offering to the gods. As a corollary of these duties, they ate only once a day, and meat was forbidden them save at religious feasts. When they first entered the college their hair was cut short, and they continued to serve until claimed in marriage. Needless to say no courting was possible under such conditions, for a young man who attempted to converse with the girls was liable to pay with his life for such temerity. Nevertheless, runaway love marriages were not by any means unknown.

Monogamy was the general rule, but persons of high rank often possessed many wives. In the Michoacan region of western Mexico a man married his mother-in-law should she become a widow. Similarly a man marrying a widow, older than himself, with a daughter, took the daughter as a second wife. Where polygamy existed among the nobility, the wives were separated, each possessing her own small dwelling close to her husband's house.

Divorce was not uncommon. Couples who had not made a success of their joint life appeared before the local judge, stating their troubles. The petitioner was almost invariably the man, for women were expected to make the best of a bad job. Grounds for separation were the idleness of the woman in her household tasks, barrenness or inability to cook, spin or weave. The judge heard both sides, and based his decision largely on whether the couple was legally married. When this was the case he did his best to compose the differences, pointing out that separation would bring disgrace on the parents who had arranged the marriage. If his efforts failed, he dismissed the pair, who were then free to separate. According to other authorities the judge himself pronounced the marriage dissolved. Were the couple not legally married a separation was more readily obtained.

Death, the close of life's cycle, was the occasion of a great many ceremonies. The Aztecs believed in three abodes of the dead. The most aristocratic of these was reserved for warriors slain in combat or on the sacrificial altar, and their feminine counterparts, women who had died in childbirth. Those lucky enough to qualify for this afterworld went to the sun. The men accompanied the sun, patron god of the warriors, in its daily course across the heavens, but only as far as the zenith. Thence to its setting it was accompanied by the women. After four years' residence in this solar paradise, the dead were converted into birds, particularly humming birds, and were free to fly down to earth. The humming bird is associated with the sun's sojourn on earth in Maya legend.

Tlalocan, the second abode of the dead, was situated on earth. This was the home of the Tlalocs, the principal rain gods. It was a land of happiness and contentment, replete, as one would expect in the home of agricultural gods, with fields of growing corn, squashes and beans. Suffering and pain were unknown in this land, but those who could enter this charming abode must first qualify by being drowned or being struck by lightning, deaths directly attributable to rain deities. However, those who had died of certain incurable skin diseases were also admitted, perhaps as a kind of compensation for their suffering on earth. Persons eligible for Tlalocan were not cremated, as was the general Aztec custom, but were interred in special burial places.

To the third abode of the dead went those that had died a natural death whether of noble or humble birth. This place was situated under the world's surface, and was known as Mictlan. Here ruled the Mexican equivalent of Pluto—Mictlantecutli and his spouse Mictecacihuatl. A corpse destined for this abode was addressed as follows: "Our son, you have finished with the sufferings and fatigues of this life. It has pleased our lord to take you away, for we have no eternal life in this world. Our existence is like the ray of the sun. It is short like the fleeting moments in winter when one warms oneself in the sun. Now has come the time for Mictlantecutli and Mictecacihuatl to take you to the abode that has already been arranged for you. . . . You must go to the land of shadows where there is no light or windows. You will never get away from there, and you must not worry about returning, for your absence will be eternal. . . ."

The journey that the deceased must make from this world to Mictlan was long and fraught with danger. First he had to pass between two mountains that were forever clashing against each other. Next he had to traverse a trail guarded by a monster snake and a croco-

PLATE VI. CREMATION AND SACRIFICE

Above: Two priests in front of funerary pyre. One has a torch in his hand
ready to set fire to the pile. The deceased wears a jaguar head-dress.
Below: Removing heart from sacrificial victim. Zouche Codex.

dile. Beyond lay eight deserts and a mountainous region known as Eight Hills. The next tribulation was a bitingly cold wind called the Wind of Knives, for it was so fierce that it tore up even the stones in the ground and cut like a razor.

The final obstacle was a great stretch of deep water, known as Eight Waters. Once this was crossed the deceased entered Mictlan, but four years had been consumed in the journey. Certain help was supplied the deceased by his mourners. Certain papers were cut out by the priests and given the deceased to aid him in his pilgrimage. All his clothes and arms were burned, for it was held that the heat engendered by their cremation would protect the deceased when he faced the Wind of Knives. With the deceased was buried a small vermilion dog with a cord of unspun cotton around its neck. The dog went straight to the far side of Eight Waters, where it awaited the arrival of its master, swimming across to meet him at the expiration of the four-year period. Riding on the dog's back with the cord to support himself, the deceased was able to cross the great sheet of water.

It was believed that only a vermilion-colored dog could help in this manner, for the white dogs excused themselves by saying that they were already washed, while the black dogs said that they were blemished by black markings, and for that reason could not pass their masters across. This belief still exists in some of the remoter parts of Mexico, but under the influence of

Christianity, the name of the stretch of water has been changed to the Jordan River.

Ceremonies at the death of a ruler were extremely elaborate. Torquemada has left a detailed account, which can be freely translated as follows:

"It was customary among the peoples of Mexico that when a ruler died, word of his death was carried with great solemnity to all the neighboring towns and to distant rulers related to the deceased. Warning was given of the time of burial, which was usually four or five days after death. When corruption started, the body was placed on specially worked mats, where it was guarded with great ceremonies until the arrival of the rulers invited to the burial. These brought presents of beautiful cloaks, green feathers and slaves, each according to his wealth, offering them for the burial ceremonies.

"Once the bidden guests were assembled, the corpse was dressed in fifteen or twenty rich cloaks, woven with many beautiful patterns, and adorned with gold and other jewelry of great value. Then a piece of jade, which the Indians call Chalchihuitl, was placed in the deceased's mouth, for it was said to serve as the deceased's heart. Locks of hair from the top of the dead ruler's head were removed, and placed with others, which had been cut from his head at birth, in a well-worked box of stone or wood carved on the inside with figures of their conception of the demon [Mictlantecutli?]. These locks of hair were kept as a memento of his birth and death. A painted mask was then placed

53

on the dead person, and a slave was slain. This was the slave who during life had served the dead ruler as chaplain, placing fire and incense on the altars and braziers, which the ruler had in his house. It was held that he was slain so that he could accompany his master to the next world, there to serve his master in the same duties.

"On the deceased were next placed the clothing of the principal god of the town, in the temple or chief house of which he was to be buried. The body was removed from the house with great solemnity, accompanied by the other rulers, relations, friends and the widows. All wept and mourned while the priests sang unaccompanied by drums. On arrival at the gate of the courtyard of the temple, the high priest and his assistants came forth to meet the procession. The deceased was placed at the foot of the staircase leading up to the temple, pitch pine, sprinkled with copal incense, was piled around and set alight. (Plate VI.)

"As the body burned and the gold ornaments and jewelry melted, large numbers of slaves, both men and women, were sacrificed. The number of these was sometimes as much as one hundred, sometimes two hundred, the number depending on the position and wealth of the deceased ruler. These were the personal slaves of the deceased or those presented by the guests. First the victims' breasts were opened and their hearts removed, as in the ordinary sacrifices, then their bodies were thrown on a funerary pyre, but not that on which the deceased ruler was burning. Among those slain in this fashion were some of his wives, and the dwarfs, hunchbacks and deformed, who had kept the dead man amused in his palace. These were slain, it was said, so that they might solace their master in the next world, where he would be provided with another palace. . . .

"On the day following these foolish and superstitious practices, the ashes and any bones that had not been burned were collected and placed in the box in which the locks of hair had already been placed. The piece of jade, which had been placed in the corpse's mouth to represent his heart, was also placed in the box. Over the box was placed a wooden statue of the deceased, decked in his clothing. In front of this the remaining widows and relations and friends made offerings. This ceremony was called *Quitonaltia,* which means 'They give him good luck.' For four days they paid him honor, and took offerings to the place where he had been burned. Indeed, many of them made the same offering twice daily, and repeated it in front of the box enclosing the hair and ashes. At the end of this period another ten or fifteen slaves were slain, for they said that at the end of four days the soul of the dead man began his march to the abode of the dead, and consequently he needed their aid. . . .

"Twenty days after the cremation four or five more slaves were sacrificed, and after another twenty days two or three more. Another twenty days later one or two more were slain, and finally eighty days after the first ceremonies ten or twelve more were sacrificed.

"This last sacrifice was as though it were the end of the year, for after this no more humans were slain. Every year, however, a memorial service was held in front of the box. Rabbits, butterflies, partridges and other birds were sacrificed, and in front of the box and the statue over it were placed much incense, offerings of food and wine, many flowers and roses, and some tubes of cane containing fragrant things to smoke [tobacco], which they call *Acayetl*. (Plate VII.) These offerings were kept up for four years, and the participants feasted and drank until they fell intoxicated. They also danced and wept, calling to memory the death of the deceased."

The custom of slaying wives and slaves of the deceased had at one time or another an almost world-wide distribution. Torquemada also gives a long description of the death and cremation of the ruler of Michoacan in western Mexico. The ceremonies were similar to those already described, but he tells us that for five days after death no maize was ground in the city, no fires were lit, and the whole population remained at home, mourning their dead ruler.

For the common people the ceremonies were, naturally, very much more simple. The bodies were cremated unless the deceased had qualified for the paradise ruled over by the Tlalocs. Offerings of food were made as in the case of the rulers, and the simple possessions of the deceased were burned with him.

Among the Zapotecan peoples of Oaxaca the cre-

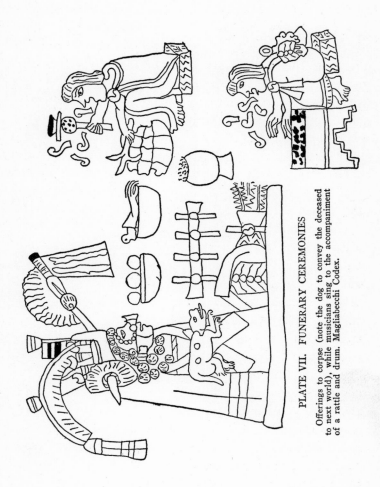

PLATE VII. FUNERARY CEREMONIES

Offerings to corpse (note the dog to convey the deceased to next world), while musicians sing to the accompaniment of a rattle and drum. Magliabecchi Codex.

mated ashes were placed in large funerary urns of pottery, on the front of which were modelled figures of the gods. (Plate XXIX.) Examples of these vessels are to be seen in almost all Mexican archæological collections. In this same area are also found large cruciform burial chambers, the walls of which are decorated with the geometrical mosaic patterns typical of this area. In the Colima district of western Mexico large well-made pottery dogs are frequently found with burials. It is not certain if these represent food offerings or the dogs slain at burials to accompany their masters to the next world. (Plate XIII.)

The eldest son of a ruler was not necessarily chosen to succeed his father. That depended on his ability. An elder son of little ability or fighting prowess might be passed over in favor of a younger son, and among the Aztecs themselves the brother of the dead ruler usually succeeded. Property usually passed to the eldest son, but he was expected to share it with the other children. Children of the masses inherited little from their fathers, for the land farmed by a man belonged to the community, and reverted to it on his death. Heirs who wasted the property that they had inherited were frequently put to death, since they did not appreciate what they had obtained from the sweat of the brow of another.

Guardians were appointed to look after the property of minors, and any dishonesty on their part was punished by death. In some of the remoter parts of Mexico, the son who inherited his father's property also inherited such of his father's widows as were childless, but this custom was not permitted among the Aztecs, who considered such a practice very reprehensible.

CHAPTER III

ARTS AND CRAFTS

Agriculture the Chief Industry. Communal Ownership of Land.
Ceremonies at Sowing Time and at Harvest. Origin of Maize.
Amaranth. Principal Agricultural Products. Cacao Beans used as
Currency. Maguey Source of Intoxicant. Prohibition for the Young.
Domesticated Dogs. Turkeys. Hunting and Fishing. Cooking. Cactus
that Produced Hallucinations. Markets. Spinning and Weaving.
Dress and Ornaments. Gold Working. Jade and Turquoise. Obsidian
Knives. Featherwork. Wood Carving. Houses. Causeways. Canals.
Bridges.

THE land, basis of Mexican civilization, was divided
between three categories of owners. The first, and most
important, was the calpulli, or geographical clan of
which there were twenty in Mexico City at the time of
the fall of the Aztec régime. Each calpulli, which comprised the inhabitants of a ward, owned a considerable
amount of land in its district. Part of this was worked
communally by all the men of the calpulli to provide
tribute and for the upkeep of the temples, priests and
religious services. The rest of the calpulli's land, roughly corresponding to the *ejidos* of a modern Mexican
village, was divided among the various families of the
clan according to their requirements. Ownership remained in the name of the calpulli, and were the land
assigned to any family to remain unworked for a period

of two years, it reverted to the community. In practice the land was to all intents and purposes the personal property of the family to which it had been assigned, passing from father to son. All the produce was the personal property of the cultivator, who was free to dispose of it as he wished, but he could not sell or transfer his rights to the land, and were a family to die out or to move to some other district, the land that had been assigned to it reverted to the calpulli.

In addition to the communally owned calpulli lands, members of the nobility and in particular relations of the rulers of the different communities possessed private estates which had been presented to them or their ancestors for services to the state. These estates normally passed from father to son, but they could be sold. Apparently the peasants in the neighborhood were under an obligation to aid in the harvests. The last category of owners was formed by the warrior class. The land they owned was situated in conquered territory. It was the Aztec custom to grant sections of the conquered territory to warriors who had taken a distinguished part in the war that had led to the incorporation of the new district into the Aztec commonwealth. In addition to serving as a reward for valor, such grants helped in the pacification of the new territories, and resulted in the planting of Aztec nuclei to guard against disaffection. These estates passed from father to son, but could not be alienated, for ownership remained in the hands of the Aztec ruler, and were the occupant to die childless, the estate reverted to the state. Labor for such estates was, presumably, supplied by the conquered peoples in the vicinity.

In the comparatively treeless plateau country the soil was apparently prepared for sowing with hoes, for no plow existed in the New World before the arrival of the Spaniards. In the lowlands preparation of the soil was more laborious owing to the prevalence of dense tropical forest. This had to be removed before planting could start, and must have presented a very serious problem to the natives, who possessed no better tool than a stone ax. Actually the soil was largely cleared by girdling the larger trees with fire so that they would die. This work began at the commencement of the dry season in January. A month or six weeks later, when the felled trees and bush were sufficiently dry, the whole was fired, and the maize sowed in the resulting ash-covered soil. The planters passed up and down the field or milpa, as such a clearing is called all over Central America, making holes at intervals of about a yard, into which three or four grains of maize were thrown and then covered with a little earth kicked into the hole. The same method of preparing the milpas may be witnessed at the present time all over the *tierra caliente* of Mexico, Guatemala and Honduras. In many parts of Mexico it was the custom for groups of as many as twenty men to unite to aid each other in the task of preparing and sowing the crops. In the plateau land it was not generally necessary to clear the land by burning, but hoeing was necessary to keep the grass down.

The day of sowing was fixed by consultation with the soothsayers, who decided on an appropriate day after consultation of the Tonalamatl (p. 169). The seed was obtained from certain ears of corn of the previous harvest, which had been blessed in the temple of Chicomecoatl at the feast held in the month Huei Totzozontli (p. 180). The goddess Chicomecoatl, spirit of the corn, was apparently believed to lurk in these ears which had been hanging in the house since their blessing. On setting forth the sower begged the bag, in which the seed was carried, and the planting stick to help him in his work. Prayers were also made to the soil to yield a bountiful harvest. Sometimes the local priest was present at the sowing. Scattering some of the seed on the ground, he cried:

"I, the priest, the holy sorcerer, am present. Listen, sister seed, remember that you are our sustainer. And you, Your Highness the soil, now that I am entrusting into your hands my sister [the seed] who gives us our maintenance, take care that you do no wrong. Do not treat this as a light matter, and do not fall into sin by making fun of it. Beware that what I bid you do is not a matter for delay. I must see my sister [the seed], our maintenance, burst forth from the soil soon and without delay, and I wish to come with rejoicing to welcome my sister, our maintenance, at her birth."

This oration, which is somewhat freely translated, strikes one as being more in the nature of a command

63

than a prayer. The Tlalocs, gods of the rains, were also invoked at this time to guard the newly sown crop against any animals that might damage it. Seven or eight days after the plants appeared above ground, the owner again prayed to the Tlalocs, burning a candle of beeswax and offering copal incense. Again, when the ear started to form, a turkey was sacrificed and candles and copal offered to Chicomecoatl. Not even a leaf might be plucked until the silk appeared, but as soon as this was visible, a number of ears were plucked together with green leaves and the first flowers of maize, and carried to the granary, where with a turkey, copal and a candle, they were offered in sacrifice.

As soon as the green corn was ready for eating, some of it was carried to altars on the hill tops, and offered there. Fire was made in honor of Xiuhtecutli, the fire god. The green ears were placed to roast on the fire, on which copal had been sprinkled. Some of the more devout drew blood, which was sprinkled, together with pulque, on the corn. Other offerings included paper smeared with crude rubber, which was sacrificed to the Tlalocs. If a plant should produce two or three ears, a sorcerer was called in by the owner of the land. After certain ceremonies the twin ears were placed at some point near the village where the trail branched. Only some one in dire need was allowed to take these ears. The fact that a maize plant with two ears was of sufficient rarity to warrant calling in the local sorcerer and the performance of a special ceremony is evidence that

64

the maize of those days could not have been anywhere near as highly developed as the modern plant.

Maize is believed to have been first cultivated in the Highlands of Mexico, where a possible wild ancestor is to be found in Teocentli, or maize of the gods, as its Aztec name means (*Euchloena mexicana*). This plant bears more resemblance to a grass than modern maize, but it has recently been suggested by a botanist that maize evolved from the accidental crossing of some species resembling sorghum with it. Once, however, it had come under cultivation, its spread was rapid, and at the time of Columbus it was cultivated from southern Canada almost without a break as far south as central Chile. Many varieties of maize were grown by the Mexicans, but in this respect they were outstripped by the ancient Peruvians.

Agriculture may have had an accidental start in the New World. The pre-agricultural peoples undoubtedly made considerable use of nuts, fruit and seeds to round out their menu of meat and fish. These seeds were collected in baskets, and brought back to the settlement for winnowing. Such is still the practice of certain primitive tribes in the United States. Under favorable circumstances seed falling to the ground during winnowing would germinate, and suggest to an observant Luther Burbank of those days the practicability of collecting and sowing the seeds in order to avoid long journeys to collect it and possible conflicts with other groups who claimed the same collecting grounds.

A food plant of considerable importance in ancient Mexico was a species of amaranth (*Amaranthus paniculatus*), which remained unidentified until a few years ago although still under cultivation in Mexico. It was known to the Aztecs as Huahutli. The grain is smaller than mustard seed, but each plant yields a prolific crop. The seed, after parching and grinding, was mixed with water to form a variety of pinol drink, but the chief importance of the plant lay in its ripening, for it was harvested at the end of the rainy season. Once the Huahutli crop was gathered the people were insured against serious want should the maize crop prove a partial failure. Its economic importance is seen in the fact that over 150,000 bushels were annually paid to Montezuma as tribute.

As a harvest thanksgiving, idols about nine inches high were made from flour of the first seed harvested kneaded with maguey sap. After baking, the idols were placed on the family altar, where offerings of flowers, candles, copal incense and pulque were made to them. The following day the ideals were ceremonially eaten. At the feast of Huitzilopochtli a large idol of the same type was made of amaranth seed flour and carried in a litter to the god's temple. The eyes were made of inlaid stones and maize grains served as teeth.

Other stable products of the Valley of Mexico included beans, squashes, sweet potatoes, chili peppers and tomatoes. In addition to these, many agricultural products of the lowlands, of which cacao was the most important, were brought in trade to the plateau country. The cacao tree, which requires a hot, damp climate and plenty of shade, was planted in groves shaded by a taller tree of thick foliage known as the mother of the cacao tree. The kernel was esteemed not only for the chocolate made from it, but also as currency. As such it was used all over Central America. Indeed, one early writer, not a cleric, tells us that in Nicaragua a lady's favors could be had at the price of eight cacao beans. The use of cacao as a currency has survived into the present century in some of the remoter parts of southern Mexico and Guatemala. Peter Martyr has the following apposite comment on this use: "O blessed money, which yeeldeth sweete, and profitable drinke for mankinde, and preserveth the possessors thereof free from the hellish pestilence of avarice, because it cannot be long kept, or hid under ground." A type of counterfeit money existed in ancient Mexico, for we are told that certain dishonest persons used to bore holes in the kernels, through which they extracted the contents, filling the hollowed kernel up once more with earth.

Chocolate, as an imported article, was always a luxury in the plateau country, seldom appearing on the menus of other than rich persons. It was frothed with a swizzle stick, and served with spices and ground maize, chili pepper frequently serving as the spice. Our English words cacao and chocolate are derived through Spanish from the Aztec, as, too, are the names tomato and aguacate.

Maguey was cultivated on a large scale in the plateau country. From the leaves a fibre was derived, and this was used in the manufacture of coarse cloth resembling jute, twine, and carrying bags. The fermented juice supplied pulque, or octli as it was called, the principal intoxicant of the plateau Mexicans. Every action in the cultivation of the maguey, such as the transplanting and drawing of the liquid, was accompanied by its appropriate prayer. On the latter occasion the copper knife employed was urged to cause the plant to weep copiously; in other words yield a bountiful supply of fluid.

Only the old people were allowed to overimbibe, intoxication among the younger people being punishable by death, although this rule did not apparently apply to the ceremonial feasts and drinking bouts, at which the devout, for religious reasons, drank to the point of insensibility. Indeed, at certain religious festivals of this nature in some parts of the country liquor was forced into the intoxicated bodies of devotees in an unnatural and disgusting manner. Generally speaking, liquor was not drunk for social but for religious reasons.

The only domesticated animal known to the Mexican was the dog. Of these large herds were kept, the females for breeding, the males for eating and for sacrificial purposes. There were several breeds, the most interesting of which was a dog with little or no hair, from which the modern Chihuahua breed is probably descended. According to one early authority, all the hairless dogs were not born this way, for some were rubbed

68

with a certain resin which caused the hair to fall out. At night these dogs were protected from the cold by being wrapped in cotton mantles. The same authority (Sahagun) adds the following description of these dogs with little hair: "They generally have a long muzzle, long and sharp teeth, ears hairy and sharply pointed, and their heads large. They are corpulent; their claws are pointed. They are tame and domesticated, and accompany or follow their masters. Habitually good-tempered, they wag their tails, growl, bark, and let their ears drop on their cheeks as a sign of friendship. They eat bread, green corn, flesh both raw and cooked, dead bodies and food that has turned bad." As explained on page 52, dogs played an important part in mortuary rites. Oviedo, an early Spanish writer, writes that stewed dog was a delicious dish.

Large flocks of turkeys were raised, and in many parts of the country a species of small stingless bee was kept in hives made from tree trunks. Hunting naturally played an important part in the economic life of a people thus handicapped by a lack of domesticated flesh-producing animals. A short description of a communal hunt will be found on page 000.

When hunting alone many ceremonies had to be undergone before setting forth. On departing to hunt deer, for example, it was very necessary that the hunter be calm and even-tempered. On reaching the hunting ground he invoked a number of deities including the earth goddess, the four winds and the Tlalocs to have pity on him and aid him in his hunt. Later he prayed to the deer to advance tamely and allow themselves to be shot so that he might be able to offer part of their flesh to Mixcoatl, the hunting god, and the goddess Xochiquetzal. The prayers are of a highly ritualistic nature, and contain many recondite allusions, some of which are difficult to understand at the present time. Similar prayers were offered whenever hunting took place. A short address made to the bees when removing the honey well illustrates the general type of these discourses: "I, who come to do this unfriendly act, come compelled by necessity, since I am poor and miserable; thus I come only to seek my maintenance, and so let none of you be afraid nor be frightened of me. I am only going to take you so that you can see my sister, the goddess Xochiquetzal—she who is called 'Precious branch!' " Fish were caught with hooks or various types of traps. Gold hooks were apparently used among the Mayas, but none have so far been definitely reported from Mexico. A kind of fish scoop of cane was much employed. This was wide-mouthed, gradually narrowing towards the point. Bait was placed in this, and it was supported in midstream by means of empty calabashes. More elaborate traps of lines of stakes were also employed as fish weirs.

When starting to fish the fish were flattered by being addressed in this manner: "My uncles, the painted ones, the ones decorated with spots. You who have chins, horns and fins like beautiful featherwork or turquoise,

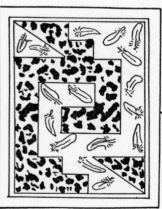

PLATE VIII. DESIGNS ON MANTLES. MAGLIABECCHI CODEX

come here and make haste to come for I seek you." The bait and the traps were also invoked to aid in the work, and flattered with soft words, while alligators were bidden to stay away. One gets the impression that these numerous hunting and fishing prayers, as well as those used in planting and harvesting the crops, are a peculiar blend of command to their hearers to fulfill their function of supporting man directly and the gods indirectly, of apology that man only disturbs them through dire necessity, and of outrageous flattery. It will be noticed that the gods are only indirectly invoked, and the prayers serve to show the strong survivals of a crude animism that underlay Mexican religion. Probably these prayers would not have been countenanced by an orthodox Aztec priest, but they demonstrate clearly the attitude of the Mexican peasant.

Game was always somewhat scarce, and the Mexican peasant was of necessity largely vegetarian. Maize, beans, and chili pepper were the three fundamental elements of his diet. Cooking was woman's task. In preparing tortillas, the form in which the maize was chiefly consumed, the maize grain was first left to soak overnight in water and lime or water and ashes. This loosened the hull of the grain. After washing in water to remove the lime, the grain was ground on a concave stone with a stone roller. The concave stone, known as the metate, a corruption of its Aztec name *Metlatl*, frequently stood on three feet. Next the prepared dough was pressed out with the fingers to very thin disks, and placed on the griddle, a circular pottery tray, which rested on the three stones of the hearth. In a few minutes with a low fire the tortilla was ready to serve. Beside its use for grinding maize for other dishes and also drinks, the metate was also used for grinding other seeds such as cacao beans. Doctor Redfield, in commenting on the time wasted in this drudgery, estimates that the average Mexican Indian woman of to-day spends six hours a day in preparing tortillas where she alone has to prepare the food for a good-sized family, using the metate.

Maize dough was also mixed with water to form *posol* drink. Rolls of dough mixed with fat and often with vegetable or meat centres were placed in maize leaves, forming the well-known tamal. In ancient times, however, tamales appear to have been eaten only during festivals, public or family. Practically all dishes were highly flavored with chili pepper, and if, as one imagines, the ancient Mexican enjoyed his food as highly spiced as does the modern Indian, he must have had a tongue with the consistency of alligator hide. For sweetening honey was used as well as a syrup obtained from the maguey plant. In addition to the more usual method of boiling, food was also cooked in stone-lined underground pits, which were warmed by lighting a fire inside. The fire was removed, and the food, wrapped in leaves, placed in the hole, which was covered with sticks supporting leaves and turf. The practice of frying appears to have been unknown.

In the houses of the humbler people meals were eaten squatting or sitting on blocks of wood around the hearth. When guests were present, the men ate first, the womenfolk of the household serving them, and eating when the men had concluded. Tables were not used, and a rolled tortilla served as spoon; teeth or fingers as knife. Pottery vessels were used to carry and store water, to boil food, and to a limited extent as dishes. A peculiar food much in demand in the Valley of Mexico was made from a kind of ooze on the surface of Lake Texcoco. This was spread out to dry on the shore, and then cut up into bricks to be sold for eating. It is referred to in the description of the market given below. Gnat-like insects from the lake were also eaten.

Certain plants resembling black mushrooms were eaten with honey before some feasts. They caused hallucinations and an effect of drunkenness. One of the early writers also mentions certain red mushrooms as having the same effect, but the mushrooms were actually dried peyote cactus flowers. Peyote seeds were the centre of a regular cult. Candles were burned in front of the packets of seeds, and offerings made to them. A drink made from these peyote seeds also caused hallucinations, but it was entirely employed in curing sickness, and for divinatory purposes. Were a person to lose any valuable possession, he called in a certain sorcerer, who after enquiring the details, drank peyote. While under its effect he had a vision in which an old man, the spirit of the peyote, appeared to him and solved the problem as to where the missing article was located, or in the case of sickness, revealed who was the maker of the black magic that had caused the sickness. Tobacco, too, was used to a limited extent in divination, as well as a plant of the same botanical genus (*Datura*) as the well-known Jimson weed.

Surplus products were taken to market where they were sold or exchanged for other products. Bernal Diaz, who took part in Cortez' march on Mexico City, describes (Maudslay translation) the market in the following words: "When we arrived at the great market place, called Tlaltelolco, we were astounded at the number of people and the quantity of merchandise that it contained, and at the good order and control that was maintained, for we had never seen such a thing before. The chieftains, who accompanied us, acted as guides. Each kind of merchandise was kept by itself and had its fixed place marked out. Let us begin with the dealers in gold, silver, and precious stones, feathers, mantles, and embroidered goods. Then there were other wares consisting of Indian slaves both men and women; and I say that they bring as many of them to that great market for sale as the Portuguese bring negroes from Guinea; and they brought them along tied to long poles, with collars around their necks so that they could not escape, and others they left free. Next there were other traders who sold great pieces of cloth and cotton, and articles of twisted thread, and there were *cacahuateros* who sold cacao. In this way one could see every kind of merchandise that is to be found in the whole of New Spain [Mexico], placed in arrangement in the same manner as they do in my own country, which is Medina del Campo, where they hold the fairs, where each line of booths has its particular kind of merchandise, and so it is in this great market. There were those who sold cloths of henequen and ropes and the sandals with which they are shod, which are made from the same plant, and sweet cooked roots, and other tubers which they get from this plant, all were kept in one part of the market in the place assigned to them. In another part there were skins of tigers and lions, of otters and jackals, deer and other animals and badgers and mountain cats, some tanned and others untanned, and other classes of merchandise.

"Let us go and speak of those who sold beans and sage and other vegetables and herbs in another part, and to those who sold fowls, cocks with wattles (turkeys), rabbits, hares, deer, mallards, young dogs and other things of that sort in their part of the market, and let us also mention the fruiterers, and the women who sold cooked food, dough and tripe in their own part of the market; then every sort of pottery made in a thousand different forms from great water jars to little jugs, and these also had a place to themselves; then those who sold honey and honey paste and other dainties like nut paste, and those who sold lumber, boards, cradles, beams, blocks, and benches, each article by itself, and the vendors of pitch-pine firewood (for

76

torches), and other things of a similar nature. I must furthermore mention, asking your pardon, that they also sold many canoes full of human excrement, and these were kept in the creeks near the market, and this they use for making salt or tanning skins, for without it they say that they cannot be well prepared. . . .

"Paper, which in this country is called *Amal*, and reeds scented with *liquidambar*, and full of tobacco, and yellow ointments and things of that sort are sold by themselves, and much cochineal is sold under the arcades which are in that great market place, and there are many vendors of herbs and other sorts of trades. There are also buildings where three magistrates sit in judgment, and there are executive officers like *Alguacils* who inspect the merchandise. I am forgetting those who sell salt, and those who make the stone knives, and how they split them off the stone itself; and the fisherwomen and others who sell some small cakes made from a sort of ooze which they get out of the great lake, which curdles, and from this they make a bread having a flavor something like cheese. There are for sale axes of brass [bronze] and copper and tin, and gourds and gaily painted jars made of wood. I could wish that I had finished telling of all the things which are sold there, but they are so numerous and of such different quality and the great market place with its surrounding arcades was so crowded with people, that one would not have been able to see and enquire about it all in two days."

77

Every town possessed its local market, which the people attended every fifth day. Scenes such as Bernal Diaz describes can still be seen in many towns of south Mexico, although, naturally, not on so vast a scale, and the merchandise is still largely transported on the back of its owner as in Bernal Diaz' time.

In addition to their work in preparing and cooking food, women were also occupied in spinning and weaving. Persons of the better class wore cotton garments, but cotton was scarce in the plateau country, since much of it was imported. Some of the finest decorated cotton mantles were imported into Mexico from Yucatan, where the Mayas had earned a high reputation for their skill in this work. Cotton did not grow in Tlaxcalan territory, hence when the inhabitants were at war with the Aztecs, which was most of the time, they were deprived of cotton goods by blockade. The Aztecs and their allies similarly cut off the Tlaxcalan imports of salt.

Cotton was spun on spindles passed through pottery whorls to give added momentum. The raw cotton was hung over the right shoulder, whence it was fed with one hand, while the other was used to twirl the spindle. Sometimes the spindle was rested on the base of a small pottery bowl. For weaving primitive hand-looms of the rod-heald type, still to be seen in the remoter villages of Mexico, were employed. The rod at the top of the warp was attached to a post, while the whole was held taut by being attached to a band which passed round

78

the weaver's waist. (Plate V.) These looms appear to have seldom or never exceeded a breadth of about eighteen inches, and for wide cloths it was necessary to sew together two or more strips. Designs were made by using different colored threads in both the warp and woof, and probably by the use of tie-dyeing in which sections of the cloth to be dyed are tied so tightly that the dye cannot penetrate, and the cloth has a mottled appearance. By extension several colors can be applied to every thread. It is also possible that the batik technique was also used, since a similar method was used in decorating pottery.

Designs were also embroidered on cloth either with colored cotton, or by sewing on feathers arranged in patterns. It is doubtful, however, if the Mexican weavers attained such high levels as were reached in ancient Peru. Dyes were obtained chiefly from the vegetable kingdom, but others derived from the soil were also employed. The most interesting dye contributed by the animal kingdom, in addition to cochineal, was a purple obtained from a sea clam (*Purpura patula*) found off the southwest coast of Mexico. The process is very similar to that used in obtaining the imperial purple of ancient Rome. This purple cloth was very highly valued both for its rarity and for the distance it had to be transported. The industry continued to flourish until the present century, when a rapid decline set in due to the cheapness of aniline dyes. Many elaborate patterns on cotton mantles are reproduced in the codices. (Plate VIII.)

79

Maguey fibre was also woven for coarse clothing and carrying bags, particularly among the poorer people. This fibre was also dyed, and simple patterns introduced. The Tlaxcalans largely wore garments of maguey fibre for the reason already given. Clothing among the Otomies also was largely of this material due to the general poverty and primitiveness of this people. Skins were also worn among the Otomies, but cloaks of rabbit skins were highly valued in most of the plateau country, and rabbit hair was woven as borders for cotton mantles.

The general costume worn by men was made up of two garments. The most important of these was a loin cloth called *maxtli*. This was wound round the waist and between the legs, the ends hanging down in front and behind. Among the poorer people this was made of a simple strip of undecorated cloth, but among the nobility the maxtli was decorated with embroidered patterns and feather fringes. The second garment, which was worn only in cold weather or during festivals, was a cloak or mantle worn round the shoulders and tied by knotting together two of the corners on the chest or under one arm. This again varied according to the wealth of the owner from rough maguey fibre to embroidered cotton or rabbit skin. Young men in the military school wore mantles of maguey fibre to which were attached small sea shells. Members of the nobility wore a similar decoration, but the shells were made of gold. Feather cloaks were also worn by the wealthy.

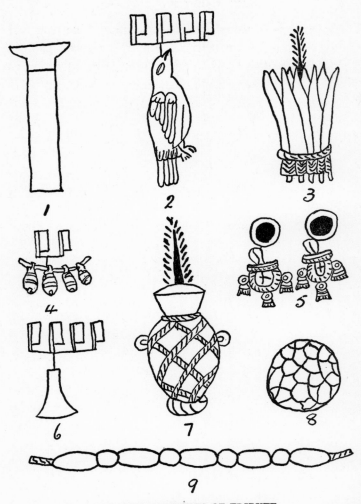

PLATE IX. ARTICLES OF TRIBUTE

1, Amber tubes; 2, Eighty plumage birds; 3, Four hundred bunches of feathers;
4, Forty strings of copper bells; 5, Sixteen thousand balls of copal incense; 6, Eighty
copper axes; 7, Four hundred jars of honey; 8, Mosaic mirror; 9, Jade necklace.
Mendoza Codex.

Sandals were made of coarse maguey fibre, the leaves of a tree called *Yecotl*, or of hide. A large number of pottery stamps are found throughout Mexico, and these, apparently, were used for stamping designs on cotton clothing as well as on the body. Many of the designs are intricately carved; one of the favorites represents a spider monkey. Body painting was a common practice particularly among the Totonacs and Huaxtecs, for very many of the figurines from this area show large areas covered with black paint. Direct evidence for tattooing does not exist among the Aztecs, although there are vague references to the custom, but since it occurred among the Mayas, it was in all probability also a Maya custom. Prostitutes stained their teeth red with cochineal, and in other parts of Mexico it was the custom to stain the teeth black. Incisor and canine teeth of the upper jaw were also occasionally inlaid with small disks of jade, examples having been reported from Oaxaca and Puebla. The drilling of the holes, which was probably done with a hollow bone or bamboo drill and sand, must have been extremely painful. Teeth were also occasionally filed, but neither of these customs was as common as among the Mayas.

Nose, lower lip and ear-plugs were worn by persons of rank. These were of jade, crystal, obsidian, or other precious stones or of metal. Persons of less rank wore plugs of pottery. Some of the jade ear-plugs, which were worn in the lobe of the ear, are of considerable size, reaching a diameter of more than two inches. One of a similar type found by the writer in a Maya ruin had a width of little short of five inches. Skillfully decorated gold and copper rings were worn, but they are comparatively scarce in archæological collections. The outer half of the circumference was frequently twice as wide as the hidden half, and carried designs often of birds' or animals' heads.

Necklaces of all descriptions were worn by the nobility. Those of jade were considered most valuable, being more prized than gold. The former consisted of globular or tubular beads with little or no decoration; the latter were made of beads of all shapes. Sometimes gold was combined with semi-precious stones. Among the treasures of Mexico sent by Cortez to the Emperor Charles V was a large collar of gold and mosaic stone-work of eight strings made up of 132 red stones and 163 jade beads with twenty-seven gold beads attached, with four stone amulets in the centre inlaid or with settings of gold. From these amulets, which probably represented gods, hung pendants. Such a necklace with such a large quantity of jade beads must have been of very great value.

Aztec gold was principally obtained from what to-day forms the State of Guerrero, although Oaxaca seems to have been the area of greatest output, but most of it was retained and worked by the Zapotecs. A third important centre was on the east coast of Mexico in the vicinity of the State of Vera Cruz. The metal was not mined but washed from river sand by the use of gourds.

The gold was usually transported as dust placed in transparent quills. Bernal Diaz in a continuation of his description of the market writes: "There were many more merchants, who, as I was told, brought gold for sale in grains, just as it is taken from the mines. The gold is placed in thin quills of the geese of the country, white quills, so that the gold can be seen through, and according to the length and thickness of the quills they arrange their accounts with one another." He uses the term mine to mean placer mining, as can be shown by extracts from other parts of his history. Gold was also occasionally transported in the form of bars. The greater part of the metal reaching Mexico was paid as tribute, codices giving lists of towns of southwest Mexico, and the quantity of gold to be paid by them.

The working of gold, like most crafts, was attributed to the Toltecs. At the close of the Aztec empire the craft was particularly developed at Azcapotzalco, once the capital of the Tepanecs, but now a suburb of Mexico City. As explained on page 180, Xipe was the patron god of the goldsmiths, who sacrificed victims in his honor. Gold was smelted in charcoal-heated crucibles. In place of bellows the smith blew down a tube. The most usual method of fashioning gold ornaments was as follows: The artificer mixed very finely ground charcoal with the clay used in pottery-making. The well-kneaded lump was cut into disks and left to dry for two days. Then being thoroughly hard it was carved into a negative of the requisite shape with a copper imple-

ment. The charcoal cast was next covered with a mixture of clarified wax and charcoal, and over the surface
of the wax was sprinkled a thin coating of charcoal
powder. Finally the whole was enclosed in a tight-fit-
ting mold of coarse charcoal and clay, leaving only a
narrow spout leading from the outside to the wax. The
whole was then heated so that the wax melted and was
poured out through the spout, and replaced by molten
gold or an alloy. As soon as this was cool, the mold was
broken, and the gold, having occupied the place of the
wax next to the negative, or mold, was of the required
shape.

In addition to this method, gold was hammered out
into the required shapes. Thin gold-leaf was also manufactured, and applied as a covering to wooden-carved
objects, such as spear-throwers, two beautiful examples
of which are to be seen in the Florence Anthropological
Museum. As illustrative of the craftsmanship of the
Mexican goldsmiths might be mentioned three or four
of the articles sent to Spain in 1525 as the king's share:
"A flower of stone set in gold like a small bell weighing
twenty-four pesos," "A collar of small melons consisting of thirty-two pieces of greenstones, made so that
they seem to issue from the flower, the flowers and
stalks being of gold," "A small scallop-shell set in gold
with a greenstone in the centre," "A butterfly of gold
with the wings of shell, and the body and head of greenstone." It must be remembered that all objects of pure
gold, with very few exceptions, were melted down, so

that we have descriptions of the objects only partially of gold that could not be melted down. Doctor Saville in his *Goldsmith's Art in Ancient Mexico* gives full lists of the shipments, and to him we are indebted for the list of objects just given.

Owing to the melting down of the gold, not a single example of this original loot has survived, and we are dependent for visual knowledge of Mexican gold work on occasional archæological finds. These are scarce, and frequently the objects even to-day find their way into the melting pot, the finders not realizing that their archæological merit is greater than their bullion value. Most modern finds of gold have been found in the state of Oaxaca, and as this chapter was being written news arrived of the finding of what will surely prove to be the greatest haul of gold objects made in Mexico in the last two hundred years. Luckily the finds were made under the supervision of Licenciado Alfonso Caso, one of Mexico's leading archæologists, consequently the specimens will enrich the national collections and not find their way to the melting pot. This gold was found in a burial chamber close to the famous ruins of Monte Alban in Oaxaca.

Gold was very frequently alloyed with copper, and sometimes with silver. The art of metal working seems to have had its New World origin in Peru or the contiguous regions, and thence spread to Colombia and the Panama-Costa Rica area. It does not appear to have been introduced into Mexico and the Maya area until some time between the eleventh and thirteenth centuries. No authenticated example of metal has ever been found in the Maya Old Empire period. Some of the Mexican gold pieces resemble those of the Panama-Costa Rica region, and doubtlessly the first gold objects known in Mexico were trade pieces from that area. Gold or copper bells of Mexican workmanship were traded far and wide, having turned up in archæological excavations in areas as distant as Honduras, Yucatan, and New Mexico. One of the strangest examples of gold work was reported from Tepic in northwest Mexico, where a pottery vessel of the plumbate glaze ware was found. This vessel, which from the nature of the clay (p. 000) was almost surely imported from far-away El Salvador, was made in the shape of a turkey with the head and neck painted bright red. The wattles are ornamented with thin leaf gold, the whole effect being extremely naturalistic.

The highly prized jade largely reached Mexico City as tribute from the conquered provinces of southwest Mexico, particularly Guerrero and northern Oaxaca. Jade is really a misnomer, as the stone is actually jadeite. For many years it was believed that this had been imported into Mexico from Asia, but chemical analysis shows the percentages of the components of Mexican jade vary slightly from those of Asiatic jade; consequently Mexican jades could not have been transported across the Pacific. No authenticated deposits of jade have been found in modern Mexico, but there are two explanations for this. Firstly, large districts of south-west Mexico have never been thoroughly examined by geologists, and secondly, ancient Mexican jade was largely obtained from water-carried boulders, as the specimens themselves frequently show. In the course of centuries this supply was practically exhausted, and hence the rarity of jade in ancient times and the failure to find it in modern times.

Jade was worked with the aid of sand. Apparently, for cutting string was rubbed up and down a groove liberally strewn with sand, but the more usual method of working was with the aid of a hollow drill of bamboo or bone, possibly operated with a bow drill, similar to that used by the Eskimo, and sand. Some thirty years ago a very beautiful onyx tablet in Field Museum was accidentally broken. The break revealed a bone drill still in position in the middle of the hole bored through the centre from top to bottom. Holes of this nature were invariably bored from both ends, and serve as a first ready test as to the authenticity of a doubtful piece, since the bore is always widest at the two mouths, gradually narrowing towards the centre and frequently the two bores do not exactly meet. Faked pieces often show that the hole, made with a modern drill, passes through from one side to another without narrowing. If only the fakers would take archæologists into partnership, it might prove profitable for them, and give some of us more lucrative appointments!

Most jade pieces show clear examples of shallow drill

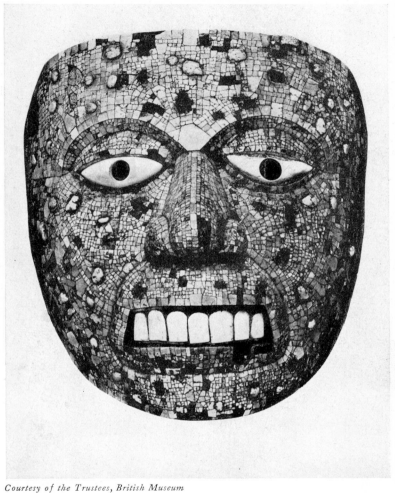

PLATE X. TURQUOISE MOSAIC MASK WITH SHELL TEETH
AND SHELL EYES

bores used to indicate the eyes and ear-plugs. Particularly is this true of the innumerable figurines from the Mixtec country of Oaxaca, where the technique is combined with the cord cutter. Mexican jades vary from apple-green to a marked gray-green. Field Museum possesses a large mask of black jade, but this is rare, and it is doubtful if the Mexicans realized that it was of the same stone. On the other hand, many other green stones were confounded with jade by the Aztecs, and even copper-stained rock crystal comes into this category, although the craftsmen must have realized the difference owing to the variable facility with which the substitutes were worked.

Turquoise was also highly valued, particularly for mosaic work. This was mined, in all probability, in the southern Vera Cruz region, although it has been claimed that it was fetched from the mines of New Mexico. Owing to its rarity it was reserved for divine use. A few beautiful examples of turquoise mosaic work are extant, particularly in the British Museum, where are preserved a number of the presents sent by Cortez to the Emperor Charles V. (Plate X.) Patterns were picked out by using different colored stones, or making the figures in low relief. Some of the best examples in the New World were found a few years ago in a cave in Mexico, and are now on exhibit in the Museum of the American Indian, Heye Foundation in New York. According to one early authority turquoise was reserved entirely for religious purposes, but we know that the Mexican rulers used a head-dress with turquoise decoration, possibly because they were considered more than semi-divine.

Most cutting implements were made of obsidian or flint, particularly the former, of which there was a plentiful supply owing to the volcanic nature of the country. From oblong hunks of this material, called cores, thin slivers were removed all round the circumference by pressure flaking. Subsequently pressure behind the angle formed by the removal of previous slivers caused the loosening of other three-faced thin slivers, which served as knife blades. (Plate XI.) The pressure was exerted by pushing with the chest on a T-shaped wooden implement, the point of which rested against the required point, the core being held between the worker's feet. A small percussion bulb marks the point of pressure. Flakes could be removed from the core until it was reduced to very small dimensions. Cores of this description may be found in large numbers in the Valley of Mexico. Ordinary thin flakes were used without retouching as knife blades, since they have an extremely sharp edge. Spear-heads of obsidian were made by retouching the larger blades with secondary pressure flaking. Flint spear-heads with secondary pressure flaking were also used, and the best rival the finest stone work of the Old World. (Plate XI.)

Implements of similar type were set in elaborate mosaic-covered wooden handles and employed as sacrificial knives. Frequently the handles appear to have been made in the shape of crouching men. Beautiful examples of such sacrificial knives are to be seen in the British Museum and the Anthropological Museum in Florence.

Obsidian was also polished to serve as mirrors and was carved into masks, long tubular beads and labrets. Rock crystal appears to have been highly prized. One of the finest examples of rock crystal carving is in the form of a very realistic human skull that formed part of the early loot sent from Mexico to Spain, and is now in the British Museum. Labrets and beads of rock crystal are also to be seen in a number of museums. Graceful vases of calcite were made in the southern part of the Vera Cruz area, and apparently were also highly prized. Small amulets and beads were made from a wide range of stones, both semi-precious and common.

Feather working was an important industry in ancient Mexico, but very few examples of this craft have come down to us. The feather workers formed a wealthy and honored guild closely united to the merchants, who brought them their finest feathers from the southern lowlands. They had seven patron gods, of whom the most important was Coyotlinauatl, a deity with the face of a coyote and long gold teeth. The feather workers lived in a certain district of Mexico City, honoring their deities with the usual sacrifices of slaves. In the simpler work feathers were merely sewn on cloth, but in the more elaborate work the feathers were arranged in mosaic fashion to form delicate patterns. In the finer work only the small delicate feathers were used, and they were arranged to overlap so that no part of the quill was visible. The most valued feathers were the long tail feathers of the quetzal and other trogons. These were sewn on head-dresses and banners. Most of the finer feathers were imported from the southern lowlands. In parts of Central America macaws were kept in captivity to supply the feather demand, and descriptions of Montezuma's aviary speak of ducks, flamingoes, macaws, parrots, and quetzals being kept there for their plumage. If quetzals were indeed kept in captivity the Aztecs had greater ornithological knowledge than modern man on this subject, for it has been found impossible to keep this bird in captivity, since it feeds off insects on the wing, hence its adoption as the national symbol of Guatemala.

Feather mosaic work was frequently combined with gold to produce the most intricate designs. Among the objects sent to the Emperor Charles V were a feather pattern with turquoise mosaic and a centre of gold, the whole with a leather backing, and a feather head-dress surrounded by sixty-eight pieces of gold and twenty turret-shaped objects of the same metal. Unfortunately the whole industry collapsed soon after the Spanish conquest, living only in the descriptions of the Spanish chroniclers and half a dozen museum pieces the worse for three centuries of neglect.

The trade of carpentry was passed on from father to son, the finest work requiring not only skill but also a high artistic ability. Copper and stone adzes were used, but for the more delicate work sharp stone implements were probably favored, together with drills for circular work and cords employed with sand for cutting straight lines.

Few examples of carved wood have survived to the present time, but of this small number the majority, comprising drums and spear-throwers, are of outstanding merit. Nearly all these fine pieces, which carry carved designs depicting deities and religious scenes, are to be seen in the European museums, although there are a few examples in the Heye Foundation in New York and one or two in Mexico.

Carved wooden stools, either with or without a back support, are depicted in the codices, but none of these have survived to the present time. The supports are usually shown as carved with the step pattern so frequently used at Mitla (p. 264). Bernal Diaz, in his description of the great market place in Tenochtitlan (p. 77), speaks of gaily painted wooden vessels. These apparently were lacquered. At the present time delicate lacquer work is done in western Mexico, and in some cases the designs are definitely native. This, together with the fact that lacquered wooden vessels were made in Peru prior to the discovery of America, suggests that the craft was not introduced by the Spaniards, but is of native origin.

From early accounts it is also known that wooden chests and boxes were manufactured, but again not a single example has survived. Of the tens of thousands of wooden idols that must have existed in Mexico five hundred years ago, practically none survive, and those very few that have come down to us, escaping the bon-fires of the missionaries, are of little merit.

Every day objects of wood, such as bows, canoes, paddles, household utensils, were presumably not made by professional carpenters, but by the man who needed them for his own use. The same, of course, applies to a number of the objects, on which we have already touched, except when they were needed for ceremonial purposes or for persons of high rank. The average man would manufacture his own spearthrower, but a skilled carpenter would be employed to carve and adorn the spearthrower carried by Montezuma or placed in the hands of some idol.

Factories were non-existent, for crafts were carried on at home. Most craftsmen carried on their trades as a side line, living in their native villages, and never neglecting to plant their crops. The goldsmiths, and possibly other metal workers, appear to have been the only craftsmen who did not conform to this practice.

Copper working was little developed in Mexico at the time of the conquest, since copper tools were fre-quently not superior to those of obsidian or stone. Cop-per axes were used to a limited extent, but the metal was mainly employed for ornaments or to be alloyed with gold. The chief purpose to which copper was put was the manufacture of the clapperless copper bells de-scribed on page 133. A few copper rings have been

Courtesy of Field Museum, Chicago

PLATE XI. COPPER AND STONE ARTIFACTS

Bell, ring, money token and hoe blade of copper; knife blade of flint; spear-heads and knife blade of obsidian; celt of jade

found in the course of excavations as well as other simple copper ornaments, but the chief use, apart from the manufacture of bells, to which copper was put, was the making of thin ax-shaped blades. These have a crescentric blade on the end of a thin haft of copper set at right angles. They are found principally in Oaxaca, and are reported to have served as currency. (Plate XI.)

Early Spanish reports speak of the natives mining tin. This, together with the results of analyses, shows that, like the Peruvians, they knew how to make bronze, but the invention must have been made very shortly before the conquest, since few of the objects so far analyzed show evidence of a deliberate intention to produce bronze.

House building was not a trade, but a task in which every one took a hand, the members of a community assisting any one who needed a new home without reward save their food during the work and a feast when the task was completed.

The average house of the poorer class Aztec was a square structure with walls of adobe, rough stones set in mud, or mud-covered wattle and cornstalks, with the outsides frequently covered with plaster. Pent-shaped roofs of thatch were most common, but flat roofs were used in the more pretentious structures. In some parts of southern Mexico and among the Huaxtec round houses were built. Houses of the poorer people usually consisted of a single windowless room, light entering through the doorways. Furniture was scarce, straw mats for beds and low wooden stools being the principal fixtures. Sometimes the kitchen was situated in one corner of the room, but more usually was located in a minor structure behind the house. In addition, a round tower-like structure with walls of maize stalks was placed in front of the house to hold maize on the cob. Often another construction, shaped like a huge vase with swelling sides, served as a second granary, being employed to hold shelled maize. This was mud-plastered.

Many families possessed sweat houses. These probably did not vary to any marked degree from those still in use to-day in many parts of central and southern Mexico. "This," to quote Redfield's description of a modern sweat house in Tepoztlan, "is made of stone set in mortar. It is rectangular, approximately square, and about five feet high at the centre. The roof is low-peaked. The one entrance is barely large enough to permit entrance of a man on hands and knees." These sweat houses were principally used for therapeutic purposes, although there appears to have been an idea of purification too in their probable use before religious ceremonies. Steam was generated by pouring hot water on heated stones. The sweat house is a very widely distributed trait of ancient American civilization both in North and Central America. Such in brief are the structures that housed the peasant household of the Aztecs and its possessions. Many families in addition owned turkeys that necessitated small fowl houses, and bees, whose hives were formed from hollowed-out sections of tree trunks stopped up at the ends, except for exits, with mud.

The houses of the wealthier members of the community ranged from the simplicity of the homes of the peasants up to the luxury of Montezuma's palatial residence described in Chapter IV.

Many of the villages and towns situated on the shores of Lake Texcoco were composed of houses set on piles. For locomotion, fishing and duck hunting these lake dwellers made use of simple dugout canoes, sometimes decorated with carved projections fore and aft, presumably made by adding a gunwale with projections at these points. (Plate XXXI.) Tenochtitlan (Mexico City) itself was situated in the middle of Lake Texcoco prior to the conquest, and the streets in many parts were canals and the outlying houses stood on piles.

The location of the Aztec capital in the middle of a lake made it an ideal defensive position. Except in canoes, it could only be approached by one of the four causeways that united the city to the mainland. These were raised above the lake level, the foundation consisting of rubble and rocks. Their defence was made easier by a number of bridges consisting of planks of wood spanning gaps in each causeway. Cortez, in one of his letters to the Emperor, writes that the bridges were so wide that ten horsemen could ride abreast. This implies that the causeways were largely used for religious and civic processions, since a people like the Aztecs, possessing no beast of burden or wheeled traffic, could have had no need for such wide roads and bridges. Raised roads of a breadth of thirty feet or more are also reported from eastern Yucatan in the Maya area. They, too, cross shallow lakes, as in the case of the causeways under discussion. Naturally, the bridges also were built to allow the water of the lake to find its own level, and to allow the passage of canoes carrying produce to different parts of the city.

The centre of the city was built on dry land laboriously built up during the early occupation of the city, but in many respects the city as first viewed by the Spaniards must have appeared as a fantastic Venice transported to the New World, with its domed churches converted into the pyramidal homes of Beelzebub.

CHAPTER IV

SOCIAL ORGANIZATION, WAR, AND TRADE

Status of Rulers. Their Election. Tribal Council. Montezuma's Palace and Gardens. Initiation of Ruler. The Geographical Clans. Their Organization. The Basis of Mexican Society. The Four Divisions of Tenochtitlan. Dual Executive. Justice. Judicial System. Slavery. Warrior Classes. Initiation Ceremonies. Warfare. Weapons. Triumphs. Trophies. Causes of War. Merchant Guild. Trade. Markets. Trade Pieces.

THE status of Montezuma and the other Aztec rulers has been hotly debated. The early Spanish writers speak of him as though he were an Emperor of unlimited power, and Prescott, the most popular writer on Mexico in English, paints Montezuma as the head of an absolute monarchy. Bandelier, who might be described as a pioneer debunker, advanced the thesis that Montezuma was little more than an elected executive with limited personal authority. Modern opinion, following the tendency of our age, favors compromise over these fundamentally different viewpoints. The Aztec ruler, the term I use in this book to describe Montezuma and his predecessors, might be compared to the chairman of a financial or industrial corporation. His authority varied according to his personality, and that of the executive council. A strong ruler with a weak council might be something very close to an absolute monarch, just as a strong chairman with a spineless board of directors concentrates power in his own hands. On the other hand a weak ruler with a strong council might find himself with little authority.

The Aztec and other Mexican rulers did not succeed their fathers, but were elected by an assembly of clan chiefs, old leaders and leading priests, whose vote had to be unanimous. The choice was limited to a single lineage (p. 28). In actual practice a younger brother of the deceased usually was elected, or failing that a son, but if the logical successor was unsuitable he was passed over. This council appears also to have had the power of deposing the ruler under exceptional circumstances. Montezuma, while a prisoner in the hands of Cortez, was deprived of his position partly on account of his pusillanimous attitude and partly because of his inability to assume the leadership while in Spanish hands.

The executive council, whose authority was in many ways supreme, apparently consisted of one representative from each of the twenty geographical clans (*calpulli*) which formed the Aztec nation. The council seems to have met once every Mexican month—that is every twenty days—but could be summoned at other times in the event of an emergency. We should probably not be far in error in comparing the relations between this council and the ruler to that of the British cabinet to the king of England, the council like the cabinet reflecting popular opinion, and the Mexican ruler acting as a constitutional monarch with somewhat more latitude than is allowed the king of England, but like him of considerable importance in state religion. As the nominal head of the Aztec nation, Montezuma was accorded very high honor.

It is related that any chief who wished to speak to the Aztec ruler, approached him with downcast eyes, barefoot, and dressed in the clothing of a person of no importance. Montezuma was usually carried in a litter, the supports of which were borne on the shoulders of four chieftains. Under no circumstances were his feet allowed to touch the soil, and to avoid this mantles were strewn in his path. This is an ancient custom of world-wide practice having its origins in magico-religious concepts. Four other chiefs held over the litter a canopy of green feathers with a fringe decorated with gold, silver, pearls and jade. No one was allowed to lift his head at the ruler's approach. We are told that even the soles of Montezuma's sandals were of gold, while the upper part was adorned with precious stones. Bernal Diaz has left us an interesting description of his habits, from which the following account of palace life is quoted:

"If it was cold they made up a large fire of live coals of a firewood made from the bark of trees which did not give off any smoke, and the scent of the bark from which the fire was made was very fragrant, and so that it should not give off more heat than he required, they placed in front of it a sort of screen adorned with idols worked in gold. He was seated on a low stool, soft and richly worked, and the table, which was also low, was made in the same style as the seats, and on it they placed the table cloths of white cloth and some rather long napkins of the same material. Four very beautiful, cleanly women brought water for his hands in a sort of deep basin which they call *Xicales* [jicara gourd], and they held others like plates below to catch the water, and they brought him towels. And two other women brought him tortilla bread, and as soon as he began to eat they placed before him a sort of wooden screen painted over with gold, so that no one should watch him eating. Then the four women stood aside, and four great chieftains who were old men came and stood beside them, and with these Montezuma now and then conversed, and asked them questions, and as a great favor he would give to each of these elders a dish of what to him tasted best. They say that these elders were his near relations, and were his counsellors and judges of law suits, and the dishes and food which Montezuma gave them they ate standing up with much reverence and without looking at his face. He was served on Cholula earthenware either red or black. . . .

"From time to time they brought him, in cup-shaped vessels of pure gold, a certain drink made from cacao. . . . Sometimes at meal-times there were present some very ugly humpbacks, very small of stature and their bodies almost broken in half, who are their jesters, and other Indians, who must have been buffoons, who told him witty sayings, and others who sang and danced, for Montezuma was fond of pleasure and song."

These dwarfs wore rubber footgear to make them bounce better—surely the first recorded case of rubber shoes. Torquemada states that children were purposely deformed to qualify as entertainers, and that albinos were also kept for entertainment, although another early chronicler (Gomara) says that the albinos were kept in the zoological gardens as though to suggest that they were not looked on as human. Albinos were also reserved for sacrifice during eclipses of the sun.

Montezuma's palace is reported to have been built around three patios in the centre of one of which there was a fountain of water brought by conduit from Chapultepec. There were one hundred bedrooms and one hundred baths, so it is clear that the Aztecs reached the American ideal of a bath for every bedroom several centuries ahead of their conquerors. The walls were made of stone and mortar bedecked on the inside with valuable stone, while the woodwork was of carved pine, cedar and palm. Montezuma had a private oratory in the building. This room was 150 feet long and 50 feet wide. The walls were covered with thick slabs of gold and silver and adorned with precious stones. An idea of the great extent of the palace buildings can be gathered from a contemporary statement that in attached buildings the soldiers of Cortez and more than 2000 Tlax-

calan allies were sheltered during the first occupation
of the city. The early accounts appear somewhat exaggerated, and it is unfortunate that they cannot be
checked archæologically. The roofs presumably were
flat like those of the houses of the nobility.

Nearby were Montezuma's zoological gardens, where
every kind of wild animal, rare bird and strange rep-
tile was kept. The reptiles included alligators and every
conceivable species of snake. Some of the zoo's inmates
were kept for eating, or, in the case of many of the birds,
for their feathers, but the majority were maintained
solely as a curiosity. There were also numerous gardens
and woods attached to the palace.

Like most semi-civilized potentates, Montezuma had
a large number of concubines, although monogamy was
the usual Mexican practice.

On being chosen to succeed to the rulership, a candidate was forced to undergo a rigid period of initiation.
At the start of the investiture the ruler clad only in a
loincloth marched in silence to the temple of Huitzilopochtli accompanied by the nobility and the allied rulers of Texcoco and Tlacopan. On his arrival the high
priest painted him from head to foot with a deep black
paint, and then on his kneeling, sprinkled him four
times with water. Next the priest decked him in a
cloak decorated with a design of bones and skulls, and
placed on his head two cloths, one black, the other blue,
decorated with similar designs. Magical powders to
ward off disease and an incense brazier were also pre-

sented to him. On the conclusion of this ceremony the high priest discoursed at length on his executive duties, to which the future ruler replied with an equally long speech, probably not differing greatly from the platitudinous discourse a modern Chief Elk or Rotarian would make under similar circumstances. Finally the future ruler retired to a small chamber.

Here he remained without stirring from the vicinity for four days, during which he fasted, eating only once a day, and spending the time in prayer and the sacrifice of blood and incense. The former was drawn from his ears and other parts of his body. At the conclusion of the four days all the chiefs, high priests and noblemen conducted him to his palace. Rulers of nations allied to or under the subjection of the Aztecs were confirmed in their office by the Aztec ruler after their election. At a later ceremony of confirmation of the investiture, many prisoners, procured in a special campaign led by the candidate, were offered in sacrifice.

The twenty calpullis that formed the Aztec nation at the time of the Spanish conquest were probably derived from original exogamous clans in which descent was through the mother, but by the time of the Aztec collapse the calpulli functioned more as a geographical organization than one based on kinship, and the descent had reverted from matrilineal back to its first probable form of patrilineal. Apparently there were no prohibitions at this last stage against marrying a fellow member of the calpulli. The calpulli, as we have seen (p.

60) held title to land, which was assigned to the different families that composed it, but apart from this important difference, and the common descent claimed by its members, the calpulli appears to have resembled in most respects the boroughs that made up a mediæval European city. While under the supreme rule of the state, the calpulli functioned in many respects as an independent entity. It had its own elected officials, of whom there appear to have been two of outstanding importance.

One was the military leader of the group, for each calpulli seems to have fought in war as a kind of local regiment; the other a civil official, whose duties appear to have included the disposal of the produce of those sections of the group's land worked in common for religious and other needs. There was also a group council, to which position all the elders of the calpulli appear to have been eligible, corresponding to the borough or parish council of the European city. Meetings were held in a large building or communal house, which served as a men's club for all adult members of the calpulli. Women were probably not admitted to this communal house. Each calpulli also possessed its own temple, and in addition its own patron god, corresponding to the patron saint of the European parish. The upkeep of this temple and its attendant priest or priests was forthcoming from the communal lands, and in all probability each calpulli got a share of the tribute paid by the subjected peoples to the Aztec city-state. Almost

certainly disputes between two members of the same
calpulli must have been settled by calpulli judges.

Mexican society can truthfully be described as having been founded on the calpulli. In early times probably independent units, they never lost their independence entirely, but were loosely federated into the
Aztec city-state. There was however an intermediate
superior union, consisting of four divisions of the tribe,
each possibly composed of five calpullis. This larger
organization presumably had a religious basis in connection with the ritualistic division into the four world
directions. Each quarter had its own deity and temple,
and the members of the different calpullis composing
a quarter considered themselves to be loosely related
by common descent. At the head of each quarter was
a war chief of very high rank, second only to the Aztec
ruler and the chief civil ruler discussed below. Apparently these war chiefs were of the "royal" lineage, since
the Aztec ruler was chosen from their number, and we
have already noted that he was always one of a certain
lineage. The four war chiefs of the quarters shared the
privilege with the Aztec ruler and the chief civil ruler
of wearing their hair bound with red leather. Each
quarter also possessed an armory and a boys' college.
The organization of each quarter probably did not differ essentially from its components—the calpullec (plu-
ral of calpulli).

We have spoken of Montezuma and his predecessors
as the Aztec rulers. This is in some respects a misnomer,

for the chief executive office was dual. Montezuma was the military and religious leader, and for that reason was of greater importance, but there was also a mysterious official of apparently similar rank rejoicing in the equally mysterious title of Snake Woman. The snake woman, who was male, appears to have been the civil Aztec leader, possibly in charge of the war commissariat and the gathering and division of tribute. Like the military and religious leader he wore the *copilli*, the mosaic-studded crown which rose to a peak in front, and faintly resembled the crown of Lower Egypt. These two leaders with the tribal council, of which little is known but which appears to have consisted of one representative from each of the twenty calpullec, were the executives of the Aztec tribe.

Despite this picture of the fundamental calpullec forming four quarters and federated under the chief Aztec ruler and Aztec civil ruler to form the Aztec city-state organization, there are many gaps in our knowledge of the social organization of the Aztecs. For instance we have no information as to the relationship of members of the nobility to their calpulli. We have also hints that certain trades may have been confined to special calpullec.

Justice was meted out with considerable severity, judging by our modern coddling of prisoners. Prisons were unknown; the only thing approaching these were the wooden cages in which prisoners were usually kept pending sacrifice. These cages, however, had as their function not the punishment of the prisoner, but the prevention of his escape. A man convicted of robbery was sold into slavery and the stolen goods restored to their owner, but if the stolen goods could not be found the thief paid with his life. Robbery was so rare and contrary to Mexican conventions that the houses had no doors. When the owner was away two sticks were placed in the doorway, and these appear to have acted as a taboo somewhat on the same lines as the taboo signs, such as crotulus leaves, left on property in many Pacific Islands to guard it.

Any one caught robbing in the market was beaten to death, while those caught stealing gold were sacrificed to Xipe, the patron god of the goldsmiths. Despite these very severe penalties, there were professional robbers. The arm of a woman who had died giving birth to her first child was considered a sovereign protection against being caught. Robbers also considered that Quetzalcoatl was their protector. When stealing at night a robber would knock twice on the ground and the lintel of the house he was going to enter, for he believed that this would cause the inmates to sleep soundly while he was robbing them.

Those who were hungry were allowed to pluck two or three ears of corn as they passed the fields, but should a man take a large quantity of corn or maliciously uproot plants in the fields, he suffered death. A man could only be condemned for adultery if there were independent witnesses, and a confession was made by the guilty party. The punishment was death by stoning in the public market; either stones were thrown by the general public or a heavy stone smashed in the offender's skull. Members of the nobility were accorded the privilege of being executed in private, hanging being a common form of execution in this case.

A man who killed his wife for adultery was punished with death, the law maintaining that no private individual had the right to mete out justice. Other crimes punishable by death were the moving of boundaries, the peculation of the property of a minor, the wasteful spending of a patrimony, and witchcraft. In the last case the guilty person was sacrificed. Drunkenness in the case of a young man was punished by death by garrotting, while a person of importance was deprived of his office, for, except during festivals, only old people were allowed to get drunk with impunity. A high priest found guilty of committing some crime or failing to remain celibate was exiled. Any member of the nobility who made use of the insignia of the chief ruler in a dance or battle suffered death and the loss of his property.

The early sources are vague and contradictory on the Aztec judicial system. Probably small cases involving members of the same calpulli were settled by a gathering of the clan elders. Above this was a series of judicial courts, one, apparently, located in each of the four quarters of Mexico City and one in each of the important districts outside the city limits. These district

courts sat all day and every day. In each court a president assisted by two other judges presided over the session, and there were three bailiffs to see that the sen-
tences were carried out. The judges were chosen from
the ranks of the nobility, only men of proved trust-
worthiness, honesty and sobriety being eligible. They
wore a distinctive dress and were maintained from the
produce of special lands set apart for this purpose.
Above these district courts was a single court of appeal
consisting again of a president and two other judges.
This was located in the chief ruler's palace, and its sessions apparently were held in secret. Here all cases
were heard in which members of the nobility were on
trial, and in addition appeals from the decisions of the
lower court were considered. Once cases of appeal had
been heard here and a verdict given, the sentence was
carried out immediately with Gilbert and Sullivan ce-
lerity, the prisoner being executed without more ado,
if such were the sentence—an example that might well
be followed in this country.

The snake woman, the Aztec co-ruler, presided over
a higher court; apparently this was to try appeals of
the nobility from the decision of the appeal court, which
for them was a lower court. The snake woman was assisted in his deliberations by thirteen elders. Some early
writers state that the cases were depicted on paper, and
the case thus put on record for transmittal to a higher
court, but Aztec hieroglyphic writing was so clumsy
that one can't conceive of much detail being noted in

such records. However, by the combined system of picture writing and glyphs it would be possible to record the prisoner's name, his crime, as for instance the theft of so many mantles, the town where the crime was committed, the name of the victim, and the sentence, if it were a case of death or some fine. No records of this nature have survived, but there is no reason to doubt that they were used as aids to memory.

In addition to the civil courts, there were special military tribunals that dealt with military crime, such as treachery and cowardice, the punishment for which was death. In the former case the whole family of the criminal was enslaved.

Slaves were sold in the market, the average price being twenty cotton mantles. Some, we have seen, were sold into slavery as punishment for some crime, while yet others, such as gamblers, of their own accord sold themselves to raise money to continue their gambling. Relations of traitors were also punished by the loss of their liberty. In Texcoco the laws seem to have been more lenient, and robbers, who could not repay what they owed or persuade their relatives to do so, were not killed but sold into slavery; and similarly the theft of maize was not punished by death but by slavery. Slavery, however, was different from our conceptions, since a slave might own property, and even possess his own slaves. Slaves, unless they were very poor, owned their own homes and in many cases could not be sold to another master. Apparently they were really more in the nature of free men who were obliged to work at certain times for their masters without payment, and it was a common custom for masters on their death-beds to liberate their slaves; if this were not done the slaves passed to the deceased's heirs. Children of slaves, moreover, were free.

Often a family in desperate circumstances would sell one of the children as a slave, and after a certain period send a younger brother as a substitute. In this way all the children might serve a few years, but were the one serving as slave to die while carrying out his master's duties, the arrangement was considered cancelled; but were the son to die at home, another member of the family must replace him. Frequently the owner would marry one of his slaves, and many cases occurred of a widow marrying one of the slaves she had inherited from her deceased husband. This clearly shows that no stigma attached to slavery. A man who succeeded in catching an incorrigible thief, or one who had committed some very serious crime was given his captive as a slave. Incorrigible slaves wore wooden yokes, and might even be sold for sacrifice, although such punishment was rare.

There is no information as to the exact duties of male slaves, but in all probability these were in most cases confined to helping their masters in their farming. Probably most of the time they only worked on occasional short jobs, while at sowing and harvest times their services were required for longer periods. Female slaves, one supposes, helped their mistresses in their domestic duties for a short daily period. In any case this mild form of slavery does not appear to have been considered a very severe hardship, since many persons voluntarily sold themselves to obtain the equivalent of money for fairly trivial purposes.

A slave who had been forced to wear the wooden yoke for incorrigible behavior was set free if he could reach the palace of the chief ruler. A slave escaping in this manner could not be impeded in his flight by any one save the owner or his sons. Indeed, any one else who tried to stop him was himself liable to slavery. The palace guards were not allowed to prevent his entrance, and once inside the building, he was free.

In time of war all men of military age were eligible for service, each calpulli supplying a force which fought as a unit of the Aztec army, but in addition to these civilians, whose military interest was secondary to their civilian occupations, there were certain military classes, that might be loosely compared to the orders of knighthood in mediæval Europe. Candidates for these orders were trained in the youths' school, and ascended in rank according to the number of prisoners that they took. The initiation into the very high rank of Tecutli among the Tlaxcalans is described in great detail by Torquemada.

The initiate had to be of high rank and of a certain age. Before the ceremonies the parents and relations of the young man might spend as much as three years collecting wealth in the form of clothing and jewelry. On a favorable day, indicated by the priests, all persons of importance were invited to the opening ceremony. Accompanied by his relations, the young man ascended the pyramid of the war god Camaxtli, and knelt down in the temple. The high priest then pierced his nostrils with a sharpened eagle's claw and a sharpened jaguar's bone, and thrust jet (basalt?) beads into the wounds. The eagle and jaguar symbolized the two highest warrior ranks. At the conclusion of this ceremony the initiate had to submit to blows and insults from his companions. His clothes were torn off, but he was not permitted to protest or defend himself from the blows rained on him.

Later he was conducted to the abode of one of the priests. Here he sat on the floor until nightfall, when a low stool was brought for him. The others present at the ceremony banqueted in front of him, but apparently he was not allowed to participate. After their departure two or three seasoned warriors remained with him. He painted his body black, made frequent offerings of copal incense and blood drawn from his body with maguey thorns. During the first four days the initiate was only allowed to sleep for very short intervals, the warrior instructors pricking him with the maguey thorns if he slept more than the alloted short intervals. In addition to this he was only allowed to eat once every twenty-four hours, the solitary meal usually being eaten at midnight after a round of the temple for sacrificial purposes. It consisted of only four small balls of maize none of them larger than a nut.

At the end of the four days the initiate returned to the temple of his calpulli, where he continued his penance and instruction for a period of a year under less severe conditions. During this time he was not allowed to visit his house. At the end of the year a lucky day was chosen for the completion of the initiation ceremonies. To obtain this the coefficients of the day of the initiate's birth and the day of the ceremony must, when totalled, reach an odd number. (Chapter VI.) Nobles from far and wide were invited to the ceremonies, and in front of the seat of each one were heaped costly gifts. The initiate was again carried, amid dancing and music, to the temple of Camaxtli, where his simple clothing was taken off and replaced with costly garments carrying the symbols of the order into which he was being initiated. His hair was tied with a red ribbon, from the ends of which featherwork hung, and a bow and arrow were placed in his hands. The ceremonies concluded with a great banquet, in which sumptuous presents were distributed among those present according to their rank. Sometimes the final ceremonies were postponed until sufficient resources could be collected to meet these requirements. The membership was restricted to those of considerable wealth, who had shown particular bravery in war or had a high reputation as statesmen. Candidates had also to attain a certain age before they were eligible for election.

PLATE XII. WARFARE

a, Warrior capturing prisoner; *b*, Warrior whose dress shows that he has captured several prisoners; *c*, Enemy tribesmen attacking merchant symbolized by his fan and stave. Mendoza Codex.

As already stated (p. 43), young warriors graduated from the training colleges. Those of high birth passed through the more rigorous Calmecac, the others received their training and education in the Telpochcalli, or clan school, of which each calpulli possessed one. The former were supposed to be officers in the making, but it is doubtful if such a rank as an officer in our modern sense of the word existed. Probably, however, the recruits from the Calmecac fought apart as a group, at the same time supplying trained leaders to the calpulli brigades.

The stages by which a young warrior won his spurs have been briefly described in the passage cited, but there appear to have been innumerable stages of promotion to higher honorary rank, each exploit carrying with it certain very prized privileges of dress and ornament. The right to wear eagle or ocelot skins was the highest reward of this nature. One early Spanish writer states that only members of the nobility were eligible for the "Eagle Order," but one suspects that in this respect he has fallen into the common error of early Spanish chroniclers of imputing a non-existent aristocratic distinction in accordance with European notions. It is often difficult to estimate exactly how democratic was the Aztec state at the time of the conquest. It is clear that it was in process of evolution from a loose democratic federation of clans into something not far short of a feudalistic empire. If the Spaniards had arrived a century later they would undoubtedly have encountered the latter. As it was they viewed a transitional stage in which a militaristic aristocracy was gradually gaining control from the clans.

The Aztec army was composed of divisions based on the clans. Each calpulli sent its own division, thus forming a force of twenty divisions, each with its own insignia and leaders. Probably, too, each calpulli was responsible for its own equipment and commissariat. The calpulli divisions were grouped in units of five calpullis corresponding to the four quarters of the Aztec city-state, and these with their respective leaders were under the orders of the chief ruler, or king, as the Spaniards erroneously called him. The chief ruler could not declare war of his own accord, for such a decision was a prerogative of the chief council.

Wars were declared to obtain prisoners for sacrifice, to avenge insults, particularly attacks on merchants, and invariably on the selection of a new ruler. Once the chief council had decided on hostilities, spies were sent into the territory to be attacked. On their return with reports as to the disposition of the enemy and information on the country to be traversed, war was declared, on a day considered suitable by the astrologers, by placing weapons, cotton cloaks, or eagle down in the enemy's territory. The advance to the attack was also made on a propitious day. There was little room for strategy, since battles were usually fought in specially chosen spots on the frontier of the country attacked. Here whichever army arrived first awaited the arrival of the enemy. The higher leaders carried banners, the poles of which fitted into a box-like contraption attached to the back. Sometimes these were of gold. The raising of these on high was the signal to attack. A Mexican army drawn up for battle must have presented a picture rivalling in color and gallantry the tournaments of mediæval Europe.

In addition to the proud wearers of the eagle and ocelot skins, other warriors were clad in costumes of bewildering color. Some wore dresses of yellow feathers, others of green feathers bedecked with gold. The chief ruler wore a costume in which red, yellow, vermilion, blue, and green feathers mingled with ornaments of gold and jade. On his back he carried a golden image, the body of which was made of gold, while the wings, which were shaped like those of a butterfly, were of green feathers. This represented Itzpapalotl, the butter-fly god, apparently a god of battle. The common soldiers usually wore a kind of quilt of thick cotton, which served as armor. Warriors who had distinguished themselves in previous combats wore their distinctive insignia on the outside of these, the designs being frequently worked in feathers.

In addition to the cotton armor fighters defended themselves with shields. These were usually round disks of wood covered with hide, and, when owned by members of the warrior orders, were decorated with featherwork and sometimes jewelry. There were also oblong shields, possibly made of slats, which could be rolled up into a small compass when not in use. Heads of the nobility were protected with wooden helmets almost buried from sight below masses of feathers and other decoration.

For long-range fighting bows and arrows were employed as well as spears hurled with the aid of a spear-thrower. This last was a thin piece of wood a little over a foot long with two holes of the diameter of a finger set on each side of it, close to the front. The top surface was grooved, while at the butt a small point projected into the groove. The spear was laid in this groove with its hollowed butt resting against the point. With the first two fingers of his hand passing through the holes, the thrower was able to cast the weapon with greater force, the implement acting as an extra arm. The implement still survives in a few localities in Mexico as a hunting adjunct. The spear points were of obsidian or flint. Slings were also employed for hurling stones.

For close fighting wooden swords were used. Into both edges of these were set a number of blades of stone or obsidian that imparted a cutting edge. The blades were glued into position with a mixture made of a root of a tree pounded up with a certain sand and birds' and bats' blood. Bernal Diaz, himself a soldier and a keen observer of military matters, writes that these blades had a better cutting edge than the steel swords of the Spaniards. These Mexican swords were carried suspended from the wrist by a leather thong, so that they could not be snatched out of their owner's hand in combat.

Before engaging in battle the hostile forces frequently exchanged insults and goaded each other on with derogatory gestures. The whole of the army was not engaged at one time, forces being held in reserve to replace the tired fighters, who retired from the combat to eat and rest. The forces advanced to the attack amid the din of shouts, the blowing of conch-shell trumpets, and the beating of drums. This together with the gruesome paint with which the warriors bedecked themselves helped to inspire the enemy with terror. Ambushes were not infrequently used in battle, and it is said that the Mexicans were adept in concealing themselves. Pits were dug in the ground. In these warriors hid, covering themselves with straw and grass. Other soldiers pretended to flee in panic, and after the enemy had passed in triumphant pursuit the hidden warriors emerged from their concealment to attack the unwary pursuers in the rear.

Most of the fighting was carried on at close range, for the object was to capture prisoners rather than to slay as large a number of the enemy as was possible. The first prisoners captured were immediately sacrificed on the battlefield, but the rest were reserved for later sacrifice. Where a dispute arose between two warriors as to which had captured a certain man, the prisoner himself was questioned, and his testimony served to settle the question. The Aztecs and confederate states were lifelong enemies of the Tlaxcalans, but they claimed that they never completely subdued the latter, since they would be deprived of a future supply of prisoners if the Tlaxcalans were weakened to such an extent as to be unable to resist them. The historian Duran recounts that on one occasion the Cholulans challenged the Aztecs to battle. The challenge was accepted and a battle fought, but after the combat had lasted all day neither side was victorious. Next morning the Aztecs sent messengers to the Cholulans to enquire if they wanted to continue the fight. The Cholulans replied that their gods were satisfied, presumably with the captives already taken. Both armies then marched home.

On the other hand, if the war was waged to subdue a revolt or to force a tribe to pay tribute, the fighting continued until the enemy was entirely routed, and their capital taken. In the hieroglyphic codices victory is shown by a picture of a burning temple and the glyph of the captured city in which it was situated.

The troops were accorded a triumphal entry to the city on their return from a victorious campaign. Priests censed the triumphant warriors with copal, and the whole population turned out to witness the arrival of the warriors with their captives. Poor people used to visit the homes of wealthy warriors to sing their praises, and were rewarded with presents of food, drink and clothing as well as a small share of the spoils. Armies of the allied nations of Texcoco and Tlacopan always took the field with the Aztecs, and the war booty was divided among the three nations, two-fifths going to the Aztecs, two-fifths to the Texcocans, and one-fifth to the Tlacopanecs.

Were the campaign a failure, the defeated army was welcomed in silence on its return, while the priests, who went out to meet it, had their hair unbound, since this was a sign of mourning or sorrow. Wooden statues were made of those warriors of noble birth who had fallen into the enemy's hands and had been sacrificed, or whose bodies had not been recovered. The statues were treated just as though they were the bodies of the dead warriors. They were dressed in costly clothing, bedecked with jewels, and then burned to simulate the cremation ceremonies of the Aztec nobility. Slaves were also sacrificed on this occasion as in the usual cremation of persons of wealth.

Tlaxcalan territory was defended by great defensive walls. These were made of mortarless stone, and are described as being twenty feet wide and nine feet high. On top was a breastwork manned by the defenders. At the occasional gateways the wall was doubled for a distance of some forty yards, the passageway which ran between this length of double wall was only ten paces wide, and consequently was difficult to force.

Night fighting was very rare, but not entirely unknown, for the battle of *noche triste*, in which the Spaniards were severely punished on their retreat from Mexico City, was, as the name implies, fought through the night. The Spaniards taken prisoner in this fight, as in others, were sacrificed. On one occasion the Spaniards

PLATE XIII.   POTTERY DOG, COLIMA

found in a temple in the Huaxtec country the heads of some of their comrades who had been captured. The heads had been skinned, and the tanned skins placed on the temple walls. The heads of sacrificed prisoners were frequently skinned and placed on poles. Eyewitnesses describe them as wrinkled up and shrunk dry to the size of children's heads. One is reminded of the Jivaro shrunken heads of Ecuador, but there is no information as to whether these Mexican heads were purposely shrunken. This is possible, but not probable, since if they had been purposely shrunken by some method similar to that used by the Jivaros, they ought not to have had a wrinkled appearance.

Usually the captor kept the hair of his prisoner as his trophy, but little golden trophy heads were also made.

While their menfolk were at the war, the women played their part to insure victory. As long as the army was in the field the women abstained from washing their faces, although the rest of the body could be washed as usual. Luckily campaigns were seldom of long duration. Early in the morning, at sunset and at midnight the women made small tortillas and other maize dishes which were offered to the household gods to protect the lives of their husbands. They also took bones of previous captives of their husbands, and hanging them from a beam, censed them and the household deities with copal incense.

The prayer offered on this occasion was a simple one.

"Lord of all that has been created, of the heaven, the earth, the air and the sun, the water and the night and day, have pity on your slave and servant, who traverses the woods and valleys, the plains and broken country offering you his sweat and breath. He is your eagle and jaguar, who without rest or repose spends this miserable life in laboring in your service. Lord, I pray and beseech you that you spare his life for some time yet that he may enjoy this world. Hear me, Lord." The description of the man as eagle and jaguar refers to his warrior rank (p. 213).

Wars, as has been said, were frequently caused through trouble with merchants or failure to pay tribute. The Aztecs fought one campaign because the enemy refused to pay a tribute of a certain kind of sand that was found in their territory, and was particularly good for polishing stonework.

The merchants, who directly or indirectly were the cause of many wars, formed an important and privileged caste in the Aztec social organization. They had their own deity, Yacatecuhtli, and formed a highly honored and in some respects almost independent group within the tribe, possessing their own judges who settled independently disputes between members of the guild. Yacatecuhtli was depicted as a merchant travelling with staff in hand. He was clothed in a blue shoulder cape and wore gold ear-plugs. His face was painted red and black, and in his free hand he carried a yellow and blue shield. He was the senior deity of a group of six brothers and one sister. In the month Panquetzaliztli the merchants made a feast in his honor of great sumptuousness, as befitted their wealth, sacrificing many slaves, whom they purchased in the slave market of Azcapotzalco.

Merchants were often absent for very long periods on trading trips, their absences sometimes exceeding a year. During a merchant's absence his wife and children only washed their heads once in every eighty days. The traders travelled in large groups accompanied by porters carrying the merchandise on their backs with the aid of a tump line. Soldiers were sometimes sent in their company to protect them from hostile tribes and to gather military information. The travellers gave a feast to the old merchants before their departure, particularly to those who had retired from active trade owing to age. A good day was chosen for the start of the enterprise, the sign 1 Coatl being considered particularly lucky for an enterprise of this nature, for often merchants would defer their departure for long periods to await the arrival of this lucky day. It was considered very unlucky to look back once the departure had been made.

The wooden staff each merchant carried was an object of particular veneration, and was believed in some way to personify the patron deity Yacatecuhtli. At the end of the day's journey these staffs were piled together. Each merchant drew blood from his tongue and other parts of his body to sprinkle on them, and copal incense was also burned in front of them.

Groups of merchants regularly traded to the southern limits of modern Mexico and even beyond, passing into western Guatemala. Indeed, most of the business was done with this southern area, for here could be obtained tropical produce not found in the central plateau region. The quetzal bird, for instance, is only found in a small mountainous area on the Chiapas-Guatemala border. This general country was known to the Aztecs as Tzinacatlan, "The region of the bats." At the present time part of Chiapas is occupied by a Maya tribe known as the Tzotzils, *Tzotz* being the Maya name for bat. It is probable, therefore, that the Aztec name Tzinacatlan referred to their territory. Merchants who traded in this country spoke the language perfectly, and disguised themselves as natives in order to trade. Products of the plateau country such as obsidian spear-points, cochineal, red ochre, rabbit-skin cloaks and bells were bartered for quetzal plumes, jaguar and other skins and amber.

The traders ran a considerable risk in penetrating this and other distant lands where Aztec influence was not dominant and the natives hostile. Those, whose disguise was penetrated, were summarily executed. In that case the deceased's relatives burned a wooden statue of the unlucky man, simulating the usual cremation ceremonies as in the case of a warrior slain in enemy territory (p. 124). Large quantities of cacao were also brought from the southern coastal areas, and jade from the Guerrero-Oaxaca region. Much gold also reached

Mexico City from the Oaxaca region, either in trade or in tribute. It is possible that cotton capes from Yucatan penetrated to Mexico City, for these were sent to the Vera Cruz area from Yucatan in exchange for cacao beans, and it is not improbable that they were re-exported from the Totonac towns of Vera Cruz to the cities of the Valley of Mexico.

Returning merchants timed their arrival home so that it would coincide with a lucky day. A great feast known as "The washing of feet" was held to celebrate the happy conclusion of a long trip. Each merchant placed his staff in his calpulli temple, treating it as though it were Yacatecuhtli himself, and making offerings of food, flowers and copal incense.

There were certain markets specializing in special products. Cholula was the centre for precious stones and valuable feather-work; buyers of textiles and richly decorated gourds journeyed to Texcoco; at Azcapotzalco and Izocan were special slave markets; while at Acolman there was a great dog market. Eyewitnesses state that even after the conquest when the demand for dogs for sacrifice had naturally ceased, and even the eating of dogs was much frowned on by the church, the number of dogs on sale at this market seldom fell below four hundred. Markets were held every five days, and all persons living within a radius of about ten miles were expected to attend, or the local market god might be expected to take their non-attendance as a slight, and vent his wrath on the negligent.

There was a peculiar superstition that it was very unlucky to sell en route anything that one was taking to market. Indeed, the superstition was supported by a law forbidding such a transaction. This old superstition seems to have lingered on, for the writer has encountered the same unwillingness to sell en route to the market among the modern Indians of Central America, although a good price was offered and a long journey to market might have been avoided.

Most of the frequenters of the market were women, who seem to have combined business with pleasure, meeting their friends there, hearing the news, and indulging in a good gossip, as in most parts of the world. Father Duran, an early priest, whose life was one long worry trying to stamp out the old practices, has the following amusing paragraph with reference to the pleasure with which the Indian women travelled from market to market: "I think that if one was to say to one of those Indian women who love to wander round the markets 'Listen, to-day is market day in such and such a place, which will you to choose, to go straight to heaven or go to the market?' I suspect that she would say 'Let me first see the market, and after that I will go to heaven,' and she would be quite contented to lose that period of Glory just so that she could go to the market, and go wandering round here and there without any purpose save to satisfy her greedy desire to see it."

The markets were invariably placed close to the prin-

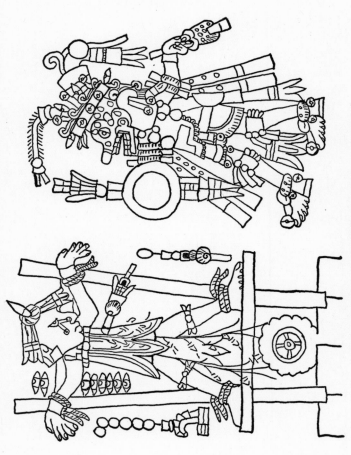

PLATE XIV. SPEARING SACRIFICIAL VICTIM

The victim, tied to a scaffold, has been pierced by a spear hurled from the spear-thrower of the warrior on the right. The latter wears a mask representing the death god and carries a shield and two spears. Zouche Codex.

cipal temple, and market day always coincided with a feast in honor of the local patron god. The market itself was walled in, and on the walls were set round stones with a centrepiece resembling the sun, around which were other carvings. This apparently must have represented Yacatecuhtli, the god of merchants. Offerings of flowers and food were made here by the vendors and buyers. Disputes that arose in the market were taken to a council of twelve old men who served as judges.

Each clan had its own market, and in addition there was a central market situated not far from the present position of the cathedral of Mexico City. A description, quoted from the conquistador and writer Bernal Diaz, has already been given of the products sold here (p. 75). Another early writer on ancient Mexico says that this main market was held every day, and that it held as many as one hundred thousand people. This figure is surely an exaggeration, but as the central market for the whole Aztec confederation, no doubt it was always thronged.

A circular fan served as the badge of office of the merchants, and this was regarded as a general mark of travel. It has been said that trade follows the flag, but in Mexico the flag followed trade. In addition to the important information on distant lands that the merchants were able to obtain on their travels, and for which they were well rewarded, the massacre of a party of merchants served the Aztecs as a valid excuse for imperialistic expansion in the same way that the murder of missionaries led to annexation of territory by the European powers in the nineteenth century. (Plate XII.)

Through archæology we can obtain confirmation of the early accounts of the wide distribution of articles of trade. In what is now the Republic of El Salvador a special clay containing a percentage of lead occurs. This when fired acquires a dull metallic lustre varying from blue-green to orange according to the intensity of the firing. The effect is very pleasing. Pottery vessels made of this clay soon acquired a high reputation on this account over a wide area, and a large export trade was built up. Quite apart from the clay, the shapes of the vessels can be recognized as of local patterns, pear-shaped jars, animal forms and vases with heads of the Tlaloc gods predominating. The extent of this trade is shown by the discovery of vessels of this type in localities as far apart as Yucatan, Jalisco, and the Vera Cruz District, while they are found in large numbers all over the Highlands of Guatemala and also in Honduras. The shapes clearly indicate that the finished vessels, and not the unworked clay, were traded. Copper clapperless bells of the same type are found over as wide an area, and, according to one of the early writers, were manufactured in the Valley of Mexico. Copper bells of this type have even been reported from a Pueblo ruin in the United States. The graceful pottery of Cholula also travelled far and wide. Trade between Cholula and Oaxaca seems to have been considerable, since much of the pottery of this latter region closely resembles that of Cholula in colors and designs. On the other hand the people of Cholula wore tunic-like ponchos of cotton, resembling those used by the Zapotecs, and it is probable that this fashion was introduced from Oaxaca.

CHAPTER V

RELIGION

Bigotry of Early Writers. Agricultural Gods. Tlalocs. Chalchihui-tlicue. Chicomecoatl. Centeotl. Xochipilli. Xipe Totec. Xochiquetzal. Tlazolteotl. Coatlicue. Drinking Gods. Sky Gods. The Sun God. The Moon. The Planet Venus. Rulers of the Underworld. Mictlan-tecutli, Mictecaciuatl, His Spouse. Miscellaneous Gods. Huitzilopoch-tli. Mixcoatl. Tezcatlipoca. Quetzalcoatl. Creation Gods and Legends. Age of the World. Human Sacrifice.

MEXICAN civilization was based on agriculture in general, and the cultivation of maize in particular. Although in later times we get a picture of a highly organized militaristic state, whose rulers were surrounded by pomp and wealth not unworthy of some eastern potentate, we must not forget that the background of this picture is formed by the fields of maize. Europe was agog in the sixteenth century with tales of wonder from the New World. Such matters as the everyday life of the people were of little import. What mattered were the stories of overwhelming wealth, of new products and bizarre customs. Mexican history is clouded by this wild enthusiasm, and, unfortunately, accounts of native religion are tinged with its consequential stressing of the new and strange.

Mexican religion, with its holocausts of sacrificial victims, appears on the surface an ugly and barbaric travesty of our conceptions of the relations between man and the heavenly powers, but we must remember, too, that we are looking at it through the jaundiced eyes of sixteenth-century bigots, who would have considered that they were in danger of falling into the clutches of his satanic majesty were they to describe features of Mexican religion in a favorable light. These zealous writers also tend to cloak their accounts of Mexican religion in classical raiments. They have left us lists of gods, grim accounts of grim ceremonies, and involved descriptions of sacerdotal beliefs, but we have no account of Mexican religion from the layman's viewpoint. Were such an account to exist, it would surely paint Mexican religion in a better light, and would probably show that many of the names given as those of distinct gods were merely variant names of a few important deities. Then, too, we could get the Mexican man-in-the-street attitude towards human sacrifice.

Although to us human sacrifice is the most horrible feature of Mexican religion, we must remember that it took the place of slaughter in war, for Mexican battles were fought to capture prisoners, not to inflict slaughter on the enemy. Had not human sacrifice existed, many times the actual number of sacrificial victims would have perished in the fighting. It was due to this practice that the Spanish losses in the capture of Mexico were so insignificant. In a sense they were not playing the game in slaughtering their enemy on the battlefield. Furthermore, sacrificial victims could count on a direct passage to the joys of the next world, and for this reason many warriors desired to finish their lives on the sacrificial block, though like the Irishman and heaven, they were in no particular hurry to get there. Probably there was not a single Mexican fighter who would not have preferred death on the sacrificial block to death in battle. Secondly in Mexican eyes human sacrifice was an absolute necessity, to keep the gods propitiated, and to ensure good crops. Aztec religion called for real devotion and abnegation; buttons in the collection were outside the Mexican's concept of religion.

The ancient Mexican was not an idealist. He looked on his gods as endowed with the same mixture of friendliness and ill-will as he saw around him. The gods, like most men, did not believe in giving something for nothing. If one expected their favors one should give something of value in return. Hence the human sacrifices and the offerings of food, copal incense, rubber, and other precious objects.

Agricultural Gods

In view of the importance of agriculture, it is not strange to find agricultural gods forming the majority of the occupants of the Mexican pantheon. They, in turn, can be divided into three classes—gods of rain, gods of the growing plants, such as maize and maguey, and gods of the actual soil. Deities of all three classes are closely connected, and frequently their functions and attributes overlap.

The Tlalocs were innumerable mountain gods, under whose control were the rains, thunder, lightning, snow and hail, and, by extension, rivers, lakes and wells. Any local hill might be considered a Tlaloc by the residents in its immediate vicinity. At the same time there was one Tlaloc who was considered the leader, and three others of importance, who with him ruled the four world directions. The relationship between these different Tlalocs is somewhat obscure, but sometimes they appear to have been looked on as a single deity in a manner resembling the orthodox Christian belief with regard to the Trinity. It is possible that the confusion is due to the clashing of two different viewpoints—that of the priest and layman. The former may have looked on the Tlalocs as a single god; the latter as being innumerable.

Be that as it may, the importance of the Tlalocs is shown by the fact that five of the major annual festivals were dedicated to their worship. (Chap. VI.) These festivals clustered around the dry season, and three of them, at least, were to intercede for rain for the crops. These fell in the dry months of February, March, and May when damp soil was required for planting, and, later, rains to aid the young maize plants.

A feature of the worship of the Tlalocs was the sacrifice of young children, and the victims sacrificed to these gods were generally supposed to weep. This is an example of sympathetic magic combining with religion, for the shedding of tears was believed to compel the

PLATE XV. (*Left*) CHICOMECOATL, MAIZE GODDESS, VALLEY OF MEXICO.
(*Right*) A WARRIOR IN COTTON QUILT ARMOR, JALISCO

sending of rain. Most of the Tlaloc festivals were held on mountain tops, but at the festival of Etzalqualiztli (p. 182) the ceremonies took place on a lake, emphasizing that the Tlalocs were also lords of the rivers and lakes. As rulers of the clouds and hail, they were also accorded worship. In the abode of the Tlalocs stood four great jars. In one was stored good rain which aided the crops; in the second rain which produced mildew and rust in the crops; in the third hail and sleet; and in the fourth rain which prevented the crops from drying so that they could be collected. From these jars the Tlalocs drew off whatever kind of rain they wished to pour down upon the earth from their homes on the mountain tops.

The chief Tlaloc was supposed to be married to Chalchihuitlicue, a goddess of water, and, although the information is nowhere given, one would suspect that there were a number of humbler counterparts of Chalchihuitlicue, each guarding her own stream, and serving as a faithful spouse of one of the junior Tlalocs. The Mexicans were a practical people, and doubtlessly they had some such arrangement to ensure the domestic bliss of the other Tlalocs.

These rain gods are among the most easily recognized of Mexican deities, for they are invariably shown with very distinctive circles around the eyes and long curved tusk-like teeth. In addition a long scroll often emerges from the mouth, either at the side or curling upwards in front of the nose. (Plate XVII, *b*.) The dress is usually painted blue or green to represent water, and the face black, possibly denoting the rain-bringing clouds. The circles around the eyes represent snakes, and in some representations of the gods are thus shown. The snake was intimately connected with rain both in Mexican and Maya belief, possibly because rain seems to bring out the snakes from their hiding places. Similarly frogs also symbolized the Tlalocs, probably because the croaking of frogs announces the imminence of rain. Indeed, Maya tradition records that frogs formed the orchestra of the Chacs, the Maya equivalents of the Tlalocs, who were also closely associated with snakes.

The Tlalocs lived in a land called Tlalocan, whither went all those who had been buried, not cremated in the usual Aztec fashion. Those who had met death at the hands of the Tlalocs, either by drowning or being struck by lightning, as well as sufferers from certain diseases formed this class (p. 49). The close connection between the Tlalocs and fertility is shown by the belief that Tlalocan was a land of abundant crops and plenty. These gods were on the whole favorably disposed toward man, but could show their bad side by withholding the rains, sending them in too great abundance at harvest time or by sending hail to ruin the crops.

The worship of these primitive mountain-dwelling fertility gods undoubtedly dates back to early times, as tradition relates. The cult was probably initiated by the agriculturalists of the pre-Maya civilization, forming part of the cultural heritage passed on to succeeding civilization of both Mexico and Central America, the names of the gods alone varying from tribe to tribe. Images of Tlalocs are found all over central and south-

PLATE XVI.   FIRE MAKING

The individuals "7 Dog" and "8 Deer" ceremonially kindling fire. Zouche Codex.

ern Mexico, and their worship extended as far as El Salvador. In this latter region pottery vessels with a Tlaloc face in relief were manufactured of a lead-bearing clay, and exported far and wide over Central America—an early example of American business enterprise.

The Tlalocs were, *par excellence,* the gods of the people as opposed to gods who found favor with the priests and nobility.

Chalchihuitlicue, wife of the chief Tlaloc, was also a goddess of water, as the numerous secondary names such as "Foam of the water" and "Water which makes waves" indicate. The name Chalchihuitlicue means "She with the jade skirt" for she was said to wear a skirt studded with green jade ornaments to represent the water. As already suggested (p. 139) there may possibly have been a considerable number of subsidiary goddesses of the same name. Chalchihuitlicue, however, does not appear to have been directly connected with rain. She is recognizable both in statuary and in the codices by a peculiar tasselled cape, corners of which usually hang down in front and behind. Among the Tlaxcalans she was known as Matlalcueye, "She of the blue robe," and was believed to live on a mountain in that region.

Chicomecoatl, whose name means "Seven snake," was believed to be a sister of Tlaloc. She was a goddess of the ripening corn as her secondary name "Seven ears of maize" indicates. She is usually shown holding two ears of corn in each hand to typify abundance. (Plate XV.) She is almost invariably depicted as red in color, and this might suggest that she is associated with the early ripening red maize. Stone statues of her, which frequently still retain traces of red paint, are very abundant in the Valley of Mexico. In addition to

142

the ears of maize, she usually wears a square headdress, on which rosettes are set.

Xilonen, whose name means "Young ears of corn," was probably nothing more than Chicomecoatl under another name, although the early Spanish writers speak of her as a separate goddess. Whereas Chicomecoatl was a goddess of the ripening maize plants as a whole, it is not improbable that she was known as Xilonen when considered not as goddess of the plant as a whole, but purely as goddess of the green ears of corn, and in particular those of the red maize. This is borne out by her name and by the fact that her festival fell when the maize was beginning to ripen. The victim who represented her was decapitated. Many of the victims of agricultural deities were sacrificed in this manner, which symbolized breaking off the ears of corn from the plant at harvest. The dress of the goddess in her guise of Xilonen typifies the young ears of corn, for her face was painted yellow and red to represent the two main species of maize, and a necklace of jade served to represent the green foliage from which the ears emerge.

Centeotl was also a maize spirit, as his name "Maize god" shows. He appears to have been primarily the spirit of the yellow maize. His features and clothing were painted yellow and green, the colors of maize, as opposed to the red and green colors of Chicomecoatl. Although primarily the god of yellow corn, there appear to have been variants of his nature, where he is known as "Red Maize god" and "White Maize god."

Usually, however, he typified the yellow maize when it was ripening. He was considered to be the son of Tlazolteotl, an earth goddess, and the brother of Xochiquetzal, a goddess of fertility and flowers. Essentially a passive spirit, he was largely dependent on the Tlalocs, for without their aid he could not flourish. The deification of the different crops is met with all over the globe, and in a modified form still survives in many parts of middle America.

Xochipilli was the flower god, as his names "Origin of the flowers" and "Five flowers" imply. Although a god of flowers in general, he seems also to have been closely associated with the flowering of the maize. As this was an occasion for great rejoicing, he came to be also the patron of all forms of pleasure, such as feasting, dancing, gambling, and the ball game. Generally he may be said to represent abundance. Seler has suggested that he is Centeotl under a different guise, and it may well be that the two gods were to a certain extent confused. The Aztecs, like the Romans, were very hospitable to alien gods, particularly those of conquered peoples. In this way several fertility gods crept into their pantheon, among whom Xochipilli may be numbered. Both as god of flowers and as patron of revelry, he came to be connected with Octli, the intoxicant made from the maguey plant. His distinctive emblem is a comb-like ornament that runs from his forehead to the back of the head.

Xipe Totec, the god of human sacrifice, appears originally to have been a maize god, hailing from the neighborhood of Oaxaca. He was the god of sacrifice by flaying, and all victims slain in his honor were thus treated. As we know that he was originally connected with agriculture, it does not seem improbable in view of our knowledge of other symbolic sacrifices that the flaying of the victim represented the husking of the corn. This did not take place when the crop was gathered, for the ears were stored with their coverings of leaves in special granaries until required. This theory that Xipe was the patron of the husked maize is borne out by the fact that the heads of victims to be sacrificed to him were first shaved, symbolizing the removal of the beard of the corn when it is husked. Xipe, however, also came to be a war god. Such a connection evolved through the necessity of capturing victims for sacrifice to insure good crops. An account of the special festival of Xipe held in the month Tlacaxipeualiztli, which fell in March, is given on page 180.

Xochiquetzal, "Flower-quetzal feather," was the female counterpart of Xochipilli, being like him a deity of flowers, pleasure, song and dancing. By extension she was also goddess of sexual pleasure, and in this aspect also patroness of prostitutes. It is more than probable that the sexual aspect of her worship had its origin in fertility rites, intercourse having the effect of inducing better crops. The Tlaxcalans held a special feast in her honor in the month Quecholli. On this occasion all prostitutes and hermaphrodites, garbed in women's dress, paraded for a sacrificial ceremony. Xochiquetzal was also the patron of weaving, and originally she appears to have been the moon goddess.

Tlazolteotl, an earth goddess, whose name means "Dirt goddess," was also called "Heart of the earth" and "Our grandmother" among a large number of minor names. That Tlazolteotl was primarily a maize goddess is shown by the decapitation of the girl who impersonated her, the employment of flowers and ears of corn at her festival, and by the fact that her face was painted yellow, the color of maize, and her dress was spotted with crude rubber, a symbol of the rain gods. Like Xochiquetzal, she was also a goddess of sexual intercourse, particularly in its lustful aspect. Strangely enough Tlazolteotl was the recipient of confessions. As one could only be absolved by her of great sin once in a lifetime, the more canny Mexicans waited till old age, when the temptations they might face no longer had their old appeal, before making their confessions. After consulting the Tonalamatl, the priest set a day for this event, and the penitent arrived with a new mat and copal incense to burn in sacrifice. If the sins were light, the penitent got off with a four-day fast, but if he had committed many grievous sins, he was ordered to march at night to the shrine of one of the drinking gods, and there make an offering. The penitent had to make this journey naked except for a paper loin-cloth. After the confession the penitent was given a certain piece of paper as a mark he had confessed. With this in his pos-

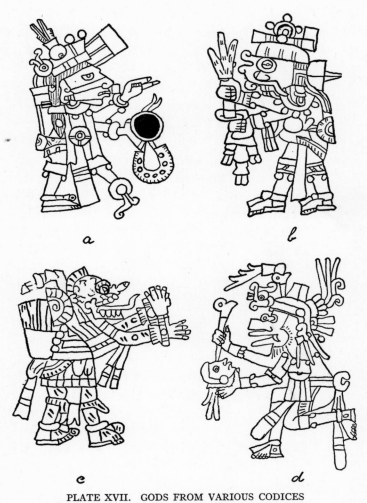

PLATE XVII.   GODS FROM VARIOUS CODICES

a, Tezcatlipoca; *b*, Tlaloc; *c*, Mictlantecutli; *d*, Quetzalcoatl as Eecatl.

session he could not be tried for any offense he had committed prior to its receipt, for as he had been forgiven by Tlazolteotl, the person against whom he had offended must also forgive him.

Coatlicue, whose name means "Serpent skirt" is chiefly famous for the enormous stone statue of her, found under the Zocalo Plaza, and now in the Mexican National Museum. This statue shows her with her skirt of snakes, and her head formed by two snakes' heads placed snout to snout. Apparently an earth goddess, she was later connected with Huitzilopochtli. Tradition relates that she was a pious god-fearing widow. One day as she was doing penance on the summit of Coatepec mountain, a ball of feathers fell at her feet. Picking it up, she placed it in her bosom. As a result of this action she became pregnant. Her numerous children, seeing her condition, were very ashamed, for, not unnaturally, they did not put much credence in this strange story. After discussing the matter among themselves, they decided to slay their mother. When they came to do so, the unborn child issued fully armed from his mother's womb, and falling upon his half brothers slew every one of them. This miraculously conceived child was Huitzilopochtli, the Aztec war god. Apparently Coatlicue was originally a fertility goddess, for flowers and green corn were offered her in the spring, the festival concluding with songs and dances.

The *Octli* gods, who were patrons of the Octli or pulque drink made from the sap of the maguey plant, were considered to be four hundred in number. This number signified innumerable to the Mexicans in somewhat the same manner as the biblical term "Seventy times seven." The Mexicans considered these gods to be innumerable since they believed that the forms of drunkenness were without number. Originally, however, these gods were spirits of the maguey plant. They were known collectively as "The four hundred rabbits," since a rabbit symbolized drunkenness. Also since the Aztecs believed a rabbit inhabited the moon, the Octli gods came to be connected with the moon. In this aspect they are easily recognizable in the codices by a peculiar crescent-shaped nose ornament they invariably wear, the stone axes they carry, and a bell-shaped ear-plug. Only the old men were allowed to become intoxicated in ancient Mexico, hence the Octli cult was in their hands. A young man who became intoxicated, except on ceremonial occasions, was in danger of being put to death as a punishment. The principal Octli gods were Tepoztecatl, Patecatl, Mayauel, a goddess, Totochtin and Macuiltochtli.

Sky Gods

Tonatiuh was, as his name implies, the sun god. Frequently he carries a back-shield representing the sun with its rays. (Plate XX.) His hair is usually flame-colored and decorated with eagle's feathers, and as patron of the warriors, he often carries shield and spears.

The fertility gods, whom we have already briefly sketched, were the gods of the rank and file of agriculturalists who formed the backbone of the state. The sun god was the patron of the parasitic class of warriors and nobles, whose chief function, whether they realized it or not, was to supply sacrificial victims so that agriculture could continue unimpaired. The intervention of the sun as a direct aid to agriculture was little sought, for in Mexico he could always be counted on to shine sufficiently to ripen the crops, but the Mexicans seem to have looked on him as the *fons et origo* of all life. It was believed that his youth must be continually renewed by human sacrifice so that he might continue his daily pilgrimage across the sky. Hence the heart of every sacrificed victim was held up to the sky after extraction, even when the sacrifice was in honor of some other deity. Because of the close connection between human sacrifice and the sun, the warriors, who were responsible for the supply of sacrificial victims, were also closely tied to the sun, and after death were believed to join him in his daily progress across the sky from sunrise to mid-day. Beyond this point women who had died in childbirth, and so indirectly aided the upkeep of the sacrificial victim supply, accompanied the sun to his setting point. The connection of the sun with sacrifice may have originated from the belief that the sun was always thirsty, and forever sucking up moisture from the earth. The sacrifices then would tend to keep him satiated with blood so that he would not suck all

the moisture out of the soil. At the same time blood
gave him greater strength than he could ever obtain
from water. Hence there was little danger of his losing
his power to shine down and envelop the earth in his
warmth.

Metztli, the moon, is depicted both as an old man
and as a woman. The Mayas considered her feminine,
and to be the wife of the sun. Both civilizations agree,
however, in recognizing a shell as the moon's symbol.
The Aztecs also believed that a rabbit was seated in the
planet, and from this derives the connection with the
Octli gods, who were known as "The four hundred rabbits" as explained on page 149. Little attention seems
to have been paid the moon, although eclipses both of
the sun and the moon were greatly feared. As already
noted Xochiquetzal was in all probability the original
moon goddess.

Tlauizcalpantecutli was the god of the planet Venus,
recognizable by the five white spots on his face. (Plate
XXIV.) The part played by Venus in Mexican religion
and calendrical calculations is explained on page 202.
His name means "Lord of the house of the dawn."

Rulers of the Underworld

Mictlantecutli, the Aztec equivalent of Pluto, ruled
over Mictlan, the underworld abode of the dead,
whither journeyed those who had not qualified as warriors to join the sun, or by burial to enter Tlalocan,

the paradise ruled over by the Tlalocs (p. 49). Although Mictlan was in the underworld and a land of darkness, it must in no wise be considered a place of punishment. The souls of the dead after many wanderings and adventures entered Mictlan four years after their death. On their arrival there they made some offerings to Mictlantecutli, and for this purpose suitable presents were interred with the ashes of the deceased. The ruler of Mictlan was aided in his duties by three assistants, duly provided with spouses, indicating, perhaps, that in the Aztec afterworld there were both marriage and giving in marriage. Mictlantecutli is usually shown with a skull in place of a head, or failing that the bared jawbone and fleshless jaws of death. (Plate XVII, c.) Frequently a flint knife is fixed in the fleshless nostrils, and crossbones are sometimes painted on his clothing.

Mictecaciuatl, "Lady of the abode of the dead," was the wife of Mictlantecutli, and has the same distinguishing skeletal features. The abode of the dead of the Aztecs was vaguely considered to be in the north, whence the Aztecs migrated to the Mexican plateau land. Many primitive or semi-civilized peoples consider the abode of their dead to be in their original home, and the Aztecs appear to be no exception. Possibly their picture of Mictlan was based on vague traditions of North America with its long winter nights, for northern branches of the great Shoshonean linguistic group, to which the Aztecs belong, are still to be found in Mon-

PLATE XVIII. POTTERY MASKS FROM VALLEY OF MEXICO

Representing Tlaloc (*left*) and possibly Tezcatlipoca

tana. The Zapotecs, on the other hand, considered their capital city Mitla to be built over the entrance to their Hades, hence its name. The Zapotecs, however, claimed that their race originated in this same region.

Miscellaneous Gods

In this small group are included several of the most important of the Aztec deities.

Huitzilopochtli was, at the time of the Spanish conquest, the tribal war god of the Aztecs, and in the eyes of the warrior-nobility class the most important god. His name has been variously translated as "Humming bird left-handed one," "Humming bird sorcerer" and "Humming bird of the south." According to tradition he was an early leader of the Aztecs during their wanderings prior to the foundation of Tenochtitlan, and after his death was elevated to divine rank as the tribal deity of the Aztecs. In addition to his functions as a war god, Huitzilopochtli was also a god of hunting. There is a great deal of doubt as to his exact functions. Doctor Seler, the great German student, was of the opinion that he was also a god of the sun and of fire, while Lewis Spence considers that he was originally a god of the maguey plant. He is recognizable by his dress of humming-bird feathers and by the spears, spearthrower and shield he usually carries, as befits a god of war and hunting. Peculiar to this god was a strange weapon called the *xiuhcoatl* or fire snake, which was shaped like a cross between a lizard and a snake. With this he was said to have slain his half brothers at his miraculous birth (p. 148).

The temple of Huitzilopochtli in ancient Mexico City was the greatest religious centre of the Aztecs. (Plate XIX.) A flight of 120 steps, flanked by balustrades formed by great stone snakes, led up to two temples on the summit of the pyramid. One of them held the statue of Huitzilopochtli, the other that of Tlaloc. In front of the temples was an open space, in the middle of which stood the sacrificial block some twenty inches high with a convex summit on which the victim's back rested. The remains of this temple can still be seen under Calle Escalerillas in the heart of modern Mexico City. A series of great stone snakes' heads which originally formed the bottom of the snake balustrades, and sections of stairways bear witness to the number of times the great structure was enlarged. In front of the temple originally stood rows and rows of racks, which were filled with the skulls of those who had been sacrificed. The high priest and assistant priests of the Huitzilopochtli cult were held in very high esteem among the Aztecs, since they interceded with Huitzilopochtli for Aztec victories. There is some doubt among the early Spanish chroniclers as to whether the statue of Huitzilopochtli that stood in the temples was of wood or stone.

Mixcoatl, which means "Cloud serpent," seems to have been nothing more than another name for Huitzilopochtli in his rôle of hunting god. It is possible that

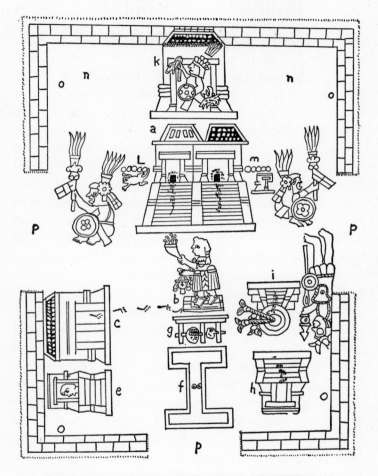

PLATE XIX.   PLAN OF GREAT COURT, TENOCHTITLAN

a, Pyramid with temples of Huitzilopochtli and Tlaloc; *b*, Sacrificial altar;
c, Priests' house; *e*, Warriors of the eagle hall; *f*, Ball court; *g*, Skull rack;
h, Temple of Coatlicue; *i*, Stone for mock combats; *k*, Temple of Colhuacan;
l, Date "5 Quetzpalin"; *m*, Date "5 Calli"; *n*, Dancing Patios; *o*, Wall of
court; *p*, Entrances to court. After Sahagun and Seler.

he was a tribal god of pre-Aztec people, and after the consolidation of Aztec influence, he became confused with Huitzilopochtli. An account of the hunting feast held in his honor in the month Quecholli is given on page 189. He is depicted in the codices as wearing a black mask or painting across his eyes. Among the Tlaxcalans he was worshipped under the name Camaxtli. Every fourth year the feast held in his honor was of unusual magnificence. The statue of the god was dressed in robes of cotton and rabbit skins, new fire was made, and the sacrifices included birds, rabbits, snakes, alligators, butterflies and prisoners of war. In one Tlaxcalan town alone five hundred captives are said to have been sacrificed in this festival. The birds and beasts were offered, naturally, because of the deity's patronage of hunting.

Tezcatlipoca, whose name means "Smoking Mirror," was, possibly, the most important god in the Aztec pantheon. He has a score of minor titles such as "The youth," "He whose slaves we are," "Dreaded enemy," and "Obsidian." It would almost appear that Aztec religion was evolving towards monotheism at the time of the conquest, and that Tezcatlipoca was on his way to becoming the sole god of the nobility. He was believed to be omnipotent, invisible and ubiquitous. As an all-powerful god, he both gave and took away life. He was a god of drought, but also a god of plenty. In the account of his great feast given on page 209 we see his association with agriculture from the fact that his

consorts impersonated fertility goddesses, and his youth
is shown by the fact that on the return of the gods, he
was the first to arrive (p. 188). His connection with
war is shown by his patronage of the college for youths,
where the young warriors graduated. According to tradition Tezcatlipoca was the great enemy of Quetzalcoatl,
and in the guise of a sorcerer caused his downfall and
the dispersal of the Toltecs.

Tezcatlipoca gets his name from the mirror he carried. In this, it was believed, he could see everything
that happened in the world. This mirror was made of
obsidian, hence its name of smoking mirror, for obsidian, has the appearance of smoked crystal rock. Divination of this nature was usually practised in Central
America with a jade sphere. Tezcatlipoca can usually
be recognized in the codices since he is generally shown
with his mirror. Most frequently it is substituted for one
of his feet (Plate XVII, *a*), but sometimes it is worn
on the breast or on the head. The great statue of the
god in Mexico City was made of obsidian bedecked with
gold and jade. In one hand the god held his obsidian
mirror in a frame of green, yellow, and blue feathers.
Sometimes the god was represented with a skull to sym-
bolize his power of life and death, or decked in contrasted red and black guises.

Quetzalcoatl, the third great god of the inhabitants
of the Mexican Plateau, and a deity worshipped all over
middle America, is almost as difficult to interpret as his
two great rivals Tezcatlipoca and Huitzilopochtli. The

name means "Quetzal snake." The feathers of the quetzal bird, which inhabits a limited mountainous area on the Guatemalan-Mexican border, were highly prized all over ancient Mexico for their rarity and great beauty. Only the three or four long tail feathers of this member of the Trogon family were of marked value. The esteem in which they were held is shown by the extension of the word quetzal to describe anything precious. Unfortunately the leading ruler of the Toltecs bore the name of Quetzalcoatl, and after his death was deified. This has added greatly to the confusion, for it is now not certain whether the god took his name from the man, or the man from the god. It is even possible that such an individual never existed, but was created in an attempt to rationalize the deity. Although definite proof is lacking, one might hazard that an unimportant deity bearing the name of Quetzalcoatl existed from the earliest times, but that the great Toltec namesake, on being promoted to divine rank, added lustre to the original Quetzalcoatl and eventually the two became so inextricably confused that the Mexicans themselves had difficulty in distinguishing between them. It is not improbable that Quetzalcoatl was in early times the Toltec tribal deity, although he appears to have been borrowed by the Toltecs from the Huaxtecs.

The great centre of his cult was the city of Cholula, where, according to tradition, the remnants of the Toltecs settled after the overthrow of their dominion. The pyramid, on which his temple stood, was the greatest in the New World, and in mass exceeded the pyramid of Cheops on the banks of the Nile. The remains of this great structure, now crowned by a Christian church, are still to be seen on the outskirts of the modern town of Cholula. Hither in ancient times came pilgrims from all parts of Mexico. As tribal god of the Toltecs, Quetzalcoatl came to be considered the great civilizer of ancient Mexico, and was credited with the introduction of metal working, the calendar, jade and other exotic products such as the quetzal feathers.

Primarily Quetzalcoatl was the wind god, and as its patron was known as Eecatl, which is the Aztec name for wind. As the wind god he was depicted with a peculiar beak-like mouth and square stumpy nose as in the hieroglyph for the day Eecatl. (Plate XXI.) In addition he wore a conical painted hat, hooked earrings, the loops of which turned outwards, and a section of a conch shell as a breast ornament. (Plate XVII, *d.*) Sometimes he wears a scraggy beard below the beak. In his guise of wind god he is very readily recognizable. Whereas the temples of all other gods were square or oblong, those dedicated to the wind god's worship were circular. Presumably they were built in this shape in order to offer the least possible resistance to the wind.

Since the winds bring the clouds, Quetzalcoatl is to a certain extent an agricultural and fertility god, and for this reason barren women prayed to him for offspring. According to some accounts Quetzalcoatl was one of the original creator gods, and was himself miraculously conceived through his mother coming in contact with a jade stone. His mother was said to have been Chal-chihuitlicue, the water-goddess wife of the chief Tlaloc. This story was clearly made to rationalize the knitting together of wind and rain.

Quetzalcoatl was also worshipped as lord of the planet Venus under the calendar name "1 Acatl," one of the days on which the Venus cycle was supposed to start. According to the tradition Quetzalcoatl was con- verted into the planet Venus at his death, and eight days after, the period of obscuration of the planet at in- ferior conjunction according to Mexican calculations, he rose again from the dead, reappearing as Venus as morning star. Every 104 years the planet Venus was supposed to return on this date, although in actual fact the Venus cycle gained about 4 days in this period. It was believed that Quetzalcoatl would return in a year 1 Acatl, and this belief was of material aid to Cortez and his followers, since they arrived in a year 1 Acatl. It was believed that Quetzalcoatl would return in a year white, and would reappear from the east. Furthermore, Quetzalcoatl wore crosses on his clothing. It is no won- der, then, that the Mexicans at first believed that their beloved god had returned with his followers when the Spaniards set foot on the mainland. They were speedily disillusioned.

The drawing of blood from different parts of the body was said to have been a custom introduced by

Quetzalcoatl, who was opposed to human sacrifice. His worship as the feathered serpent was very widespread all over Mexico and the Maya country. A serpent with feathers attached to its scales is the commonest art motif in aboriginal middle America, and this doubtlessly represents the god. (Plate III.) Frequently a human face is shown in the snake's open jaws. These representations range from the purely naturalistic to the extremes of conventionalization. The fact that the quetzal bird is not indigenous to the Mexican plateau shows that the quetzal-bird-snake concept must have been introduced from the south. Representations of feathered serpents occur in Old Empire Maya art, and it is more than probable that the cult penetrated into Mexico at an early period, acquiring great importance at a later period.

Tonacatecutli and *Tonacaciuatl* were the male and female creator gods. They were believed to have been responsible for the creation of the world and of the gods. Little attention was paid them since it was believed that they were so far removed from human affairs that they would scarcely intervene in mundane matters.

Creation Legends

The early Spanish chroniclers give several accounts of the creation, which, unfortunately, are at variance with one another. It is more than probable that there were a number of distinct local legends which account for the conflicting stories. Space forbids a full summary of all these versions, but below is given an outline of these beliefs compiled from various sources.

The world was first created by Tonacatecutli and Tonacaciuatl, who placed a great dragon-like monster in the primal waters. The back of this monster, which was called Cipactli, the name of the first day sign, formed the earth. After a number of the more important gods had been created, Tonacaciuatl gave birth to a flint knife, which was immediately thrown to earth. As soon as it touched earth sixteen hundred gods sprang forth. After deliberation these decided that they would like to create man. They asked permission of their mother, Tonacaciuatl, who told them to apply to Mictlantecutli, the lord of the underworld. Quetzalcoatl, or according to one version Xolotl, the dog-headed god, was sent. He managed to get bones from Mictlantecutli, but on hurrying back, he dropped them. Thereupon Ciuacoatl, an earth goddess, crushed the bones, making the first pair of humans from the powder. In the other version, Xolotl obtained a very large bone, which was placed in a vessel. All the gods drew blood from their bodies, and this was poured on the bone. On the fourth day a young man emerged from the vessel, and at the end of a further four days, a young woman also emerged. The world was peopled by their descendants.

At this time the world was still in darkness, for the sun had not yet been created. The gods assembled at

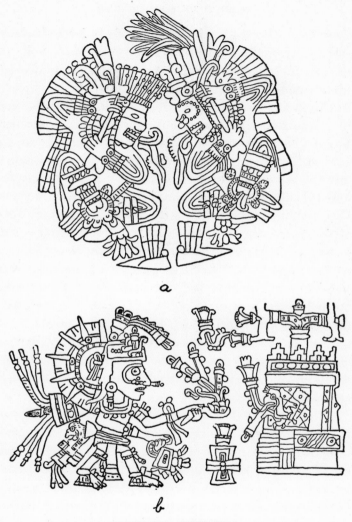

a

b

PLATE XX. OFFERINGS

a, Priests dressed as the God Tezcatlipoca piercing ears to draw blood for sacrifice. *b*, Tonatiuh, the sun god, or a priest in his garb holding a brazier of copal incense in front of a temple in which a turkey stands.

Teotihuacan to discuss its creation. In order to become the sun, it was necessary that a god first throw himself into a fire. Nanahuatzin, the syphilitic god, volunteered for the sacrifice, since he had little desire to live owing to the dread disease from which he suffered. Prior to his immolation, Nanahuatzin spent four days in penance and sacrifice, drawing blood from his own body as an offering. At midnight of the chosen day he cast himself into the fire in the presence of all the gods, and after an interval appeared as the rising sun in the east. He was very red, and none of the gods could look at him. The moon rose at the same time, its brightness being equal to that of the sun, but one of the gods threw a rabbit in its face, and that dimmed its light. The sun remained stationary in the sky, and the gods on earth were so burned by the heat of its rays that they decided to commit suicide. Quetzalcoatl, as the wind god, slew the gods one by one. When all were dead Quetzalcoatl exerted all his strength, and moved the sun by the force of the winds he controlled. Since then the sun has always moved across the sky.

After the world had existed a little more than four thousand years it was destroyed by a great flood, and most men were turned into fish. This first period was called "Water sun." A little more than 4000 years later the world was again destroyed. This time the destruction was due to violent winds, and, with few exceptions, all men were turned into monkeys. This period, which was called "Wind sun," was succeeded by another of slightly longer duration, which was known as "Fire sun," since it ended by the almost complete destruction of the world by fire. Some 5000 years later mankind was again almost destroyed by famine. The present age, in which we are living, would be destroyed by earthquakes, it was believed.

The famous calendar stone, now in the National Museum in Mexico City, refers to these five periods of the earth's history. In the centre is the sign 4 Olin, or in English "4 Earthquakes," the day on which, it was believed, the world would eventually be destroyed by earthquakes. Each corner of the Olin sign is occupied by one of the days that marked a previous end of the world. At the bottom left corner is 4 Quiauitl or 4 Rain, the date that ended the world by flood. At the top left corner stands 4 Eecatl or 4 Wind, the day that marked the destruction of the world by wind. The top and bottom corners on the right contain respectively 4 Ocelotl and 4 Atl, the days that marked the other destructions of the world. Around the circumference are placed two snakes, the heads of which meet face to face at the base. In each open mouth is a human face, while on the sides of the snakes' bodies are depicted the twenty day signs.

The Tlaxcalans were many centuries ahead of their contemporaries in their theories of the world's origin. They believed that it had not been deliberately created, but originated merely by chance. Indeed, all Middle American peoples held more modern ideas as to the length of the world's existence than those imposed on them by their European conquerors. The Aztecs, as we have seen, placed the beginning of the earth some 20,000 years ago, whereas Maya computations carried the count possibly millions of years into the past.

Human Sacrifice

Human sacrifice played such a part in Mexican religion, and is mentioned so frequently in these pages that the following account from a very early source is of peculiar interest, quite apart from the quaint phraseology of its Shakespearean English. The account is from Peter Martyr, who wrote a few years after the conquest of Mexico. The present translation from the Latin was published in 1612.

"When any moved through piety towards any divine power, determineth to dedicate an Image thereunto, he endeavoureth to gather together of seedes fit to bee eaten, such an heape, as may suffice for the height of that Image which he hath purposed to erect, bruising those seedes, and grinding them to meale. But oh cruell wickednes, oh horrible barbarousness, they teare in peeces so many boyes, and girles, or so many slaves, before the meale which is to be baked, while they draw so much blood, as in stead of luke warme water may suffice to temper the lumpe, which by the hellish butchers of that art, without any perturbation of the stomacke being sufficiently kneaded, while it is moyst and soft, even as a potter of the clay, or a wax chandler of wax, so doth

this image maker, admitted and chosen to be maister of
this damned & cursed worke. I have else where said,
if I mistake not, that these sacrifices are not slaine, by
cutting of the throat, but by thrusting a knife through
the short ribs neer unto the hart, so that their hart is
pulled out, to be sacrificed while they be yet living, &
behold their own miserable condition: with the blod
which is next unto the hart they annoint their godds lips,
but burne the heart it selfe, who thereby suppose the
displeasure of their godds to be appeased, and this pro-
digious act, the priests perswade the people to be acceptable to their Idols. But many wil demand, & that
rightly, what they do with the flesh & members of those
miserable sacrifices: O wicked yawning & gaping, oh
loathsom provocation to vomit: as the Jewes somtimes
eate the lambs which were sacrificed by the old law, so
do they eate mans flesh, casting only away the hands,
feet, & bowels. . . . In the halles, which as we sayd
before, were in the temples, were the great Images of
thir godds, & in the halles were darke inner roomes, into
the which they enter by narrow & strait dores, where-
unto the priests only have accesse. . . . Some of Cortes
his familiars, entred into those narrow, & darke chappels,
against the keepers wils, and when by torchlight they
saw the wals besmeared with a redd colour, they made
proofe with the pointes of their poniardes, what it should
be, and breake the walles. O bruitish minds: the walles
were not only besprinckled with the blood of humane
sacrifices, but they found blood added upon blood two

fingers thicke, oh loathing to the stomacke, out of the holes they made with their poniardes they say, an intolerable hellish stincke issued from the blood which lay hidd under the fresh."

It cannot be too often reiterated that human sacrifice was man's side of the bargain with the gods. Man gave life to have life: he offered blood in return for rain. Few religions endow their deities with the belief that it is better to give than to receive, and the Mexicans lived too close to nature to suppose that its personifications were less harsh.

We have passed in hasty review the principal characters of the Aztec pantheon. Most of them we have traced back to the soil, whose cultivators first conceived them, but the functions and development of a few baffle us. Nevertheless, we can be sure that far in the past the rude rustic molded them from the plants, the elements, and the soil, that together filled his life. "Scratch a Russian and find a Tartar" runs the old saw. Strip a Mexican god and you will find nature. This love of the soil survives undiminished in modern Mexico, for only the land hunger of the peons brought Mexico's Maderos and Zapatas to the fore, and made possible the overthrow of Porfirio Diaz.

CHAPTER VI

THE CALENDAR AND THE FEASTS

Methods of Reckoning Time. The Day Signs. The Weeks with
Their Varying Fortune. The Solar Year. The Religious Festivals
Month by Month. The Five Unlucky Days. The Concurrent Double
Count. The Reckoning of Years. The Writing of Dates. New Fire
Ceremony Held Every Fifty-two Years. The Sacred and Divinatory
Nature of the Tonalamatl. World Directions and Colors. The Planet
Venus. Zapotecan Count. Origin of the Mexican Calendar. Slaying
of the Representative of the God Tezcatlipoca. The Human Sacrifice
to the Sun.

THE Mexican calendar, which was far simpler than
that of the Maya, played a very important part in the
daily life of the Mexicans. It consisted of two concurrent counts. The first of these was a sacred almanac
called the *Tonalamatl*, which consisted of only 260 days,
and functioned primarily for ceremonial and divinatory computations. The second count was an approxi-
mation to the solar year, for it was a 365-day year,
consisting of 18 months of 20 days each and a final
group of 5 odd days, the last being a period of very
bad omen, during which the minimum amount of work
was undertaken. No correction was made to the calendar for leap years, but it is probable that the advance
made by the calendar over the tropical year through
the lack of intercalation was computed, and the required
correction noted. This, at least, we know was the Maya
practice.

With. these two systems running concurrently a day in the *Tonalamatl* could not coincide again with a day in the 365-day year for 52 years (18,980 days). This is so because the highest common factor of the two numbers is only five, hence the interval that must elapse between such coincidences was $365 \times 260 \div 5 = 18,980$.

The sacred almanac or *Tonalamatl* was formed by twenty day signs running concurrently with the numbers one to thirteen. These two sequences repeated themselves in unchanging order. Since there is no common factor of thirteen and twenty, the same day sign and number could not coincide for 260 days. In this way no day, complete with name and number, could repeat in a single *Tonalamatl*. Below are given the first thirty days of the almanac. During this period, it will be noted, the thirteen numbers have repeated, and are started on

1 Cipactli (Mythical water-monster)	3 Cozcaquauhtli (Vulture)
2 Eecatl (Wind)	4 Olin (Movement)
3 Calli (House)	5 Tecpatl (Stone knife)
4 Quetzpalin (Iguana Lizard)	6 Quiauitl (Rain)
5 Coatl (Snake)	7 Xochitl (Flower)
6 Miquiztli (Death)	8 Cipactli
7 Mazatl (Deer)	9 Eecatl
8 Tochtli (Rabbit)	10 Calli
9 Atl (Water)	11 Quetzpalin
10 Itzcuintli (Dog)	12 Coatl
11 Ozomatli (Howling monkey)	13 Miquiztli
12 Malinalli (Grass)	1 Mazatl
13 Acatl (Reed)	2 Tochtli
1 Ocelotl (Ocelot)	3 Atl
2 Quauhtli (Eagle)	4 Itzcuintli, *etc.*

PLATE XXI. HIEROGLYPHS FOR THE TWENTY DAYS

1, Cipactli; 2, Eecatl; 3, Calli; 4, Quetzpalin; 5, Coatl; 6, Miquiztli; 7, Mazatl;
8, Tochtli; 9, Atl; 10, Itzcuintli; 11, Ozomatli; 12, Malinalli; 13, Acatl; 14, Ocelotl;
15, Quauhtli; 16, Cozcaquauhtli; 17, Olin; 18, Tecpatl; 19, Quiauitl; 20, Xochitl.

their third round, while ten of the day names have repeated, but naturally with different numbers. In parentheses are given the English translations of the Aztec names. The actual glyphs for these days are given on Plate XXI, the numbers were written with dots, one dot for each number. (Plate XXIII.)

At its next recurrence Cipactli will have the numeral 2 attached to it, for in the twenty-day interval from its last appearance the numeral 8 will have reached 13 twice, and advanced to the second position $(8 + 20 = 28 \div 13$; remainder of 2$)$. At its next occurrence still twenty days later, the attached number will be 9, until 260 days from the start the attached number will be 1 again.

The *Tonalamatl* was divided into periods of thirteen days, which, for convenience, we can term weeks. Each period or week started with a day, the attached number of which was one. After thirteen days, of course, the number one repeats, but the day name is thirteen positions later in the *Tonalamatl*. Each period was ruled over by a patron god, and on the auspiciousness or ill auspiciousness of this first day depended the fortune of the whole week, but a lucky day in an unlucky period was considered to be of good omen. These weeks were much used by the sorcerers and astrologers in prophesying the careers of newly born babies, and in arranging suitable occasions for all undertakings. The starting days of the periods were in their correct order as follows:

1 Cipactli. The week ushered in by this sign was of

good omen, and those born in it would be happy and fortunate.

1 Ocelotl. The week starting with this day was unlucky. Men born during this period would be immoral. They would be taken prisoners of war, and finish their lives on the sacrificial block, or through want would be forced to sell themselves into slavery. Women born under this sign would be taken in adultery, and would be put to death as a consequence.

1 Mazatl. The period was lucky.

1 Xochitl. Men born during this week were gay, witty and fond of music. Ladies, whose birthday fell in this week, were inclined to be a little too liberal with their favors.

1 Acatl. Liars, bearers of false witness and scandalmongers were born in the 1 Acatl week. The period, which was under the patronage of Quetzalcoatl, was considered to be unlucky.

1 Miquiztli. Neither particularly lucky nor unlucky. Tezcatlipoca was the patron god.

1 Quiauitl. A disastrous period. On the first day the *Ciuateteo*, who were the malevolent spirits of women who had died in childbirth, descended on the world, bringing all sorts of sickness to children. Parents guarded against this by making their children stay indoors on this day. The next eight days of the week were of similar bad omen, but the last four days were more auspicious.

1 Malinalli. An unlucky sign. Those born under it would be happy for some time, but sooner or later bad

173

luck would overtake them. Many would die in adolescence.

1 Coatl. A lucky week especially for merchants and travellers.

1 Tecpatl. Huitzilopochtli was the patron god, and the period opened with a great feast in his honor.

1 Ozomatli. A fairly lucky period. The Ciuateteo were believed to return to earth, sowing sickness and death. Those who were very ill at this time were left to die, as it was believed that they would not live.

1 Quetzpalin. An auspicious period. Boys born in this week would be brave. They would receive no hurt from falls, since the lizard, under whose sign (Quetzpalin) they were born, can similarly fall from great heights and land unhurt on its feet.

1 Olin. Neither lucky nor unlucky. If parents took good care of the education of their children, they would turn out well, but the reverse if neglected in their youth.

1 Itzcuintli. A very lucky period. It was under the patronage of Xiuhtecutli, the fire god. Special feasts were held in his honor, and food offerings were thrown in the fire. Specially manufactured pieces of paper decorated with jade and rich feathers covered his image.

1 Calli. A very unlucky week. The Ciuateteo were active again, spreading disease, and those born under this sign must expect to die "with their boots on."

1 Cozcaquauhtli. A long and happy life was in store for those born on this day.

1 Atl. The period, which was of very bad omen,

was ruled over by the water goddess Chalchihuitlicue. On the first day those who travelled much by water made their offerings to her.

1 Eecatl. Quetzalcoatl was the patron, and the period was considered to be unlucky. Those born during its course would turn out to be traitors, sorcerers and witches. They would have the power to turn themselves into animals.

1 Quauhtli. The Ciuateteo were active again, and the week was generally unlucky. Men born under this sign would be brave but haughty and overbearing, and much given to flattery. Women born under this same sign would not be all that they should be.

1 Tochtli. The last period. The patron god was Izquitecatl, the Mexican equivalent of Bacchus. Those born under this sign consequently were drunkards. Nevertheless the period was lucky, and those born in it would be prosperous and happy with the sole drawback just noted. The next week began the round again with 1 Cipactli.

The division of the *Tonalamatl* into these twenty weeks was made purely for divinatory purposes, and possessed no civil connotation.

The solar year, as already pointed out, consisted of eighteen months of twenty days each with five supernumerary days added at the close. Each month had its special feast, and a brief list and description of these gives a certain insight into Mexican religious observances. The days of Maya months were numbered from

0 to 19, but Mexican months bore the numbers 1 to 20. The months with their principal feasts were as follows:

Atlcoualco, the first month, was dedicated to the Tlaloc rain gods and Chalchihuitlicue, a water goddess and the wife of the chief Tlaloc. The name means "The buying of the rains," for during its course special ceremonies were held to insure a plentiful rainfall at the close of the dry season. Large numbers of children were sacrificed on the mountain tops, where the Tlalocs were believed to live. The doomed children were carried thither in litters bedecked with flowers and feathers. Were the children to weep much *en route,* heavy rains might be expected, the tears insuring this—a good example of sympathetic magic, in which like begets like. War captives were also sacrificed to Xipe, the god of flaying and secondarily of agriculture. Each captive was attached to a stone altar by a rope round his ankle, and given a blunt wooden sword. He was then forced to fight warriors armed with the usual weapons. (Plate XXII.) After the mock combat, the prisoner was carried to a stone altar, on which he was laid. The priest then cut out his heart with an obsidian knife, and raised it in offering to the sun and the four world directions. The body of the victim was rolled down the pyramid steps to the crowd below. There it was cut up and eaten as a kind of communion with the gods. At the time of the conquest this month started on February 12 (Gregorian).

Tlacaxipeualiztli, the second month, was dedicated to

176

PLATE XXII. GLADIATORIAL COMBAT

The sacrificial victim tied to a stone, and armed only with a paper sword defends himself against the warrior, clad in a jaguar skin, who has a real sword. Magliabecchi Codex.

Xipe, the god of flaying. A great feast in his honor was held on the last day of the month. Warriors dragged their prisoners by their hair up the steps of the principal pyramid, where they were sacrificed. After their hearts had been removed, the bodies were rolled down the steps to priests below, who removed the skins. Old men then cut up the bodies in the presence of their captors, and the flesh was eaten with corn in solemn communion.

Next day more captives were sacrificed to Xipe, but this time the same ceremony of gladiatorial combats described for the previous month was held. The captives were dragged up the steps by their hair, attached one by one to the stones, and then with wooden sword made to fight four warriors one after the other. These warriors were dressed in jaguar skins or eagle plumes. Many of the captives were so exhausted after their rough handling in mounting the steps, that they were unable to resist, but others wore out their adversaries. In that case a fifth warrior, who was left-handed, came forward, and raising the exhausted man in his arms, dashed him to the ground. He was then dragged to the sacrificial stone. Prior to the combat the victim had been given a cup of pulque, which, after offering to the world directions, he drank through a reed—Dutch courage for the combat.

The hearts of the victims were thrown into wooden tubs, and from the lacerated hollows, that had held the victims' hearts, priests drew off blood in tubes, which was offered to the sun god. The captor of a victim filled another bowl with his blood, and went to the different statues of the gods, smearing their lips with the blood. Subsequently he took the body to his house, where it served as a ritualistic feast for his friends, although he himself did not eat the flesh. The body had previously been flayed, and men donning the skins danced in the streets. Finally a great dance was held, in which the captors danced carrying in their hands the heads of their victims.

It is said that men of the cities, with which the Aztecs were at war, frequently attended this ceremony, but they were not molested, for it was considered that they would be duly awed at seeing the fate that awaited so many prisoners of war.

Next day another great dance was held, apparently of an agricultural significance, since the participants wore collars and garlands of tamales and corn cakes, and carried feathers and stalks of young maize.

Twenty days after the flaying ceremony those who wore the skins of the victims removed them, and the wearers were bathed in maize flour and water in a kind of absolution ceremony, the captors doing penance for having slain their victims. The captor meanwhile had erected a kind of tripod in his courtyard surmounted by a mat, on which rested the paper ornaments of his victim. He lent these to a friend of his, a courageous young man, who went through the town as if looking for wicked people. If he caught any one he seized the man's possessions, and took them back to his friend, the captor. The captor also celebrated his victory and the sacrifice of his victim by erecting a column as a sign that he had taken prisoners, and placing on top of it the thigh bone of his captive ornamented with sacrificial papers.

Xipe was the patron of the goldsmiths' guild, and it, too, celebrated his month by sacrificing victims. The connection between the god of flaying and the goldsmiths seems to lie in the fact that the skins of the victims worn at his festival were depicted as yellow, and thus might be said to resemble the gold-plated products of their trade.

Tozoztontli, the third month, was dedicated to the Tlalocs and Coatlicue, a rain goddess and patroness of agriculture. Spring was now well advanced, and a special feast of flowers was held. Until this event no one was allowed to smell any flowers. More children were sacrificed to the Tlalocs that rains might fall in time for the maize crop. Some of the ceremonies already described in connection with the Xipe sacrifices did not terminate until this month. The name of the month means vigil or fast.

Huei Tozoztli, the fourth month, was dedicated to Centeotl, the maize god, and Chicomecoatl, a goddess of maize. The faithful drew blood from their ears, with which they smeared reeds. With these and branches of a certain sacred tree they decorated their houses and their household gods. Young maize plants were brought from the fields to deck the altars of the men's houses, and offerings of food were made.

In the temple of Chicomecoatl special ceremonies were held. Hither came a procession of young girls bearing on the backs by means of tump lines loads of ears of corn from the previous harvest. These were presented to the goddess and then taken back to the houses, having been, so to speak, blessed. These ears of corn were kept for sowing the next crop, and some were placed in the middle of the grain stored in the granary to protect it from mildew and damage.

Toxcatl, the fifth month, was dedicated to Tezcatlipoca. At this time took place the sacrifice of the youth, who had been impersonating this god during the past year. This event is described in full detail on page 206. In addition to the Tezcatlipoca festival, an important feast was held in honor of Huitzilopochtli. An image of this god was made of Tzoalli flour, the bones being made of the sacred mizquitl wood. The image, richly garbed, was placed on a large litter carved with snakes' bodies, and carried with singing and dancing to another temple. In front an enormous sheet of thick paper was carried by youths. Next morning copal and food were offered to the household images of the god. Subsequently offerings, which included the sacrifice of partridges, were made, and special dances were performed by young girls. The ceremonies closed with the sacrifice of a youth, who for a year past had impersonated Huitzilopochtli in a manner somewhat similar to the impersonation of Tezcatlipoca described on page 206.

This sacrifice varied from the usual practice in that

the victim was not sacrificed on a convex stone, but was held in the arms of the priests while his heart was removed, and secondly the victim chose his own time for being sacrificed. Prior to this he took part in the dances held in his honor, leaving this of his own free will for death. Some, it is said, were in haste to die, others delayed their end, but none, it would appear, required persuasion, for it was believed that since the victim impersonated the great god Huitzilopochtli, he took divine rank, and might expect great honor and glory in the next world. The victim's head was removed immediately after his death and placed on a pole alongside of that of the impersonator of Tezcatlipoca. Many other prisoners were sacrificed, and the ceremonies concluded with a general dance and incense-burning ceremony. A feature of the ceremonies was that all the children were given small cuts on the chest, stomach, and the arms with stone or obsidian knives.

Etzalqualiztli, the sixth month, took its name from certain special dishes resembling our modern succotash, which were eaten at this time. During this month more ceremonies were made to insure that the Tlalocs would send rain for the young crops. The priests and leaders of Mexico City made a pilgrimage to a lake near Citlaltepec, north of the city to seek special reeds used to adorn the altars of the Tlalocs. On this journey a precedent was set for the modern hold-up man, for it was permissible to rob any one met in the road, taking from him even his clothes. The victim was not permitted to resist, and even those bearing tribute to the Aztec ruler received the same treatment. Any one who was rash enough to resist was slain or, at the least, very badly hurt. Needless to say every one took good care to keep out of the way of these holy "Gentlemen of the Road."

One of the most pathetic ceremonies of propitiation of the Tlalocs centred round the death of a young boy and girl. They were placed in a canoe together with the hearts of many other sacrificed victims, and towed to the centre of this same lake, where the canoe was sunk, and the children allowed to drown. At this same ceremony such priests of the Tlalocs as had done some wrong in the past year were punished by being half drowned in this same lake.

Tecuhilhuitontli, the seventh month, was noted for the feasts held in honor of Huixtocihuatl, the goddess of salt. This festival was of importance in Mexico City because of the large number of persons who earned a living by extracting salt from Lake Texcoco. The most important ceremony was a dance in which only women took part. They danced wreathed in flowers and linked together with floral ropes. In their centre danced a woman who represented the salt goddess. At the end of the ceremony she was doomed to sacrifice. Ceremonies were also held to propitiate the Tlalocs, for it was believed that Huixtocihuatl was their sister, a natural assumption in that salt was not mined to any extent in ancient Mexico, but was extracted from salt water.

Hueitecuhilhuitl, the eighth month, means in Nahua

"The great feast of the rulers." It was under the patronage of Xilonen, the goddess of the tender ears of corn, which at this time (July) were beginning to ripen. The feast in her honor lasted eight days, and during this time the women wore their hair loose. This, an example of sympathetic magic, in which like produces like, was to insure that the maize would grow large and develop a good beard. Any one who visited the temple of Xilonen during this period was given as much corn as he could eat and a special kind of pinol. A slave girl impersonated the maize goddess, dancing continuously during these eight days. It was believed that if she danced vigorously the new crop of corn would be abundant and healthy, but should she dance listlessly, a good crop could not be expected. After dancing all night the girl was sacrificed at daybreak. A priest lifted her on his back, while another cut off her head, and subsequently removed her heart. As soon as the sacrifice was completed the people were free to eat new corn, which up to then had been forbidden to them. Decapitation, symbolizing the gathering of the corn, was the usual practice in agricultural sacrifices.

Tlaxuchimaco, the ninth month, was dedicated to Huitzilopochtli, the Aztec war god. Large numbers of turkeys were killed, and tamales prepared for a great feast to be held on the following day. The images of Huitzilopochtli and other gods were wreathed with flowers, and a great dance was held. This varied from the usual run of dances, in which men and women danced apart or only one sex took part, for in this dance the men placed their arms around the women's necks. In this same month the merchants honored their patron god Yacatecuhtli with sacrifices.

Xocotlhuetzi, the tenth month, was dedicated to the fire god, who was called Xiuhtecutli or Huehueteotl, "The old old god." A revolting ceremony was held in connection with this festival. Prisoners of war were first made to take part in a ceremony, in which they danced side by side with their captors. Next day the prisoners were taken by their captors to the top of the pyramid. There the captors cast a certain powder in their faces. This was made from Yauhtli (*Tagetes lucida*), and had the effect of an anæsthetic, deadening their sensibilities for the terrible ordeal that was to come. Then lifting the captives, who were bound hand and foot, they danced round a great furnace, each man with his captive on his back. Then one by one as they circled round the furnace, each captor threw his captive into the great fire. Just before death put an end to the wretched man's sufferings, he was quickly dragged out with the aid of large hooks by the priests, who promptly removed the heart from its half-burned body.

A feature of the ceremonies in connection with the fire god centred round a great pole 150 feet high. This had on its summit an image, that probably represented the fire god, made of dough of Tzoalli (amaranth flour). This was dressed in a huipil and decorated with paper ornaments. At the conclusion of the ceremonies a wild scramble took place among the young men to see who could first climb up the smooth pole. The lucky winner scattered the dough to the crowd below, and seized the spears, spear-thrower and shield that the figure wore. As a reward he was presented with certain ornaments and a mantle of a type that no one else was allowed to wear. Furthermore he was carried by the priests to his home to the accompaniment of music.

Ochpaniztli, the eleventh month, was marked by feasts in honor of Teteoinan, mother of the gods, who was also known as Tocitzin, and was secondarily a goddess of the ripe maize. A woman, who impersonated the goddess, was sacrificed at the close of the ceremonies. It was considered very important that she should not weep, probably for fear that that would cause heavy rains at the coming harvest. With this end in view special games and buffoonery were indulged in in her presence. The woman had no knowledge that she was to be sacrificed. Indeed, when she was being prepared for the sacrifice, she was informed that she was being dressed in this manner so that she might become the mistress of one of the rulers that night. This was not far from the truth, since she was to sleep with death so soon.

When the fatal moment arrived, she was placed on the back of another woman, and her head cut off. The body was immediately skinned, and a robust youth donned the skin. Wearing this he was carried by the nobles and priests to the temple of Huitzilopochtli, where he sacrificed other prisoners. Afterwards, mimicking the goddess he impersonated, he went through fertility rites with Huitzilopochtli. Meanwhile a section of the skin removed from the slain woman's thigh was carried to the temple of Centeotl, the god of maize and son of Teteoinan. Prior to this it had been worn by a youth impersonating this god.

A great military review took place after these ceremonies. The Aztec ruler, seated on a throne covered with an ocelot skin and with his feet on a hassock of eagle feathers, distributed mantles and other insignia of rank to those who had deserved promotion for their valor. The ocelot and eagle were the emblems of the two orders of warriors, hence their employment in this ceremony.

An interesting ceremony in connection with these festivals of the earth goddess in her dual aspect of keeper of the crops and patroness of warriors was held at the close of the festivals. Certain priests, dressed in the flayed skins of sacrificial victims, scattered maize of all colors, white, red, yellow and brown, as well as calabash seeds on the crowd waiting below. This seed was considered sacred, and a wild scramble ensued to gather it. Doubtless such seed was reserved for sowing in the following crop.

Teotleco, which means "The return of the gods," was the name of the twelfth month. The Aztecs believed that during part of the year the gods were absent, but returned on the eighteenth day of this month, corresponding to October 10. On the eve of this return a mat was laid at the entrance of the principal temple, and on this fine maize flour was spread. The chief priest kept watch during the night for signs of the gods' return, which was usually manifested after midnight by a foot-print appearing in the flour. As soon as this appeared the waiting priest shouted the glad tidings, and the people who had been awaiting the signal, rushed to the temple, where they danced and rejoiced till daybreak.

It was believed that the first god to arrive was Tezcatlipoca, since he was eternally youthful and robust. During the day all the other gods, who had travelled more slowly, arrived save two. These were Xiuhtecuhtli, the fire god, and Yacatecuhtli, the god of merchants. The former was delayed because of his great age, for he was always called the old, old god; the second also arrived late since, as a merchant, he would be expected to wander off the beaten track in search of business.

A great orgy of drinking and the burning of captives in a furnace closed this festival. According to one early authority the arrival of Tezcatlipoca was played by a youth, who, like all other god impersonators, met his death by sacrifice at the close of the feast.

Tepeilhuitl, the thirteenth month, was dedicated to the gods of the mountains, who were merely an aspect of the Tlalocs. Wooden snakes were made in honor of the Tlalocs, for the snake was their emblem, and many little figurines, which were covered with amaranth paste. Some of these little figures were made in honor of the

Tlalocs, others in memory of those who died under certain circumstances that qualified them for the afterworld ruled over by the Tlalocs (see page 49). Four women and a man impersonated certain of these gods, and, arrayed in costly fabrics bespattered with crude rubber, were carried in procession to one of the temples, where they were sacrificed. After the heads had been cut off and stuck on poles, the bodies were cooked and eaten by the principal members of the community in a kind of communion.

Quecholli, the fourteenth month, was presided over by Mixcoatl, a god of hunting and, by extension, of war. Arrows and spears for use in war were made at this time. During the four days that this occupation lasted a general penance ceremony was held. Blood was drawn from different parts of the body and offered in sacrifice. The old people, who alone were permitted to carouse, abstained from liquor during this period, and husbands did not cohabit with their wives. Small darts and tamales were placed on the graves of the deceased.

On the tenth day the men of Mexico City with the Tlatelucans took part in a great hunting expedition held on the slopes of Cacetepec mountain, which was considered to be a goddess and was known as "Our mother." On the top of this an altar had previously been erected. The hunters formed a ring round the mountain, and started to drive the game toward the summit, shouting, beating drums and firing the grass as they advanced. The ring of hunters gradually converged on the summit, where large quantities of game had been pent up in this manner. Eventually these were shot by the hunters. Some were sacrificed to Mixcoatl on the altar, and the rest was taken back to the cities. A great banquet ensued, followed by dances and acting in honor of the patron of the feast.

Panquetzaliztli, the fifteenth month, was signalized by a great festival in honor of Huitzilopochtli, the war god. Every day for twenty days a dance was held each night from sunset to about 9 P.M. On the last day captives were sacrificed, and a mock battle was held between two groups of prisoners destined for sacrifice. One group, recruited from captive warriors, was armed with mock weapons; the other group, drawn from the slaves to be sacrificed, was armed with the regular wooden swords set with blades of obsidian. The fighting that ensued was sufficiently serious as to lead to the death of some of the combatants, but whether they died in the combat or not, they were not allowed to live, for the survivors were sacrificed.

In connection with these ceremonies occurred an incident of unusual archæological interest. Certain of the captives, prior to their death, were taken to the houses of their masters. Each one on arriving at his destination dipped his hands in a bowl of red, black or blue paint, and pressed them on the jambs and pillars of the house. He did the same thing at the home of his family. Hand prints of this type, impressed in red paint, are found on buildings in many parts of the world, and are common on Maya temples. Doubtless there is more than one explanation of their presence, but it is interesting to find this evidence, supplied from an early Spanish source, of one of their causes.

Atemoztli, the sixteenth month, was given up to more festivals in honor of the Tlalocs, the rain and thunder gods of the mountains. For five days prior to the festival the priests allowed no water to touch their heads, and abstained from cohabitation. Long poles from which hung paper streamers coated with crude rubber were set up outside the houses, and each household fashioned little paste images of the Tlalocs to which food and drink offerings were made. All night vigils were held, the people singing and playing before their *penates* and making fresh offerings. The middle of this month coincided with the winter solstice at the time of conquest. Rain was needed at this time prior to the dry period ushered in about the middle of January.

Tititl, the seventeenth month, was marked by a feast in honor of Ilamatecuhtli—"The old princess." As in the usual Mexican method, a woman impersonating this goddess was sacrificed. She was permitted, indeed expected, to weep and sigh to a large extent as she danced alone before being sacrificed. This would suggest that the festival was held primarily to obtain rain, just as the children were supposed to weep in the rain-making ceremony held in the first month of the year. On this same day the men made small bags, which they filled with straw, dried grass and other soft materials. Carrying these under their cloaks, they sallied forth, giving any woman they met a swipe with the bag. The children used to beat them so hard that they would weep. It may well be that this was the object of this pillow fighting, the tears helping to bring the needed rain.

Izcalli, the eighteenth and last month of the year, was dedicated to Xiuhtecutli, the fire god. Every four years captives were sacrificed, but on the other years the ceremonies were carried out without this usual accompaniment of Aztec religious ceremonies. A great hunt, that lasted ten days, preceded the festival. All the young men took part. On the eve of the young men's return the sacred fire was put out, and new fire made at midnight by twirling one stick of hard wood in a hole in a board of softer wood. All the game brought by the hunters was cooked next morning with the newly made fire. The meat was served to the priests and nobles, whereas the hunters had to be content with certain tamales.

Every four years, when, as stated above, captives were sacrificed, the young children had their ears and lips pierced for ornaments. In the town of Quauhtitlan, about twelve miles from Mexico City, a peculiar ceremony was held at this time. Two women were sacrificed and flayed. Then two leaders of the community dressed in their complete skins, and carrying in their hands the leg bones of the victims, slowly descended the altar steps, roaring the while like wild animals. While they danced round large numbers of birds were sacrificed.

People came from many miles around for this ceremony, and it is related that the birds sacrificed on one occasion passed the 8000 mark. Subsequently six prisoners were placed at the tops of high poles, and shot at by the multitude below with their bows and arrows until they fell dead to the ground. (Plate XIV.) Then, inevitably, their hearts were removed. That night the bodies were eaten at a banquet.

The five odd days at the end of the year were called Nemontemi. They were considered extremely unlucky, and no work save what was absolutely indispensable was performed on them. Quarrels were especially to be avoided during this period. There is some doubt as to the position these days should occupy in the year. They were supposed to come at the end of the year, but most early sources agree that new year's day fell on the first day of the month Toxcatl, but the unlucky five days apparently came after the eighteenth month.

The ceremonies described above have been given only in the barest outline. Early writers devoted as much as a chapter to the ceremonies of each month. Such a description as has been given above naturally lacks much of the color and romance attached to this series of great feasts that made up the ritual year of the Mexicans, but at least it serves to indicate the general lines of Mexican religious observance without the endless repetition of human sacrifices that gives a wrong impression of Mexican worship.

These months of the solar year, to return to the in-

terrupted discussion of the calendar, ran concurrently
with the sacred almanac of 260 days, called the Tonalamatl. Since both 365 and 260 have a common factor
of 5, only every fifth day of the Tonalamatl could
coincide with any given day of the solar calendar. In
actual practice the day Calli was one of the five days that
could fall on the first day of a Mexican month; the other
days of the Tonalamatl that could fill this position were
Tochtli, Acatl and Tecpatl, each of which is five days
later than the day in front of it. Below is given a short
section of the two counts functioning side by side. This
count starts from an arbitrary 1 Calli 1 Toxcatl, which
was in fact the new year's day of the Aztec year corresponding to 1493.

1 Calli	1 Toxcatl	1 Cozcaquauhtli	14 Toxcatl
2 Quetzpalin	2 Toxcatl	2 Olin	15 Toxcatl
3 Coatl	3 Toxcatl	3 Tecpatl	16 Toxcatl
4 Miquiztli	4 Toxcatl	4 Quiauitl	17 Toxcatl
5 Mazatl	5 Toxcatl	5 Xochitl	18 Toxcatl
6 Tochtli	6 Toxcatl	6 Cipactli	19 Toxcatl
7 Atl	7 Toxcatl	7 Eecatl	20 Toxcatl
8 Itzcuintli	8 Toxcatl	8 Calli	1 Etzalqualiztli
9 Ozomatli	9 Toxcatl	9 Quetzpalin	2 Etzalqualiztli
10 Malinalli	10 Toxcatl	10 Coatl	3 Etzalqualiztli
11 Acatl	11 Toxcatl	11 Miquiztli	4 Etzalqualiztli
12 Ocelotl	12 Toxcatl	12 Mazatl	5 Etzalqualiztli
13 Quauhtli	13 Toxcatl	13 Tochtli	6 Etzalqualiztli
		1 Atl	7 Etzalqualiztli

It will be seen that the day of the Tonalamatl that
coincides with 1 Toxcatl, will coincide with the first day
of every other month in the current year, since there are

194

twenty day signs and twenty month signs, but the attached number will increase by seven each month, since
there are but thirteen numbers. Were the year of only
360 days the same day sign would recur at the beginning of every year, since 360 is divisible by 20 without
remainder. Since there are 365 days in the Aztec year,
the day is five positions later in the Tonalamatl, and
the numerical coefficient is one greater for 365 divided
by 13 leaves a remainder of 1. The positions in the
Tonalamatl that can serve as new-year days run in the
following order:

1 Calli	5 Calli	9 Calli	13 Calli
2 Tochtli	6 Tochtli	10 Tochtli	1 Tochtli
3 Acatl	7 Acatl	11 Acatl	2 Acatl
4 Tecpatl	8 Tecpatl	12 Tecpatl	3 Tecpatl, etc.

Since there are only four day signs and thirteen attached numbers, the position 1 Calli will recur as a
new year on 1 Toxcatl only after all the fifty-two possible permutations have been run off, or in other words
once in fifty-two years.

This supplied the Mexicans with a very convenient
system for differentiating every year in a fifty-two-year
cycle, just as we, if we took no account of leap years,
might differentiate any year in a seven-year cycle by
calling the years Sunday year, Monday year, Tuesday
year . . . Sunday year, since, omitting leap years, each
year starts a day later in the week than the year that
preceded it. Similarly no double date of Tonalamatl day
and number combined with the position in the 365-day

year could recur during this period of fifty-two years. By writing 5 Ocelotl 17 Quecholli, for example, one could be certain that this date would not occur again within fifty-two years, and the day was thus differentiated in a manner impossible in our calendar. It is true 17 Quecholli will recur after 365 days, but then it will be accompanied by the Tonalamatl position 6 Quiauitl, and the next time it is associated with the original Ocelotl sign, this will have changed its numerical coefficient, and will have become 9 Ocelotl.

Although the Aztecs used this system to a certain extent, they made more use of a method of giving the Tonalamatl date of the new year in combination with a sign rather like a capital A, following it by the Tonalamatl position of the date to be given. A date of this type, registering 6 Coatl in a year 12 Tochtli and a second giving 13 Quauhtli in a year 5 Acatl are shown in Plate XXIII. This would be an equally satisfactory system were it not that a day of the Tonalamatl may occur twice in a solar year, since the latter count is 105 days longer than the former. The Mexicans got round this difficulty in the following ingenious way. There existed a series of nine gods, known as "The Lords of the Nights," who ruled over successive nights in a strict unending rotation, so that if a certain Lord ruled during the night of 1 Calli, he would not rule again until 10 Malinalli—nine days later. Since 260 days, the length of the Tonalamatl, is not divisible by 9 without remainder, the same god would not be the Lord of the

PLATE XXIII. GLYPHS FOR TOWNS AND DATES

a, Acayocan (Place of Reeds); *b*, Tecpayocan (Place of Flints); *c*, Cihuateo-
pan (Temple of Cihuacoatl); *d*, Aculco (Twisted Water); *e*, Coatepec (Snake
Hill); *f*, Cuernavaca (Near the Tree); *g*, Day 6 Coatl in a year 12 Tochtli;
h, Day 13 Quauhtli in a year 5 Acatl.

night on the next occurrence of 1 Calli, but his turn would come the following night—2 Quetzpalin. The Aztecs appear to have differentiated a repetition of the same day in the same year by adding the glyph of the corresponding Lord of the Night.

The end of the fifty-two-year cycle, when a double date would recur for the first time, was the occasion of very important ceremonies. This event took place in the 2 Acatl years. Previously the cycle had ended in the year 1 Tochtli, but owing to a run of bad luck in the 1 Tochtli years, the date of the ceremony was shifted to a year 2 Tochtli. Torquemada has left a detailed account of these ceremonies which is given below in a more abbreviated form.

The natives believed that at the end of this fifty-two-year period the world might come to an end, and would only continue if the gods showed that they were favorably disposed by permitting new fire to be kindled. Consequently their ceremonies were an appeasement of the gods and a token that the people would faithfully serve them if spared such a dreadful fate. All idols, both in the temples and private houses, were replaced. The implements, braziers and furnishings used in the temple services were renewed, and all buildings whitewashed and renovated.

At sunset on the evening before the fatal day, the priests, robing themselves in the vestments of Quetzalcoatl, Tlaloc and other important gods, silently set forth in solemn procession to the summit of a hill called Hui-

xachtecatl, situated about six miles from Tenochtitlan.
The priests, who were accompanied by a large part of
the populace, so timed themselves that they reached
their destination a little before midnight. Meanwhile
throughout the length and breadth of the land every
fire in home and temple had been extinguished.

Exactly at midnight a captive was sacrificed by the
usual method of tearing out the heart. In the cavity,
caused by its removal, new fire was made by twirling a
stick on a flat board of softer wood. As soon as the first
wisp of flame was visible, a great shout arose from the
spectators, for this was the sign that the world would
not come to an end, but would endure for at least another fifty-two years. From the newly kindled fire a
great bonfire was lit so that the people for miles around
might know that the gods were favorable, and the world
had been spared once more. Among the spectators were
many fleet runners. These carried pine torches, which
they lit in the flames, then sped forth on the road to
their villages. Fresh runners, placed along the route,
relayed the torches through the night until the new fire
reached the farthest provinces. As soon as the runners
reached Mexico City, the fire was lit from their torches
on a special altar in the temple of Huitzilopochtli.
Hither came all the people to carry the new fire back
into their homes. The early chronicler describes the
night being as bright as day because of the multitude
of torches carried by the crowds.

While waiting to know if the new fire would be lit

and the world continue, every one was filled with great anxiety. Families assembled on the flat roofs of their houses to await the outcome. Pregnant women were shut up in the maize granaries and their faces covered with special masks made of maguey leaves, for it was believed that, should there be difficulty in making new fire, women in this condition would turn into wild animals. Children also were masked, and great care was taken to see that they did not fall asleep while waiting for new fire to be made, as it was believed that they would turn into rats should sleep overtake them.

Until midday following the new fire ceremony, every one fasted, even the drinking of water was prohibited. At noon prisoners were sacrificed, the pregnant women were released from the granaries, and each family sat down to a meal of special cakes made of honey and a certain kind of flour. Copal was burned and birds sacrificed to the gods of the four world directions, and the day concluded with general rejoicings. Such in short was the festival of *Toxiuhmolpilia*, or "The tying up of the years" as the name means. Despite its simplicity, this must have been the most impressive spectacle in ancient Mexico.

It is no exaggeration to say that the Tonalamatl and its operation closely affected the lives and movements of every member of the community from ruler to slave. Examples of its use in connection with birth and marriage are given in Chapter II, but illustrations of such uses might be multiplied a hundredfold. No important action from birth to death was undertaken without reference to it. No man, for example, would set out on a hunting trip without first discovering whether the day was propitious for such an undertaking. Similarly such tasks as the preparation of the fields, the sowing and harvesting of the crops, the building of houses, and the making of pottery could only be started on lucky days. The departure of merchants for distant lands and declarations of war were likewise governed by the Tonalamatl.

It is difficult for us to realize to what an extent everyday life was governed by such astrological and religious rules and regulations. In addition to the permutations of lucky and unlucky days, the numbers attached to the day signs had benevolent and malevolent values. Thirteen, for instance, was of very good augury; four was man's lucky number because of the four directions of the world, and three was women's auspicious number since three stones formed the hearth, around which a woman's life revolved.

Divisions of the Tonalamatl were also associated with the four world directions and colors. Starting from Cipactli, which was associated with the east, the days were assigned in order to the directions in an anti-clockwise manner, Eecatl pertaining to the north, Calli to the west, Quetzpalin to the south, and Coatl again coinciding with the east. In the same way the years were associated with the four world directions and primary colors, as well as the gods of the world directions. In addition to the four points of the compass, the centre of the world was considered of ceremonial importance. These directions are symbolized in the codices by trees, on the branches of which perch birds. It was believed that at the creation a red, yellow, white and blue tree were planted, one at each compass point.

The Aztecs possessed a double 52-year cycle based on the movements of the planet Venus. The Venus year consists of a fraction less than 584 days, 5 Venus years equalling 8 solar years of the Aztec type (2920 days). At the end of 13 times this interval 65 Venus years, 104 Aztec solar years and 146 Tonalamatls had passed, and the three counts coincided again for the first time. This great period of 104 years formed the double 52-year cycle. Actually the fractional loss of the Venus year had amounted to about four days at the end of this period, and the next Venus period started four days earlier in the Tonalamatl.

The Venus year was counted from the heliacal rising of the planet, the period of inferior conjunction preceding this being calculated at eight days. The reappearance of the planet was considered to be of ill omen. The holes in the roofs of houses, through which smoke from the fire escaped, were stopped up so that the light of the planet's rays should not enter the houses. The rays of light were looked upon as arrows shot by the Venus god, Tlauizcalpantecutli, and they were considered to bring ill to different classes of individuals in different years. In the 1 Acatl years, for example, rulers

were smitten, and in the 1 Olin years warriors and maidens were the victims. These beliefs are portrayed in
different codices where Tlauizcalpantecutli with five

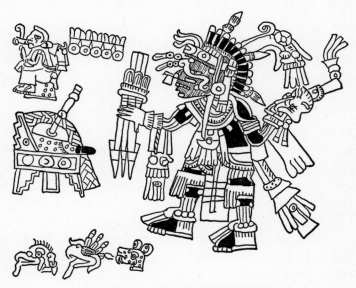

PLATE XXIV. TLAUIZCALPANTECUTLI
Venus god hurling spears at ruler's throne. Codex Vatican 3773.

white spots on his face, one on the tip of his nose and
the others on the cheeks, hurls spears earthwards with
the aid of his spearthrower, slaying kings and warriors.
(Plate XXIV.) The white spots on his face show a connection with Maya practice, for in the Maya inscriptions the hieroglyph of the planet Venus consists of five
circles arranged in a similar manner. To appease the

wrath of the Venus god a human sacrifice was offered at heliacal rising, and the devotees of the cult continued to offer copal incense and blood drawn from their ears and other parts of their bodies during the ensuing period of the planet's greatest brilliance.

A similar calendar to that of the Aztecs was in use among the Zapotecs of Oaxaca, but the day names differed. It is very probable that every tribe in the central and Southern Mexican regions possessed its own distinctive names for the days and months, but in most cases these have not survived. Inscribed dates on stone are fairly rare in the plateau region, and with very few exceptions those that have been recovered can be dated on stylistic grounds as belonging to the Aztec period. At the great site of Teotihuacan no calendrical inscriptions have been so far recovered. From this it has been argued that the calendar did not reach the Mexican plateau until quite late in history, and it has been claimed that it was introduced from Yucatan by Quetzalcoatl, the Toltec ruler in the twelfth century of our era.

It is clear that the calendar certainly did not originate in the plateau region, for several of the day signs represent animals not indigenous to this region. Among these are the howling monkey, glyph of the day Ozomatli, the ocelot, glyph of the day Ocelotl, and the blue iguana, glyph of the day Quetzpalin. However, by the twelfth century Yucatecan Maya differed so much from the archaic Maya that many of the glyphs had become meaningless in name and representation. Nevertheless, from survivals in the Maya calendars of Guatemala we know that the eleventh day of the Maya Tonalamatl was originally called Batz—howling monkey —whereas the Yucatecan name for this day, Chuen, is meaningless, and the glyph bears no resemblance to a monkey. Similarly the name of the fourteenth day Ix has no meaning in Yucatecan Maya, but has the meaning of jaguar in the Kekchi-Maya language, and corresponds to the Aztec Ocelotl. Perhaps we would not be wrong in inferring that the archaic Maya name for this day meant jaguar, and has survived only in the Kekchi, just as we find Latin words surviving in one Romance language, but not in the rest.

Secondly, Mexican colonists settled in Nicaragua in Toltec times, carrying with them the Mexican day names spelt in Toltec fashion, but they did not apparently carry with them the worship of Quetzalcoatl. Had these settlers left their homes after the time of Quetzalcoatl they would undoubtedly have carried with them this new and very important religion. From this we can infer that the Tonalamatl existed in Mexico before the time of Quetzalcoatl.

From these two lines of evidence we might deduce that the Tonalamatl probably originated at a very early time in the lowlands among a pre-Maya people, and with maize, cotton, pottery making and fundamental religious concepts was among the cultural traits inherited by the later civilizations, both Maya and Mexican. In other words the Mexicans did not borrow their calendar either directly or indirectly from the Mayas, nor the Mayas from the Mexicans, but both civilizations were co-heirs of an earlier culture. Presumably the Mayas added their system of reckoning in 20 and 400 year periods at a later date, for such a system was unknown to the Mexicans, whereas had the Mexicans received their calendar from Yucatan in the twelfth century, they could hardly have failed to take over also this method of reckoning years.

A brief outline of the principal Aztec feasts has been given in the list of the months. In order to supply a fuller insight into Aztec ritual and religious concepts, accounts of two important ceremonies are given below in full detail. The first is that of Tezcatlipoca. The account is taken from Sahagun's monumental account of the ancient Mexicans. The translation is free, and the punctuation and lengths of paragraphs have been altered.

"The fifth month is called Toxcatl. In it they make a special feast in honor of their principal god called Tezcatlipoca. He is also known as Titlacaoan, Yautl, Telpuchtli, or Tlamatzincatl.

"In this feast they kill a youth of a polished disposition. This youth had been kept for a year in idle enjoyment, for they said that he was the living personification of Tezcatlipoca. They had a large number of these young men set aside, and from them one was chosen and kept apart for a year as soon as the previous candidate had been sacrificed. The candidates who were chosen from among the prisoners of war were all of noble blood, of good disposition, clever and without any corporal blemish. The youth who was to be slain was carefully taught to play on the flute. He was also coached in carrying the reed tobacco tubes, and to wander round smoking and smelling bouquets of flowers as was the custom of the Aztec nobility. The Calpixques, in whose power the youth was kept until chosen to act the part of the living god, took great pains to teach the candidates good manners, such as how to salute or address persons they met, for once they had been chosen for the part, every one who met them treated them with great reverence, kissing the ground [*i.e.*, touching the ground with the fingers, and placing them to the lips. This was the Aztec manner of showing humility]. If the youths became too fat, they were given salt water to reduce their weight.

"Once the youth had been chosen to die, he began to wander through the streets, playing his flute, smoking and smelling his bouquets of flowers. He was free to wander both by night and by day, but wherever he went he was accompanied by eight attendants dressed as though they were pages of the Aztec chief ruler. The chief ruler, once the youth had been proclaimed as the next to die in this feast, dressed him in costly and strange clothing, since he was now considered to be a substitute for the god. They painted his face and body and decorated his head with white feathers attached by means of resin. His hair reached to his waist.

"After dressing him they placed on him a garland of flowers, which they call Yzquisuchitl, and a long wreath of the same flowers hanging from the shoulder to the arm-pit on both sides. In his ears they placed ornaments like gold ear-rings, and round his neck a string of precious stones. From this hung a white precious stone which reached to the breast. A long lip-plug made of cockle [conch?] shell was placed [in his lower lip]. On his shoulders he carried a bag-like ornament, a palm's width square, made of white cloth with tasselled fringes.

"They placed gold bracelets on both arms around the fleshy parts above the elbows and strings of precious stones were wound round the fore-arms covering them almost entirely from wrist to elbow. They covered him with a beautiful cloak made in a netted technique and supplied with a very curious trimmed edge.

"They placed around his waist a piece of cloth called maxtlatl, which they use to cover their private parts. The ends, which hung down in front almost to the knee, were elaborately decorated, and the whole was about a palm in width. Gold bells were placed around the legs, and these tinkled wherever the youth wandered. On his feet were placed sandals which were very curious and covered with paint. In this manner was the youth dressed at the beginning of his year of impersonation.

"Twenty days before the actual feast they changed these clothes, with which he had made so much display up to then, and washed off the paint from his head and body. They cut his hair short in the style adopted by warrior captains, tying it up in a lock on the crown of the head, and leaving a curious fringe. To the lock of hair was tied a tuft of feathers and rabbit hair decorated with gold and buttons. At the same time they married him to four maidens, whose company he enjoyed for the remaining twenty days of his life.

"These maidens also had been raised in great luxury for this rôle. They were given the names of four goddesses. One was named Xochiquetzal [goddess of flowers and pleasure], the second Xilonen [goddess of maize], the third Atlatonan [our mother, the water], and the fourth Uixtocioatl [goddess of salt, elder sister of Tlaloc].

"Five days before the feast, when the youth was to be sacrificed, they honored him as god. The Aztec ruler remained alone in his house, but all persons of rank followed him [the youth], performing dances and giving banquets attired in their richest clothing.

"The first day they made a celebration in his honor in the quarter called Tecanman; the second day in the quarter where the statue of Tezcatlipoca was kept; the third day on the little hill called Tepetzinco in the lake; the fourth day on another little hill called Tepelpulco, also in the lake. At the close of this fourth feast he and his women, who went to console him, were placed in a canoe with an awning, in which the Aztec ruler used to travel. Leaving Tepelpulco, they journeyed in the canoe to Tlapitzaoayan, near the Ystapalapan-Chalco road, where there is a little hill called Acaquilpan or Cabaltepec. Here he left his women and the crowd, returning to the city unaccompanied save by the eight attendants, who had been with him constantly during the past year.

"They guided him to a small, poorly adorned pyramid at the side of the road, a league or nearly that from the city, and situated in an uninhabited district. On reaching the foot of the steps, he began to climb up unattended. At the first step he broke one of the flutes on which he used to play during his time of good fortune; at the second step he broke another and at the third yet another. In this way he destroyed all of them one by one as he climbed the steps.

"At the top of the pyramid the priests were ready for him, and as soon as he reached the top, they seized him and placed him on his back upon the stone block. Priests held his hands, legs and head, while the one with the knife plunged it into his breast with a great blow. Removing the knife, the priest thrust his hand into the wound, and tearing out the heart, immediately offered it to the sun. In this way they slew all those to be sacrificed [an untrue statement]. The body in this case was not thrown down the steps, as was the usual custom, but four priests carried it down to the court below. There they cut off the head and stuck it on a post called Tzonpantli [skull rack].

"In this way he who had been honored and showered with gifts for a year ended his life. They said that this

PLATE XXV. PLAYERS IN A BALL-COURT
Note the rings and death heads. Magliabecchi Codex.

ceremony signified that those who had had riches and pleasures during their life would in the end come to poverty and pain."

The second feast to be described in full is that held by the warrior group in honor of the sun every 260 days. The account is translated from that given by Duran, an early writer on Aztec history and customs.

"There existed in this land an order of knights who made a profession of arms. They had vowed to die in defense of their country, and not to turn their backs on the enemy even if ten or twelve attacked [one of] them at the same time. These knights considered the sun to be their god and the head of their order, just as the Spanish knights are under the patronage of glorious Saint James.

"All those who entered this order were illustrious and courageous persons. Only the sons of knights and nobles were admissible, persons of humble birth not being eligible however brave they might be. The feast of these knights and nobles was made in honor of their god, the sun, whom they called *Nauholin,* which means Four Movements. . . . [Duran goes on to state that this feast was held on the day 4 Olin. The reason for the choice of this day was that the present age, called "Four Suns," was supposed to have started on the day 4 Olin. The sun's regular name was Tonatiuh, but here, following a fairly common Mexican custom, he is given the day of his feast as a second name.]

"This temple [of the order] was situated on the

very spot where they are now building Mexico cathedral. It was called Cuacuauhtinchan, which means the house of the eagles. [Plate XIX.] The title of eagle or jaguar they gave to men who had done brave deeds as a sort of mark of honor to commemorate their bravery. Thus the house of eagles really meant the house of brave men. The metaphor was employed because the eagle is one of the bravest of birds, and the jaguar the fiercest and most savage of four-footed animals.

"At the top of this temple [pyramid?] there was a room next to a court, which as we said in the previous chapter, was about forty feet square and smoothly finished with lime. On one side of this court was this room of which I speak. Inside there was an altar, above which hung a cloth with a representation of the sun painted on it. This painting was in the shape of a butterfly with outspread wings, and around this there was a circle of gold with dazzling rays radiating from it. [The sign was not a butterfly, as Duran states, but the day sign Olin, which bears a slight resemblance to a butterfly. See Plate XXI.] The rest of the room was gaily decorated and well arranged. To reach this room there was a staircase of about forty steps.

"In this temple all the ceremonies practiced in the other temples were also performed. For instance, the idol was carried out in solemn procession to be shown to the people four times a day, and all the ceremonies of offerings and sacrifices were performed as in the case of the other gods. For this purpose they [the eagle knights] had their priests and dignitaries with full rank and the same privileges as the other priests. They solemnized this feast in the following manner.

"This day [4 Olin] all the people of the city observed a strict fast. This was so rigorous that not even children or sick persons were allowed to eat until the sun, pursuing its course, was overhead at midday. At that moment the priests and ministers of that temple took some shells [conch shell trumpets] and trumpets and gave the signal to the people to assemble at the temple. This they immediately did with the same attention and haste as they now flock to Mass on Sunday.

"As soon as the people were assembled at this sound of the shells and trumpets, an Indian prisoner of war was brought forth. He was accompanied by a throng of nobles, who surrounded him. His legs were painted with white stripes, half his face was reddened, and white plumage was stuck on his hair. In one hand he carried a staff handsomely decorated with loops and knots of leather, in which feathers were inserted. In the other hand he held a shield with five balls of cotton on it. On his back he carried a bundle containing pieces of red ochre, eagle feathers, gypsum, pinewood soot, and pieces of paper decorated with stripes of raw rubber. . . .

"They placed the prisoner at the foot of the steps leading to the temple, addressing him in a loud voice so that all the people might hear. 'Sir,' they said, 'we beg you to go to our god, the sun, and salute him on our behalf. Tell him that his children, the knights and chiefs, who remain here [on earth] beg him to remember us and favor us from where he is [in the sky]. Ask him to receive this small present which we send him. Give him this staff to walk with, and this shield to defend himself, together with the other objects which you carry in the bundle.'

"The Indian [prisoner], on hearing this address, replied that he would be pleased to do so. Thereupon he was released. Slowly he began to climb to the temple, stopping for a considerable time on each step. The delay on each step was according to instructions, for this dilatory climb symbolized the slow passage of the sun. When at last he had reached the summit, he walked to the stone called cuauhxicalli, which has in the centre the symbol of the sun. On to this he climbed.

"Standing there, he addressed in a loud voice the image of the sun hanging above the altar of the room, turning occasionally towards the real sun. As soon as he had concluded, four priests climbed to the top of the stone, each one ascending by one of the four flights of steps which, as I have said, the stone possessed. They took away the staff, the shield and the bundle which he carried; then they grasped his hands and feet. Next the high priest, ascending with his knife in his hand, cut the prisoner's throat, bidding him go with his message to the real sun [whom he would meet] in his next life.

"They [the other priests] poured the blood into the font. From there, passing down a canal, it spilt out in front of the chamber of the sun and the image of the sun painted on the stone. As soon as all the blood had drained away, they opened his [the victim's] breast, and took out the heart. Raising it on high, one of them presented it to the sun, holding it aloft until it ceased steaming, and grew cold. Thus did the unfortunate messenger to the sun come to the end of his life, going [instead] to hell with his message, there to give an account of the great blindness in which the people yet lived.

"The sacrifice of the Indian had been witnessed by the whole populace without breaking their fast. The ceremony was so cleverly timed that it was exactly midday when the Indian ascended to the sacrificial stone. As soon as the throat cutting and the rest of the ceremony was concluded, the temple priests blew the shells and trumpets. This was the signal that the fast was over and all might now eat. The fast had been kept very strictly up to this moment. No one dared break it for fear of incurring the wrath of the sun, for all kinds of evils were foretold should they do so.

"As soon as the signal was given, all went to eat. Some retired to their houses, others, who had travelled a long distance, had brought their food with them, and ate it there. While the people were eating, the priests were not idle. First they took the bundle of presents, the staff and the shield, which the Indian had carried, and placed them beside the image of the sun. Then they took [the body of] the sacrificed man, and returned it to its owner [*i.e.*, the captor].

"He [the captor] solemnized the feast with the flesh, for the flesh of all sacrificial victims was considered sacred and holy. They ate it with as much reverence and with as many ceremonies as if it were some heavenly thing. The common people never ate this flesh, but only the nobles and chiefs.

"After eating their repast, all the populace returned on the signal being given with those instruments [*i.e.*, the conch shells and trumpets], which served in the same way as we now use bells. When the temple [the court?] was again full, the youths of the nobility came forth. Each one had some small knives in one hand, and in the other a bundle of thin smooth sticks of osier. Sitting down in their correct order, they practiced a peculiar form of self-sacrifice.

"This consisted of making wounds in the fleshy part of their left arms above the elbow. The wounds, which were about an inch long, passed between the skin and the flesh. Through these they passed the sticks one by one, drawing them out at the other end covered with blood. These sticks they threw down in front of the image of the sun. The one who drew most sticks [through the wound] was considered the most pious and possessed of most fortitude, and was accorded most glory. This particular sacrifice was only performed on the day of the feast. [Plate XX.]

"When the sacrifice was finished, they [the participants] went to bathe. Afterwards they brought out the drums, and made a great dance. In this only the chiefs and nobles took part, the rest of the populace not being permitted to participate. In this dance the chiefs wore many beautiful jewels, curious featherwork and very fine necklaces. Especially was this the case with the knights of the [eagle] order, who had the symbol of their patron, the sun, on their shields and feather work."

It has been suggested that the great calendar stone (p. 165) was the sacrificial stone mentioned in this account. This is quite probable in view of the fact that the glyph 4 Olin occupies the most prominent position on the stone. Part of the stone has been broken off, and it is quite possible that it was originally square. Small steps of wood or lime-coated rubble may have existed on all four sides, as Duran suggests.

Only a fraction of the religious feasts of the Aztecs have been discussed in this chapter. Nevertheless, one gets a very forceful impression that the Mexican's daily life was so hedged in by these countless ceremonies and practices that a strict observance must have been well-nigh impossible for any one except the zealot. We should probably not be far in error in supposing that the average layman managed to get round many of the tabus and omens of bad augury with as much success as the average Christian avoids strict application of the advanced idealism of the New Testament. Whatever the priest and diviner may have thought, the Mexican man in the street probably reached the conclusion that the Tonalamatl and the continuous round of feasts were made for man, and not man for them. Probably he compromised accordingly in their observance, devoutly participating in those which most closely affected his wellbeing, but inwardly little moved by the feasts of the warrior group.

CHAPTER VII

PRIESTHOOD, SPORTS, AND WRITINGS

Need for Numerous Priests. Two High Priests. Sacred Priests of
Tehuacan. Blood Drawing. Dress. Daily Life. Divination by the
Calendar. Soothsayers. Auguries and Superstitions. Divination by
Maize. Witch Doctors. Curing of Illness. Magicians. Sacred Ball
Game. Used to Settled Disputes. Flying Game. Game Like Back-
gammon. Riddles. Dancing. Sometimes 3000 Participants. Instruc-
tion in Dances. Musical Instruments. Life of Eight Deer. Hiero-
glyphic Codices.

THE bewildering multiplicity of gods, the innumerable religious festivals and the large numbers of temples and sacred structures necessarily required a large
and well-organized priesthood. Such existed, every calpulli having its own temple and priests in addition to
the large tribal temples with their attendant sacerdotal
organization. Torquemada claims that there were no less
than 5000 persons employed in the service of the great
temple of Huitzilopochtli in Mexico City, including
priests of various classes, probationers, vestal virgins and
boys from the schools. Although it may well be that
this number is somewhat exaggerated, there is little doubt
that the priesthood was of enormous importance both in
numbers and in influence. It could hardly be otherwise
with a people of such religious intensity as the ancient
Mexicans.

At the head of the Aztec priesthood stood two priests
of equal rank. One of these, who bore the title of Quet-

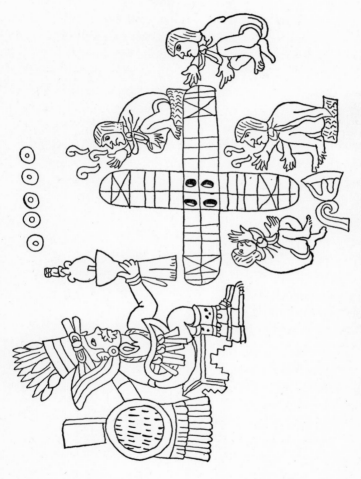

PLATE XXVI. PLAYING THE PATOLLI GAME

The patron god of games is seated on a stool, watching the game. Magliabecchi Codex.

zalcoatl Totec, was the high priest of the cult of Huitzilopochtli, the Aztec war god. The other was the chief
of the order of priests of Tlaloc, and bore this god's
name. According to Sahagun these were chosen entirely
on the grounds of piety and wisdom by the council of
elders of the tribe, but Acosta states that the priest of
Huitzilopochtli must have belonged to a certain lineage, presumably that from which the Aztec chief rulers
were also chosen. Below them was the priest in charge
of the Calmecac, or tribal school for the sons of the
nobility. The education here was largely of a religious
nature (p. 41), and the position of chief instructor was
considered of very great importance, since the holder
would be largely responsible for the proper upbringing
of the coming generation of civil and religious leaders.
The cult of every important god had its chief priest,
under whom were the ordinary priests, junior priests,
corresponding roughly to the deacons of the Episcopal
Church, and finally initiates.

Among the Totonacs of the Vera Cruz region there
was a special order of priests of the maize deity Centeotl
(p. 143), who had a very high reputation for sanctity
all over Mexico. Only men over sixty years of age and of
unblemished reputation could be elected. They were
vowed to perpetual silence except when consulted on
questions of policy or ritual. They wore fox or coyote
skins and never ate meat. In addition to the advice they
imparted, they were occupied largely in painting hieroglyphic codices.

At Tehuacan there was another order of priests of very high renown, who were consulted by persons from near and far. Among those who sought their advice were the Aztec chief rulers, although their temple was outside real Aztec territory. A group of four held office for a period of four years, at the end of which time they were replaced by another group of four. During this period those in office underwent a rigorous course of prayer, penance and fasting. They slept on mats, using a stone for a pillow, and even in winter were allowed only a thin cotton cloak and cotton breech-clout as clothing. Except on feast days they only ate once every twenty-four hours, their meal consisting of one tortilla, weighing about two ounces, and a little posol. No other food was allowed them, not even salt or chili pepper, but every twenty days when a religious festival took place, they were free to eat as much as they wished.

Every twenty days they drew blood from their bodies by piercing their ears, and passing sixty reeds through the wounds. The blood-stained reeds, which were of the average thickness of a finger, were piled up in a gradually mounting heap, until at the end of the four years of office each priest burned his pile in front of the image of the patron god. As a result of the abnormal life they led, for in addition to fasting, they spent long periods in vigil, they received many visions. The advice they gave was based on these, and were one of the group to die during his period of office, dire calamity was expected to overtake the whole community. The penalty for a serious lapse from piety during the incumbency of this office was death.

Generally speaking Mexican priests wore long white cotton skirts and a fringed cape of the same material knotted over one shoulder. Aztec priests never cut their hair, nor permitted it to be combed or washed. As the blood of sacrificial victims often spurted over the priest's head, one can imagine its condition. The early Spanish conquerors, who themselves never paid much attention to the precept that cleanliness is next to godliness, were full of disgust for this revolting custom, writing that the priests were not only lousy, but that their heads smelt in a disgusting manner. There is no doubt that this custom was followed for religious reasons since the ancient Mexican was as a rule scrupulously clean. The hair was worn in long hank-like masses, but for occasions of mourning it was worn loose.

For religious ceremonies priests blackened their faces, hands, arms and legs. For special occasions a peculiar mixture of insects such as scorpions, tarantulas, wasps and centipedes was ground up with poisonous snakes, tobacco and peyote, and the whole burned. The ashes, after being offered in the temple, were used to blacken the priests' faces. It was believed that this admixture gave its wearer additional courage. Small boys from the schools were sent out to get the raw material, and rapidly became expert in catching all the required specimens of poisonous vermin. Among the Totonacs priests were consecrated after election by being anointed with a liquid

Photograph by Ministry of Education, Mexico

Pyramid near Papantla, Vera Cruz

After Peñáfiel through courtesy of Doctor Robert Redfield

Xochicalco. Feathered serpent sculpture

PLATE XXVII

composed of crude rubber and children's blood, crude rubber being one of the insignia of rain and fertility deities.

In addition to the regular religious services and special festivals, each priest made an offering of his own blood and copal incense four times during the day and five times during the night. This was done in honor of the sun god, who was saluted as Tonatiuh during the day, while at night he was worshipped under the name of Yoaltecuhtli. The priests and initiates also spent long periods chanting prayers to the accompaniment of hollow log drums. A sacred fire always burned in each temple. This was only put out at the end of the fifty-two-year period (p. 198), and were it to be allowed to go out through carelessness, a serious calamity affecting the whole community was to be expected. Needless to say the person responsible for such carelessness was severely punished.

In addition to the idols, many incense burners and braziers for the sacred fires were kept in the temples. Most of the vessels used in the religious services were of pottery, but some were of gold or silver. Priests kept supplies of maguey thorns, reeds and cord for passing through the wounds inflicted for drawing blood. The blood of sacrificial victims was sprinkled on the idols by means of a kind of hyssop of red feathers. The sprinkling ceremony was the cause of the thick coatings of blood on the temple walls, of which Peter Martyr speaks with horror (p. 167).

Junior priests made frequent pilgrimages into the forests, sallying forth at night to make offerings of pine wood and copal to the mountain gods. On these occasions they covered themselves with the peculiar concoction of poisonous insects, snakes, tobacco and peyote mentioned above. This was believed to give them "Dutch courage," so that they had no fear of the woods at night. Sometimes on these nocturnal expeditions they heard a peculiar sound like that of a man cutting down a tree. This was considered a very bad omen, presaging grave misfortune. The ancient Mexicans seem to have had a great fear of going out at night in the forest unaccompanied, a fear shared by their modern descendants and the modern Mayas, for the latter have a strange repugnance to going out alone after dark.

The regular priests were occupied with the temple functions and sacrifices, the hearing of confessions, fasting and penance, chanting and the supervision of sacred dances. The junior priests slept in the Calmecac, but there were probably living quarters attached to all the important temples. Of these there were a very large number in Mexico City, for in addition to those of the normal Aztec gods, there were also edifices dedicated to the worship of foreign deities. In their willingness to accept deities of conquered peoples, the Aztecs resembled the Romans. All priests had an intimate knowledge of the Tonalamatl or 260-day sacred almanac, for they were continually engaged in consultations as to suitable occasions to undertake any task or celebrate any event. By this means the priesthood controlled every action of the people from the declaration of war by the tribe to the building of a bird coop by one of its humblest members.

In contrast to the priests, who were professionals supported by the whole clan or local calpulli, and usually celibate, there were a large number of humbler soothsayers and healers, who carried on their normal occupations, occasionally serving in these secondary capacities. They were largely consulted by the humbler agriculturalists as to when to sow or harvest, as well as for domestic reasons. Their answers were governed either by the Tonalamatl or by visions which came to them after eating peyote or certain other narcotic herbs (p. 231).

There were a very large number of superstitions current among the people. The calls of certain birds, such as the owl, presaged death, and similarly if a rabbit or a skunk were to enter the house, the inmates might expect bad luck. Rats played an important part in these beliefs. A person who ate food that had been gnawed by rats would be falsely accused of theft or adultery. If an occupant of a house committed adultery, the rats would eat his or her clothing. One imagines that this superstition must have been the cause of many baseless matrimonial recriminations. If a householder wished to rid his home of rats by setting traps for them, he first placed the corn-grinding roller outside, otherwise the roller would warn the rats of the danger that awaited them.

227

There were also a number of superstitions connected with the preparation of maize. If one were to lick the grinding stone, one's teeth would fall out. The curling of tortillas on the griddle announced a visitor or the return of an absent husband. A woman who broke her grinding stone would die within a short time. If a person were to upset some grains of corn on the ground, he must pick them up, otherwise they would invoke a curse on him for not showing them due respect. If maize cobs were burned in a house where a baby had been recently born, he would become spotty and covered with freckles unless one just touched the child's face with the cobs before placing them on the fire. A soldier, who ate a tamale that had stuck to the side of the pot, would thereafter prove a poor marksman. Green corn eaten at night would cause toothache unless it were first warmed at the fire. If the first fire lit in a new house burned well from the start, the inmates of that house would live long and happily; if the fire burned badly, the contrary might be expected.

Two peculiar beliefs existed in connection with the growth of children. It was thought that were a person to step over a child, the latter would cease to grow, but the remedy was simple. All one had to do to break the spell was to step over the child again in the contrary direction. When an earthquake was felt, parents lifted their children up by their heads, or, it was believed, they would not grow any more. Children were not allowed to play around the corner posts of the house, for it was held that proximity to the posts would cause them to develop into liars. Merchants had the peculiar superstition of carrying the arm of a female monkey with them. This improved their salesmanship powers. If merchandise still remained unsold at the end of the day, the merchant offered chili peppers to the monkey arm to induce higher-powered salesmanship the following day. Among the Huaxtec a man who had died from the bite of a certain snake must be buried face downwards, otherwise serious floods would devastate his native town.

Divination was largely practised by the soothsayer-medicine man. A common method to know how long a sick person would live was by measuring the left forearm with the right hand. The palm was laid across the arm, and the distance measured off. If at the last measurement the outside of the hand coincided with the points of the fingers, the patient would promptly die. If there was a wide space over, the patient would live for a long time. The medicine men bunched up their hands or lay them flat to reach the desired result, which probably depended on a shrewd examination of the patient before divining his fate.

Often maize was used in divination. Grains of maize were thrown into a jug of water. If all sank to the bottom, good fortune might be expected; if some floated on the surface, misfortune or death was to come. The medicine man controlled these results by a careful selection of the grain he wished to employ, since good grain sank immediately to the bottom, whereas rotten or worm-eaten grain floated. In another method twenty-five grains of maize were taken. Four grains were placed in each corner of a mat, the sorcerer holding the remaining nine in his hand. Passing the handful over each corner group in turn, he threw the nine grains in the centre of the mat. If the majority fell face upwards good luck might be expected.

A sick child was held over a deep bowl of water. If the face was clearly mirrored in the water, recovery would take place; if the reflection was blurred, the child would die, or if it lived would be pursued by bad luck.

All these divinations were accompanied by set prayers, of which I shall quote only that used with the divination last cited in connection with holding a child over water.

"Behold now my mother, jade, you with the skirt and huipil blouse of jade stones, you the white woman. Let us see if this child is sick because her star, her good luck has deserted her." The mother with the jade skirt and huipil is the goddess Chalchiuitlicue, goddess of water. Naturally she is invoked in this ceremony that involves water. The reference to a star may be due to European concepts having influenced the priest who gives this prayer. The good luck refers to the deity to whom the child has been dedicated.

In all cases of sickness it was first necessary to find out by divination what caused the sickness. The Mexican, like most primitive peoples, did not believe that illness was due to natural causes. It might be caused by the sorcery of some evilly disposed person, or by bad winds, or be sent as a punishment for evil living, or some lack of respect toward a deity. Divination was primarily directed to finding out which of these was the cause of the illness. If the divination showed that an individual was responsible, the diviner proceeded to find out who was the author.

Counter magic was the chief means of curing illness, but herbs and other remedies were used as well. Toothache was treated by dropping a little burning copal on the offending tooth. Swollen throat was treated by covering the swelling with arnatto and then squeezing. Sometimes the soothsayer pricked the sore place with a needle a large number of times, as though he or she were tattooing the patient. Copal mixed with water was applied as a poultice to inflammations. Peyote cactus was also very frequently used as a medicine as well as a plant closely allied to Jimson weed. These last remedies owed their efficacy to their divine nature.

Of the divinatory narcotics that known as ololiuhqui (Datura meteloides) was the most important. The plant was considered particularly sacred, and packets of it were placed on many household altars and were the recipients of prayers and offerings, such as food and copal incense. These packets were considered so sacred that they might never be opened, nor even removed from their original locations, and the duty of guarding them descended from father to son. In many ways the ololiuhqui cult is reminiscent of that of the sacred bundles of the plains Indians of North America.

The medicine man, on taking some ololiuhqui, had a vision in which the ololiuhqui deity appeared to him and supplied the answer to the problem over which he had been consulted, whether it were the cause of some disease, the whereabouts of a lost relative or the location of stolen property. These medicine men, at their initiation, were believed to die, returning to life after three days, during which time they received their powers from gods or dead relatives.

In many of their cures the medicine men used tobacco, frequently pulverized when green and mixed with lime. Tobacco, too, was a divine plant, being inferior in this respect only to ololiuhqui, peyote and one or two food plants. The employment in medical work of daturas and tobacco mixed with lime is very probably of South American origin.

Often the medicine man used to suck the patient's chest or stomach, and then, producing small stones, bones or hair, claim that he had sucked them out of the patient's body, thereby curing him.

Apart from the medicine men and priests there were also magicians who combined divination and medicine with conjuring tricks. The Huaxtec had a reputation all over Mexico for their magic. It is related that they were able to produce a spring with fishes swimming in it in the middle of a waterless country, or produce an illusion of a burning house where no house existed. It

PLATE XXVIII. INTERIOR COURT OF PALACE, MITLA

is even claimed that they killed themselves, cut themselves in pieces, and then brought themselves back to life. The Quiche Mayas have traditions of similar tricks performed by their heroes. One is reminded of the tricks of the Indian fakirs. Among the Mayas the ceremony of running bare-foot across red-hot embers was regularly performed without apparent hurt to the performers, and it is quite probable that the Aztecs had a similar ceremony. This fire ceremony is of wide distribution in the Old World.

Closely connected with religion and the priesthood was the sacred ball game. Every town of importance had at least one court in which to play, and cities of importance had several. These were always placed in close proximity to the important temples. The courts varied in size; 200 feet long was not exceptional with an average breadth of some 30 feet. In ground plan they resembled two T's placed base to base, for while long in the centre they broadened at the ends. (Plate XXV.) The sides of the courts were formed by walls, of an average height of about fifteen feet. These were faced with smooth slabs of stone interspersed with carved decoration. The walls of the broad ends were usually very low. High up half way down the length of each wall was placed a stone ring, the hole through the centre of which was about two feet in diameter. Often the carving was made so that a figure of Xochipilli, the patron god of games, held the ring in his arms. Around the court were planted trees, particularly palm trees, and sometimes temples were attached to the courts. The game was played with a rubber ball, the players hitting it with the hips or the knees, for it was forbidden to hit the ball with the hands or feet. However, beginners and indifferent players were, apparently, allowed to use their hands and feet, but this wasn't considered the real thing. The players on one side were supposed to put the ball through the ring on one wall, while their opponents endeavored to drive it through the other ring. This, however, very rarely happened. The games were always well attended, the watchers standing on top of the walls that flanked the court.

Custom decreed that in the event of a player driving the ball through the proper ring, he was entitled to the clothes of the onlookers and any possessions they might happen to be carrying with them at the time. Whenever this happened a regular scrimmage developed, the victor's friends aiding him to catch onlookers and strip them of their possessions before they could escape. However, this event was so rare that the rooters ran little risk of literally losing the shirts off their backs.

One early Spanish writer, who had witnessed many games, says that sometimes the play would last an hour without the players once missing a hit with hip or knee. Apparently it was not entirely unusual for a player to die of exhaustion after a very hard game.

The descriptions that have come down to us of the method of playing are sometimes vague, for we do not even know how many players there were on each side.

A green or black line ran along the ground from ring to ring, and it was necessary for the ball to cross this line to save a fault. It would seem that the wide ends had to be defended, and that if the ball entered these courts the side that had driven it there scored. In addition to the right of seizing the property of the onlookers, the player who scored a ring shot was given a prize of featherwork or clothing, and every one gathered round him, dancing and singing his praises as a renowned player. Indeed, the fame of a first-rate player was bruited far and wide, and his exploits discussed. In pecuniary reward alone he failed to rival a Babe Ruth.

A good player also added to his skill by appropriate magical ceremonies. A simple method to insure victory consisted in placing the grinding stone and griddle in one's home upside down and placing the grinding roller in one corner of the house. At night a player placed the rubber ball in a clean plate and hung the leather hip and knee pads on a pole. Then squatting down in front of them, he proceeded to pray to them and a large number of other deities including those of games and sport, begging them to grant him victory in the morrow's play. When the prayer was concluded the player burned incense in front of the instruments of play, finally offering them food and pulque. The vigil was kept up all night, but at dawn the player ate the offerings he had made.

Sometimes games were played to decide personal arguments or tribal quarrels. Thus the chief of one tribe would play against another tribal chieftain to settle some point of difference. Nevertheless games were usually played for stakes, poor persons betting with maize or other produce of their farms, while those of rank staked jades, featherwork, gold and other valuable possessions. There were many inveterate gamblers, and frequently a man would gamble his own liberty in a ball game or some other game of skill or chance.

A peculiar religious function symbolizing the passage of the year was held in all the principal towns once a year. A very high pole was set up in an open space. There was a small platform at the top of the pole, and to this ascended four picked performers. After dancing for some time on the narrow platform, each player, who was dressed in a distinctive costume to represent various different birds, attached to his belt the end of a rope wound round the pole. Then one by one the performers cast themselves off the platform, swinging round and round the pole, as the rope to which they were attached gradually unwound. The lengths of the ropes were so adjusted that the performers reached the ground after making thirteen revolutions in the air. The four performers by each making thirteen revolutions symbolized the fifty-two years into which the small Aztec cycle of years was divided. Some of the players swung in the air with only their feet attached to the rope. This ceremony still survives as a popular amusement in outlying districts of Middle America, for it has been reported in recent years from Papantla in the state of

Vera Cruz, and from more than one town in Guatemala, the latter suggesting that it was also a Maya custom. Modern poles are often as much as one hundred feet in height.

A favorite game of the ancient Mexicans resembled our modern ludo. The game, which was called patolli, was played on a mat on which was a design like a St. Andrew's cross. (Plate XXVI.) This was marked off into a series of little sections. The dice were beans, the surfaces of which were painted white and numbers painted on them. Each player usually threw five beans, and advanced down the course accordingly. Tylor, the great English anthropologist of the nineteenth century, believed that patolli had been derived from the Hindu game parchesi, and used this close resemblance as an argument for Asiatic influences in ancient Mexico.

In another somewhat similar game scoring was made with sections of a bamboo-like reed slit down the centre. These were thrown on the mat, and a point scored for each reed that fell with the hollow centre upwards. A similar game exists to the present day among the Tarahumare of northern Mexico. Just as the crap shooter talks to his dice, the players of these games used to speak to the beans or reeds, invoking their aid. The ancient Mexicans went further, for they burned incense to the mat and dice to win their favor. Large stakes were gambled on these games of chance as on the ball game.

Riddles and conundrums supplied an innocent form of entertainment popular among the Aztecs as well as

237

other peoples of Middle America. A few examples of these are given below:

Q. What is it that one catches in a black forest and kills in a treeless bare country?

A. Lice, which are caught in the hair and killed on the thumb nail.

Q. What is the mirror that resides in a house made of pine branches?

A. The eye behind eyelashes.

Q. What is it that goes through a valley with its entrails hanging out behind?

A. The needle when one is sewing. The threaded cotton is the entrails.

Q. What is the blue gourd with toasted maize grains scattered on it?

A. The blue gourd is the sky; the toasted maize grains are the stars.

Q. What is it that howls when one scratches its ribs?

A. The bone rasp used as a musical instrument.

Dances played an important part in religious life. They wound up practically every important festival, sometimes lasting for several days, or rather nights, for most of the dancing took place at night. In the great majority of dances the sexes were kept apart, the most important exception being the dance held in honor of the deity Huitzilopochtli, when men danced with their arms round the women's shoulders (p. 184). Sometimes, however, men impersonated women in the dances, and on other occasions women danced alone. Although there was great variation in the different dances, it would be tedious to enumerate them. Instead a description of a dance held in Montezuma's honor is given below. The account is somewhat abbreviated from that given by Gomara.

"After eating they started to execute a dance of rejoicing and goodwill, called Netoteliztli. Long before the dance commenced they stretched a great mat over the floor of Montezuma's patio, and on this they placed two drums. One was small of the type they call Teponaztli, the other large and high. With these as an accompaniment they sang cheerful, happy songs or some romance in honor of the past kings, recounting their wars and victories, the risks they ran and such matters. These adventures were sung in regular verse. When it was time for the dance to start, eight men whistled loudly, whereupon the drums were beaten softly, and the arrival of the dancers was no longer delayed. They wore beautiful cloaks, some white, some red, green or yellow, and all decorated with rich embroideries. In their hands they carried bouquets of roses, feather fans or fans made of both feathers and gold, and many carried wreaths of sweet-smelling flowers. Many too wore feather head-dresses or masks in the form of heads of eagles, crocodiles, jaguars or other wild beasts. Often as many as 1000 took part in the dance, and the number never fell below 400.

"All who take part in the dance are chiefs or persons of rank, and the higher the rank of a performer, the closer he dances to the drums. They dance in two long lines with linked arms one behind the other. Two well-trained dancers head the lines; the others follow them in their movements. When the two leaders sing the rest reply, or if the arrangement calls for it, only a few. All together they raise or lower their arms and heads, achieving a graceful unison as they move together as though they were all one single dancer.

"At the start they dance slowly as they sing romantic histories. Singers do not raise their voices, dancing with serious mien, while the drums are softly beaten. As they get worked up, they start to sing cheerful songs and the pace of the dance is quickened. Soon all are dancing rapidly and with great animation. As the dances last for a long time, there are intervals when servers bring cups (of pulque). Sometimes certain men start to imitate the men of other nations, wearing their clothes and burlesquing their speech. They also indulge in other kinds of buffoonery, pretending that they are drunk or crazy, or imitating old women. These turns cause great amusement and laughter among the dancers and on-lookers. All those who have seen this dance, say it is a sight well worth seeing and better than the *Zambra* dance of the Moors which is performed here in Spain. It is better still if women dance instead of men, but in Mexico the women do not dance this in public."

Torquemada states that in the really big dances as many as 3000 or 4000 take part. A favorite dance of the Aztecs was held in honor of Xochiquetzal,

Photographs by Professor Charles J. Chamberlain

PLATE XXIX. INTERIORS OF THE PALACE ROOMS, MITLA

goddess of flowers and dancing. A bower of roses was erected, and in this the statue of Xochiquetzal was seated. Close by imitation trees decorated with sweet-smelling flowers were set up. While the dance proceeded, youths dressed in costumes made of multi-colored feathers to imitate birds and butterflies climbed up these trees. Next they passed from branch to branch, pretending to sip the dew on the flowers. While they were engaged in this task, priests issued from the temple armed with blow-guns, and taking aim, pretended to shoot them down.

In another dance the performers wore masks of old hunchbacks, and this dance provoked great mirth. Some of the dances, however, were of an obscene nature, and were probably performed in connection with fertility rites to assure successful crops.

Great care was taken in instructing the young men in the manner of dancing, for this formed an important item of education in the calpulli schools. At the same time as the boys learned the dances, they were acquiring a good knowledge of tribal tradition and lineage.

Musical instruments were used in all ceremonies and dances, but the range of these was small. There were two distinctive types of drums. The Teponaztli, already mentioned, was made of a section of log laboriously hollowed out so that a thin tongue of wood projected forward from the tops of both ends. Music was produced by striking these tongues with drumsticks, the knob-like ends of which were tipped with rubber. A deep sound was emitted. Early writers claim that this could be heard at distances of several miles. The second type of drum was upright, standing on three wooden legs and with its mouth covered with deer hide or occasionally snake skin. (Plate VII.) The outsides of both kinds of drums were elaborately carved. Animal figures, gods and religious scenes were frequently depicted.

Four-fingered flutes of bamboo or pottery were also used. Those of pottery were sometimes carved with human heads or other devices. Smaller whistles with two-finger holes were much used, and are found in large quantities in Aztec deposits. They generally carry conventionalized birds in low relief. The Mexicans possessed no string instruments with the possible exception of the musical bow. This simple instrument with a gourd resonator is used at the present time in many parts of Middle America, but may be of African origin.

The carapaces of turtles were beaten with antlers, and rasps were made from the cores of conch shells or by notching human bones, preferably femurs. The sound was produced by rubbing a stick or antler along their surfaces. Conch shells with their tips sawn off served as trumpets, the sound carrying a very long distance. Smaller univalve shells strung on strings were worn on the legs and arms, producing a pleasant sound as they jingled together when their wearer danced.

The same effect was produced by small clapperless bells worn in a similar manner (see p. 94). These were usually of copper, but occasionally of gold. More in the nature of curiosities were whistling jars of the same type as those found in the Late Chimu horizon of ancient Peru. In Mexico these were never common as in Peru. The vessels have two compartments joined by a narrow passage. As the water is poured out through the spout, air, rushing into the second compartment through a very small intake, causes the whistling sound. The same effect is also produced by swishing the water from one compartment to another.

Simple whistles were also manufactured to imitate the calls of deer and other wild animals. These were used by hunters to decoy game.

It can be seen that the range of musical instruments was very restricted. Indeed, the Aztecs, like most American Indians, were not a musical nation. The modern Indians of middle America have, however, taken to the marimba, an importation from Africa, with great gusto, until now it has become the national musical instrument of Guatemala and to a certain extent of Mexico as well. No examples of ancient music have survived, but we have translations of a number of poems or hymns of a religious or historical nature. In many cases these reveal a high standard of poetic imagery such as would be expected from a people so devoted to oratory. Unfortunately many of them are couched in metaphorical language, containing so many obscure references of a symbolic or religious nature, that they have little meaning for us.

Although many of the traditions and historical events sung at dances and festivals were transmitted orally, similar records were also kept in hieroglyphic books. Some years ago the life history of an individual named 8 Deer was worked out by Mr. J. Cooper Clark. His adventures were found depicted in various allied codices, all dating from a period before the arrival of the Spaniards.

He was born in the year 12 Acatl, corresponding to the year A.D. 1439, and, following a fairly general Mexican custom, was named 8 Deer since he was born on that day (8 Mazatl). His father similarly was named 5 Cipactli and his mother 9 Quauhtli. He had two sisters and one brother. One sister was two years older than he, the other sister was a year younger, and his brother was four years younger. Various scenes in the codices represent events in his life. In one scene we see him playing in a ball court with an individual named 1 Olin, and between the ages of twenty-one and thirty he is almost continuously engaged in warfare. During these campaigns he took part in the capture of no less than twenty-six towns and villages. Over and over again we see him hurling spears with the aid of his spear-thrower into some town.

One scene shows him undergoing the rite of having his ears pierced, presumably for the insertion of ear-plugs. Another scene shows the piercing of his nostrils for the insertion of a nose-plug. This event takes place when he is thirty-four years of age. He lies on his back on a kind of couch, on which is spread a jaguar skin, while the priest, holding his nose with the left hand, is on the point of piercing his nostrils with the pointed bone instrument he holds in his right hand. This ceremony was a mark of honor. Previous to this, but in the same year 7 Calli, 8 Deer is shown bringing in a prisoner with a rope around his neck, and perhaps this capture qualified him for the nose-piercing ceremony. Two years later we see him kindling the sacred fire in the usual method of twirling sticks. (Plate XVI.)

In 1474 his brother 9 Xochitl, then aged thirty-one, is sacrificed in his presence. Although this must have been a severe shock to 8 Deer, we must remember that death by sacrifice was a fate to be expected by warriors, and by dying in this manner, one was assured of entrance to the land of the sun instead of the less delectable underworld ruled over by Mictlantecuhtli. Apparently 9 Xochitl was sacrificed by his fellow tribesmen, for had he died at the hands of enemies, 8 Deer would scarcely have been present at his death.

Another scene shows 8 Deer and other chiefs in a canoe. Maritime shells clearly demonstrate that the water shown is the sea, and not a lake. 8 Deer and his companions are armed, and obviously are on the warpath, probably on the point of attacking a coastal town. The attack must have been successful since the next scene shows the sacrifice of a captured chief. In 1486 8 Deer was the aggressor in a gladiatorial fight similar to that described on page 176 and illustrated on Plate XXII. The weeping captive is tied to a circular stone, and defends himself with mock weapons. An adjoining scene shows the prisoner bound to a wooden frame, where he is speared to death. (Plate XIV.)

In the year 13 Acatl (1479) he marries a girl called 13 Coatl. As he is now forty years old, the marriage is presumably not his first, for most Mexicans married at about the age of twenty. Two years later a boy, 6 Calli, is born. Another scene shows the parents, 8 Deer and 13 Coatl making a thank-offering of copal and maize for the safe deliverance of the child.

At the age of fifty-two 8 Deer's life comes to an abrupt close. The year is 12 Acatl, the same name as the year in which he was born and the year in which Columbus discovered America. Apparently he was taken prisoner in an attack on a city. The last scenes show him stretched out on the sacrificial block while a priest plunges a knife into his breast to remove his heart in accepted Aztec style. Eleven days later, on the day 12 Calli, his body was cremated. The codex depicts his mummy bundle tied up and adorned with a feather head-dress ready for the cremation ceremonies.

The careers of other individuals can also be traced through the codices, although none, apparently, with as full detail as that of 8 Deer. Undoubtedly he was an important personage, but it has not been possible to identify him with any particular town or people.

The Mexican hieroglyphic codices, however, treat little of individuals, but devote much space to religious matters, and divinations as to lucky and unlucky days. Although many of the deities can be identified and some of the ceremonies recognized, we are still far from possessing a thorough grasp of the contents of these books. One can hazard a meaning for many of the scenes, but there is no way of proving or disproving one's theories.

Some codices, apparently, were devoted to the listing of tributes paid by vassal peoples of the Aztecs, others to the history of the Aztecs and other tribes, while a third class may have been filled with legal matters (p. 111). Of the first class there are no strictly aboriginal survivals, but the Mendoza codex, a prized possession of the Bodleian Library of Oxford University, is a copy on European paper of an Aztec tribute roll, and contains in addition much information on the upbringing of children, the ranks of different classes of warriors and other invaluable material. It was made by native scribes soon after the conquest, and is accompanied by a Spanish translation.

Of the truly pre-Columbian hieroglyphic codices only fourteen have survived. Five of these are in England, four in Italy, two in France, one each in the United States, Austria and Mexico. Except the last and the one now in the United States, all probably formed part of the loot sent over to Europe by Cortez and other conquistadores. At the time of the Spanish conquest there must have been many hundreds in existence, but nearly all of these were destroyed by church authorities as works of the devil. All that we can say is that the Mexican codices have been luckier than those of the Mayas, since only three of the latter have survived to the present day.

The hieroglyphic books consisted of a single long sheet, of an average width of six or seven inches and in one case as much as thirty-four feet in length. This sheet was folded up screen fashion. At each end were covers of wood or hide to protect the contents. In one case jade ornaments were let into the wooden cover, and have survived to the present time. The sheet, which was painted on both sides with the text, was made of a coarse maguey or amatl paper or hide. The surface of this was covered with a very thin coating of fine lime to receive the text. The pictographs and hieroglyphs were painted in a wide range of colors. These included red, blue, green, black, white, yellow, orange, brown and purple. Most of the prime colors were shown in more than one shade, and, for the most part, were of vegetable origin. All colors were outlined in black.

The text was read from left to right across the folds of the page, both back and front. Sometimes the sheet was divided into two or three sections by horizontal lines. In that case the text of the lower section or sections was read after the top section was concluded. The texts were a mixture of hieroglyphic and pictographic writings. Hieroglyphs were used for the day signs (Plate XXI), for the names of towns, for the names of persons, such as 8 Deer, for numbers and for certain objects, such as gold, jade, etc. Hieroglyphs for towns were made on the same principle as rebus writing. Thus Mazatlan's glyph was a deer's head, since *Mazatl* means deer in Aztec. The glyph of a town called Ecatepec was

PLATE XXX.   OAXACA POTTERY

Note the ears of corn on the funerary urn, the "scroll and fret" pattern on the large tripod
bowl, and the feet patterned as snakes of the bowl in the centre

written by placing the head of the wind god above the glyph for a mountain. The Aztec equivalents of these are *Eecatl* and *Tepec*. Similarly the glyph of the Aztec ruler Itzcoatl was a snake from the body of which project obsidian knives. *Itztli* means obsidian knives, and *Coatl* means snake. (Plate XXIII.)

The Mexican numerical system was, like that of the Mayas, vigesimal. Numbers 1 to 19 were written by a corresponding number of circles. Twenty was indicated by a conventionalized banner. Four hundred, the next highest digit, was expressed by a drawing of a pine tree, and the next unit, 8000, was shown by a pouch for holding copal. These numerical glyphs occur frequently in the tribute rolls. (Plate IX.)

There were certain conventionalized pictures which were well on the way to becoming glyphs. The conquest of a town, for instance, was shown by a temple with a spear driven through it, and the glyph of the town in question juxtaposed, or simply by the glyph of the town with a spear driven through it. Similarly a prisoner was shown as being dragged along by his hair.

Other scenes, such as many described in the life of 8 Deer, were shown by means of pictures, hieroglyphs being employed only for the dates and the names of the participants. Needless to say, the glyph for 8 Deer was written with the day sign for deer (Mazatl) with eight dots attached. (Plate XVI.)

Paper, called Amatl, was largely used for sacrificial purposes, and for ornamenting statues of deities. Sacrifices of paper covered with crude rubber were particularly common in the Tlaloc rites. This same paper is still made in one or two small Mexican towns. It is now cut into human and other shapes, and employed in sorcery—a sad degeneracy.

Maps were also made, and paintings of different objects were made for informative purposes. Thus when Cortez landed on the Mexican coast, paintings of the Spaniards, their horses, ships and other novelties were made and sent to Montezuma to supplement verbal information.

Historical codices also existed, giving the migrations of the Aztecs, and a general outline of their history. Migrations were shown by painting footsteps passing from the hieroglyph of one town to that of another, together with the hieroglyphs of the dates.

Actually the codices were more in the nature of mnemonic aids. Regular stories were probably attached to each historical picture, and the teller, by an occasional glance at the text could preserve the sequence of the events he was narrating. Primitive story tellers develop an extraordinarily retentive memory, unknown in modern civilization, since we can fall back on the written word to refresh our memories, and the accuracy with which long genealogical tables were recited in Polynesia, for example, is almost unparalleled in civilized communities. Similar retentive powers were doubtlessly possessed by the ancient Mexicans, but the codices prevented errors creeping in. Recourse was also made to the codices at all times for divinatory purposes in con-nection with the Tonalamatl. In addition codices were doubtlessly used in the schools of instruction and in the training of initiates into the priesthood. Neverthe-less, the number of persons who could interpret the texts was probably quite small.

Visitors to Mexico should be warned that there are a number of fraudulent hieroglyphic codices and paint-ings on deer hide in existence. Some of these are skillful fakes. *Caveat emptor.*

CHAPTER VIII

TEMPLES AND TOMBS

Archæological Wealth. Pyramid of Sun at Teotihuacan. Construction. Stone Carving. Pyramid of Quetzalcoatl. Xochicalco. Tajin. Circular Structures. Monte Alban. Possible Maya Influences. Mitla. The Palaces. Mosaic Stone Decoration. Tepoztlan Temple. Teopanzolco. Frescoes at Tizatlan, Teotihuacan and Mitla. Idols. Braziers. Quauhxicalli. Pottery. "Yokes." "Palmas." Funerary Urns. Tombs. Mexican Cultures and Their Neighbors. Theories of Atlantis and Egyptian Origins. American Cultures Overwhelmingly Native.

IN the previous chapters, with the partial exception of Chapter I, we have looked at ancient Mexico mainly through the eyes of Spanish writers of the sixteenth and seventeenth centuries. In this chapter we shall depend for our information largely on the supplementary evidence supplied by the finds of archæologists. Archæologists are the rag-pickers of ancient history. If the rubbish heap is that of a rich culture, the pickings are good, and the information imparted by the relationship of the objects one to another correspondingly important. Mexico is in this respect a rich country, although climatic conditions have caused the destruction of all textile, wood and basketry objects. Nevertheless little scientific work has so far been done outside of the Valley of Mexico, and for large areas we are dependent on the little information supplied by the undocumented finds of the old-time pot-hunters and grave-robbers—a species unfortunately not yet extinct.

In this chapter little attention will be paid to the various cultural areas into which Mexico has been divided. These divisions are merely temporary, and there is no doubt that with more archæological field work the simple pattern of Mexican cultures evolved around the beginning of this century will have to be radically altered. Areas, off-handedly assigned to a single civilization, will doubtlessly be found to house half a dozen local cultures each divisible into time periods.

Almost without exception all Mexican religious structures were placed on the summits of raised mounds, frequently in the form of a truncated four-sided pyramid. The most famous structure now surviving in Mexico is undoubtedly the Pyramid of the Sun at Teotihuacan, about twenty-eight miles northeast of Mexico City. Actually there is no evidence that this structure was devoted to solar worship. Indeed, there is no reason to believe that much attention was paid to the sun by the ancient inhabitants of Teotihuacan, and the name has been given to the structure since the Spanish conquest. In general principles this pyramid doesn't differ radically from all other pyramids erected in central Mexico from the earliest known example, probably that of Cuicuilco, to the latest Aztec structure of the late fifteenth century. Accordingly in describing this pyramid we are describing all ancient Mexican pyramids, allowing for differences in size, ornamentation and minor elements, such as arrangement of stairways and the number of terraces.

The pyramid of the sun has a present height of no less than 215 feet, and covers an area of over half a million feet with a frontage of 716 feet. Actually the present measurements are considerably less than those of the original structure, for about two decades ago a thick layer was removed from the whole surface of the pyramid in the course of some very unscientific excavations.

The structure is divided into five sections by setbacks in the sloping walls. These form narrow terraces, around which processions of priests, presumably, once wended their way in ceremonial ascents or descents. On the front, which is the west side, one ascends by means of an enormous stairway, which is double between the second and third terraces. Actually there is at the present time a small pyramid immediately in front of the west face, which may have been a later addition. As a result of its presence the staircase forks at this point, one spur descending to the north, the other to the south of the obstruction. In passing it may be noted that the forking at the base and the short double section are features not met with in most stairways.

The summit of the pyramid is a level platform originally covered with a plaster floor, and measuring about 130 feet square. On this formerly stood the temple, but as this was made of perishable materials, no traces of it survive.

Of the exterior facing of the pyramid nothing now remains, thanks to the vandalism to which reference

PLATE XXXI.   SMALL STONE MASK AND SQUATTING FIGURE, VERA CRUZ

has already been made. There is some reason to believe the finish was similar to that of most Teotihuacan substructures. That is, the upper section of each sloping wall was decorated with a sunken perpendicular panel running the whole length of the face and enclosed in a raised panel. (Plate III.) Apparently these decorative panels, which in turn were frequently ornamented with simple circles and other geometric designs, were added to the structure after the construction of the sloping sides. As they were not firmly welded into the sloping walls, their eventual collapse was assured.

A tunnel driven into the interior of the pyramidal core brought to light many pottery figurine heads of the Early Teotihuacan period. As no typical Middle or Late Teotihuacan heads were recovered, it is fairly certain that the work of constructing this enormous pile started during the Early Teotihuacan period at about the same time as the Cuicuilco pyramid was erected. It appears, however, that the original structure was subsequently enlarged during the height of the Teotihuacan period.

The first task in erecting a pyramid of this type was to clear the turf off the ground. Next, apparently, rough walls were erected to enclose the area to be covered by the structure. These were made of stone, set in mud or adobe, or cut blocks of tepetate conglomerate, and the corners were not bonded. The space enclosed by these walls was then filled with a mass of stone, tepetate conglomerate and earth. In Maya structures this rubble mass was not thrown in haphazard, but independent rectangular sections were built up to the required height until the whole area was thus filled. A somewhat similar method was followed in ancient Peru, and it has been conjectured that each section was a task for a gang. Although there is no specific information as to the Teotihuacan practice, it is probable that here too this method was employed.

The sloping walls of the outer face were next added. An inclined bank, roughly of the required shape, was made of small stones. The exterior slope of this bank was then covered with a three-inch layer of concrete. Thin slabs of andesite were laid horizontally so that their butts penetrated into the core and their outer faces projected beyond the concrete layer. These slabs carried the weight of the sunken panels and their frames. The exterior was finally covered with a wash of lime, on which frescoes were usually painted.

The summits of structures were finished off in a similar manner. Over the loose interior fill a layer of closely packed small stones or tepetate blocks was placed. Over this again was laid concrete with a lime or plaster finish.

Well-cut stone was rarely employed in Mexican structures except for decorative purposes, for an even finish could be easily obtained by a concrete or plaster surface over undressed stone or roughly finished blocks of tepetate. Nevertheless, in some structures well-carved stone ornaments served as secondary ornamentation. One of the most frequent forms of this kind of decoration was the carving of balustrades in the form of feathered serpents. These are very common on Aztec pyramids, but also occur in the Teotihuacan period. The bodies of the serpents served as the balustrades, the tails were in relief at the top of the stairway, while the enormous heads projected at the base.

The pyramid of Quetzalcoatl at Teotihuacan possibly supplies a prototype of this decoration. Here serpent heads are set at intervals the whole length of each balustrade. Each head projects from a feather ruffle, and the open jaws display a terrifying set of non-ophidian teeth. The framed panels below each terrace also display these same feathered serpent heads. They alternate with conventionalized masks of the rain god Tlaloc. Scattered along the panels are also small representations of shells in low relief, while the lower aprons are adorned with full-length snakes also in low relief. (Plate III and frontispiece.)

This temple of Quetzalcoatl was subsequently covered by another pyramid placed immediately in front of it. This second structure, which is clearly of later date, is without relief decoration. It forms the centre of a large group misnamed the citadel, consisting of a hollow square flanked on all four sides by fifteen smaller pyramids of the same type. There are four of these on all flanks except that behind, that is the west side, there are only three.

Another profusely decorated pyramid is that of

Xochicalco. This is situated in the State of Morelos, not far from Cuernavaca. Here again the feathered serpent is the principal ornament. The balustrades carry a decoration of serpent scales, while the sides of the squat pyramid are ornamented with a series of writhing feathered serpents in low relief. The designs are more realistic than those of the temple of Quetzalcoatl at Teotihuacan. On the west, or front side, there is a feathered serpent on each side of the stairway. Owing to lack of space each serpent has its head turned back looking at its tail, which is curled forward so that the projecting feathers are touching the out-thrust bifurcated tongue. The effect is very striking. (Plate XXVII.)

In addition to the plumed serpents there are a number of human figures set into the design. These are seated cross-legged. The heads, which are in profile, are crowned with huge plumed snake head-dresses. They are strangely reminiscent of Maya sculpture, but the representations of the serpents and certain interspersed glyphs are certainly not Maya. The whole structure was originally painted in various colors. Green and vermilion predominate, but red, blue, and black also occur. There are also the remains of a stone temple on the summit of the pyramid.

Probably the structure was erected by a Nahua people who had been affected by influences emanating from southern Mexico. It has been suggested that the structure was built around the year A.D. 1100. This would place it as belonging to a pre-Aztec horizon, and make it contemporaneous with late middle Teotihuacan, the period which probably witnessed the erection of the Quetzalcoatl pyramid at Teotihuacan.

In the Puebla-Vera Cruz frontier area occurs a peculiar type of architecture remarkable for the use of niches set in the pyramidal walls as decorative features. Until a few years ago the only known example of this type of architecture was the famous pyramid at Tajin, near Papantla, in the State of Vera Cruz. (Plate XXVII.) In recent years Mr. Enrique Palacios, the well-known Mexican archæologist, has discovered a similar type of decoration on several pyramidal structures at Yohualichan, near Cuetzalan, and in the same general region. The Tajin pyramid is in Totonacan linguistic territory, while the ruins of Yohualichan are in an area where a Nahua language is spoken. This type of architecture is generally ascribed to the Totonacs, but there is no actual evidence for this.

The niches, together with the rest of the pyramidal facings, are constructed of well-cut neatly finished blocks of stone, affording a marked contrast to the rough finish of pyramids in the Valley of Mexico when stripped of their concrete or stucco veneer. In many cases the slabs at the back of the niches retain traces of red paint over the stucco. Red paint is also found elsewhere, suggesting that the whole structure was once painted in this color. The pyramid of Tajin has seven set-backs. The total number of niches is a multiple of seven; the cornices are formed by seven slabs; finally

the spaces between the niches are occupied by seven little seat-like arrangements. This strange use of the number seven must be more than a coincidence. Perhaps the
explanation lies in the structure having been dedicated
to Chicomecoatl, or a local variant of this goddess, whose
name means "Seven Snake."

The greatest pyramidal structure in ancient Mexico
was that of Quetzalcoatl at Cholula. The base of this
has been calculated at about a dozen yards short of 500
yards. The pyramid, which has sadly lost its original
form, is now crowned by a Christian church. It presents
no feature of interest other than its enormous size,
which in ground area exceeds that of any other pyramid
in the whole world, Egypt not excepted.

Of peculiar interest is the circular temple at Calixtla-
huaca in the Toluca Valley, west of the Valley of Mexico. Excavation of this strange five-story structure is
now being carried out by archæologists of the Mexican
Ministry of Education. A stairway on the east side ascends steeply to the summit, on which, presumably, once
stood a circular wooden temple. Round temples were
once common in ancient Mexico, but this is the only one
known to exist at the present time outside of the Maya
area, and differs from the four known from Maya land
in possessing no less than five terraces.

These circular temples were dedicated to Quetzalcoatl in his rôle of Eecatl, the wind god. Early Spanish writers hint that circular structures were more suitable for the worship of the wind god, for the absence

of corners moderated the gusts one often meets on turning the corner of a building. Presumably the wind god was therefore less hindered in his wanderings when he encountered a circular wall, and for that reason inclined to assume a more benevolent attitude toward his worshippers. The early pyramid at Cuicuilco is also roughly circular, but there is no evidence that it was connected with the worship of Quetzalcoatl-Eecatl.

The Toluca Valley, in which the round structure is situated, was the home of the Matlatzincas (the deer people), but it was subdued by the Aztecs in the course of their imperialistic expansion. Settlements of Aztecs were then placed in the valley to act as a kind of garrison and prevent any uprising by the Matlatzincas. Information at present available does not indicate what people was responsible for the erection of the wind-god temple. Pottery found in the structure will eventually give the answer to this question. It is known, however, that the building had been enlarged at some period, following a fairly general Mexican-Maya custom.

Monte Alban in the State of Oaxaca is now famous for the wealth recently extracted from its tombs by Mr. Caso and other trained Mexican archæologists, but the site has been of archæological importance for many years for quite different reasons. Here pyramids and mounds are arranged in an orderly manner more reminiscent of part of the Maya area than of central Mexico. The ruins consist of a vast system of level courts forming terraces in the mountain-side and bordered by a great series of pyramids. The original side of the mountain has been so excavated in ancient times to form these terraces and courts that practically no part of the terrain remained unworked.

At Teotihuacan there is a certain rather vague arrangement of structures, but for a close parallel to the Monte Alban courts one must turn to the Peten District of the Maya area. The masonry of Monte Alban is poorly dressed, but this is probably due to the absence of easily worked stone in the immediate vicinity. Monte Alban lies in Zapotecan linguistic territory, but close to the territory inhabited by the Mixtecs. The recent finds show that the city must have been used right up to the time of the conquest, for the contents of the tombs clearly date from the late fifteenth century, but the site is at the same time of great antiquity. There is no definite evidence as to the race that originally inhabited the city.

The presence of stela-like stones inscribed with hieroglyphs in cartouches is suggestive of Maya influences. In addition the number five is written on these Monte Alban monuments with a bar in the Maya style instead of with five dots, as was the Aztec custom. These similarities, while suggesting possible Maya influences, do not necessarily imply a Maya invasion; culture can, and usually does, travel without being carried by immigrants or invaders.

At the nearby site of Mitla are the so-called Palaces with their mosaic decorations. Mitla was the ancient holy place of the Zapotecs, to whom it was known as Yoopaa, for Mitla is a corruption of the Aztec name Mictlan, which means the underworld. The Zapotecan name seems to carry the same meaning, for the word means the resting place, carrying the idea by related words of a burial place. The name seems to have been derived from the fact that, according to local belief, the entrance to the underworld was situated here. Mitla was conquered by the Aztecs in the year 1494 according to one native source, but Aztec domination probably never sat very heavily on the Zapotecans. One or two military colonies were planted in their territory, and an annual tribute was exacted, but the Zapotecans continued to govern themselves under their own ruling chiefs until the arrival of the Spaniards.

The ruins of Mitla do not show the orderly arrangement characteristic of the site of Monte Alban. Here are to be seen the remains of four palace buildings and two pyramidal structures with adjacent minor mounds, but the different groups are placed haphazard with no particular arrangement one to another, although the structures forming a group are arranged around quadrangular courts.

The best-preserved building is Palace II, as it is called by archæologists. (Plates XXVIII and XXIX.) It consists of a long hall running the whole length of the south side. This is the front, which is approached by a wide flight of steps. One enters this hall through a triple doorway divided by two short sections of wall and bridged by heavy stone lintels, each carved from a single stone. Immediately behind the hall is a small enclosed court, flanked by rooms on all sides. There are five of these rooms, of which two are on the east side. A doorway from the main hall communicates with the southernmost of the two eastern rooms. This in turn, like the other four rooms, has a doorway leading into the interior court. All five rooms are very narrow, having only about half the breadth of the main hall.

The roofs were made of beams of wood passing across the breadth of the rooms. Over these were laid smaller pieces of wood at right angles; these in turn were covered with a layer of small stones finished off with a covering of cement. As the main hall was too wide to be spanned by single beams, six stone pillars were placed in line down the centre of the room. On these rested long beams placed end to end so that they ran the whole length of the hall. On these in turn rested transversal beams so that two spanned the breadth.

The walls of the whole building are decorated inside and out with elaborate mosaic patterns. These are without exception of geometric origin, and can clearly be traced to textile designs. Frets or grecques attached to a step design form the majority of the patterns, no less than eight different combinations or variations of these two designs occurring together. (Plate XXVIII.) Another frequent motif consists of step designs arranged in a diamond pattern with a small cross in the

PLATE XXXII.   CHOLULA POLYCHROME BOWL

centre. Sometimes a second diamond is placed inside the first.

Each stone forming part of one of the decorative panels carries a small part of the design in relief. These blocks, of which no less than 80,000 were used in the designs of the walls of the court alone, were cut and carved with the required design before being fitted into their positions on the walls. Each stone is supplied with a tenoned back which was set into the rubble mass of the interior of the walls. The whole, therefore, forms an example of mosaic work on a gigantic scale, but with the same technique employed as in the designing of mosaic decorations on turquoise shields or other minor *objets d'art*.

The whole structure, as was apparently the case with all Mexican and Maya structures, was covered with stucco. Every few years a new coat of stucco was given every building, and as the old was not usually scraped off, an amazing number of coats are frequently found on such parts of a building as have been well sheltered from the elements. In the background of the decorative panels of the building in question traces of red may be seen. It is possible that the whole building was originally painted red, or red may have been used as a background to set off the cream-white of the mosaic decorations. The Mexicans and Mayas shared with the Greeks the custom of painting all their sculptures. Although this is barbarous taste in our eyes, one must not forget that the beautiful stonework of the Gothic cathedrals of England was similarly covered with layers of limewash in mediæval times.

According to Father Burgoa, who relied on documents as well as traditions current among the Indians during his time (seventeenth century), these buildings were used as residences of the high priests and nobility. The following passage is taken from the translation given by Seler:

"One of the rooms above ground was the palace of the high priest, where he sat and slept, for the apartment offered room and opportunity for everything. The throne was like a high cushion with a high back to lean against, all of tiger skin, stuffed entirely with delicate feathers or with fine grass which was used for this purpose. The other seats were smaller, even when the king came to visit him. The authority of this devilish priest was so great that there was no one who dared to cross the court, and to avoid this the other three chambers had doors in the rear, through which even the kings entered. . . .

"The second chamber above ground was that of the priests and the assistants of the high priests. The third was that of the king when he came. The fourth was that of the other chieftains and captains. . . . All the rooms were clean and well furnished with mats. It was not the custom to sleep on bedsteads, however great a lord might be. They used very tastefully braided mats, which were spread on the floor, and soft skins of animals killed in the hunt; deer, rabbits, armadillos, etc., and also birds, which they killed with snares or arrows."

This description hardly fits Palace II, for there are no traces of a back entrance, and the rooms are six in number, counting the hall, not four, as Father Burgoa says. The description probably applies to one of the other palace groups now in ruins. Father Burgoa also speaks of a range of rooms beneath. Nothing corresponding to this is known at Mitla, although under one of the buildings was found a cruciform burial structure of a type to be described later.

The term "palace" is used archæologically to describe multiple-room structures such as these, although there is little evidence that they were used as residences. The word is used to differentiate them from the obvious temple structures perched on the tops of pyramids, the palaces, in contrast, standing only on low substructures.

Typical pyramidal substructures have already been described, but it is more difficult to describe the actual temple structures since few of these have survived. Undoubtedly the majority were made of wood and thatch, and for that reason have long since perished.

Near Tepoztlan in the District of Cuernavaca are to be seen the remains of a temple crowning a steep pyramid. This, apparently, was dedicated to Tepoztecatl, one of the pulque gods. One enters the temple through a doorway divided into three entrances by two stucco-covered pillars. A low stucco-covered bench adjoins the side and back walls of the temple on the inside. Two short walls, projecting from each lateral wall, divide the temple proper into an outer and an inner chamber. These short walls carry decorations in stucco. Against the back wall of the inner chamber stood an idol, believed to have been that of Tepoztecatl, but this was thrown down and smashed by a Christian priest in 1592. The fragments were built into a nearby church.

On the face of the bench are a number of crude hieroglyphs. It has lately been claimed that these show Maya influences, but the evidence for this is very weak, and the identification extremely dubious.

Very similar are the two temples of Teopanzolco recently excavated by Mexican archæologists. These are situated close to Cuernavaca station. Two flights of parallel stairs on the west side lead to two temples at the summit. One of these is similar to that of Tepoztlan in possessing an inner chamber and a bench against the back wall. The second lacks the division into two chambers, but has a bench at the back and square pillars at each corner, possibly to support the roof. The outside of the walls are decorated with small rather crude animal heads. The pyramidal substructure is enclosed by another and later pyramid. This later addition is not so high as the original structure.

Some six years ago archæologists of the Ministry of Education uncovered very important ruins on the top of a natural hill at Tizatlan in the State of Tlaxcala. A flight of steps leads to a much-destroyed temple facing a little east of north. A stucco-covered bench runs along the back wall of the temple, while two pairs of semicircular columns serve to mark off a kind of inner sanctuary, and presumably once carried roof beams. Immediately in front of these are two low oblong altars with their long axis running north and south. The sides of these, except where they touch the columns, are covered with frescoes in a remarkable state of preservation.

The front of one shows Tezcatlipoca with his telltale leg (p. 157) facing Mictlantecutli, the death god, while the sides of the altar have a pattern of alternating death heads, hands, hearts, and what may be shields. The second altar has on the front two complicated mythical scenes with a lower border of geometric patterns of grecques and steps similar to those at Mitla. The sides carry a series of conventionalized signs with a similar border at the base. The colors, which still retain their original brightness, comprise blue, gray, black, yellow, white, pink, red and brown. Some of these colors are shown in several shades, and the whole presents an exceptionally vivid picture. The treatment is very close to that of the codices, except that the different scenes are shown with painted backgrounds, while in the codices the background is almost invariably unpainted.

A number of very beautiful frescoes have also been uncovered at Teotihuacan. A scene on the walls of the so-called Temple of Agriculture at this site is of particular interest. This showed, for it has unfortunately been destroyed, every-day functions in connection with the temple services. Priests are shown approaching with offerings of copal or some similar substance placed between two bowls placed lip to lip, while on top of the altar flames and clouds of copal smoke belch forth. Other priests approach with offerings of birds and other objects and women prepare maize bread. Above there is a representation of a divination ceremony in which note is made of how tortillas or something of that nature fall when tossed onto a mat. As in the codices there is no scale, distant figures being shown as the same size as those in the foreground, but distance is shown by placing those farthest away at the top, and those supposed to be nearest the observer at the base.

Other frescoes at Teotihuacan show priests with plumed head-dresses facing each other; the scrolls, representing speech, make a particularly well-balanced composition, while the portraiture is superior to that usually found in the codices. At Mitla, again, are found frescoes representing recognizable deities and others, presumably, of local origin. A form of negative painting is employed, for the figures in white stand out against a red background. Black is also sparingly used as face marks and occasional details of costumes. Unfortunately only the upper sections of these frescoes survive. Part of the building, in which some of them were situated, had been turned into a stable, and others looked down from their walls on a hog sty. This situation has been remedied since the present Anthropological Department of the Ministry of Education undertook its energetic campaign to protect the ancient monuments of Mexico.

Richly embroidered cotton curtains hung across the temple doorways, and in temples of stone little light can have penetrated when these were in position. Unfortunately there is no good account of the contents of a Mexican temple in ancient times, although casual references enable us to reconstruct the furniture with fair accuracy. The principal object was naturally the idol of the god to whom the temple was dedicated.

Idols were made of stone or wood. As in the codices, each had its distinguishing mark by which it could be recognized by the humbler devotees. The ordinary worshipper would recognize the god as easily as the good Catholic recognizes Saint Andrew by his X-shaped cross or Saint Peter by his keys. The attributes of the idols were the same as those of the gods depicted in the codices. The idols were also dressed in clothing and given head-dresses which also helped to differentiate them. Naturally the clothing has perished, and consequently gods are frequently not recognizable without them. A few, however, can be easily recognized. Xochipilli idols, for example, almost always carry the comb-like crest typical of this god and Tlaloc heads are shown with the goggle eyes and tusks in the mouths. (Plate XVIII.)

Occasionally idols in the temples were made of pottery or even obsidian, and the household gods appear to have, usually, been made of pottery. The features of the patron god of a temple were also portrayed on many of the utensils used in his service, one can assume. Thus masks of Tlaloc were presumably used in his temple; and the pottery vessels with his head in relief were supposedly employed in his worship.

Of ceremonial importance were the copal braziers and incense burners. Sometimes the Aztecs used portable braziers consisting of a bowl in which the copal was burned, and to this was attached a long handle. This was frequently in the shape of a snake, the body forming the arm of the handle and the head reposing in the the priest's hand. Usually these arms were hollow and contained a clay pellet which rattled when the brazier was moved. A vessel of this type may be seen in the hand of the sun god in Plate XX. Other braziers of the Aztec period have two lugs by which they could be suspended from the ceiling of a temple. One might conjecture that these held the sacred fire.

Another type has an elaborate lid. This depicts the bust of a god complete with ear-plugs and other paraphernalia, and, like those described above, was made of pottery, but there were also stone braziers. Of these the most characteristic are braziers representing the squatting fire god. He is invariably shown as a wrinkled old man owing to his name of the Old Old God. The top of his head-dress is hollowed out to form a flat-bottomed bowl. Braziers of this type vary greatly in size,

PLATE XXXIII. JADE ORNAMENTS FROM OAXACA

but all can, apparently, be safely attributed to the Teotihuacan horizon.

An important utensil of Aztec temples was the *Quauhxicalli* or receptacle into which the hearts and blood of sacrificed victims were cast after first being held aloft to the sun. The name literally means "Eagle gourd," and it played an important part in Aztec ritual. After the sacrifice, a priest dipped a feather-tipped reed in the blood that had been poured into it, and proceeded to asperge the different idols with this ghastly liquid. This is the reason why the Spanish conquerors found the temple walls so thickly caked with blood (p. 167).

The quauhxicalli were often beautifully carved with intricate designs, and were usually in the shapes of deep, flat-based bowls. It has been conjectured that certain stone vessels in the shapes of jaguars and with hollows in the centres served the same purpose. From Duran's account we also get the impression that the term was applied to the famous calendar stone. This is more than likely, since this was closely connected with sun worship, as were the quauhxicalli. It will be remembered that the eagle was the name of the Aztec warrior order, whose patron was the sun, and also that the jaguar was the name of a similar order under the patronage of the sun god. In fact both these animals were closely connected with sun worship.

Carved stone boxes are occasionally discovered, and it is a fair assumption that these were used in the temples, particularly as they are often carved with religious symbolism. A beautiful example in Field Museum has the four day signs, on which the years started, carved on the inside, one sign being carved on each of the four sides. The base of this box has a feathered serpent with saurian features carved in low relief on the base. Sometimes these boxes carry carvings that show different gods piercing their ears in sacrifice, a feature occasionally met with on the quauhxicalli. This would suggest that the boxes also served as blood receptacles.

The sacrificial block seems always to have been placed outside the temple, doubtlessly in order that the public might witness the sacrificial ceremonies from below (p. 217). On the terraces, to judge by Maya practice, stood supports in which the butts of standard masts stood. These standards or flags, again according to Maya custom, were in all probability constructed of featherwork, and fluttered horizontally to the ground.

From statements of the early writers we know that pottery vessels were used in religious services to hold the offerings of food and precious objects. There is no information as to what vessels were used for this purpose, but it is a fair assumption that the best was employed in the service of the gods. To go into full details of the principal types of pottery manufactured in Mexico would be outside the scope of this book, but a few outstanding types will be discussed below.

The finest ware produced at Azcapotzalco was a rare development resembling the well-known cloisonné.

This was produced by cutting away the background so as to leave the required design in low relief and flush with the untreated surface of the rest of the vessel. The deep background was then filled flush with the rest of the surface with color, or merely painted. Vessels of this type are very rare, and it is possible they were imported from the region of Zacatecas, where they also occur. Typical Teotihuacan vessels of the pre-Aztec period are monochrome, either of a polished brown or black. Frequently these vessels are supplied with three small teat legs or three legs like flat blocks of wood standing on end. Sometimes the outer faces of these latter feet are carved. Vases covered with beautiful designs in painted stucco are also found at Teotihuacan.

Undoubtedly the most beautiful pottery produced was that of Cholula. This ware, which is of late date, often reaches six or seven colors. The surface is very highly burnished, but there is no glaze, such a practice being unknown in the New World. (Plates XVIII and XXXII.) The only exception is the plumbate ware already described (p. 133), and in this case the semi-glaze was accidental. Intricate designs are found on this best Cholulan ware, which with local variations are also found in Tlaxcala. The decoration is frequently reminiscent of the paintings on the codices, but the high burnish brings out the deep richness of the brown, orange, and chocolate shades to an extent unparalleled in the codices.

Tripod dishes are particularly typical of this ware,

the legs being frequently shaped as animal or human heads, but many other shapes are met with. In the nearby Tlaxcalan territory tall cylindrical jars with flaring bases are most typical. These also carry elaborate polychrome designs, sometimes of a somewhat grim nature, skull and cross-bones being a by no means rare motif.

The best pottery from northwest Oaxaca is very similar to that of the Cholulans, but the shapes are different. A shape peculiar to this region is provided with a wide pouring lip, resembling our old-fashioned cream jugs. In addition to the colors employed at Cholula, this Oaxaca polychrome ware includes a rich purple, probably obtained from a shell fish (p. 79). Other typical shapes are shown on Plate XXX. One vessel shown has the three feet shaped as snakes. This ware has been attributed to the Mixtecs, but this association is premature in view of the lack of excavation in this region.

In the vicinity of the Panuco River on the northeast coast of Mexico are found peculiar spouted vessels resembling our teapots. These are generally assigned to the Huaxtec culture because this people was inhabiting the region in which they are found at the time of the conquest. The designs are painted in black on a white background.

The best Aztec pottery is divisible into two main classes. In the first the ware is covered with a fine lightly polished orange-yellow slip. Simple geometric or highly conventionalized designs are painted in black, usually in delicate thin lines. The commonest shape is the tripod bowl, the legs being either square or thin circular supports tapering to a point. Often the bases of these vessels are scored with crisscross lines. These, it is believed, served for grinding chili peppers. Miniature vessels of this same ware are frequently found; some of these, apparently, served as supports for spindles when cotton was being spun, while others may have been used to hold ointments and precious liquids.

The second class of fine ware manufactured by the Aztecs was covered with a highly burnished deep-red slip, which was often decorated with simple designs in black, and less frequently in black and white. The commonest shape resembles a diablo toy, consisting of a cone-shaped cup standing on a flaring base which resembles a second, but inverted, cone. Low wide-mouthed bowls of this ware are also frequently found, and the designs, when they occur, are frequently very decorative. This ware was taken over by the Aztecs from their predecessors in the Valley of Mexico.

Each area has its distinctive shapes, the greatest variety occurring in the Jalisco and Michoacan areas of the west and the Vera Cruz District in the southeast.

Typical of this last area are two peculiar forms of stone sculpture. The first of these groups is composed of the famous "yokes," about which there has been so much controversy. In shape these are like a capital U, averaging a depth from the open mouth to the curve

277

at the base of about eighteen inches. Some are plain, but the majority are elaborately carved both inside and out. The ends, too, usually carry designs. Examples of these peculiar carvings have been found over a wide area, one having been found as far away as El Salvador, and a fragment of another in the great Maya city of Palenque. These were, apparently, trade pieces.

Theories put forward as to their use vary from the suggestion that they were used to hold down the sacrificial victims or as yokes for slaves to their having served as supports to hold the deceased in an upright position in the grave. None of these explanations are satisfactory. Recently a burial has been described in which the body lay full length with the head placed inside the yoke, which lay flat. The open ends of the yoke reached to the person's shoulders. Joyce has suggested that the yokes represent the gaping jaws of the earth monster ready to receive the dead, and this is a feasible suggestion since such scenes are frequently depicted in the codices. In any case only persons of considerable importance can have been honored with such elaborate carvings. The yokes are generally attributed to the Totonacan civilization, although this attribution is based solely on the fact that they are generally found in Totonacan territory. It is certain that the burials are not Nahua, for among the Nahua cremation was the general practice except in certain cases already noted (p. 49).

In this same area are found other remarkable stone

carvings generally known by the Spanish name of "Palmas." The purpose which these served is equally mysterious, for no satisfactory function, which they might have filled, has ever been suggested. Whereas the yokes are almost invariably of a well-polished stone, usually diorite, the palmas are unpolished and made of a volcanic rock. The designs are of great variety; some are carved as birds, human figures, or human heads (Plate I), whereas others represent featherwork or carry simple conventionalized patterns.

With few exceptions they are carved on all four sides except for a small strip close to the base of the rear side. Almost without exception the base is hollowed out from one side to the other, giving it a cusp-like support. This suggests that the stones were placed on horizontal poles, and that there was a small support fixed to the pole, against which the bottom of the back rested. As the backs are usually carved, except for this small section at the base, it is clear the palmas did not stand on poles on the fronts of structures. It is possible, however, that they were placed on a cross-bar over the entrance to a temple courtyard, or, conceivably, on the cross-bar of some processional litter.

Very striking are the ornate funerary urns of pottery found in parts of Oaxaca, especially in the vicinity of Monte Alban. These consist of a box-like base, from the back of which rises a tapering funnel, while, masking it, a grotesque figure is seated in front. (Plate XXX.) These funerary urns vary greatly in size, some reaching a height of over two feet, but all, apparently, were originally covered with paint. In most cases this seems to have been a simple red wash, but sometimes as many as four colors are found painted on a single urn. Most of the urns represent anthropomorphic deities, but a group are modelled as jaguars. The human type usually wears a shoulder cape, loin cloth, ornaments, such as ear-plugs and breast pendants, and an elaborate head-dress of feathers with a glyph in the centre.

Most of the figures represent a grotesque deity with an elongated nose and the bifurcated tongue of a snake. The face, which closely resembles the early masks on a primitive pyramid at the Maya site of Uaxactun, undoubtedly represents a rain deity. Others represent a youthful deity who is clearly a maize god, as he is often shown with ears of maize in his hands or in his head-dress.

These urns are usually found in groups of fives, placed above, or in front of, tombs. Occasionally they have been found fixed in a long shallow niche above the entrance to the tomb. It has been suggested that they represent deities who will guide the deceased on his journey to the next world. This does not seem very probable, as the figures do not seem to represent any deities associated with the underworld.

The tombs with which these urns are associated are long vaults with roofs made of flat stone slabs and a regular doorway with stone lintel and sealed with large stones. Sometimes the walls are provided with niches, in which the bones of the deceased, or at least a part of them, are frequently placed. In one case the walls of the tomb had been covered with frescoes, but these, unfortunately, were in too bad a state of preservation to be copied. In another case the lintel of the doorway was carved with a hieroglyphic inscription.

Very frequently the bones of the dead persons, for several corpses are sometimes found in one tomb, had been painted red or vermilion. This naturally implies a secondary burial. Possibly the bodies were allowed to rot, and, after complete decomposition, were cleaned, painted, and placed in the tombs. The bones of a dog, painted a rose color, were also found in one grave, suggesting that the belief was also held in this region that a dog helped the soul of the deceased in his journey to the next world.

In one case the skeleton of an individual had been placed immediately above the roof of the tomb. This may have been the body of some slave sacrificed to accompany the soul of his late master to the next world, for, naturally, only persons of rank were buried in these imposing vaults. In one case decapitated heads were found in a mound containing one of these tombs. Each was covered with an inverted dish. Heads treated in a similar manner and lacking a body have been found in different parts of the Maya area, notably British Honduras and the Peten area, and it has been conjectured that they were the heads of sacrificial victims.

Drain pipes of pottery are found in some of the

mounds covering these tombs. They consist of short sections of tubing, tapering slightly at one end, so that the narrow end fits into the wider mouth of the adjacent tube, the juncture being made water-tight by the addition of cement. These drains, which, apparently, served to carry the water from the centre of the mound, in one case reach a length of thirty-six feet. In this case the drain carried the water from the floor supporting a tomb. Underground piping of this type has not been noted from any other part of middle America.

At Mitla and in the near vicinity are found even more remarkable burial vaults decorated with carved mosaic designs on the walls similar to those of the Mitla "palaces" already described. These tombs are built in the shape of crosses roofed with flat stone roof slabs and with a doorway at the end of one of the arms. The most elaborate of these is situated under one of the Mitla temples. The doorway, which was below the court in front of the temple, had apparently been concealed in ancient times, but during the colonial period the entrance appears to have been discovered, and the tomb robbed of its contents. The length from the end of the north arm to the extremity of the south arm is slightly more than forty feet, and the length between the extremes of the east and west arms is thirty-four feet. The arms are each slightly over five feet wide and about six and a half feet high. At the intersection of the four arms of the cross the roof is supported by a single round column. In a number of cases a short flight

of steps leads down to the entrance to the tomb, for
the floor of the tomb is in all known cases below ground
level.

The fact that these tombs are in the shape of a cross
does not imply any connection with Christianity, for
the cross was a common symbol in ancient middle
America, where it was primarily a sign for the four
world directions and their guardians. It is probable that
these tombs were built in this shape in honor of the
four lords of the world directions. Sometimes the centre of the world was considered to be a fifth world direction, and in this connection it is interesting to recall
that the funerary urns outside the other type of tomb,
already described, were placed in groups of fives. It is
true that the figures are often the same, whereas one
would expect to find five different deities, one representing each direction, but all can be shown to be connected with agricultural gods, if one considers the beliefs of the neighboring Mayas. The long-nosed rain
gods were associated with the world directions. They
are sometimes called *Balaam*, which is the Maya word
for jaguar, and it will be remembered that some of the
Oaxaca funerary urns are in the shape of jaguars. Finally
these rain gods of the world directions are closely associated with the crops, and, as already noticed, some of
the figures on the urns carry ears of corn. The evidence
is not conclusive, but is, at least, suggestive.

Before bringing this chapter to a close it would be
well to include a short survey of the relations of Mexi-

can civilization to those of its neighbors. As one passes northward from the centre of Mexico, there is a marked falling off in culture. The Pueblo cultures of the south-western United States have clearly been influenced by cultural emanations from Mexico, although there are a few local developments. Culture spends its force as it travels. Districts which are far removed from the centre of culture and difficult of access receive fewer cultural impulses from the point of radiation than do those areas which are close to the point of diffusion or, although distant, are geographically or physically brought close to the centre by the absence of barriers. The cultural stream overlaps its banks, depositing the rich mud of its progress in the most accessible points.

It would be a mistake to attribute to Mexican influences all features which Pueblo culture holds in common with Mexico. Many of these features undoubtedly date back to an early period before the rise of the individualized Mexican civilizations. These same features can also be found in the cultural areas of South America.

Mexican influences made themselves felt more strongly in the lower Mississippi Valley, where such middle-American features as human sacrifice and pyramidal structures occurred. The reason why these features are found in the far-away Mississippi Valley while they are absent in the more contiguous Pueblo area is not far to seek. Access to the Pueblo district was difficult, whereas by following the easy route that skirts the Gulf of Mexico, influences could easily pass from the Panuco region into the lower Mississippi Valley. Nevertheless, these cultures to the north were mere recipients, not cultural donors.

To the south of Mexico lies the Maya area. Mention of Maya civilization has been made many times in these pages, but it is doubtful if much in Mexican culture can be attributed directly to the Maya. Maya civilization was a late specialized development, and there is little reason to credit the hoary antiquity usually attributed to it.

It is very probable that the cultures of Mexico and those of Central America, including the Maya, are off-shoots of an earlier civilization that arose at about the time agriculture was developing in the new world. This civilization, if we can accord it such rank, must have comprised many independent peoples with their local languages and local arts, but united in sharing their cultural attainments and fairly uniform religious concepts based on agriculture. This does not imply that the same type of vessel was made in all parts in which this culture was found, nor that the same deity was worshipped with exactly the same rites and under the same name all over the area, but rather that the resemblances were far greater than the local differences. Naturally the most isolated parts diverged most strongly from the mean. Hence we find that the Maya and Mexican civilizations, assuming for the sake of clarity that all Mexican civilizations had the same origin, developed along fairly similar lines. Early divergences would in some cases be accentuated, but contacts between the different branches would close up the gaps in other cases. Resemblances might have been closer had it not been for the influx of the hordes of Nahua-speaking peoples from the north. They naturally imparted fresh ideas and religious concepts. Deities such as Huitzilopochtli and Tezcatlipoca are quite foreign to Maya ideas, but these are precisely the deities which were the patrons of the invaders from the north. The old gods, such as the Tlalocs or the god of the planet Venus, might pass any day as Maya gods with a change of name. Like Judith O'Grady and the colonel's lady, they are the same under the skin.

When one turns to Peru, the resemblances are found to be less close. This is due to the great distance between the two areas. Contact was practically lost at an early period, and there was no consequent check on divergences. Peru specialized on metallurgy, Central America on mathematics. A concrete discovery, such as the working of copper, was able to bridge the gap, and appears in middle America at a much later date. Mathematics, lacking the impulse of utility, was impeded in the counter flow. That contact between the pre-specialized cultures reached as far as Peru is shown by distribution of all the early agricultural plants, as well as pottery making, agricultural deities, and even myths.

A backwash at a later time carried other agricultural plants of South American domestication back into middle America, possibly at the same time as the north-ward spread of metals. In the centuries immediately preceding the arrival of the Spaniards, Peru seemed to have made more contributions to cultural advance than did Central America, for there are more inventions found only in Peru than are found only in the latter region. Colombia also seems to have made its solid contribution to advancement, but the other areas, including the United States, merely donated buttons to the cultural offertory plate. As in communities, so in nations; a few lead, the rest are pulled along, lagging far behind.

In recent years there has been a revival of the old wild theories that claim Atlantis or a sunken continent of the Pacific as the source of American civilization. These theories are put forward by cranks or persons with no real knowledge of aboriginal American culture. On a few superficial resemblances between Old and New World cultures these fantastic schemes are reared. They are contradicted by geologists and qualified archæologists without exception. Nothing is too impossible to be put forward by the proponents of this rubbish. It has even been claimed that the Greek alphabet is a Maya hymn recounting the submergence of Atlantis! "The Star-Spangled Banner" might just as well have been substituted for the Greek alphabet. One could probably produce from it by the same methods a Maya hymn every bit as plausible.

It has also been claimed that American civilization

has been derived from Egypt via the Pacific. Against this theory is the fact that every cultivated plant in the New World, with three possible exceptions, was unknown in the Old World prior to the time of Columbus. The exceptions are cotton, gourds, and sweet potatoes. In the case of cotton the varieties of Old and New World origin are different, and in the case of the third the question is not yet settled as to whether or not the sweet potato was known outside of America before 1492. Now had the civilization of America been derived from Egypt via the Pacific, it is inconceivable that the invaders would not have introduced with them the plants of the Old World. Not only were the staples of the Old World, such as wheat, barley, yams, bananas, and rice totally unknown in America, but also a very long period would have been required to domesticate the wild plants of the New World, and the invaders and their descendants would have reverted to barbarism long before the first crops were gathered, allowing leisure for the building up of a new civilization. Even had this been possible, the evidence of the maize plant itself refutes its feasibility. With the exception of rice, a plant requiring entirely different methods, all Old World grasses are sown broadcast. Maize also is derived from a grass. Had it been first cultivated in the same way as the people of the Old World cultivated their other grasses, it would have been sown broadcast. It would then have developed like other grasses into a short, multiple-stemmed plant, but its present form clearly shows that each plant was sown individually with an adequate space between it and its neighbor, enabling it to develop one massive and high stalk.

Metal working is definitely absent from all periods of middle-American history prior to three or four centuries before the conquest. If these civilizers had come from Egypt or Asia, it is to be presumed that they would have brought with them the knowledge of working metals. Similarly the wheel was totally unknown in the New World. If the invaders were able to introduce so many religious features, as are claimed by them, it is strange that they did not utilize their knowledge of the wheel. Furthermore, no Asiatic artifact has ever been found in the New World under conditions that would preclude its having been introduced in the post-conquest period. All such finds must be very carefully investigated, as the following clearly shows. Some years ago an indubitable Maya flint was dredged out of the Thames River near London. It was subsequently found to have come from a spot where ships from British Honduras were accustomed to dump ballast. In a second case large numbers of Egyptian scarabs were found on a farm in Scotland. It was subsequently discovered that the farmer had given the field a dressing of manure. This manure, it was learned, had come from Egypt, and there is no doubt that the scarabs were scooped up with the manure in Egypt. These two illustrations serve to show the need of very careful investigation of all such finds.

Certain middle-American sculptures and paintings of Maya and Aztec origin are cited as clear proofs of Asiatic influences, since they appear to portray elephants. In most cases these supposed elephants' trunks are the snouts of the long-nosed rain gods, and are clearly of ophidian origin, but in one or two cases the trunks are certainly very elephantine. The explanation is probably to be found, not in an Asiatic prototype, but in a half-forgotten tradition of the mastodon. Recent discoveries have now shown that the mastodon lingered on for many centuries as a contemporary of man in the New World, and there is some evidence that in Ecuador one was slain by man not more than 3000 years ago, as the polychrome pottery associated with it attests. This massive animal would naturally leave a tremendous impression on the minds of its human contemporaries, and would in all probability be accorded worship, like other important fauna.

Clearly American civilization was not imported wholesale from Asia, but there is a certain case to be answered for Pacific influences in South America. The question is complex and too involved to be stated here. Suffice it to say that the evidence is very far from being conclusive at the present time. It is possible that the argument will never be definitely settled, but it is the duty of all Americanists to keep an open mind. Whatever may be the outcome, there will never be any serious question that the great bulk of native culture of the New World should be stamped "Made in America."

SELECTED BIBLIOGRAPHY

Clark, J. C.—*The Story of "Eight Deer" in Codex Colombino*. London, 1912.

Diaz, Bernal—*The True History of the Conquest of New Spain*. Translated by A. P. Maudslay. Hakluyt Society. 5 vols. London, 1911–16.

Holmes, W. H.—*Archæological Studies Among the Ancient Cities of Mexico*. Field Museum Anthropological Papers, vol. I, Chicago, 1895.

Joyce, T. A.—*Mexican Archæology*. London and New York, 1914. *Maya and Mexican Art*. London (The Studio), 1927.

Saville, M. H.—*The Goldsmith's Art in Ancient Mexico*. Museum of the American Indian: Heye Foundation. New York, 1920. *Turquois Mosaic Art in Ancient Mexico*. Museum of the American Indian: Heye Foundation. New York, 1922. *The Woodcarver's Art in Ancient Mexico*. Museum of the American Indian: Heye Foundation. New York, 1925.

Spence, L.—*The Gods of Mexico*. London, 1923.

Spinden, H. J.—*Ancient Civilizations of Mexico*. American Museum of Natural History, New York, 1927.

English editions of Peter Martyr, Herrera, Gomara, and Acosta exist, but are rare. They may be consulted in larger libraries. There is a French translation of Sahagun as well as one into German. Torquemada and Duran alone of the great historians have not been translated from Spanish.

Both Spinden and Joyce (1927) give bibliographies to which readers are referred. The above list only includes books of non-technical and general interest written in English.

The Best
of Times,
The Worst
of Times

The Best of Times, The Worst

ERRATA

Page 2 — para 1 should read as follows:

The Depression had hit, not hard enough to leave the family penniless, but hard enough to destroy years and years of their father's effort and hope. Greeley never mentioned the Great Crash to his children, but its lesson did not escape his only son: a lifetime of work can be washed away in a single moment; even the promise of summer can be broken. No one—no matter how honest, how fair, or how generous—is exempt. For as long as he can remember, that son has had a recurring dream. He is in a summer house on the lake watching great waves wash up at the foot of the house. They are beautiful, awesome waves. They begin to lap into the house and fill up the porch and front room. But they go no farther and the home is left intact.

Nelson-Hall Company nh *Chicago*

Library of Congress Cataloging in Publication Data

Kotre, John N
    The best of times, the worst of times.

    "Books by Andrew M. Greeley": p.
    Bibliography: p.
    Includes index.
    1. Greeley, Andrew M., 1928-   2. Catholic Church—Clergy—Biography.   3. Clergy—United States—Biography.   4. Catholic Church in the United States—History.   I. Title.
BX4705.G6185K67   282'.092'4 [B]   78-14224
ISBN 0-88229-380-X (cloth)
ISBN 0-88229-597-7 (paper)

To: John F. Kotre, Elizabeth
C. Dyker, and the corner of
Bell and Chase

Acknowledgments

For help extended along the way I wish to thank the staff of the Rebecca Crown Library of Rosary College, Philip Scharper, Sue Ann Holden, and my wife, Ann Marie. To Robert Coles I owe special thanks: for gracing this book with a foreword, but especially for passing on in his own work a certain spirit that spoke, long before I ever conceived of this project, to some of the things I hoped to become. I am also grateful to one Charles Dickens for providing the title to a volume that is very much a tale of two cities—and of a man caught between them.

Contents

Foreword

There are many ways to come to know a particular society. The subject of this biographical effort has done more than his share to tell us about ourselves—through a strenuous outpouring of articles, essays, published data, newspaper columns, and not least, books containing a wide range of inquiry and comment. Moreover, Father Greeley has recently been moving toward additional genres—stories, poems. He is a remarkably conscientious, determined, steadfast observer and writer—only one citizen, but an important asset for a nation that badly needs to understand what it is about. He is also a man of considerable courage, who has not felt the need to fall in line —to yield to the intellectual "powers and principalities" which have their own special ways of demanding compliance, conformity.

For years now Father Greeley has walked a number of tightropes with dignity, persistence, and a smile that has indicated a certain rebellious amusement at his own fate. An intellectual of broad and deep sensibility, he has refused to distance himself (in spirit or in the nature of his work, his concerns) from the working people of this country. A man of obvious social compassion, he has kept a keen eye on the hypocrisies and pretenses, and worse, the smug arrogance that can more than occasionally bedevil those who want to "reform" society. A social scientist, adept at various quantitative "instruments" of research, he writes strong, clear, often quite touching prose—a much needed example to his colleagues. A Catholic priest, he has dared show his love for the Church by pointing out exactly where he thinks it stands, where it is headed—and at what cost to its flock.

In a sense, Father Greeley combines in a striking and gifted manner the pastoral and prophetic elements of the priesthood—and of the secular priesthood which we call "social science." He has made dozens of important interpretations, clarifications, analyses, and predictions—thereby telling us what is happening to a large, rich, powerful, but sometimes rather torn and confused nation. He has also kept close to his own roots and to those of many other Americans— their memories, hopes, worries, dreams. And always, he has shunned the faddish, the clever postures that upper-middle-class intellectuals no less than others are susceptible to. He offers us not only opinion and shrewd observation, but mounds of carefully sifted and evaluated evidence—some of it, over these past few decades, a wonderful reminder that all too much of the received wisdom of the day is, in fact, a porridge of self-serving distortions or rationalizations.

Father Greeley's working man—Irish or Italian or Slavic, or yes, black—is not always the liberal or radical intellectual's version of the same. He knows and has tried to do justice to the ironies, ambiguities, contradictions, inconsistencies, and paradoxes of our social, economic, political life. He comprehends and does not fear acknowledging the conflicts in men and women all to readily written off as "prejudiced" or "narrow-minded" or "provincial"—by those who have their own wordy, self-important ways of exhibiting meanness, a limited intelligence, and thorough insularity. And as his recent, exceptionally instructive and movine book *Neighborhood* reveals, he knows what people crave, and still have, if lucky, despite the easy and clever dismissals of various critics: a sense of place, a sense of tradition, a sense of affiliation, all concretely realized in streets, houses, stores, schools, and playgrounds, where relatives and friends are to be found—neighbors in much more than the spatial or incidental meaning of the word.

This is the book of a young colleague who has found a decent, imaginative, independent-minded mentor and has chosen to celebrate that discovery—not to mention the considerable body of work that has a life of its own, once put into print. John Kotre's writing is lucid and forceful, a fitting tribute to the man whose complicated, unusual, vigorous life is evoked in these pages. A lot of people who know and love Andy Greeley will be grateful for this book; but one hopes his critics will find their way to it and will have the courage to face its thrust with an open-minded, inquiring spirit. Andrew Greeley has never issued heavy-handed, dour fiats—is himself a man of wit, liveliness, and wide-ranging concerns. He has never been anyone's (in the secular world) piece of property, and he deserves an attentive, reflective audience, willing to learn from him, and one hopes, to appreciate his singular, rewarding presence on the American religious, scholarly, and journalistic scene.

—Robert Coles
April, 1978

Preface

Andrew M. Greeley is an Irish Catholic priest of the Archdiocese of Chicago and a sociologist whose Center for the Study of American Pluralism is located at the University of Chicago. But as I write, neither the archdiocese nor the university wants anything to do with him. In 1950 Greeley was hidden in a seminary, four years from ordination, thinking of anything but a career in writing. In 1975, he was beginning his third decade in the priesthood and contemplating his sixtieth book. In the twenty-five intervening years, American Catholicism, and the country itself, had undergone enormous change. This is a record of one very expressive man, living through those times of change, loving them, hating them, taking hope from them, despairing of them, and always—*always*, in the case of Andrew Greeley—doing battle with them. It was the best of times; it was the worst of times; and somehow for this Irish Catholic priest— and for American Catholicism along with him—they came in that order.

Greeley *is* expressive; his books are coming out more rapidly than ever before. They bear such diverse titles as *The Education of Catholic Americans, Come Blow Your Mind with Me, The Jesus Myth, Sexual Intimacy, Building Coalitions.* He has published hundreds of articles—in *Commonweal, America,* and the *Critic*; in the *New Republic, Redbook,* the *Village Voice,* and the *New York Times Magazine*; in the *American Journal of Sociology,* the *American Sociological Review,* and the *Public Opinion Quarterly*; in the *Scientific American,* the *Bulletin of the Atomic Scientists,* and dozens of other journals. Add to that a weekly column syndicated to fifty Catholic diocesan newspapers, biweekly columns in fifty city newspapers, meditations mailed out twice a month to subscribers of the Thomas More Association, another continuous assignment that is published anonymously, and whatever else he writes but fails to mention in an interview because his work comes forth almost unconsciously. He was asked to write his first book, and 80 to 90 percent of what he has produced since then has been initiated at the request of a publisher or an editor. A volume he described to me as his *magnum opus* (a misnomer—he has written no *magna opera*), which was reviewed as "generous, intelligent, and often courageous theology," was dictated from notes in a single week—more than three hundred pages of typewritten copy. Better, he has said, to write an incomplete book at the right time than a complete book at the wrong time. Is he repetitious? Absolutely. Predictable? Even his loudest critics say no. Clear? For his own good, probably too clear.

Within a period of a few years, one and the same man, Andrew Greeley, wrote all of the following:

> It is also interesting to note that there is relatively little short-circuiting going on in the model. Most variables exercise their influence "further down the line," indirectly rather than directly. There are only three short-circuit linkages, the -.20 already mentioned between age and a desire to marry, the -.21 between age and loneliness, and the -.50 between age and modern values. Age, then, is the only variable in the model that is likely to cause short circuits.[1]

> And the woman will be semiconsciously dwelling on similar questions. When will he start? Will it begin even before supper or will he wait? Where will his hands and his mouth go first? Will he be in one of those moods when he wants to strip me leisurely? Shall I turn the tables on him tonight and strip him first, or will I surprise him with my plan to trap him at his work in the library when I approach him wearing only panties and a martini pitcher—or maybe only the martini pitcher? Will I kneel on top of him, forcing my body down on his?[2]

> I know what you're going to say. You were indeed quite explicit about the need to become like little children. And what you meant was that we should have the faith and the trust and the enthusiasm of little children. But you were just speaking figuratively, weren't you, Lord? You really don't expect me to become like that small creature? It would be absurd. Wouldn't it?
> *Amen.*[3]

> As I sat on an eroding Lake Michigan dune watching the Democratic party destroy itself in July of 1972, I kept asking myself what

picture these people had of the American public. Do they really
know what it does to the American voter to be told that Bella
Abzug, Shirley MacLaine, Jesse Jackson, Bill Singer, Walter
Fauntleroy, Robert Drinan, Abbie Hoffman, Jerry Rubin, and the
Minnesota and New York representatives of gay liberation be-
longed on the floor of the Democratic convention while Richard
Daley did not?[4]

Q. *(Triumph)* Most Holy Father—
A. I'm not Holy, and I'm certainly not Most Holy, and I'm also
certainly not your father or anybody else's, so call me Pope, or Mr.
Pope, or Bishop, and drop the rest of that nonsense.[5]

Critics accuse him of spreading himself too thin. Only a dilet-
tante, they say, could possibly cover the ground that he does, and, if
he has a wide readership, it is because he is a "popularizer" and not
a "serious scholar." There is suspicion of the man settling, like the
medieval Jew, on the fringe of our intellectual domains, who has
connections with other lands and other ways of thinking, who wants
to be part of us yet not assimilate our premises, who has the gall, the
chutzpah (may Greeley's patron saints forgive me) to tell us—his
hosts—that our assumptions are only culturally relative. Much as
we mouth the value of "cross-fertilization," we are likely to view the
outsider as one who brings germs, not seeds, and our impulse is to
treat him like the first astronaut back from the moon: two weeks in
an isolation chamber to make sure we are not "fertilized" by his
parasites.

When one adds to the role of migrant intellectual the personality of Andrew Greeley, who crosses borders to plant mines as
often as he does to sow seeds, who is in such a blur of motion that
one can project anything onto his person (he has been called a
"sunny optimist" and a "gloomy pessimist," a "stereotypical New
Leftist" as well as an "apologist for Daley"), who loves to get his
readers flowing one way and then to cut back against the grain, one
has conflict of the highest—and, I might add, the most instructive—
order.

I first met Andrew Greeley when I walked into his office with an
idea for dissertation research on young adults from Catholic backgrounds: Why did some of them wish to retain their identity as
Catholics and why did others wish to sever themselves from the
Church? I was, of course, studying myself. Father Greeley was receptive to the idea and proved to be an ideal dissertation director: he

left me alone except for suggestions at critical moments and was on the phone to me with immediate feedback whenever I dropped several chapters off at his office. At the same time I sat through his course in the Sociology of Religion—now the books *Unsecular Man* and *The Denominational Society*—attending perhaps half the sessions, watching the attendance dwindle from a crowd in the beginning to a handful at the end. The course left no great impression on me, simply memories of a Roman collar, of percentages on the blackboard, of Freudian slips, of quips about illiterate bishops, of springtime growing outside a dirty window.

I saw little of Father Greeley after I left the University of Chicago in 1969. I remember reading his condemnation of sensitivity training and recall columns in which he psychoanalyzed those who were leaving the priesthood (and, it seemed, anyone else who disagreed with him). A *Commonweal* column, entitled "Andrew Greeley, Divine Sociologist," accused him of "sneers, name-calling, and distortion . . . a cavalier attitude toward the truth."[6] I saw a brief appearance on the national news in which he expressed the growing anger of lower-middle-class whites at being "left out," and I did not miss his scathing attack on the Catholic hierarchy; "morally, intellectually, and religiously bankrupt" was the delicate way he spoke of the nation's bishops. It seemed that a new book was being advertised or reviewed every few months, but I paid little attention because "it was just Greeley sounding off again."

At the time I was involved in the impersonal mathematics of survey research at the University of Michigan. Something in me had to counter that excess of rationality and logic; it led to a book on fantasy and the search for a genre that would enable me, as a social psychologist, to touch the lives of people more directly. People had so much more to offer than variables. They were concrete, reactive, emotional—and they unified and focused issues in a way that abstracts of research did not. I read Robert Coles's book on Erik Erikson and said, yes, that is something I would like to do, and it was not long thereafter that I decided to try it with Andrew Greeley.

I chose Andrew Greeley because there was always a stir about him, because he was saying things at that time that were not being said in my environs, because at the core of his polemic there often appeared a kernel of truth that could not be shucked. Here was a man who had lived and breathed, encouraged and fought American

Catholicism during some of its most tempestuous years, who knew its people from the inside, who researched their social, political, economic, and religious behavior, who wrote about the spiritual underpinnings of their existence. Through him, through what he had studied and what he had lived, one could tell the story (true, *his* story) of the American Catholic people over the past quarter of a century.

And so I wrote Father Greeley with a proposal to get all that he had written into one volume. He told me he was astonished and flattered at the idea, offered to cooperate in any way he could, and sent me an up-to-date bibliography (which wasn't up-to-date at all). I began, then, not as an intimate of Andrew Greeley, but as a former student. Over a period of four years I got to know him well, reading nearly everything he had written, interviewing him extensively, consulting the archive of his materials available at Rosary College in River Forest, Illinois. Through it all, my goal was not to systematize his thought (that would have been impossible) nor to tear it apart (that was being attended to quite nicely) but simply to return it to its source—the ebbs and flows of a single human life.

I like to think that this book is about the *eyes* of Andrew Greeley. When Father Greeley speaks to you, his eyes are in constant motion, working hard, dancing nervously about the room, seeking not so much the variety there as that which exists in his own mind. The eyes are on the trail of ironies and paradoxes—primal unities in diversity—that surprise, perplex, confuse, yet capture truth. They pounce on one-liners that offend one person and make another laugh (of a Pentecostal meeting: "The Holy Spirit had bad breath"). Greeley has argued, in his public life, that the metropolis is not an even mass but a patchwork of ethnic color. He has championed the unstable pluralism from which the American political system emerged and shouted out for those parts of the system not being heard. Of schools, of the organizational Catholic Church, of the priesthood he has said that without experimentation in alternative structures they will decay. He believes the unfaithful spouse is one who is monotonous, who fails to explore and surprise, in the marriage bed. He believes that life itself is a preparation for the surprise of death and that God was drunk when He created the universe, so great and colorful is the variegation that exists within it.

1 A Recurring Dream

In the early 1930s a number of Chicago's newly affluent Irish Catholics spent their summers at a Knights of Columbus camp in Twin Lakes, Wisconsin. Among them was the family of Andrew T. Greeley. Each Fourth of July, they boarded a train for a trip through Illinois chain-o'-lakes country, through Lake Zurich, Crystal Lake, McHenry, and Genoa City, to a tiny station just across the state line. Then, the children's excitement growing, they climbed aboard a truck for a bumpy ride to an old castlelike building atop a great green lawn that ran between outlying wooden cabins and sloped down to the shimmering water.

They had returned! For two months it was all little Andy and his sisters could ask for: charging madly down the hill to the beach, shooting down the metal slide to the lake, devouring roast beef with potatoes and gravy in the screened-in porch of the clubhouse, staying up in the stone-and-concrete "pergola" to watch the moon dancing on the water's surface. One night at the end of summer all the wooden crates that had been stored in the kitchen would be set ablaze, and the flames, it seemed, would light the entire sky.

Twin Lakes meant a great deal to the Greeleys. It was there that Andrew Greeley, Sr., just starting his own stocks and bonds business, had met his wife Grace McNichols, a clerk at Sears. To the children who came along—Andy, Grace, and Mary Jule—it became the promise of joy as regular as the return of summer. The Depression was raging elsewhere, but it kept its distance from Twin Lakes.

At least for a time it did.

On one of those glorious vacation days Greeley, Sr., arrived from Chicago and spoke quietly, alone, and very seriously with his wife. After that everything seemed to change. Greeley still worked as hard as ever, he still went to church faithfully, he still avoided "the creature" (unlike others in the clan), he still read voraciously. He kept the respect of family, friends, and neighbors. But a leprechaun, a lover of play, had flitted off and left behind a somber, silent, distant man. The joy had left Twin Lakes, and the Greeleys rarely returned.

The Depression had hit, not hard enough to leave the family penniless, but hard enough to destroy years and years of their father's effort and hope. Greeley never mentioned the Great Crash to his children, but its lesson did not escape his only son: a lifetime of work can be washed away in a single moment; even the promise of summer can be broken. No one—no matter how honest, how fair, or how generous—is exempt. He is in a summer house on a lake watching great waves wash up at the foot of the house. They are beautiful, awesome waves. They begin to lap into the house and fill up the porch and front room. But they go no father and the home is left intact.

The dreamer, Andrew Moran Greeley, was born on February 5, 1928, in the Chicago suburb of Oak Park, just across Austin Boulevard from the city itself. Both his parents were the children of immigrants from County Mayo on the west of Ireland, but beyond that, little is known of their roots. Andrew's father grew up in what is now Old Town in Chicago, and his father's mother taught school. Perhaps it was she who instilled in her son an insatiable passion for ideas.

Though Andrew T. Greeley had only a high-school education, he was a bright, energetic man and an omnivorous reader—far and away the best read man among his peers. He loved to argue, says his son, "but he never held an argument against you." He was a writer, too, for newspapers and magazines of the Knights of Columbus (an organization of Catholic laymen to which he was deeply committed) and for another of his loves, the *Indoor Baseball Guidebook*. He was not an "intellectual" and probably knew no intellectuals, but, in the words of his son, "knowledge was respected," and to judge from the picture of his father reading everything in sight, it was not only respected but devoured. That was unusual for Austin Boulevard in the 1930s.

Andrew's mother, Grace McNichols, had been born fifth in a

family of seven children and grew up on Western Avenue in the Holy Family–St. Ignatius district of Chicago. Both her parents died when she was in her early teens, her father, from years of working in the sewers, her mother, of the plague, so she and the rest of the family were raised by an older sister. Grace went to St. Mary's High School for two years, thought about becoming a nun but decided against it, and went to work at Sears for five dollars a week. She continued at Sears for a decade and a half until she married in her early thirties. While the crash was borne by his father in silence, Greeley recollects, it rocked his mother visibly. She spoke of it to her son, of what it had done to them, of what it had done to his father. The family was not poor after the crash (they were able to purchase a brick bungalow in 1937), but they were "hurting," especially in view of what might have been theirs—indeed, if hard work gets its just desserts, in view of what *should* have been theirs.

The family atmosphere, Greeley recalls, was "even." "There were not highs, and there were not lows." There were few shows of affection, little demonstration of feeling, absolutely *no* conflict that ever came to the surface. The children succeeded, and their success was noted without any further comment. Were failures criticized? "We didn't fail," Greeley says matter-of-factly. Young Andrew was obedient; he lived by the rules. But he was curious, extraordinarily so, inquisitive in a pushy way, constantly asking questions, delighting to tell others (even, for a while, the nuns who taught him) that they had gotten something backward.

It was assumed in grammar school that all the children, the girls included, would go to college. It was unusual for any of the Irish of that time and place to think of college for their children, and singularly remarkable that plans for higher education should include daughters as well as sons. But Greeley, Sr., was incapable of imagining anything else. "Politically, my father was a New Deal Democrat. In mainstream, nonideological liberalism, you don't discriminate against people because of sex; I mean, you just don't." No crisis, no conflict, no heated arguments about the matter—it was just one of the assumptions of that silent, even atmosphere, and only in retrospect does it seem in any way out of the ordinary.

Not that the children *had* to go to college. They were not manipulated, never held in check or forced to conform by that middle-class Irish respectability that Greeley would criticize in years to come, not cut down to size by "What will people say?" and "Who do you think you are?" There was nothing of "Irish ridicule" in his family, save from his sister Grace. The children, all of them, were free to do what they wanted. A decision would be greeted with "Fine"—no more, no less, in the same tone, and seemingly with the same involvement, with which one commented on the weather.

The Greeleys were not extraordinarily pious. "Being a Catholic was as natural as breathing," says Greeley. The family attended Mass each Sunday at St. Angela's (his father rarely went to communion), and when the children were old enough, they went to the parish school. The family was not active in parish organizations. They did have great respect for the nuns who taught their children and for the priests who said Mass and administered the sacraments (one of the elder Greeley's closest friends, in fact, was a priest on the same softball team as he). But God and religion, like so many things, were rarely mentioned in the home; rather, *they were absorbed*. With this absorbed religion came a belief (hardly formulated as such) in what Greeley calls the "ultimate graciousness of reality." Their God gave the Greeleys hope, not joyous expectation, surely, but the resilience to bounce back from the effects of a devastating financial loss. Their religion kept them going, enabled them to survive. "They were Irish," Father Greeley says—three words and a thousand years of history.

St. Angela's was truly a center of young Andrew's boyhood years. It was a depression parish, the streets lined with tidy bungalows and two-flats, the atmosphere as stable and gray as that in the Greeley home. The parishioners were almost entirely Irish, with a handful of Germans and Italians (when the latter moved in, residents feared that the neighborhood would soon "go Italian"). The people got around on foot and on streetcars and buses. The children played baseball in empty lots (called "prairies"), touch football on the asphalt streets, and basketball on the backs of garages. In winter they had snowball fights with the "publics." People didn't say they were from Austin or Mayfield Avenue; they said they were from St. Angela's. It was a world so entirely Irish and Catholic that one was not self-conscious about it; one could not imagine anything else. Indeed, its people simply felt they were "Americans."

The church itself was a frame building, later replaced by a gymnasium that served as a "temporary" church for almost two decades. The monsignor was a kindly man in failing health; the curates were friendly, affable, wisecracking. Young Father Hayes (an early hero of Greeley's) was teaching the doctrine of the Mystical Body, organizing Catholic action groups, and even saying a dialogue Mass as early as the mid-thirties. Some of the nuns in the parish schools were "crabs" and some were "nice," but they did their job. The children were orderly and always looked up the Legion of Decency rating for a movie before trotting off to see it at the Manor or the Iris. The parish had carnivals and raffles, novenas and missions, and repeated appeals to build the new church. Without bothering to think about it, you knew it was where you belonged.

One incident stands out in Greeley's memories of his early years of grammar school, something that happened when he was in the second grade. "This nun said one day, 'How many of you are going to be priests when you grow up?' About half of us raised up our hands, and she said, 'Well, maybe one of you will be one,' and I thought to myself, OK, that'll be me. And I've never really had any second thoughts about that. I made up my mind then and never really changed it."

In the early years of elementary school Andrew was insatiably curious. He loved history and geography, thought the religion books dull. He was outspoken, too, realizing now that he must have "threatened the hell out of the nuns" but having no idea of it then. But after the fourth grade, he became quieter. The criticism of teachers began to take its toll; classmates were nastier; there was no longer the hope of Twin Lakes; his father was more somber than ever. At home, there was no reinforcement of any kind, positive or negative. There emerged "a certain silence, a certain feeling of being different." He was still inquisitive, still read a good deal, still had friends, but he was "the odd one." And if he was a gifted child, he would have been astonished to know it. Friends who knew him in the later years of grammar school can hardly believe that the same person is today so brazenly articulate.

When Andrew told his parents that he wished to be a priest, they said, "Fine." His mother made it clear that it was *his* vocation, not hers, that he was free to change his mind at any time. In Septem-

ber, 1942, then, Andy Greeley and five of his friends from St. Angela's began their daily excursion to Quigley Preparatory Seminary.
He caught the Central Avenue bus, met the others at the corner of
Chicago Avenue (you had to be there by 8:10 A.M. or miss them), and
rode the "red rocket" down Chicago Avenue, through Polish and
Italian neighborhoods, to the gray Gothic building with the beautiful stained glass windows on Chicago's Near North Side. The trip
lasted an hour; along the way, the city's diversity got on the streetcar, paid its fare, and rode along beside you.

Students came to Quigley from all over Chicago. "Looking
back on it, I, probably more than most people of my generation, was
aware of the ethnic complexity of the city because Quigley was probably the most ethnically heterogeneous high school that there was.
One became aware of Poles and Czechs and Lithuanians and
Slovaks and Slovenes and Italians." The diversity was tolerated but
played down. St. Patrick's Day was celebrated but only as "First Rec-
tor's Day," the birthday of the school's first principal. The faculty,
like the clergy in Chicago at large, was predominantly Irish, but
national languages were taught because students would be returning to their communities after ordination—and they had to hear
confessions. "In retrospect," says Greeley, "Quigley's attitude toward ethnicity was a pure assimilationist perspective, but it was a
tolerant assimilation. They were going to let people assimilate in
their own time."

The regimen at Quigley was demanding, but neither strict nor
stern. No smoking was allowed (but the smoke pouring out of the
washrooms was ignored by passing faculty) and students could not
date (though there was no way of checking whether students dated
or not). Each student was expected to attend Mass every day before
coming to school. School was in session on Saturday, but Thursday
was free. Once a week all the students were herded into chapel for a
spiritual conference, and twice a year each one spent twenty minutes
in a counseling session with his spiritual director. Homework was
not excessive—Andy usually had it done by the time he got off the
Chicago Avenue streetcar. Quigley was a good place—Father Greeley has fond memories of it. There were spiritual directors like
Father Mohan, teachers like Father Grady. He wanted to be like
these men. He kept the rules. "I was very happy there, actually. The

people who attended it were nice people. I mean there was just a lot less negative reaction to me there than there was in grammar school. Now there was some, surely, but a lot less, both from the faculty and from the students. I didn't threaten the faculty and the students nearly as much as I did in grammar school. I was very happy at Quigley. Extremely happy. They were five good years."

Quigley is where Andrew Greeley came alive intellectually. He discovered John Henry Newman, Joseph Conrad, Charles Dickens, William Shakespeare. He followed politics in *Time* (which his father brought home every week) and read the *front* half of the newspaper. He lived the saga of World War II. "I was old enough to be fascinated by it and young enough not to be able to understand all the suffering," he says. At the end of his first year at Quigley he was given as a prize Theodore Maynard's *The Story of American Catholicism*, and he devoured it. It awakened him to history, "not history as something one read about in textbooks, but history as a drama, history as something on which one stood." He happened to pick up a Father Brown mystery story from a paperback rack and learned of G. K. Chesterton. *The Everlasting Man. Orthodoxy. The Ballad of the White Horse.* Chesterton was romantic and hopeful, and he had a way of saying things. "Life is too serious to be taken seriously." "Hope is a virtue only when the situation is hopeless." "It's not that Christianity has been tried and found wanting; it's that Christianity has been found hard and not tried." The paradoxes would appear time and again in years to come.

Greeley graduated from Quigley in 1947 and began major seminary at St. Mary of the Lake in Mundelein, Illinois, in September of that year. Ten days after he arrived he received news of his father's death. The elder Greeley had been ill, but everyone thought he was getting better, so the death came as a shock, an overwhelming one. "Characteristically," says Greeley, "I don't think any of us could really express grief at it. Even today, probably, some of that grief is still locked up inside." There was never a thought that Andrew would have to leave the seminary to support his mother. She did not complain, even adjusted with "some ease and elegance." The crash, it seemed, was harder for her because of what it did to *him*. After his death, Mrs. Greeley bounced back and went to work. She was Irish. She had her religion.

The years at St. Mary of the Lake were pleasant and leisurely. There was no tuition. Greeley calls the seminary a "comfortable, well-appointed ivory tower. There was no chance to mature there. All the decisions were made for you—when you got up, when you went to bed, what you ate, how you spent your time." The teaching was from textbooks. No attempt was made to return to sources or to encounter the major trends of contemporary American thought. Philosophy courses relived the hoary controversies of the Middle Ages. Spirituality was just as up-to-date. Theology was better, but that was because Greeley was reading so much on his own. The best that could be said of the atmosphere at the major seminary is that it provided the opportunity for self-education.

During his years at Quigley, Andrew held a variety of summer jobs. He was a conductor on Chicago's "el," a clerk for the Pullman Company, a stockboy at Carson Pirie Scott. There was always a week or two for a trip north, and on one of them he returned to Twin Lakes. During major seminary he worked in the summers in the warehouse of the Catholic school board. And in his last three summers at St. Mary of the Lake, there was a six-week "villa" at the diocese campground near Eagle River, Wisconsin. "A glorious, glorious place," he remembers, "six weeks—every, every second of it, every day of it, a joy. It was supposed to remove us from the cares and the worries and the temptations of the world. It didn't, but it was an awfully nice place—the lake, golf, tennis, movies every night. Splendid."

In the summer of 1950 Greeley was introduced by John Crean, a friend who had recently left the seminary, to a group of Catholics in graduate school at the University of Chicago. Most of them were there because of the GI Bill and many would be gone in a few years. They were in economics, sociology, social psychology, physics—a broad range of fields. For a brief interlude these people were a vigorous, creative Catholic presence on campus. They founded communes like the Greenwood Community; read *Concord*, a Young Christian Student (YCS) publication from Notre Dame; and traveled to Notre Dame in the summer to hear the French theologian Jean Daniélou. Says Greeley, "They encountered the secular university world with a combination of zeal and inferiority. They were going to drag the rest of the Church along with them, and they had things they thought they wanted to say to the secular university world. They were, in a way, militant Catholics and militant intellectuals.

"I remember standing on an elevated platform after a conversation with some of these people, saying to myself, in 1950, these are the first Catholics to be in this. I don't know where in the world, at that stage of the game, I was capable of having that insight—but they were. It dawned on me that, well, these are our first intellectuals."

Greeley visited the Catholic community at the University of Chicago every summer until after his ordination. By that time its fervor was declining (the Korean War had something to do with that, and so did the encyclical *Humani Generis*), and he was too busy with parish work. He felt great respect for the university at those times—he found it open, tolerant, dispassionate, a "font of knowledge." He understood something of the friction between an emerging Catholic intelligentsia and the established Church. But he had no intention of becoming a student at the university. He still wished to be a parish priest like Father Hayes, Father Mohan, Father Grady, and the upperclassmen who were by now ordained and in parish work.

It was through these contacts at Chicago (ironically, hardly at all through faculty at St. Mary of the Lake) that Greeley learned of the new thinking of the French theologians. He could read French, and so, during the years of his theological training, he would send away for the latest work of Jean Daniélou, Henri de Lubac, or Yves Congar and study it. One or two friends discussed the "new theology" with him; and Father Edward Brueggeman, a teacher of French and sacramental theology who had been to school with some of the theologians, kept him abreast of the latest titles. In the main, however, it was a journey he made alone. He returned from it absorbed in a vision of a Church as people, not hierarchy, of religious ideas as open-ended, not immutably fixed.

Near the end of his stay at St. Mary's, Greeley culminated his study of French thought with a paper, "On the Nature of the Act of Faith." Daniélou, de Lubac, and Congar, he discovered, had their roots in the French phenomenological theologians of the early twentieth century—in Pierre Rousselot, Ambrose Gardeil, Maurice

Blondell—and these in turn were influenced by (an old friend now) John Henry Newman. The earlier French theologians opened for Greeley "a whole new style of theologizing." He saw them as the source of the "new theology" of the late forties and early fifties, as forerunners of Pierre Teilhard de Chardin. In retrospect, these were seeds, planted even before World War I, of the growth that would culminate in the Second Vatican Council. Faith, Greeley concluded in his paper, was more than intellectual assent; it was the commitment of the entire personality. The position was one that enabled Greeley to find company, a decade later, with Mircea Eliade, Clifford Geertz, and Langdon Gilkey, a position evident in his later reflections on religious myths and symbols.

But scholars of religion could not have been more remote from the mind of the young man who was ordained a priest on May 5, 1954. Nor could he possibly have foreseen himself as a writer, particularly as one criticized for being too prolific. Father Greeley's mind was filled instead with a vision as grand as the waves of his dream. He saw a vibrant new parish of the people, modeled on the blueprint of French theology.

Yet the grandeur of his vision, like that of his dream, triggered a fear. What if I fail? What if the crash comes back? What if the waves destroy me? A parish priest had to deal with people, not just think about them, and Andy Greeley, isolated for years in the seminary, was sure he could not. "I was particularly afraid, literally afraid, of dealing with kids."

2

The Young of Beverly Hills - and a New Breed

In June of 1954, a few weeks after his first Mass at St. Angela's, a letter reached the brick bungalow where Andy Greeley had spent his childhood years. Its content was straightforward: You have been assigned to Christ the King parish in the Beverly Hills district of Chicago. Greeley phoned the pastor and asked when he should report The answer: I'll schedule you for Mass next Sunday.

Years later Greeley reflected on his first moments at Christ the King:

> The first day I drove down the broad tree-lined streets of the parish, with its wide expanses of neatly manicured lawns surrounding large and gracious suburban homes, I knew I was in a different world from St. Angela. My first view of the almost finished parish church, the first modern church in our diocese, confirmed my hunch that I was involved in a whole new ball game. I had been trained for a place like St. Angela but I had been sent to a parish whose existence had completely escaped our seminary faculty.[1]

Never before had American Catholicism seen the likes of Christ the King. In the beautiful homes of Beverly Hills lived the American Irish who had "arrived"—successful, well-educated business and professional men, their handsome, well-groomed wives, and their baffling and talented children. "Spoiled rich kids," the older priests and nuns told the new curate. "Their parents have given them everything. They respect nothing and nobody."

Greeley's first months at his new assignment, coming after seven years of prolonged adolescence, left him reeling. "I lost twenty-five pounds," he remembers. "I couldn't eat." He was swept up in bake sales, bridge clubs, plays, concerts, picnics, basketball games, discussion groups, dances, teen clubs—and hundreds of "spoiled rich kids." The surprise was that he loved his work and was good at it. And Christ the King, it seemed, was ready to become his new parish. "Loyalty to the parish, enthusiasm over the church—at least as it was perceived—generosity with time and money, commitment to every new project that the parish sponsored (be it the Christian Family Movement or bridge marathons) in Christ the King made St. Angela's look stodgy by comparison."[2] The enthusiasm of the parishioners was a strange mixture of the old and the new: Sorrowful Mother novenas next to Cana conferences, October and May rosaries side by side with Gelineau psalms, *Our Sunday Visitor* and *Commonweal* on the same pamphlet rack. Some people read *Extension*, others the *New Republic*. Some were obsessed with the fear of Negro "immigration"; others were organizing to bring about racial integration. But there was enthusiasm. The people were active, intelligent, intensely loyal, religiously committed (at least insofar as they understood religious commitment). They were coming into money, power, positions of social and political leadership. It was probably the most favorable environment in the diocese for an energetic priest, fresh from the seminary and bristling with ideas from the new French theology.

Still, there were problems. When one's priestly training had been aimed at "cap-and-sweater" people, what did he make of country clubs and Cadillacs? How did Christian asceticism relate to these? And how was the new theology to be applied? Seven years ago at St. Angela's, nobody thought of college for their children; here, everybody did. There, aspirations to move up were few indeed; here, "making it" was an obsession. In the quiet of seven ivory-tower years a remarkable transformation had taken place in the Catholic Church of Andrew Greeley's experience.

There were more questions. European clergy writing in the Catholic press were predicting that the Americanization of the children and grandchildren of Catholic immigrants would bring about a *decline* in religious observance—to the level, say, of that in France. But there was none of that at Christ the King—just the opposite, in fact. On the other hand, *Commonweal* was insisting on greater lay participation in the Church. It was the laity's Church, too; *they* should be in positions of power. But no one was beating down the rectory door at Christ the King and demanding an expanded role in the Church. In what, then, did the religiousness of these people consist? What did their loyalty, their enthusiasm, mean?

That Greeley began to puzzle over these questions on paper he regards as ironic, one of the "tricks of the Spirit." From his seminary days on he knew he could write—he completed assignments rapidly and got good grades—but no one told him he had talent; no one encouraged him to develop his writing skills. (On the other hand no one discouraged him—the environment was as silent as the one at home.) Besides, diocesan priests, expecially young ones, were not supposed to write. If they did, their pastors and bishops said, who was going to hear confessions?

The Spirit's first trick, apparently, was to put Greeley's name in the ears of editors of two Catholic magazines for teen-agers. One of them, based in Milwaukee, was called *High Time*, and the other, situated in Chicago and edited by John Cogley, was known as *Today*. Asked to write articles of a catechetical nature, Greeley demurred and then responded with a trick of his own, submitting several under the pseudonym "Lawrence Moran."

His principal response to the challenge of suburbia's "spoiled, rich kids," however, was both more open and more ambitious. Organizing them into study groups, he exposed them to the American Church's finest thinkers, people such as Godfrey Diekman, Gustave Weigel, Sydney Callahan, and Daniel Berrigan. Greeley's confederation of student groups, drawn from parishes throughout Chicago, was known as the Student Lay Apostolate Conference (SLAC). SLAC's first study week took place in the summer of 1956 at St. Procopius College (now Illinois Benedictine College) in Lisle, Illinois, just outside Chicago. *Ave Maria* editor Donald Thorman happened to arrive early for a speaking engagement at the conference and dropped in on a talk being given by Father Greeley. Like many Catholic editors at the time, Thorman was on the lookout for new authors. He approached Greeley and asked him to write up his talk for *Ave Maria*. Greeley agreed, and Philip Scharper, a new editor at Sheed and Ward, happened to read the results. Shortly thereafter he spent an afternoon at Christ the King planning the first book of Andrew Greeley's prolific career.

Greeley's decision to write that first book was not made easily.

Writers were still suspect in the archdiocese, and he had dropped his pseudonym for the *Ave Maria* piece. But older friends in the priest-hood—men such as George Higgins, Jack Egan, and Bill Quinn—not only encouraged him to go ahead but also secured the approval of Cardinal Samuel Stritch and even convinced the chancellor of the archdiocese to write an introduction.

The book that Greeley produced for Scharper was entitled *The Church and the Suburbs* (1959). In it, he reflected on his experience at Christ the King, analyzed its suburban soul, and inquired about its spiritual possibilities. "I am fully aware that suburban Catholi-cism is impressive, that the material affluence of the suburbs repre-sents a remarkable triumph over poverty and misery," he said. But "the purpose of the book is not to pay compliments or describe happy living, but rather to ask questions and pose problems."[3]

What is suburbia? he asked. It is first of all a place to live, com-plete with climate—simple, inexpensive, crowded housing for the newlyweds just getting started; a brick home with basement and three or four bedrooms for families moving up; curving, tree-shaded streets, well-manicured lawns, a choice of house styles for middle-rung executives, engineers, insurance brokers, businessmen, and union business agents who, at the age of forty, are successful but not yet rich; and finally, the fashionable homes of the old families and top-bracket executives for the few who had the fortune or had made the extra effort to afford them. Suburbia is color TV, freezers, big hi-fis, barbecue pits, two cars in the garage—the good life. At a deeper level, it is an escape from the city, "a new humanism, an attempt to build as perfect an earthly paradise as is possible."[4]

Suburbia is affluence, Greeley said, but there's a catch; its economic security is not now but just around the corner, at the next stop, in the next development. And so suburbia is also bleeding ul-cers, nervous breakdowns, heart attacks, and tranquilizers in every medicine cabinet.

The suburbanite participates fully, frantically, in social af-fairs—in Cub Scouts, PTA, Little League, and the country club, in T-Groups, S-Groups, and C-Groups. In his quest for community is a longing for the primary group ties that industrialization in the city has weakened, and yet, tragically, community in the Promised Land appears to mean little more than conformism. If the Protestant ethic is hard at work in suburbia, so, too, is the social ethic, soliciting the residents to be well rounded, well adjusted, and well balanced. The suburbanite is buying it all—groupism, team spirit, other-directedness, togetherness. It has even become fashionable to be a nonconformist—just like everybody else.

There are three or four children in every house. If there were not, Greeley said, mothers would not feel needed and fathers would not have a refuge from the rat race of making a living. Indeed, fathers have become more and more domesticated. They are dishwashers, repairmen, recreational supervisors (in part to expiate the guilt of devoting so much time to their careers). Families are doing more and more together. The intimacy of the family is very important, even critical, yet husbands and wives, parents and children, often feel as though they are sharing a roof with strangers.

Suburbia, Greeley continued, means crowded churches (and if the church has yet to be built, it means folding chairs in an auditorium), long lines at communion rails, meetings of the Christian Family Movement, and two thousand children per parish wanting Catholic education but having no place to be educated. The move to suburbia has brought with it a religious revival, a nationwide increase in church membership that began in the late forties, the sociological evidence for which is unquestioned. What the return to religion *means*, however, is not so certain. Highbrow journals ridicule it; others speak of it as an opportunity for spiritual growth. The suburban religious revival is paradoxical and complex—St. Christopher medals in Cadillacs, the penitential ashes of Lent beside a Florida swimming pool.

For his analysis of the safe, button-down mentality of suburbia Greeley drew upon social scientists of the day—David Riesman, William Whyte, Margaret Mead, Peter Berger, Robert Lynd, John Kenneth Galbraith—and upon greats of the past—Max Weber, Emile Durkheim, Charles Horton Cooley. The influence of Will Herberg was decisive. In *Protestant, Catholic, Jew*, Herberg had written that religions in America served the function of superethnic groups, giving people a sense of location in a context of fantastic religious and cultural pluralism. *That* was it, said Greeley. *That* explained the high levels of religious observance in Beverly Hills. People sought not only meaning from their religion but also a sense of belonging. As the residents became more American they were becoming more, not less, Catholic. Social observers like Herberg were frequently cited in *The Church and the Suburbs*, much more so than spiritual or theological writers. They were never questioned or criticized, merely used as experts to open one's eyes or to drive home a point the author was bent on making. Occasionally they had to be legitimized to an audience new to them, and so Greeley pointed out that what they said had been said before by great spiritual writers.

If Greeley's diagnoses of suburbia came from a fusion of personal experience and popular social science, his prescriptions for Christian living (and prescriptions were obligatory in a book written by a Catholic priest for a Catholic audience) were drawn from traditional Catholic theology. Mortification, he advised, one of the oldest ascetical principles, could never have been more necessary than in the affluence of suburbia. The suburbanite had to become the master of his gadgets, not their slave, and the only way to do that was to deny himself some of them. Generosity was necessary, too—not merely financial generosity, but the giving of one's whole person in works of active charity or active social justice. To the dilemma of conformity versus community Greeley offered the Church's view of itself as the Mystical Body of Christ. "The Catholic Church is sympathetic to modern man's quest for community; but its idea of community is considerably different from the narrow self-contained little world of the modern conformist." The Church was not to be a place of escape but a source of strength to go forth and "transform the institutions in which men must live and work and try to save their souls." Greeley's prescriptions ranged far and wide—good taste, for example (you get closer to God on FM than AM), and intellectual curiosity ("the biggest single need of the American Church is more lay people who read").[5]

As for the young—it was the era of rock and roll, Ivy League clothes, movies like *Hot Rod Rumble* and *Juvenile Jungle*—they needed to become engaged, committed. If they did not, they would become victims of Erich Fromm's "guilt" or David Riesman's "suburban sadness." It was a point at which Greeley hammered away. Chapters of *The Church and the Suburbs* were entitled "The Young People of Suburbia—Not Exactly 'Shook Up,'" "The Waning of Enthusiasm," "Beat, Cool—and Lonely." In December of 1959 Greeley asked the readers of *America* why hero worship had become a thing of the past. Why did not Tom Dooley stir up the enthusiasm that Charles Lindbergh had in 1927? Because "we want to be left alone," he answered, "so we can enjoy our Good Life free from social responsibilities."[6] Three months later he was back in the pages of *America* (a magazine fighting contraception and communism at the time) with "No More Radicals?" Wrote Greeley, "The young people of the 1960's may drink too much and may be much more relaxed about sexual morality, but at heart they are dyed-in-the-wool conservatives."[7] They are selfish, he said, incapable of commitment to anything save beer, marriage, and having a family. Where are the poets to come from, Greeley complained, the planners, the artists, the prophets, the philosophers, the saints?

"Oh, they loved to be told they were apathetic," says Greeley of that era's youth. "Of course, the apathetic people were the ones who weren't as·excited as I was."

Assured early in his ministry that he could communicate with teen-agers, Greeley was now torn between conflicting feelings. "There was a good deal of ambivalence because these were people I liked and found attractive—and yet also maddening. They were so reluctant to move, so mired in their own parochialism. I can remember walking over to the church one Holy Thursday evening and thinking about them when suddenly I saw a book. I came back after services and wrote an outline. By Pentecost the book was off to the publishers."

He called the slim volume *Strangers in the House* (1961). In it he revealed in the souls of his docile, unimaginative teen-agers not sins but neuroses. Do they drink? The reason, he said, is to kill the pain of a bleak, ready-made future, one with no alternatives, with nothing to capture imagination, vigor, and commitment. Do they go steady (and going steady was "morally dangerous" and "socially and psychologically harmful")? They do that to prove their·success in the social marketplace and thus to establish their value as persons. Do they cheat? If so, it is because their parents think nothing of cheating, because policemen think nothing of taking bribes, because TV quiz contestants who take answers in advance (one of the scandals of the day) say that everybody's doing it—and so do Korean War prisoners who make propaganda broadcasts for the enemy.

Teen-agers are immature because their parents neurotically maneuver and manipulate them into making exactly the decisions the parents want. Despite their superficial poise and self-control, the young are not in sufficient possession of themselves. "Their emotional state is such that many of them use the confusion of their society as a means of punishing themselves for the vague but powerful guilt which torments them." Entrapped by the need to be liked, to adjust to any group in which they find themselves, they lack the personal force to exclude unwanted elements from their personality and build an identity out of the elements they truly desire. This, then, is the ultimate cause of the age of apathy: "Young Americans are apathetic because they feel that they are no one, and they are right."[8]

Like *The Church and the Suburbs, Strangers in the House* contained prescription, advice, suggestion, what to do and how to do it—less of the practical, perhaps, than much of the Catholic "spiritual writing" of the time but still, in retrospect, a great deal. Young people, for example, had to be taught the proper use of alcohol. Alcohol was a creature of God and therefore good, but its use had to be limited and restrained by periodic abstinence. For parents of steady daters Greeley advised not adamant opposition but "killing it with kindness." As for cheating, the Rx was simple: let the parents stop first. And, in general, let parents love their children for their own inherent worth as human beings and not for what they might produce. Let them guide (and even punish) their children, but let their guidance not be manipulative nor their punishment excessive.

For the young themselves Greeley asked, "Can an organization man be a saint?" It was like other questions he posed, all of them asking whether the separate worlds of his experience could be brought together. "Of course he can," was the answer—if, that is, he engaged in regular contemplation, if he made a yearly retreat and a monthly day of recollection, if he developed a *spirit* of poverty (the Cris-Craft didn't *have* to go), if he practiced personal charity. The advice came from Greeley's seminary days and its details, really, are unimportant. What matters is the hope behind them, the hope that suburbia could move in the direction of its best impulses, that it could become Christian, and (even more) that this new event in

American Catholicism—the upper-middle-class parish—could become the salt of the earth.

The promise of the Christ the Kings appearing throughout America was in its young, in its "saving remnant" (so Greeley separated the sheep from the goats). In 1960 the saving remnant were the graduates of ordinarily stupefying Catholic colleges "who have caught a glimpse of something beyond the ordinary, the mediocre, the banal. Each year a few of these search for something more and find it. They are ordinary people with ordinary talents and ordinary problems. The extraordinary thing about them is that they have refused to believe that there are no more opportunities for greatness." Curious, generous, courageous, the saving remnant has had first-hand experience of involvement in challenging and satisfying action; it has known the meaning of group spirit and enthusiasm; it has felt the power of attractive individuals who radiate the Christian vision. The saving remnant is John Martin, Mary Jo Shultz, Kevin McCarthy, Mike O'Donnell—fictitious names for real people involved in racial and poverty work, leading sections of CCD, YCS, CFM, and other Catholic action organizations. They are not yet saints, "but at least they are living proof that the twenty thousand graduates each year will never be able to plead lack of opportunity or lack of challenge as an excuse for mediocrity."[9]

Strangers in the House won accolades: a favorable judgment in the *Saturday Review* ("the first big review I ever got," Greeley says), a Thomas Alva Edison award when Greeley broadcast excerpts from it on the "Catholic Hour" radio series. The *New York Post* called it a "sensitive and compassionate work of sociology," and most of the Catholic press agreed. The Divine Word Press in Techny, Illinois, asked Greeley for some pamphlets on teen-agers, and he quickly delivered. Apparently people were interested in what he had to say. It was a time to be inspired.

Hope begets new attitudes toward progeny, gentler attitudes, more fatherly ones, the sense that one does, after all, have something of value to pass on. Greeley's burgeoning hope, his sense of fatherliness, came to express itself in the form of letters to his young parishioners. The letters—in another time they might have been called epistles—were first published as pamphlets (to date, they have sold over a million copies) and later expanded into books. *And Young Men Shall See Visions* (1964) was addressed to "John"—and to all the male members of the saving remnant. *Letters to Nancy* (1964) was addressed to a young woman of Christ the King—and to her counterparts everywhere.

And Young Men Shall See Visions found John alone in Paris for his junior year of college. It was very important that he was away from home, away from the influence of suburbia:

Dear John,

The more I think about it the more I become convinced that your journey abroad this year may be one of the most important things that has happened to you during your life. I remember when we talked about it last fall in Worcester I thought I might be in Europe at the same time and that we would drive from Paris to Rome together. But it was good for you things didn't turn out that way. The best part of your year in Europe is not meeting new people and getting to know an ancient civilization and a style of life different from your own. What is really important is that you have gotten away from the neighborhood, from your family, your crowd, your various romances, your parish . . .

What the good Lord has done for you in the last couple of years, John, is to give you your life. He gave it to you physically, of course, long before, but now He has given it to you for your very own. It is no longer—at least on the level of ideas—under the direction of your parents or your teachers or your clergy, at least in any way near the fashion it used to be. It is yours to do with as you will. It is only the beginnings of life, only the first tiny, very hesitant movings of thought and love. It will take long and diligent practice, John, before you have mastered the skills and the discipline necessary for mature thought. You will have to be wrong many times before you are so close to being right that you will be able to admit your mistakes. You will have to make many missteps and undergo considerable sacrifice and suffering before you begin to know the meaning of love. But the Lord has opened to you during these few years the possibility of growth. He has said to you, "You are a man, you can think and love if you wish; be yourself and you will grow. What is still very small and frail in you can become great and strong, so great and so strong that it will sweep the world before you. If you wish, turn away from this possibility of growth; be content with mediocrity, but do not blame Me if you are unhappy."

All of these marvelous possibilities begin to materialize at precisely your age because now you can think for yourself, form your own ideas, and be free. This is the great decision you must take before you return from Paris. Are you going to give the weak spark of freedom within you a chance to turn into a steely flame or are you going to blow it out?

God bless,[10]

In ensuing letters Greeley repeated recent Church teaching on the role of the laity. "The Church is not just the bishops and the priests and the religious; it is every follower of Christ sharing in the work of Christ. As Pope Pius XII pointed out—*you* are the Church, *you* are Christ working in the world, *you* are Christ bringing life to men and order and truth and light to the confusion which death has caused in the world." The liturgy of the Eucharist is to be the core of one's life. Without it, "social action can readily become frantic activity without depth or purpose." As for one's career—and "career" is such a concern of John's contemporaries—let it be a way of achieving excellence and so reflecting the goodness of the One who brings life. "One bears witness to Christ, as Cardinal Suhard has put it, not by engaging in propaganda but by living one's life in such a way that one would be fooled if Christ were not the Son of God."[11]

In his very first letter to John, Greeley had stressed the intellect:

Do you remember the first idea that you ever had that was really yours and not someone else's . . . At that point, when you discovered that you had the basic human faculty—the intellect—you began to emerge as a human being. I am sure you remember the thrill of discovery that followed that experience, a thrill which is still going on as the joy of intellectual discovery increases. For suddenly there was the WORLD, no longer a *given*, no longer a closed system, no longer to be summed up in a few adolescent cliches. Now it was a place of fascination and mystery, a splendid and confusing place which demanded an explanation and which was going to be compelled to stand before you so that you might pass judgment on it.[12]

Half a year later came advice on education and intellectual growth, complete with "some prejudiced suggestions" for reading. The lay apostle, Greeley wrote, has to be up-to-date theologically. He should read Karl Rahner, Hans Küng, Daniélou, de Lubac, John

Courtney Murray, John McKenzie, Roland Murphy, Bruce Vawter,
Clifford Howell, Joseph Jungmann. Sociological works are a
must—books such as *The Organization Man; The Lonely Crowd;
Street Corner Society; Protestant, Catholic, Jew; The Exploding
Metropolis; The Politics of Urban Renewal.* "Nor can you pass up
volumes on the race question, particularly *The American Dilemma, Black Metropolis, Negro Politics,* or *The Nature of Prejudice.*" The *New York Times* is essential, said Greeley. Periodicals
like the *New Republic, Atlantic, Harper's,* the *Saturday Review,* and
the *Reporter* all got his recommendation. The liberal Catholic point
of view is presented in *Commonweal, America,* and the *Catholic Reporter.* And for strictly spiritual reading, there are the works of
Hubert Van Zeller, Gerald Vann, and Thomas Merton, though "I
am somewhat prejudiced in favor of the books of my friend Daniel
Berrigan."[13]

Throughout his young friend's year in Europe, Father Greeley
urged him to faith, to patience, to anger, to the intellectual life, to
risk-taking, to independence, to the "harsh reality of choice." He
called him away from the stagnation of the lonely but powerful
crowd of Beverly Hills and to—perhaps the best summation—*freedom.* For John, freedom meant not a moratorium on the Christianity of his upbringing—a time, say, to experience other world views,
other religions—but a call to greater Christian enthusiasm:

> These are great days to be alive. The lay vocation has always
> existed in the Church but only in our time has its full meaning be-
> come clear. It is perhaps more exciting to be a Catholic today than
> for any time in the last thousand years. With the II Vatican Coun-
> cil the Popes have thrown open the window and the strong winds
> of change are blowing. You are riding the wave of the future. For
> millennia to come, people will look back on our time and say,
> "how wonderful it must have been to be alive in those days."
> God bless,[14]

In *Letters to Nancy,* Greeley passed on new looks in old theological concepts. Grace he defined as not so much the "absence of
mortal sin" or even a "supernatural gift of God" but "God calling
on us to be as thoroughly human as we can possibly be." Sin was refusing to become one's best self, because "when you turn away from
yourself, you are turning away from God." Regarding the Cross, he

wrote, "it is the work of the Christian to keep human suffering at an absolute minimum," but suffering for the purpose of perfecting human love, suffering leading to triumph—that is what is symbolized by the Cross. Poverty was "not being satisfied with superficial goals in life," devoting a bare minimum of one's time to material things because one realizes they are unimportant. Chastity was power, not weakness, disciplined power like that of the artist, "the harnessing and focusing of sex so that it will operate in the proper fashion."[15]

Greeley's strongest caveats to Nancy regarded the "marriage mania." Betty Friedan's *The Feminine Mystique* had just been published, and he recommended it to his young correspondent:

> I would like to submit that the notion that motherhood is *the* feminine role is nonsense and is in fact dangerously close to heresy. . . . You can be fully a woman before you are married (indeed, you better be or you won't be much of a wife) and fully a woman if you should lose your husband. You can be happy before you have children, or after your children are dead, or even if you cannot have children. You can survive and you can survive very happily without husband and children and you can survive as a happy *woman*. You need not be afraid that you will feel useless or unfulfilled or unloved or unlovely.[16]

He was not opposed to matrimony or parenthood, Greeley explained, merely to the way these are approached in our society. He was especially embittered by the fact that the marriage mania had called so many promising young women from the vision.

Greeley had other names for the same sin: the family heresy, the housewife heresy, the good parent heresy. Girls in particular, he said, are prone to it. It would not be easy, he said, for Nancy to resist the temptations that would increase over the next few years. Great love *would* come to her life, said Greeley, but, he advised, "do not push, do not hunt it down relentlessly, do not compulsively look for it with every boy you meet. . . . Look not for weakness you can mother nor for force which will overpower your identity. Look rather for strength which will match your strength, for maturity which will supplement your maturity, for vision which corresponds to your vision." Sex is not something to be exploited (much less something to be ashamed of); it is a resource to strengthen and deepen the personality, giving a girl in particular the vigor to make sustained sacrifices for the one she loves. "Our Vision demands that we give; sex teaches us how to give."[17] Because sex is so powerful, however, it needs control, the discipline of a poet, a ballet dancer, or a great painter. That is why the traditional Judeo-Christian standards of premarital chastity are so important.

"Intelligence in a woman—what a fascinating subject." Girls get better marks in school than boys, said Greeley, but they try to cover their intelligence so they will not threaten fathers, brothers, suitors, husbands, teachers. They take copious notes in the lecture hall and study hard for tests but do not ask tough, critical questions. Greeley urged Nancy to be intellectually alive, though he wrote, "I do not really think I need urge this on one whose mind is as keen as yours." Our spiritual life *is* our intellectual life. "The intellect is the spark of the divine in us and when it seeks its object—Truth—it is also seeking Him who is Truth. . . . God can be in contact, through special grace, with a non-intellectual, but it is difficult, indeed, for Him to be in contact with an anti-intellectual, with one who denies the importance of that very faculty which distinguishes man from the beast." Because, in our culture, the intelligence of women seems to concentrate on the practical and the concrete and that of men on the theoretical and abstract, "I would think that the purpose of educating a girl is in part to add a masculine element to her thought processes, just as the purpose of educating a boy is, in part, to add a feminine element to his thought processes."[18]

At the end of the school year Greeley closed his correspondence with Nancy as he did with John. It was a great era in the Church, the best in nineteen hundred years.

> Enough. There is just so much your friends can do for you or say to you. Your decisions or series of decisions in the next few months are going to have to be made alone—in the chill loneliness that each soul must endure when it is locked with its God in the awful moments when its destiny is determined. Your own restless temperament which makes your longings for the Absolute more powerful will both drive you to a decision and make the decision more agonizing. During these moments there is very little we can do; watch, wait, if need be, listen, pray. What will happen? None of us knows for sure, but, appearances to the contrary, I am an incurable optimist.
>
> God bless,[19]

Never again would such fatherliness flow from the pen of Andrew Greeley, but then never again would he exude such hope. *Letters to Nancy*, a book that was stimulated by Greeley's friendship with feminist Alice Rossi, won the Catholic Press Award in 1965 as the best book of the year for young people.

In these early works Greeley's intellect was in the service of his pastorate. He thought of himself as a parish priest, not a writer, an academic, or a scholar. He wished to explain to his people (it turned out that his readers were mainly priests and nuns) the stuff of sociology and theology, to make it clear to them, to tell them what difference it ought to make in their lives, to tell them—since they always asked—what to do. Greeley called *And Young Men Shall See Visions* "middle-range spirituality," existing somewhere between the general principles of ascetic theology and the grassroots experience of people living in parishes, parts of the book "little more than a watered-down version of my dimly remembered ascetics course in the seminary."[20]

An expression can be found in these books, an aphorism of the times, one that did not look to the past as much as it opened up a future. "Grace builds on nature and nature prepares the way for grace," it read.[21] Though not of recent coinage, the words resonated with new theological overtones that had reached Greeley in his later seminary years. It meant the Spirit was no longer at war with the flesh, the church-in-here at odds with the world-out-there. The world and the flesh were "nature," not evils to be dominated, infidels to be converted, but the soil into which God poured His grace. One's task, therefore, was to prepare nature for the action of God— to see, for example, to the basic economic security of people before one spoke to them of salvation. Another expression, cited by Greeley in an article that antedated *The Church and the Suburbs*, revealed the same spirit: "The majors of our syllogisms might come from a papal encyclical, but the minors have to be supplied by realistic economics and sociology."[22]

One needed experts, then, in the "natural" or the "temporal" order. Experts were the Catholic laity in general but also professionals, Catholic and non-Catholic, in sciences like sociology. "To describe what sociology does in terms which are relevant to theology we could say that sociology studies the natural social base on

which grace and supernature must build"—that was for a symposium on "New Horizons in Catholic Thought" in the summer of
1962.[23] What was exciting in this new outlook was the belief (which
was really more of a hope) that, if each were fully understood, grace
did not contradict nature; the two were in harmony. Thus what sociology discovered as true about man could not conflict with Catholic
doctrine. As Greeley wrote in 1964, "We know that grace does not
destroy nature and so if a seemingly Christian insight is contrary to
a valid natural insight—then it is not really Christian."[24] What's
more, Catholic doctrine could speak to many of the temporal order
dilemmas of which sociologists spoke (such as that of conformism
versus community) and bring to it a solution (such as the concept of
the Mystical Body). Sociological in tone, Greeley's first books nevertheless carried the *nihil obstat* and *imprimatur*, ecclesiastical guar-
antees that they were free of moral or doctrinal error.

All his expectations in these, the best of times, reached a peak in
an article that appeared in *America* on May 23, 1964. The piece,
called "A New Breed," was one of those rare instances of perfect
timing. "I doubt," he wrote two years later, "if anything I have ever
written has created quite this volume of reaction."[25] No data were
used in the article, but none were needed, for the description itself,
naked as it was, had the power of persuasion. A month after its appearance *America* devoted the cover and substance of an issue to the
comments of readers. Ninety-five percent were favorable; 100 percent agreed with the portrait drawn. People felt understood for the
first time. A few thought Greeley had created a monster. Soon thereafter the article became a pamphlet and its title a catchword, a
slogan, a cliche. Readers took hope, a result that bears testimony to
the power of a name.

> There has risen up a New Breed that was all but invisible five years
> ago. There are not very many of them; they might not show up in
> any sample; the majority of their classmates in the colleges, the
> seminaries, the juniorates of the country continue to be listless and
> indifferent. But the New Breed is making so much noise that one
> hardly has time to notice the majority. Almost any college presi-
> dent or seminary rector will admit their existence and will confess
> puzzlement about what they want.[26]

The major impression Greeley had of the New Breed was their concern for honesty, integrity, and authenticity. Those in the semi-naries—and particularly the young Jesuits—suddenly wanted to sit down and discuss the reasons for an order before they obeyed. Their honesty, however, was a two-edged sword; it also brought a total lack of tact, patience, and diplomacy. "Truth must be spoken even if speaking it does no good and may even cause harm. To do less would be to debase one's authenticity. . . . They seem to feel that the mere repetition of what they take to be true will eventually carry the day."[27]

The New Breed is intensely worried about personal fulfill-ment, Greeley went on. "They feel that they can help others only if they can relate as persons and that they cannot relate unless there is a possibility of 'fulfillment' in the relationship." They are uncertain about their ability to love. "They have no doubt that they can be sexually stimulated, but they are not sure that they can be 'friends,' that they can 'encounter' a sexual partner or anyone else."[28]

Because they want to be liked, because they are wedded to no ideology, they are not radicals, not the Catholic equivalent of the New Left. They work for civil rights, enter the Peace Corps, the Papal Volunteers for Latin America, and the Extension home missions and even, on occasion, throw up picket lines, but they are not active in militant civil rights groups or the peace movement. They are interested in politics, but their approach is pragmatic rather then ideological. Above all, "The New Breed wants to help people and wants to be loved by them." They say, "We're getting more out of it than the people we are supposed to be helping."[29]

They are not, for all that, naive do-gooders. Once they have de-cided on a course of action they proceed with a cool competence that is anything but amateurish. They know how to handle committees, write brochures, give speeches, raise money, and issue press releases. Indeed, CALM (Chicago Area Lay Movement) "managed to get stories into the newspapers about its work *before it had begun to work*—which is surely the height of something or other . . . . Grace Ann Carroll, the cofounder of CALM, spoke for most of the New Breed when she said, 'Before we're finished, we're going to think up a lot more things to do, so that everyone who wants, no matter what their age or responsibilities, can get involved.' " The New Breed proceeds with the supreme confidence "that they will live to bury those who stand in their way."[30]

Since everything is a matter of principle to them, changes cannot be put off until tomorrow. They may mellow in this regard, especially if they see progress, said Greeley, but don't count on it. Whatever the case, do not expect them to leave the Church; they have been told they are the Church so often that they actually believe it, and, if they are restless with the organization, it is the restlessness one has toward the fair bride he loves.

The prophet of the New Breed is Teilhard de Chardin, its patron saint John Kennedy. The latter's "youthfulness, his pragmatism, his restlessness, his desire for challenge and service, his vision of a new freedom, reflected in so many ways what the New Breed wants to be."[31]

The New Breed is a puzzling lot, Greeley concluded, self-confident yet anxious, organizationally efficient but ignorant of diplomacy, eager to engage in dialogue but often inarticulate, generous with the poor and suffering yet terribly harsh in their judgments of elders and superiors:

> It should be clear that I am ambivalent about the New Breed. I am fascinated by them and I admire their courage; yet they frighten me. In another quarter of a century they will be taking over the American Church. . . . I don't know quite what their Church will look like and I wonder how much room there will be in it for someone like me. The New Breed has reason to be confident. Everything is on their side—their youth, time, the wave of history, and, one suspects, the Holy Spirit.[32]

Yes, the Spirit was alive in those days. From a listless generation sprouted new bearers of the vision. The life of this young curate knew frustration, anger, and depression, but it was all *for something*, it was *going somewhere*; and if there were thorny problems, he had the drive to seize them by their roots and dispose of them. During his years of youth work Father Greeley began and completed a doctoral program at the University of Chicago and published his first effort in empirical sociology. And the marvelous thing was that they all seemed to fit—work with youth and intellectual curiosity, theology and sociology, Christ the King and the University of Chicago, the spiritual and the temporal, grace and nature.

The country and the Church, too, were brightened by a spring-time. Freedom rides and lunchroom sit-ins bore witness to the conscience of a nation quickening to centuries of racial injustice. Russian satellites scored their trails in the darkness about the earth, and in response *we* were going to put a man on the moon. Money was pouring into the sciences, and a good deal found its way into the sciences of man. There were new leaders, new theology, a new Council, new grassroots organizations. In the Church, seminaries were full and growing but still could not meet the demand for priests; schools were bursting at the seams; publishing houses were booming. Whatever its meaning, there *was* a suburban religious revival and the promise of a new spirituality.

And a solitary priest commuted from a local parish to a neighboring school, living the rapprochement between church and university, between religion and science. His God told him to go forth, to send others forth, into a land that was no longer hostile but open and receptive. He was to bring out the best in that world and (the same thing, really) to restore it in Christ. His journey was a seed; all of these events were seeds. They brought the promise of life, yet carried, as a secret all their own, the unrelenting mechanism of future death.

3

Where Are the Catholic Intellectuals?

In the mid-fifties, when American intellectuals were bemoaning their image as eggheads, John Tracy Ellis, a Church historian at Catholic University, caught the spirit of the times and decried the pitiful contribution of the Catholic Church to American intellectual life. In an article for the Fordham University Quarterly *Thought* (Autumn 1955), he marshalled data to support an observation made over a decade earlier by Denis Brogan, a professor of political science at Cambridge University, that "in no Western society is the intellectual prestige of Catholicism lower than in the country where, in such respects as wealth, numbers, and strength of organization, it is so powerful."[1] Though part of the explanation for the failure of the American Church to produce went back as far as the original English settlers and their virulent anti-Catholicism, the chief blame, Monsignor Ellis contended, lay with Catholics themselves and "their frequently self-imposed ghetto mentality."[2]

His sober essay released a torrent of commentary in the Catholic media, some of it adopting his self-critical stance and arguing it more forcibly, some of it denying the problem altogether. Those in Ellis's camp maintained that the authoritarianism of American Catholicism inhibited the development of scientific curiosity, that the clergy dominated American Catholic life and steered the "smart boys" into the priesthood instead of scholarly careers, that Catholic emphasis on the other world led to a neglect of this-worldly scientific research, that, indeed, Catholics *feared* scientific knowledge and the whole "liberal" aura of the intellectual life. In Catholic thinking, Thomas O'Dea argued, the intellect was subordinated to a "more holistic orientation of man towards God"[3] or simply to "obedience." Catholics suffered from "formalism," "moralism," "indoctrination," "control." Some of the self-critics took note of the immigrant status of Catholic groups and asked in a sympathetic vein how one could think of the intellectual life when he was trying to survive in a strange country. But the principal target of the in-house Catholic critics, and it was hit time and again, was the "defensive mentality of the ghetto," brought on perhaps (but only perhaps) by the experience of immigration. It dictated loyalty above all and smothered the voices of criticism as so many threats to existence. How could the intellectual life flourish in such a restrictive environment? Hard questions were asked and harsh judgments pronounced, and it was all done with a vengeance.

The works of Ellis and O'Dea, along with an essay by Gustave Weigel, had been commissioned by William Rooney, a Chicago priest on the faculty of Catholic University, in his role as secretary of the Catholic Commission on Intellectual and Cultural Affairs. Father Greeley had been at Christ the King for little more than a year when Ellis's critique (which was the first) made its appearance, and it had an immediate impact on him—upon his work with youth (SLAC was geared to the intellectual life of its participants), upon his books about suburbia, upon his letters of inspiration to John and Nancy. But it never occurred to Greeley that he himself might fill the void at which the critics were so appalled. The Church needed trained scholars and Greeley *was* thinking of graduate school, but only at the urging of Fathers Quinn and Egan, who wanted someone to acquire the practical skills that would make Cana, CFM, and other action programs more effective.

Quinn and Egan urged Cardinal Stritch to send Greeley to graduate school, but their efforts were in vain. The archdiocese believed there was a shortage of priests; ideas, scholarship, and graduate training were fine ideas, but they were luxuries to be indulged in only in an era when personnel were abundant.

When Stritch died in 1958, Albert Meyer came to Chicago as archbishop. Meyer shocked Greeley by calling him in and saying he liked what he had written. In the future, Meyer said, keep me informed of what you are writing, not because I want to censor it, but because I want to be prepared for repercussions. Of that simple meeting, of that simple, unsolicited show of support, Greeley says emphatically, "It was *decisive* in my life."

When Greeley returned to the archbishop's office with the galleys of *Strangers in the House*, Meyer looked them over and said he would be sure to read the book. Then he added, "Is there anything I can do to help you?" Greeley saw his opportunity and broached the question of graduate training.

"Oh," the archbishop said, "that's a good idea. You're probably going to do more of this and you should get the professional skills. But we're just so short of priests here—could you continue with Christ the King too?"

"If you clear it with the pastor," Greeley replied.

"Well, you could go to Loyola, then."

"Or Chicago."

"Yes, that's closer to you, isn't it?"

That's closer to you. Greeley remembers that phrase with astonishment. For thirty years no priest of the archdiocese had been permitted even to think of attending classes at the University of Chicago. It was an evil, pagan place—"Moscow Tech." And now a long period of estrangement would end because an archbishop with a deep respect for knowledge made the very practical observation that Chicago was closer.

So Andrew Greeley began the double life of curate and graduate student while he set about to obtain a master's degree in sociology. He still thought he was learning skills that would make him a more effective parish priest. He began his program in September 1960 and found the first few months "absolutely befuddling." He had not seen a mathematics text in seventeen years and, although he seemed to follow his professors, he could not fathom his fellow students. "These kids seemed so bright—I didn't understand what they were talking about." An *A* on a midterm exam turned things around for him. "I felt great that day. I said, 'I've got this place cased.'" One of his professors, James Davis ("the best teacher I ever had"), offered him a job at the National Opinion Research Center, but Greeley turned him down because he was in a hurry to finish. In June 1961 his M.A. was completed, his thesis an examination of golf partnerships at "Westwood" (in actuality it was Beverly Hills) Country Club. Though Protestants and Catholics were "integrated" at the club, he wrote, Catholics from "St. Praxides" (Christ the King) chose fellow parishioners as golf partners seven times

more frequently than they would have had there been no seg-
regation on the fairways (and everyone insisted there was none).
Friendship ties were clearly cut along religious-ethnic lines. Will
Herberg's model was alive and well in the community of
"Westwood."

Half a year into his program Greeley discovered that Meyer
would give him the green light—and the tuition—for a Ph.D. In the
back of the archbishop's mind was a diocesan office for planning
and research, and he was grooming Greeley to run it. The prospect
of sociological research for the archdiocese, combined with parish
work, could not have pleased Greeley more.

So his thoughts turned to doctoral research, and he recalled the
study that Davis was undertaking at NORC—a study of the career
plans of the June 1961 college graduates. This was an excellent opportunity, thought Greeley, to obtain data on the very things of
which Ellis and O'Dea had written. He approached Davis and
NORC director Peter Rossi and asked whether they needed someone to analyze the impact of religion on career choice. Specifically,
were Catholics failing to choose academic careers as the self-critics
had charged? Davis and Rossi offered to hire Greeley, but he replied, "Don't pay me. Just let me analyze the data."

When Greeley joined the project, the completed questionnaires
were just beginning to trickle in. As the bulk of them arrived over
the ensuing months, Greeley reviewed the available literature on
Catholics and anti-intellectual values.

There was not *that* much evidence, he found—at least since
World War II—to substantiate the claims of the self-critics. The best
was a two-volume study of the origins of scientists and scholars co-
authored by Robert H. Knapp.[4] In it he reported that Catholic colleges were far below average in the proportion of future scientists
they graduated, even though science was the field of their strongest
contribution. The overall pattern discovered by Knapp, and it was
known to Ellis, was that Catholic colleges were "exceptionally un-
productive in all areas of scholarship."[5]

In 1958, three years after the Ellis article, a study of the Detroit
area by Gerhard Lenski revealed that its Catholics were more "anti-
scientific" than its Protestants. In addition, they scored lower than
Protestants on questionnaire items indicative of "economic ration-

ality." To the surprise of many sociologists, the Protestant ethic was alive and well in the Motor City, and the Catholic ethic—which, according to Lenski, valued obedience above intellectual autonomy and put the family and kin group above other relations—was continuing to work at conscious and subconscious levels to inhibit the development of scientific careers.[6]

While Knapp's data referred to graduates before 1950 and Lenski's concerned itself with the Detroit area alone, they carried a great deal of weight, for there were simply no other data in existence that contradicted them.

It was with the expectation that more of the same would turn up that Greeley drew up a set of hypotheses about the 1961 graduates of the nation's colleges. If the intellectual life of American Catholics was at the low point its critics insisted it was, then a number of predictions could be made, principally (1) that fewer Catholics than non-Catholics would *be* in college and graduating in 1961, (2) that fewer Catholic graduates would be planning to attend graduate school, (3) that those Catholics planning to attend graduate school would steer away from the arts and sciences, and especially from the physical sciences, and (4) that those Catholics who, in spite of everything, headed for the arts and sciences, would be "less Catholic" than other Catholic graduates and on the verge of abandoning their faith.

In May and June 1961 over 33,000 seniors from 135 colleges across the country spent half an hour responding to NORC Survey 431. One has to remember that this was *not* a study of intellectuals or scholars and so could not address itself to some of the contentions of the self-critics. It did, however, sample the graduating seniors at 135 representative schools. It is hard to imagine more forward-looking (and therefore more tenuous) data. The data were about twenty-one-year-olds, about their hopes, their dreams, their aspirations, what they *planned* to do rather than what they actually had accomplished. But then a good deal of what the Catholic self-critics had to say was about precisely that—the hopes, dreams, and aspirations the Church instilled in its young.

One morning in the fall of 1961 Greeley drove over to NORC to pick up the first tables that had been compiled from the completed data. When he arrived he found that Davis had written something across the top of the first page: "It looks like Notre Dame beats Southern Methodist this year." It did not take Greeley long to flip through the printout pages and discover what Davis had meant.

Were Catholics underrepresented in the nation's colleges? Apparently not. The 1957 census put Catholics in the country at 25.7 percent of the population, and Catholics constituted 25 percent of the June 1961 graduates. Were Catholics less likely to plan to attend graduate school? Thirty-four percent—compared with 28 percent of the Protestants and 47 percent of the Jews (who were 8 percent of the graduates)—were to begin graduate training in the fall. Were the Catholics who planned to attend graduate school avoiding the arts and sciences? Clearly not. Forty-six percent of them—compared with 43 percent of the prospective Protestant and 39 percent of the prospective Jewish graduate students—were choosing these fields of specialization. And what, in particular, of the physical sciences? The answer was the same. Looking at enrollees in arts and sciences, only a statistical hairsbreadth separated the proportions of the two religious groups entering the physical sciences. Finally, were there signs that potential Catholic scholars in the arts and sciences were "less Catholic" than other Catholic graduates? If there were hints of future apostasy, they were only the vaguest. While potential Catholic scholars did attend church somewhat less regularly than other Catholic graduates, and while 2 percent more of them were already apostates, the future Catholic scholars were astonishingly loyal to their faith.

Page after page, ream after ream of printout filled in the details of the same story. Catholic graduates, looking to the future, saw themselves in scientific, intellectual roles and at the same time saw themselves as Catholics. Nor did the story break down or show even the slightest crack when a host of controls was brought to bear on the findings. The results could not be explained away when sex, hometown size, socioeconomic status, income, parents' education, and a variety of other background variables were taken into account, nor when Protestant graduates were examined denomination by denomination. It did not matter whether the Catholics came from Catholic or secular campuses—in fact, the Catholics from Catholic schools were more "intellectual" and "Protestant" than Catholics from non-Catholic schools. If one looked at measures

other than future career plans, Catholic graduates were still as intellectually oriented as the rest of the sample. They expressed as much
interest in the science and math courses they had taken as under-
graduates, and they were as Protestant as the Protestants in their
reasons for choosing an occupation. The findings regarding the
anti-intellectual and anti-scientific hypotheses were entirely negative. Catholic seniors were indistinguishable from the great American mean, "no more anti-intellectual than anyone else."[7]

It was a rude but pleasant surprise. To a man concerned about
the development of a Catholic intelligentsia, here was hope that the
intelligentsia was on its way. Either things had happened in the past
decade that the critics were not attuned to, or indeed the critics had
been remarkably effective in the span of five years. Whatever the
case, this was good news, welcome positive reinforcement during a
time of collective self-punishment.

Greeley reflects on the discovery as "an immense experience. At
that moment you and you alone know something that no one else in
the world knows." It taught him the importance of *data*—those
simple statistics said more about social change than anything he had
witnessed in his move from St. Angela's to Christ the King. Says he,
"I sensed changes in the Church at Christ the King, but I didn't
know they were happening that rapidly or that dramatically."

With time, the data were analyzed more carefully, and a theory
of what had happened emerged. An apparently minor detail provided a clue: It was the brightest students at Catholic colleges who
reported the most faculty influence on career plans, whereas at secular colleges the situation was reversed—the least gifted had reported
the most faculty influence. Davis provided an interpretation of that
fact: Schools wanting to improve their status concentrate on their
best students, trying to steer them into prestigious graduate schools,
while schools secure in their status focus on less gifted students on
the premise that these are the ones most in need of assistance.
Alumni with Ph.D.'s are status symbols to be collected by schools on
the upgrade, and it was apparent that the Catholic colleges wanted
to corner a goodly share of the symbols. There were strong suggestions in the data that the cries of the self-critics had not been
wasted on Catholic schools and that those schools were recruiting
their most gifted students for academic careers.

On a larger scale the class of 1961 may have represented a milestone in the Catholic acculturation process, indicating that the immigrant trauma was over at last. Catholic immigrants apparently had taken care of first things first, establishing a secure financial and political base and leaving it to their progeny to "prove themselves" in intellectual matters. Perhaps it was World War II and the GI Bill that turned the tide. Certainly the efforts of the self-critics and the resultant recruiting by teachers and counselors at Catholic colleges hastened the process of turning Catholics to scholarly careers.

Yes, the data represented good news, and their interpretation was fascinating, but it was all too good to be true—or, rather, too good *to be perceived* as being true.

Greeley wrote up his results quickly. In June 1962, twenty months after he began his graduate program, his dissertation was completed and his Ph.D. in hand. When Peter Rossi extended to him an offer to stay on at NORC, Greeley had to check first with his archbishop. Meyer said it was a fine idea; Greeley would get more training and it would reflect favorably on the Church. Greeley's pastor at Christ the King thought otherwise—what good was it to him to have someone who was an assistant in name only? But Meyer prevailed and Greeley accepted the offer, specifying that his salary would be for a half-time position.

Greeley asked Philip Scharper if Sheed and Ward would be interested in publishing his dissertation. (Greeley was, at this time, beginning work on *And Young Men Shall See Visions* and *Letters to Nancy*.) Scharper said they would—they wouldn't make any money on the book, but it was important that it be published. Greeley's findings on the anti-intellectualism hypothesis appeared in 1963 under the title *Religion and Career*.

When the book came out sociologists began to pick at it. Gerhard Lenski, who had argued the opposite side in *The Religious Factor*, had doubts about the adequacy of the sample, saying it was unwittingly stacked with students from the better Catholic schools. Controls were inadequate, he said, other research on Catholic anti-intellectualism was ignored—and, besides, if this was a study of potential intellectual leaders, why did it not focus on the portion of the class from which those leaders were most likely to come—that is, "the brightest and best trained males"? Catholic graduates received National Science Foundation, Woodrow Wilson, and other national awards at only *half* the national rate. Did this portend the preeminence that Greeley saw on the horizon? Another reviewer asked whether Catholic graduates were being accepted at *quality* graduate schools. After all, the data did not distinguish between seniors hoping to complete ten graduate hours in education at a local Catholic university and those envisaging a Ph.D. in nuclear physics from Harvard. Other lines of questioning should have been pursued in the survey. More data were needed. They had to be analyzed more carefully. *Relevant* comparisons had to be made if the charges of Catholic anti-intellectualism were to be dismissed definitively.

But the real hostility was to come from Catholic audiences. Greeley wrote about one meeting of Catholic educators in which he and several NORC colleagues presented the survey results:

> The reaction from the floor of the meeting was violent. It was perfectly clear to our listeners that their colleges had to be inferior; the very thought they were average was quite intolerable. Finally, one questioner exploded, "You people just don't know all the anti-intellectual deans that we have to put up with." My colleague, Peter Rossi, leaned over and whispered in my ear, "What the hell makes him think he has a monopoly on anti-intellectual deans?"[8]

A decade later Greeley told me that people just would not *believe* the data. Greeley was an optimist, critics said: he wanted to be a bishop. They simply would not acknowledge the promise spelled out in his statistics. "The very hostile reaction to that book in the national Catholic liberal community was a real surprise, and a blow, and a disillusionment to me," says Greeley. "I think John Ellis has never forgiven me for our findings."

A principal contention of those who resisted the data was that the results were only the self-projections of graduating seniors. As George Shuster said in *Commonweal*, "not every rosy-fingered dawn blossoms out into a bright day."[9] John Donovan observed in the same journal that Greeley could talk only about the intellectuals Catholics *might* have some day in the distant future, not about intellectuals they had *now*. And besides, "Father Greeley's empiricist concern with the hard facts of computer sociology barely conceals its own modest anti-intellectualism"[10]

Donovan's charge of anti-intellectualism aside, there was a point here. Would the aspirations of these intelligent-but-not-yet-intellectual graduates stand the test of time? Fortunately, there was enough government and private foundation interest in the class of 1961 at large for the answer to come forth. In June 1962, a year after graduation, a second questionnaire was sent to the original respondents. Of those who said they were going to graduate school the autumn after graduation, 80 percent of the Catholics, 81 percent of the Protestants, and 87 percent of the Jews had actually done so. Catholics were in arts and sciences programs at the *top twelve* graduate schools in the same proportion as Protestants (though both groups trailed Jews). Of all the 1961 graduates, 21 percent of the Catholics, compared with 22 percent of the Protestants and 24 percent of the Jews, affirmed their intention of getting a Ph.D. Apparently Catholics in graduate school were not just getting ten hours of education credits at the local Catholic college. Nor were they finding their religion incompatible with graduate school life. At the end of a year there was only a meager drop in the percentage of those identifying themselves as Catholic and attending church weekly, and the situation at the top twelve schools was no different from that at graduate schools in general.

In 1963 and again in 1964 the class of 1961 was surveyed with no modification in the basic findings. Protestants and Catholics were very much alike in their graduate school experience, though both were still less oriented toward Ph.D.'s than were Jews. Catholics were just as successful in graduate school, including the very best schools, as were Jews and Protestants. And Catholics *from Catholic schools* (alleged bastions of anti-intellectualism) were closer to receiving their Ph.D.'s than Catholics from secular schools. Their allegiance to Catholicism, in the meantime, had changed very little. At the top twelve universities 98 percent of the graduates of Catholic colleges professed the same religion they did in 1961 (this compared with 54 percent of the Catholic graduates of non-Catholic institutions). In addition, an *independent* NORC sampling of June 1964 graduates found nothing that failed to confirm the conclusion of *Religion and Career*. Lenski's doubts about sampling variation could now be laid to rest.

Data from an altogether different source—a survey of scientists in 1960—confirmed both the picture drawn by the self-critics (respondents from parochial schools *were* underrepresented among scientists) and the change predicted by Greeley (parochial school graduates were underrepresented because they *took longer* to secure their highest degree; among the *youngest* scientists, parochial school attendance showed no inhibiting effect). And in 1968, when the 1961 graduates were tapped for a fifth time, their story had not changed: 4.3 percent of the Catholic college alumni (and 5.8 percent of those whose education through college was exclusively Catholic)—in contrast to the national average of 3.9 percent—had received the doctoral degree. Pages of the *American Journal of Sociology*, the *American Sociological Review*, the *Journal for the Scientific Study of Religion*, the *Journal of Higher Education*, the *American Catholic Sociological Review*, and its offspring *Sociological Analysis* were peppered with notes, communications, letters, and articles to this effect.

In reporting his data in the Catholic press Greeley came to refer to the "breast-beating," the "self-flagellation," the "mass masochism" of the critics who would not accept the implications of his findings. They were reveling in an "orgy of self-criticism," those Manhattan Catholics standing in awe of the prestigious Eastern universities, dazzled by European Catholicism. He would never budge from that perception. In a 1967 volume and again in 1969 he spoke of a massive "inferiority complex, . . . one of the grave weaknesses of East Coast Catholicism . . . so very powerful in the American Church."[11] And while he did what he could to beat down the masochism of the self-critics, they proceeded on, describing their efforts as "a process of intellectual fermentation," "a valuable service," "a spur to reform."[12]

Greeley also applied his findings to secular sociology, picking this time on the prima donna of sociological theories—the Protestant ethic hypothesis. Created by Max Weber at the turn of the century to interpret the rise of capitalism several centuries earlier, this theory was still revered enough to be called upon to explain economic achievement in mid-twentieth-century America. The hypothesis had many variants, but its basic tenet was that Protestants were more economically ambitious than Catholics because of their different theological and political orientation. As summarized by R. W.

Mack, R. J. Murphy, and S. Yellin in the *American Sociological Review*:

> The Catholic ethic propounded a culturally established emphasis
> on otherworldliness; the rationale for the performance of earthly
> tasks was otherworldly: reparation for sins and purification
> through humility. Luther and Calvin sanctified work; they made
> virtues of industry, thrift and self-denial. Wesley preached that the
> fruits of labor were the signs of salvation. The culmination of the
> Protestant Reformation, then, was to give divine sanction to the
> drive to excel."[13]

In a paper presented at a meeting of Catholic sociologists—and
later published in an issue of *Sociological Analysis* honoring Max
Weber—Greeley asked that the hypothesis be given a decent burial.[14]
Why should it be allowed to live—more than that, to inseminate research—when eight separate studies in the past decade had failed to
confirm it? Take the work of Mack, Murphy, and Yellin. Using a
nonrandom sample of 2,205 white males in three white-collar professions, the authors found no differences in the social mobility patterns or aspiration levels of Protestant and Catholic respondents. Or
take the work of Joseph Veroff, Sheila Feld, and Gerald Gurin. They
employed TAT tests with a representative national sample and
found that Protestants lagged behind Jews *and* Catholics in mani-
festing a need to achieve. The least Protestant of the respondents,
it turned out, were the Protestants themselves.[15]

If the facts indicate that the hypothesis is over the hill, why do
sociologists disagree? Ignorance of the pluralistic nature of Catholicism is one reason. Wrote Greeley, "David McClelland states, as
though he had just discovered it, that Catholicism is a congeries of
subcultures; but, of course, one feels like saying, this ought to have
been obvious to everyone . . . Sociologists still think that if they
find one manual that says, for example, that Catholics ought not to
be interested in worldly gain, they have uncovered the official
Catholic position as well as the practical orientation of most 'good'
Catholics. When someone tells them this is not so, they feel that the
rules of the game have been violated." In particular there is an in-
carnational, humanistic, "Christ in culture" orientation, long a part
of Catholicism—springing in fact from the same humanistic ration-

alism that produced the Calvinistic ethic—that supports worldly striving. "Indeed the rationalization of human striving attributed to the Calvinists can with equal justice be attributed to the Jesuits. Ignatius of Loyola was the last of the Calvinists (or the first of the Methodists)." Sociologists, however, are quite unaware of it all. "The blunt fact is that most sociologists are uninformed about Catholicism and hence when they try to summarize what they take to be Catholic theology or practice end up with distorted cliches and caricatures which become truth if they are repeated often enough."[16]

The Protestant ethic mythology lingers on, too, because of a misunderstanding of Max Weber. Just before he died, Weber wrote another introduction to *The Protestant Ethic and the Spirit of Capitalism*, and in it he bent over backward to insist that he did not claim that Protestantism "caused" capitalism. In fact, having spent a number of years in the study of Eastern religions, he now felt that it was the rationalizing tendency of the West, a tendency antedating the Protestant Reformation by several millennia, that, as much as anything else, explained the rise of capitalism. Protestantism and capitalism were related, to be sure, not because one led to the other, but because both sprang from a common source. And, Greeley added, there is a strong rationalist tradition in Catholicism that is as much a manifestation of the occidental spirit as are Protestantism and capitalism.

If the data were used to lay to rest at one and the same time the Protestant ethic and the Catholic anti-intellectualism hypotheses (and few people were reading the obituary in those days) they were also a harbinger of future development. A constant complaint of Greeley was that no one, especially Lenski, bothered to look at obvious ethnic differences within the Catholic population. And these differences were telling. Immigrant groups, such as Italians and Eastern Europeans, that came in later waves no doubt experienced slower acculturation than those—like the Irish, Germans, and British—who came earlier. Hence they would be less inclined to plan college attendance and academic careers or to be oriented toward economic achievement.

But no one seemed to be interested in ethnicity. In the first NORC wave of questionnaires to the 1961 seniors, not one ethnic question was asked. Sociologists went right on accepting the melting pot theory—along with the Protestant ethic and Catholic anti-intellectualism theories—and it was their loss. Wrote Greeley:

> If sociologists do not soon put aside the outmoded melting pot assumption and return to the study of what is *happening* to the ethnic groups, then what may well be the most significant sociological experience that has gone on in America—or indeed anywhere anytime—will be forever beyond our comprehension.[17]

By intent or not, Greeley had now assumed the role of the empiricist in possession of the fact that could be used to burst the bubbles of contemporary wisdom. "This is . . . perhaps the most delightful thing that sociology can do—debunk myths," he said in the summer of 1962. "Make fun of statistics if you will, but there is no surer way of cutting through the accumulated nonsense of the conventional wisdom than a modest statistical table."[18] Was he an antitheoretical empiricist, because of his "concern with the hard facts of computer sociology?" In the closing lines of his paper calling for a moratorium on the Protestant ethic hypothesis, Greeley lamented that:

> . . . instead of plunging into research that will enable us to fashion new theory, we turn to the past and obtain antecedent theory from the few people who seem to have fashioned it for the sociology of religion—which is to say Max Weber, Emile Durkheim, and Ernst Troeltsch. Even when the categories which these men devised have ceased to be fruitful in research projects, we continue to use them because they are "theory" and "theory" we must have.[19]

Real theory, not Parsonian intellectual exercise, generates testable hypotheses, predicts or fails to predict variance. It can be confronted with reality, quantified reality. "The only numbers in Peter Berger's work," he once complained of a fellow sociologist, "are the page numbers."

If the early NORC years drew Greeley into the role of an empiricist attacking the conventional wisdom, they also indicated something about the Catholic people of whom he was one—and, more specifically, about the ones who were the "intellectuals." That something he discovered empirically, not with the highly quantified empiricism of computerized research but with the unmistakably direct empiricism of a fighter being pummeled by, and pummeling in return, a friend who had become a foe. What he thought was good news preached to the Catholic self-critics turned out to be an unwelcome intrusion. To understand why, one must crawl inside that now infamous ghetto mentality of apologetic Catholicism—a mentality whose existence was acknowledged by Greeley *and* his critics—and capture it just as it was opening up to the world outside the walls.

For there were essentially two explanations for the absence of Catholics from the intellectual life of this country. The first was that the problem was theological, somehow inherent in Catholicism itself, and the second was that it was historical, lying in circumstances attendant upon Catholicism's arrival in America. The first explanation—really, the first way of *blaming*—struck deeper, hit harder, hurt more, while the second deflected blame onto nonessentials. And the irony of the situation is that those outside the Church who argued the merits of the first, the more strongly indicting, explanation were outdone in their zeal by Catholics who felt a need to punish the Church of their upbringing. For to them the demon was no longer *out there* but *in here*, inside the very walls of the garrison.

The mechanism of what, in retrospect, was such a rapid transposition need not concern us. It does seem that by 1960 Catholicism, with a secure political and economic base, was ready for America and that America, with John Kennedy about to enter the White House, was ready for Catholicism. Outside the United States, the Church was taking a new look at the modern world. Teilhard de Chardin had experienced that world as a divine milieu and Pope John had blessed it and legitimized entrance into it with the convening of Vatican II. The world was a place where young men with vision were to be sent to find Christ even more than to bring Christ. God was with Freud and Darwin as He had been with Luther and Calvin. He was with modern science, with the secular humanists, with the agnostics, and even in His own mysterious way with the atheists. So much was good about the world. So much was to be learned there—beyond the barriers erected by parochial schools, parishes, diocesan newspapers, Catholic bookstores, seminaries, colleges, and universities.

So the world was entered, tasted, and found to be sweet, and, as it was, questions were asked. Why were we so afraid before? What did we have to fear from *them*? What could the freely searching intellect discover that would destroy us? Did not the mind seek Truth? And was there not Goodness out here? And more: whence these eyes that made us see people only as Catholic or non-Catholic? How arrogant of us to think that only through our Church could these "outsiders" be saved! And who separated us from the God out here—the real God, not the commandant back there barking out orders and telling us to listen or be damned?

These questions, of course, came from those who were raised within the fort—surely not from their fathers who struggled to build the fort in the first place. And the answers were likewise those of the later generation. We were cut off from our secular brothers and their God by this very Catholic garrison, by these very Catholics maintaining it, and by this very Catholic part of ourselves that led us to distrust the world's aspirations for a richer, more complete humanity. The evil was not the open, trusting, and trustworthy world, but the narrow, defensive, restrictive ghetto. The enemy wasn't them, it was our very selves.

Such was the climate into which Andrew Greeley brought his apparently well-founded message of hope. His claims were not extravagant. The underachievement of American Catholics in the intellectual life was not being questioned. Nor did Greeley assert, at least until the evidence was in, that the Catholic graduates of 1961 would follow through on their scholarly aspirations. His strongest assertion was the unspectacular "We have become average." We—the products of these confining parochial schools—have come abreast of the rest of the American population. And this thoroughly unimpressive statement nearly always was juxtaposed with "average is not good enough" and a whole series of practical prescriptions for how to become better. As Greeley wrote in *Commonweal*, "We cannot be content until Catholic scholarship is better than any other kind; we can bear adequate witness to the Lord in the intellectual world only when we are the very best; and to be no worse than the average is a long, long way from being the best."[20]

But even a glimmer of hope, if its source was the ghetto, was too much. Heads were turned the other way, eyes dazzled by the undiferentiated aura of goodness just over the wall. That peculiar Catholic penchant for punishment had completed its tragic cycle: Catholicism itself was now the target. And perhaps something else was at work—something that Sigmund Freud called the narcissism of slight differences. People who are much alike often exaggerate the slight discrepancies that exist between them and do so to the detriment of the other (and to the increment·of the hostility between them). Greeley *was* a self-critic, a Church liberal, if you will, someone encouraging the young to fill the Catholic gap in American intellectual life, someone filling the void with his own person. Yet it was precisely the self-critical, liberal element of Catholicism that he found himself aligned against in the anti-intellectualism debate. And, on the other hand, there he was, "hailed by people with whom I could not possibly ally myself."[21]

Secular academia seemed much more receptive to him at this time. It harbored stereotypes of the Catholic that annoyed him, true enough, but there was a curiosity, an openness, even a warmth there that caught him by surprise. In a letter to *Commonweal* in March 1963, Greeley wrote of an "atmosphere of sympathetic curiosity about Catholicism to be discovered in many parts of the intellectual world, an attitude of interested friendliness which would have been impossible even five years ago."[22] Later he examined "The Catholic Message and the American Intellectual" for readers of the *Critic*. Despite the prejudices of intellectuals against the Catholic Church, he said ("When an American Bishop makes a statement, the WASP intellectual hears from the dim memory of childhood the voice of Innocent III or Cardinal Torquemada"), despite the ways in which Catholics often give substance to those prejudices, despite the fact that intellectuals are "liberal, pragmatic, empiricist, critical, and personalistic" while the Church of recent history is "authoritarian, dogmatic, deductive, conservative and often less than human," despite even the intellectual's shrug of the shoulders at the question of a Transcendent—despite all of these, Greeley said he had seen the beginnings of dialogue between the church and the university. "It seems that there has never been a time when intellectuals were more fascinated by the Church or more eager to hear about it."[23]

Oh, there were ironies in the events and feelings of the years of the "great debate." Their pattern would be repeated in the unfolding argument over Catholic education and in the year of God's death. And a decade later, Father Andrew Greeley, the emerging Catholic intellectual, would be turned around 180 degrees. No longer would his statistics demonstrate that Catholics were as good Americans (read now: as good Protestants) as everybody else, but that they were different from everybody else and that what mattered were precisely those differences.

4 The Education of Catholic Americans

"I believe in the Spirit," Andrew Greeley answered my query about his future. "I listen to what the Spirit is trying to tell me."

Whether it was the Spirit or sheer accident that brought Greeley to the National Opinion Research Center in June 1961, the consequences were enormous. Much of the feud over Catholic anti-intellectualism, in fact, falls into place when one realizes that one of the protagonists was engaged in survey research. National probability sampling is more than a sociological method; it is a pair of eyes. When faced with a confusing array of stimuli, the eyes center on the great American mean and then see everything in relation to it—not to set ideals, surely, but simply to determine one's location. Is one above average or below? To the left of center or to the right? Typical or atypical? To an elite group concerned with the ideal, the mean is too drab, too gray, too run-of-the-mill—too *real*. It jars the assumption that one's self is the microcosm of the world, that what is happening to *me* is also happening to *all of them*. The pollster, on the other hand, may forget that the modal is not the model; or worse, he may exaggerate the power of the mean to predict the future and use it as a cudgel with which to batter his ideological enemy.

Catholics had come abreast of the population economically and socially and were well on their way intellectually. That was an impressive accomplishment, Greeley asserted in *Religion and Career*, fully aware that the mainstream of intellectual life in America was not at all distinguished. "Not at all impressive—deficient, in fact," was the judgment of the Catholic self-critics, standing in the presence of the great Eastern universities, unaware of the countless lesser institutions that made up the texture of American intellectual life. In this case, in an argument where the mean was used for the first time, it *would* have mattered to ask again and again: impressive *compared with what?*

Religion and Career gave Greeley the skills and the eyes that would determine his position in a variety of battles to come. He was an empirical sociologist now, possessed of a certain style, with a new role in the Catholic intellectual community; and much of what he would produce would bulge with tables of percentages, coefficients of association, statements of probability, appendices—all the appurtenances of survey research "facts." His advice to the young, even when he tried to inspire, had always been realistic and down to earth. So now would be his sociology.

A book appeared in the early months of 1964, just a bit before Greeley placed his finger on the New Breed in the pages of *America*. Like the child puzzled by the emperor's lack of clothes, it asked an innocent question, and, like the child, it drew a bevy of gasps, cheers, and outright anger. A New Hampshire woman, Mary Perkins Ryan, wondered in the title of a book *Are Parochial Schools the Answer?*[1] And in its 176 pages she did more than wonder—she answered in the negative. The Catholic school system, she said, was an obstacle to the Catholic mission of witnessing to the presence and activity of Christ.

Would not the Church and the world be better served if the child-centered parish became an adult-centered Christian community? Ryan asked. If the home became (as it once was) the seat of religious formation? If all the resources poured into the Catholic school system were freed from "what is essentially an auxiliary service"? Think of the time, she mused, that a bishop would have at his disposal, "time now spent in attending commencements, laying cornerstones, opening new buildings, and giving awards for spelling bees." Think of 13,000 priests, 5,000 brothers, 103,000 sisters, 62,000 lay teachers freed for other work. What a witness the Church would make if its people came out and let their light shine, "if enough priests and religious worked on secular campuses so that they could come to be known by great numbers of young people, Catholic and non-Catholic!"[2]

"Mrs. Ryan's little book landed like a stink-bomb in the little old schoolhouse," one commentator observed; "the response was nearly a public relations panic."[3] The Brooklyn *Tablet* attacked it as a denunciation of the very idea of Christian education. An official of the National Catholic Education Association called it "incredibly naive" and "foolish." Though Ryan was not on the program of the ensuing meeting of the NCEA, she was a major topic of conversation and practically the only one discussed in the news. At a press conference four Catholic school superintendents "took strong exception" to the book, and three of the four predicted "immense harm and confusion" from it. Just as the case for federal aid to parochial schools was gaining momentum, Ryan's critics fumed, here was a book urging Catholics to abandon the fight.

The Catholic school system of which Ryan spoke (and the word "system" was really a euphemism) comprised, in the early sixties, more than 300 institutions of higher learning, 2,500 secondary schools, and 10,000 elementary schools. Nearly three-fifths of the Catholic parishes in the country had their own elementary schools. Catholic schools accounted for more than six million students, or about 14 percent of the country's student population. No other modernized country had a system of such extensive coverage financed by nongovernmental sources. The history of the schools went back to the middle of the nineteenth century when the Catholic minority began to feel uneasy about nativist America. At that time the country was committing itself to mass public education, but the nondenominational schools that sprang up turned out to be Protestant. Catholics, in response, became defensive, feeling they could survive only in the security of their own schools; and in the 1840s such schools began to appear in New York. Forty years later the American hierarchy decreed that a Catholic school be established in every parish and that every Catholic child be in a Catholic school. The necessity of separate schools was strongly defended at the turn of the century by Catholic immigrants, especially Germans and Poles, to whom Catholic schools were a way of preserving what was theirs in the old country. Begun, then, for reasons that were largely defensive, the school system flourished even when the need for protection was gone. In the period after World War II, for example, Catholic schools experienced a remarkable surge in growth.

But now, in the 1960s, were the schools necessary? Did Catholic parents really want them for their children? The questions were

17 4158

hotly debated by Catholic educators, and Ryan's book was merely the tip of the iceberg. Were the schools divisive? Did they tend to preserve ethnic solidarities, to prevent immigrant groups from being absorbed into American life? Did it not take *common* educational experiences to produce cultural consensus in the United States? These questions came from outside the Church—and, more recently, from within it. And behind all the polemics lay a most sensitive issue: Was it now time for parochial schools to receive financial assistance from the government?

Even before *Are Parochial Schools the Answer?* was on bookstore shelves, Greeley and Peter Rossi were in the pages of the *Critic* describing a study of Catholic education to be undertaken by NORC.[4] The two took note of the grim things Ryan had to say about Catholic schools in her forthcoming book—as well as of recent forecasts of trouble in *Look* and *Newsweek*. But they parted company with Ryan. All schools can do, they argued, was pass on knowledge—*in*form, not form. What Ryan wanted, no school could accomplish. Further, there was absolutely no sign that the Catholic school system was moribund. While only one-third of the Catholic adults in the country had been to parochial schools, more than two-fifths of the Catholic children were in such schools in 1963. It was hardly the sign of a dying system.

As readers of the *Critic* and the *School Review* were being advised of these optimistic data, NORC interviewers were knocking on the doors of more than 2,700 randomly selected Catholics throughout the country, asking for their cooperation in a study of the kinds of schools people had attended. Funded by the Carnegie Corporation, NORC Survey 476 was the first national survey ever made of the Catholic population in the United States. Greeley and Rossi were investigating three basic questions:

1. Were Catholic schools effective as religious educators? "Effective" meant different things to different people. To Bishop Ernest Primeau, who wrote the foreword to *Are Parochial Schools the Answer?*, it meant "forming a people acceptable to God." To the sociologists at NORC, however, it meant something more tangible. Did Catholic-school Catholics, they phrased the question, *adhere more completely to the norms of Catholicism* than public-school

Catholics? Did they attend Mass and receive the sacraments more frequently? Did they hold more orthodox beliefs? Did they accept more completely the authority of the Church? Were they, therefore, "better" Catholics?

2. Were Catholic schools divisive? "Divisive," too, had a multiplicity of meanings, but the researchers settled on these questions to find their answer: Were Catholic-school Catholics isolated from non-Catholics? Were they disinterested in secular community affairs? Were they intolerant of other groups? Were they prejudiced toward them?

3. Did Catholic schools impede the economic and occupational achievement of those who attended them? The question concerned possible academic deficiencies in the schools and possible anti-intellectual, otherworldly orientations that hampered their students in later life. It was another attempt to test the longevity of the so-called "Catholic Ethic."

Despite its appearances, the study that would be written up as *The Education of Catholic Americans* (1966) was actually historical in nature. The sample surveyed were Catholics between 23 and 57 years of age. Thus, they had been in school sometime in the half century between 1910 and 1960, and the subject of investigation was Catholic education of *that* period—with *its* methods and *its* conception of goals. That, of course, made the controversy over the schools stickier, for the educators in Ryan's camp were arguing that it was precisely the goals of the first half of the twentieth century that had to be abandoned.

Nevertheless, given those goals (which were all the researchers had to work with), did Catholic education produce "better" Catholics? Yes, wrote Greeley, Rossi, and Leonard Pinto in the October-November 1964 *Critic*, but the differences between Catholic-school Catholics and public-school Catholics were not that convincing. "To confirm the undramatic is a pedestrian task, especially when the researcher finds that the facts place him squarely between two positions in a controversy."[5] To sample the results: 86 percent of the All Catholic group (those whose primary and secondary education was exclusively Catholic) attended Mass weekly; 73 percent of the Some Catholic group (part of whose education was in Catholic schools) and 64 percent of the No Catholic group (Catholics whose education was entirely public) did likewise. The figures for receiving communion "at least several times a month" were 38 percent, 25 percent, and 17 percent, respectively, and those for confessing at least once a month 51 percent, 38 percent, and 32 percent. Catholic-school Catholics were more likely to accept the Church's teaching role on such subjects as race, birth control, and education. They also proved, on a brief test of religious knowledge, to be better informed regarding the fine points of Catholic doctrine, and they were more orthodox in their own acceptance of doctrine (89 percent of the All Catholic group, for example, compared with 75 and 61 percent of the others, respectively, agreed that "Jesus directly handed over the leadership of His Church to Peter and the popes"). They showed greater assent to Catholic moral dictates, especially in matters that set Catholics apart from other Americans (81 percent of the All Catholic group, compared with 74 and 71 percent of the others, disagreed with the statement "It is not really wrong for an engaged couple to have some sexual relations before they are married"). They also were more likely to participate in the organizational activity of the Church and contribute money to it. Catholics from Catholic schools *did* adhere to the official norms of Catholicism more than did their confreres from public schools.

But was not this apparent impact of Catholic education due to selectivity, to the fact that those who enrolled in Catholic schools came from "better" Catholic families? And, therefore, was not the religiousness of Catholic school graduates due not to the schools but to the families that sent their children to the schools—one of the points of Mary Ryan's book?

Those questions led to the biggest surprise the data held for Greeley and Rossi (and also ensured that the data would be misunderstood by the public). It *was* true that parents who chose Catholic education for their children were more devout than those who did not. Far from duplicating what was accomplished at home, however, Catholic schools, it was found, had impressive independent effects on children from highly religious families. Indeed, for these children, a multiplier effect seemed to be operative, so that "religiousness of home and school reinforce each other, and when they are working in concert, the level of religious behavior increases in some sort of exponential fashion."[6] The effect of Catholic schooling was increased even more if a student went on to a Catholic college and married a practicing Catholic. Those highly devout families who were not able to send their children to Catholic schools simply were not able to develop an adequate compensatory mechanism.

On the other hand, for students from less devout backgrounds—approximately three-quarters of the children in the schools—Catholic education accomplished little in the area of religious and value formation. "Catholic school administrators could reasonably assume that, at least in the past, they were wasting their time with the vast majority of their students . . . . In theory at least, there was not much point in admitting children who were not from very devout families."[7]

Lest this result come as a surprise, Greeley and Rossi cautioned, we must remember that most sociological inquiries have shown that the intimate settings of home, neighborhood, and workplace are a good deal more effective in the process of socialization than is formal education. With that in mind, the authors concluded that "the Catholic experiment in value-oriented education has been a moderate (though expensive) success." *Given the goals* of the Catholic schools from 1910 to 1960—to ensure participation at Mass and in the sacraments, to accept the Church as an authoritative teacher (especially in the area of sexual morality), to "keep the faith"—the schools had done "a reasonably adequate job."[8]

Given the limited success of Catholic schools in religious and value formation, it was not surprising to discover that they failed to show the slightest trace of divisiveness—the second major concern of the study. The divisiveness theory, in fact, remained "spectacularly unproven." To be sure, Catholics from Catholic schools were less likely to associate with non-Catholics while they were in school, but in adult life they had as many non-Catholic visitors, friends, neighbors, and co-workers as public-school Catholics. Nor were they any less interested than public-school Catholics in community affairs. They were no more or less anti-Negro, anti-Semitic, or anti-Protestant, no more or less "Manichaean," religiously extreme, or permissive. The only difference in cultural attitudes was that Catholics from Catholic schools were more tolerant regarding civil liberties than their co-religionists from public schools. Even when a battery of controls was introduced, the answer to the question of divisiveness was a resounding no. Again, the results were not surprising. "There is ample reason in social theory to expect that, just as schools produce different values only with great difficulty, so they will separate peoples only with great difficulty."[9]

The defenders of Catholic education would do well to moderate their joy at this second finding, Greeley and Rossi commented, for was not the goal of the schools, especially in view of Church teachings on social justice, to produce adults not *as* tolerant as others but considerably *more* tolerant? Why, the critics of the schools would surely ask, did the products of Catholic education show no more love of neighbor than fellow Catholics from public schools? Still, there was a glimmer of hope in the data. The youngest, best-educated products of Catholic schooling stood out from their public-school counterparts in their degree of tolerance and social consciousness.

The third question of the Carnegie study—whether Catholic schools impeded the occupational and economic success of Catholics—yielded an even stronger negative answer. Far from hampering their graduates, Catholic schools seemed to give them a boost. Even with key social and demographic variables controlled, Catholics who went to Catholic schools were more successful than Catholics who did not. Again, a multiplier effect seemed to be at work. Catholic schooling had the greatest effect in improved socioeconomic status on those students from impressive socioeconomic backgrounds. To others it was of little or no help.

If one level of Catholic education had to be jettisoned, the researchers asked, which should it be—elementary school, secondary school, or college? The question was simple enough and so was its answer—none could be safely eliminated; the data showed the effects of Catholic education to be cumulative. And how important was Catholic higher education in the entire process? The question had not been asked to this point because so few in the sample had been to college. But when those few were inspected, striking differences appeared between graduates of Catholic and secular universities, differences of 25, 30, and 39 percentage points on various indices. It was not the colleges themselves that were so influential; rather, the differences were the result of attending a Catholic college after a Catholic high school after a Catholic grammar school. Not only were those with sixteen years of exclusively Catholic education "better" Catholics, but they were considerably more tolerant— giving substance to the hypothesis that integration into one's own religious-ethnic community enables him to relate more openly to the rest of society, giving hope to Catholic educators concerned about the social awareness, the "charity," of their graduates. The effect of comprehensive religious education with college as its culmination was so strong that the authors concluded:

> If one wishes to prevent American Catholicism from developing through its school system an elite which is both religious and socially rather impressive, one would do all in one's power to eliminate Catholic higher education. . . . This would apparently deprive the Roman Church in America of many of its most fervent future leaders; it would also quite possibly deprive the larger society of a group of citizens who would be more socially conscious and enlightened than many.[10]

Finally, what was the future of Catholic education? Was it, as some journalists suggested, in its death throes, or was there continued growth on the horizon? Wrote Greeley and Rossi, "The data strongly indicate that growth is precisely what is going to happen."[11] Demand for Catholic education was high. In areas where a Catholic school was available, 70 percent had attended it. Furthermore, demand increased as socioeconomic status improved, and Catholics were rising in socioeconomic status. The prediction was simply an extrapolation of present trends. Expansion of the schools would (and should) not be unlimited, however; never had more than two-thirds of the Catholic population desired religious education for their children and, besides, the birth rate in the country was beginning to level off. The only danger to the schools, the authors concluded, "would be the teacher situation." (It was, in retrospect, an ominous phrase.) If the "vocation shortage" increased, more lay teachers would have to be hired, costs would skyrocket, and the system could be in financial jeopardy.

Greeley and Rossi were not arguing for or against continued growth in the Catholic school system. They were simply making a prediction that the expansion of the past quarter-century would not be reversed and might even continue:

> Our opinion, for what it is worth, is that discussion by Catholics
> and non-Catholics alike concerning whether there will be Catho-
> lic schools is quite irrelevant. . . . Being for or against a school sys-
> tem with over five million students is like being for or against the
> Rocky Mountains: it is great fun but it does not notably alter
> reality.[12]

And like the Rocky Mountains (or the Sahara Desert, depending on your point of view), *The Education of Catholic Americans* was there—sober, complex, comprehensive. It did not notably
alter the positions taken in the argument over the schools, but it did
lend a measure of precision—and a good deal of ammunition—to
both sides. *America* reported that the Greeley-Rossi study showed
that the schools made a substantial difference and editorialized that
yes, they were worth it.[13] The Brooklyn *Tablet* headlined its story
"Study Sees Significant Relationship in Catholic Schooling, Adult
Life,"[14] but the *New York Times,* in an article that infuriated
Greeley, said, "Education in Roman Catholic schools has been
'virtually wasted' on three quarters of the students."[15] And *Commonweal* called it the way the *New York Times* did.[16]

Other reactions to the Greeley-Rossi report were mixed. *Time*
summarized it well.[17] *Newsweek* said it was "mired in qualifications."[18] Robert Cross of Columbia University, a non-Catholic
specializing in Catholic church history, referred to the "skimpi-
ness" of parochial school success;[19] and Daniel Callahan let it be
known in *Commentary* that he still saw the future a different way:
"Sooner or later it is bound to dawn on more Catholics that the
much-desired reform of the Church cannot take place as long as so
much of its money is channeled into education.[20]

And Mary Perkins Ryan said the report really didn't answer her
question; or, rather, it had not affected her answer. The areas in
which the schools were successful were not exactly "the 'component
parts' of the Christian life as set out either in the New Testament or
the documents of Vatican II," she wrote in a review of the Greeley-
Rossi study. Where was the association between Catholic education
and charity. (One paritcularly infamous item in the study asked
whether it was more important to avoid meat on Friday or to love
your neighbor, and only 53 percent of the Catholic-school Catholics
chose love.) The institution for Christian socialization, Ryan said
again, must be the group of two or three, or ten or twenty, gathered

to celebrate the Eucharist. As for formal religious education, the study showed, it "can, by itself, have very little lasting effect even if given in a Catholic school."[21]

Overlooked in the controversy was Greeley and Rossi's documentation of the spectacular influence of the Catholic college— when experience in a Catholic college followed twelve years of all-Catholic education. Eliminate the Catholic college, concluded *The Education of Catholic Americans*, and you destroy what you have painstakingly constructed for twelve years.

Long before that conclusion reached the public, Father Greeley was off on another project, touring the United States for an eye-witness look at the level of Catholic education responsible for its most dramatic effects. With assistants William van Cleve and Grace Ann Carroll (and with more support from Carnegie) he logged two to five days at thirty-six schools, amassing fifteen hundred interviews with faculty, students, and administrators. His impressions of Catholic higher education in 1965–1966 were delivered in the Catholic press and in a monograph called *The Changing Catholic College* (1967).

Why had some Catholic institutions grown rapidly and others failed to grow in the previous decade? The strongest correlate of improvement, Greeley found, was not the market potential of certain geographic locations (though that was important), not school size, not the proportion of laymen in administrative positions, not any one of a dozen other variables. It was the competence of the top administrator, his independence from the religious order that "owned" the school, his overall charisma. It seems that Greeley and his colleagues chanced to visit Catholic colleges at a time when their presidents had immense power and the freedom to exercise it. The presidents were not as yet hemmed in by faculty organizations; the trustees were in their hands because they were members of the religious community (and the president was frequently their religious superior); the students were, by and large, cowed. Hence a president could make a substantial difference. "The great-man theory of history, if it applies anywhere, most assuredly applies to an institution of higher education": thus Greeley apprised readers of the *Critic* in the fall of 1966.[22]

Schools that Greeley classified as Rapid-Improvement had a

good deal going for them—size, resources, reputation, a national image—but without top leadership, Greeley asserted, their growth would not have been what it was. Charismatic leaders were on his mind at this time (he was simultaneously digging into American Catholic history and finding such leaders for a book to be called *The Catholic Experience*), and when he found them in the flesh in those presidents' offices, he was enthusiastic. One president, with his Gaelic charm and wit, reminded Greeley and his colleagues of Spencer Tracy playing Frank Skeffington in *The Last Hurrah*. Another's assistant brought to mind "a powerful diesel locomotive proceeding down an open track at full speed, spitting out ideas and plans much as locomotive wheels spit out sparks." Had these men not been priests, "it would be a safe guess to say that all of them would be college presidents in any event (if they had not become major political figures in the Kennedy administration)."[23]

What about Medium-Improvement schools? Had they the leadership just depicted, Greeley claimed, they too would have been on their way. But as matters stood, growth had occurred only by accident. "They are better than they were, but through no fault of their own."[24] As for schools at the bottom of the list, not even a brilliant president could have ended the stagnation. In some cases their geographic location was unfavorable; in one, concentration on physical expansion had overshadowed concern for qualitative improvement; in another, the ecclesiastical background was so conservative that movement was impossible.

Faculty status at Catholic schools had improved considerably, Greeley reported. Salaries were up, teaching loads down, research competence developing. And there were the "new professors"—young people with the best of credentials, oriented toward research and scholarship, who turned down offers to more prestigious institutions because Catholic schools needed their help. "Their enthusiasm and willingness to make a fair amount of sacrifices for Catholic colleges is one of the bright spots on the Catholic higher education horizon."[25] On the debit side, however, were disillusioning administrative policies likely to drive the new professors away, the low morale of religious faculty, and the sorry state of departments of theology.

As for students, their plight could be summarized by revising a joke about the Taft-Hartley Law. "Higher education is heaven for faculty, . . . purgatory for administrators, and hell for students." Because of the tenacious influence of religious communities on the student life of "their" campuses, because religious communities think their role is to act *in loco parentis*, students are highly regimented—and in some cases their civil rights are even violated. Freedom of the student press is restricted; organizations are not free to invite speakers to campus; disciplinary boards, often fair and not arbitrary, still do not guarantee due process. The basic assumption is that one cannot trust people. "Even though Catholic theology takes a rather benign and optimistic view of human nature, by the time this theology is filtered down to the practical operation of student life in many Catholic campuses it has become highly Calvinistic."[26]

Greeley insisted that *The Changing Catholic College* was not, for all its realism, pessimistic. Still angry over the reaction to *The Education of Catholic Americans*, he warned that those who quoted this book out of context did so at their own risk. Nobody projected anything but a continued exponential increase in enrollment for Catholic colleges—and that set the stage for innovation. Yes, for all their problems, Catholic schools *did* have opportunities. There were charismatic leaders who did not suffer from inferiority complexes. There were model schools, too, the Johns and Nancys, the saving remnant, of academic institutions. Greeley closed *The Changing Catholic College* as he did *Strangers in the House*, describing one of the schools. Its name was changed to St. Mary's.

St. Mary's *looked* like a poor school—unpretentious buildings in the middle of a large American city, corridors lined with boxes, crowded offices and classrooms, the smell of a chemistry lab next to the president's office. But its budget was $1.3 million, with no deficit, and its library was recently ranked in the top 20 percent of all liberal arts college libraries. And something else was happening in its dilapidated halls:

> One member of the research team remarked after the first hour and a half in the school, "Everybody's laughing here—the sisters, the laymen, and the girls. They're laughing all the time. What in the world is the matter with them?" What is the matter with students, faculty, and administration at St. Mary's is something that is not

the matter with most other colleges in the country—Catholic, or non-Catholic. The people at St. Mary's are happy. As a matter of fact, they are happier than anybody has a right to be, especially the students.[27]

What was going on? Imaginative, creative instruction from well-trained sister and lay faculty, voluntary theology workshops to which students swarmed, programs that brought a quarter of the student body to work in the inner city. A relaxed, playful atmosphere, "one that is difficult to believe even when one is in the midst of it, and even more difficult to believe once one has departed (and it is by no means easy to depart)."[28]

There was magic in St. Mary's past, one Mother Jeremia, the former superior of St. Mary's religious order. "We believe, in this religious order," she told Greeley, "that our function is to create an atmosphere in which each of the nuns is able to develop her own talents and personality to its fullest. We don't want to mold our sisters into any pattern. We want them to be themselves in the best possible way." Of the college she added, "We decided fifty years ago that you could either build beautiful buildings or educate young women, and we chose to do the latter."[29]

So there *was* a great administrator in St. Mary's history. There was also a spirit of flexibility on the part of the entire religious order, a feeling that if they were going into the work of education then they would do that work in the most efficient way possible. Young sisters, therefore, were sent to secular graduate schools (long before it became a practice of other religious communities) and laymen moved into key positions at St. Mary's (without the fear that they would try to take the school away). Freedom and permissiveness were encouraged within the order and within the school. Pressure from outside ecclesiastical authorities was resisted. Here was an instance in which the ownership of a college by a religious community did not deaden education but filled it with spirit.

The places and the people Father Greeley loves to describe have much in common—intellectual curiosity, love of play, belief in the potency of the person, of their own person. They are *brilliant*, not awe-inspiring, but shining, sparkling (like diamonds in the rough, not cut, polished, and well cemented in a setting). St. Mary's may not have been the best institution, academically, of those he visited, but, humanly, none was its equal. At the end of his visit Greeley facetiously warned the president against a plan to move the school to a campus with several non-Catholic liberal arts colleges:

> "You have too much going for you here, Sister," he [Greeley] noted, "don't take the risk of losing it by moving."
>
> "But," Sister President replied, "what is important here is not buildings; it's people, and the people will be the same out there as they are here."
>
> "Yes, but the people out there will be more than just your college, Sister, and a lot of them take higher education very, very seriously."
>
> The Sister President's eyes sparkled. "How much do you want to bet that we change them before they change us?"[30]

Sister President, in Greeley's opinion, had a lot more going for her than Mary Perkins Ryan—and so did the other charismatic leaders in Catholic education. When Greeley attended that infamous National Catholic Education Association meeting in April 1964 (in Atlantic City), he did not hear the death knell that certain journalists did. Though they described the convention as if it were a pitched battle between the Monsignori and Ryan, Greeley said:

> I came away convinced that there were profound and dynamic forces for growth in Catholic education. Despite all the weaknesses that are so patent, some of those in the Church who are most gifted with insight were at that convention, and the direction of their thoughts made the terms of the controversy between Mrs. Ryan and the Monsignori seem quite irrelevant.[31]

Were parochial schools the answer? Greeley thought *The Changing Catholic College* was a hopeful book, a photograph that revealed how far Catholic higher education had come, what possibilities were open to it, and how to seize upon them. But Doris Grumbach read the same book and reached a different conclusion:

> On every score the climate is seen to be dismal, the intellectual tone of these schools gray and discouraging, the student bodies of even the best schools "deficient in both social awareness and social commitment," the quality of campus religious life so poor that "most

alert,. intelligent and potentially dedicated students at Catholic colleges are being turned against the organized institutional Church."
Most pathetic is the resistance to innovation of any sort.[32]

Daniel Callahan, who earlier, in response to *The Education of
Catholic Americans*, had still predicted trouble for the parochial
schools, likewise turned Greeley's findings against him, but in a
different way. Greeley made a convincing case, Callahan said, that
the more "professional," the more "American," the more "secular"
a college's leadership, the more successful that college would be.
What Greeley's book *really* shows, he said in the *Saturday Review*, is
that the secularization of Catholic schools is imminent. They soon
will lose their distinctive characteristics—or at least they will if they
wish to improve. Of Greeley's position that Catholicism and success
in American higher education are compatible, he added, *"The
Changing Catholic College* implicitly tears that case apart more
effectively than any outside critic ever could."[33]
     And so the battle wore on, the lines drawn as before: gloomy
liberals from the East versus an optimistic nose-counter from the
Midwest. For them it was either prolonged illness or death for
Catholic colleges; for him it was an "explosion of college enrollment" and an unparalleled opportunity to innovate. *They* said the
Church was a spiritual community that did not belong in "organized" education. *He* replied that an unorganized community was a
contradiction in terms. *They* said a Catholic university was unecu-
menical. *He* insisted the Church had to do its own thinking before it
could engage in dialogue. *They* said inquiry in a Catholic university
could never be free. *He* countered that the free university came into
being in a world overwhelmingly Catholic. *They* said Catholic
universities would end up as Catholic as Harvard is Congregational-
ist. *He* rebutted: only if you despair of the vitality of the Catholic
faith. Well, they said, we need more lay administrators and lay
trustees. No, he came back, we need more great administrators, and
the lay trustees we have are being co-opted by conservative boards.
Even if you're right, they said, there is still no money for a first-rate
Catholic university. He replied: organize the alumni; they are no
longer impoverished. And he added: why do academicians in
Catholic colleges have to ape all that is bad in American higher
education? Just as the multiversities are trying to rehumanize

themselves, the better Catholic institutions are trying to prove that they, too, can become multiversities. If we could experiment, if Notre Dame, for example, could stop trying to be a Catholic Princeton, "then we could conceivably see the day when Princeton will claim—God save us all—that it is striving to be a non-Catholic Notre Dame."[34]

If nothing else, Greeley's research opened up for him a career as a sociologist of higher education. He began to serve on national committees concerned with student life, became an editor of the *Journal of Higher Education*, and in April 1968 was named program director in higher education at NORC. The year before he had been approached by a committee in the Department of Education—a unit of the University of Chicago distinct from NORC—as a possible chairman of their program in higher education. He was interested. It was customary for NORC researchers to have tenured appointments in university departments; for one thing, such appointments eased the strain on the NORC budget. During the summer of 1967 he negotiated with the department, and they unanimously recommended his appointment. But by September the offer had not come and the matter was closed.

What, and/or who, had killed his appointment? Greeley became curious. Was it his close association with Jack Egan and Peter Rossi that did him in? (Father Egan had fought the university's plans to "redevelop" surrounding neighborhoods in Hyde Park, and Rossi had justified Egan's role in *The Politics of Urban Renewal*.) Was it even, just possibly, his Catholicism, his priesthood? The answers did not come in 1967, but seeds of suspicion about the "free" and "open" University of Chicago were already germinating in Greeley's mind.

Nevertheless, he continued to concentrate his scholarly activity on higher education. His description of the New Breed brought an invitation from the Hazen Foundation of New Haven, Connecticut, to join Yale's Kenneth Keniston, Stanford's Joseph Katz, Wisconsin's Joseph Kauffman, and a half dozen others to examine higher education from the students' point of view. Greeley came to the committee's deliberations with Grace Ann Carroll and memories of John Henry Newman. The influence of both was evident in the final report, which Greeley authored and entitled *The Student in Higher Education* (1968).

The students who were the subjects of the book were not leftists dedicated to tearing down the established power structure nor rightists trying to reestablish the simplicities of the past, not the senior at Harvard looking ahead to a career in nuclear physics nor the freshman at Michigan State crying to herself at night because she is homesick, but rather the large numbers of ordinary students in between. These students were searching for purpose, but were skeptical of formal ideology. They believed in "flower power," in open, trusting, and undemanding relationships. They were poised and sophisticated on the exterior but hesitant and uncertain below the surface. It was rare for a middle-class youth, subject throughout his life to evaluations, rankings, and comparisons, to have experienced unconditional acceptance as he grew up. "Under such circumstances, self-doubt, self-rejection, self-hatred, and self-punishment become almost endemic to the collegiate culture."[35]

When such a student, filled with doubts about himself, suspicious of organizations and their administrators, arrives at college, it takes only a few months for his expectations to plummet and his curiosity to be extinguished, the report went on. During orientation week he learns where the bookstore is, where his laundry goes, where he collects his mail. If he feels lonely, there is a counseling center. If he gets sick, there are student health services. Should he have academic difficulties, he has been assigned an advisor. If he has religious doubts, there is a chaplain somewhere. All his needs have been seen to, but somehow he gets the impression that they have not been taken care of but disposed of, and in such a way as to make life as easy as possible for the faculty and administration.

He will probably be forced to take several introductory courses taught by fledgling teaching assistants in lecture halls that seat from 100 to 500 students. The assistant will want to communicate a "body of knowledge" which the student must master. If the student fails (and it is secretly hoped that the less "qualified" students will fail), he will drop out of the system before the coddled full professors (who, by virtue of their lengthy list of publications lend "distinction" to the school) have to deal with him. It is an efficient process, but it has precious little to do with education, which must, in plain English, begin where the student is and build on his inherent curiosity.

The Student in Higher Education advocated a "developmental" college experience, one that integrated the student's cognitive growth with that of his entire personality. To be sure, the primary task of universities was to develop the intellect. But "to split 'intellectual' from 'other' development seems highly analytic, for in practice, when dealing with an individual, it becomes virtually impossible to separate intellectual from moral and emotional growth."[36] The cognitive and the noncognitive had to be integrated.

In the face of predictions from the quantitative experts in higher education (those who spoke of growth in body counts and provided a dollar figure for each body), the Hazen Foundation committee was speaking *qualitatively*. Their recommendations were numerous: Do not "pass on knowledge" in the first year, but rather, orient the student toward learning; leave the material that must be "passed on" to teaching machines and use faculty in as many tutorials and individual seminars as possible; make grades optional; hire only those Ph.D.'s (and there will be a surplus to choose from in the early seventies) interested in the developmental experiences of their students and pay them as much as—or even more than—their research-oriented colleagues; increase student participation in policy-making; democratize the making and enforcing of rules; create new physical structures (especially housing and eating facilities) that promote the formation of intimate communities; make room for volunteer student service outside the universities instead of treating it as a burden; bring liberal education to Everyman, not simply to elites with IQs of better than 120. Above all, experiment:

> The university should say to a handful of its more gifted faculty and administrators, "Find some students who are interested in the experiment you want to try and then go ahead and do it. We will guarantee to do all in our power to get the students into graduate schools, and we will keep the accrediting agencies at bay. Go ahead and experiment to your heart's content and don't worry about the lamentations of administrators and the wailing of faculty colleagues. You may have to work outside the structure of the guild-dominated regular course of instruction, but don't worry about the guilds. We'll protect you from them too."[37]

In 1969 it seemed there would be a chance for Greeley to do some experimenting of his own when he became a full professor (on a joint basis with NORC) at the Chicago Circle Campus of the University of Illinois. He was to create a graduate program in higher education, but three weeks after he signed the contract of appointment, the dean with whom he had been negotiating resigned. Left in the lurch, Greeley found that the massive bureaucracies of the state universities were simply beyond him. In March 1971, having accomplished nothing, he resigned the position.

There followed three years on the board of trustees of Rosary College in River Forest, Illinois. Again, none of his dreams came to fruition. In the early seventies, Rosary, like so many colleges, was fighting for its life. "Innovative education" was in another world now, far from the day-to-day realities of enrollments and finances. Greeley realized that the opportunities of the middle sixties had disappeared. The schools had "blown it"; campus unrest diverted attention from educational experimentation and caused alumni and legislators to back off from financial help for universities and support for educational research. There were signs as early as 1968 that the bright expectations for education would come crashing down, and by 1970, after Cambodia and Kent State, Greeley recognized that it had "all gone down the drain."

So his career as a researcher in higher education would be no more than a costly interlude. Before it ended he produced two other books on the subject, both of them resulting from his longstanding relationship with the Carnegie Corporation. *From Backwater to Mainstream* was published in 1969 (Clark Kerr had asked him to write it) and *Recent Alumni and Higher Education* (which he co-authored with Joe L. Spaeth of NORC) in 1970. The former reiterated much of what Greeley said in *The Changing Catholic College* (indeed, it contained entire passages from that book), but this time Greeley named names. "Spencer Tracy," we learn, was Father Michael Walsh, and his university, Boston College. Along with Notre Dame and Holy Cross, it was one of three Rapid-Improvement schools profiled. "St. Mary's" was Immaculate Heart College of Los Angeles, soon to join the Claremont College Group. Greeley described the history of Catholic higher education in the United States as one of serendipitous founding, helter-skelter expansionism—and high mortality. Two-thirds of the colleges for men founded before 1956, for example, were no longer in existence.

The schools that survived were being, for weal or woe, "secularized" (Callahan's forecast had been correct after all)—the great leveling force of the accrediting agencies was seeing to that. And in the feverish debate over the existence of Catholic schools, stark financial realities were looming larger, in some cases even deciding the question. Catholic schools, Greeley reported, were no worse off than the typical private institution—which placed them in plenty of trouble. Several years earlier he had forecast two decades of rising demand for desks at Catholic colleges; now the picture was different— unstable enrollments and the prospect, with increasing tuition, of severe decline. Contributed services of religious faculty were diminishing, the salaries of lay faculty increasing. Fund-raising was often inept; besides, "it would seem that American Catholics are not as generous in contributions as Jews or Protestants." The church-state issue made government help uncertain in some areas of the country. "It is safe to predict that many of the smaller and weaker Catholic schools may not survive into the 1980s; the larger and better schools probably will, but it will be a perilous adventure."[38]

Recent Alumni and Higher Education reported on the fifth survey, in 1968, of the class of 1961. Greeley had already used some of the findings in the anti-intellectualism debate, telling readers, Catholic and non-Catholic, that alumni of Catholic colleges *had* fulfilled their ambitions of combining scholarship with Catholicism. In an article for *America* he worked on another "dogma to which many Catholic liberals cling despite all proof to the contrary." Catholic alumni in 1968 were *not* dissatisfied with their schools. They were critical of them, true; they knew the curriculum, the library, the professional standing of the faculty were something less than perfect. Yet the Catholic alumnus was still more likely to be strongly attached to his college than the typical alumnus and to say he wanted his children to attend the school that he did. "One might even go so far as to say that the alumni seem to be more confident of Catholic higher education in the future than do many Catholic educators."[39]

The reason for alumni loyalty was not that they thought they had attended quality schools. To the contrary, only 14 percent of the Catholic college graduates rated their alma mater in the top quartile of American colleges. This contrasted with 52 percent of the alumni of private universities and 53 percent of those from liberal arts colleges—a finding Greeley did not emphasize in the *America* article. No, the alumni were loyal for a different reason. They esteemed their alma mater's role in value formation, and to a greater extent than alumni from all other types of institution. *The Education of Catholic Americans* concluded that experience in a Catholic college, following experiences in Catholic elementary and secondary schools, had a significant impact on value formation. The alumni of Catholic institutions saw it the same way.

Alumni expect a lot from higher education, Greeley said in a postscript to *Recent Alumni and Higher Education*. Colleges are supposed to be "parent, priest, psychiatrist, master craftsman, confidant, charismatic leader, prophet, social reformer"—but they cannot be all of these, and it would be well if society, and the colleges themselves, recognized this fact.[40] Reflecting on the class of 1969, Greeley offered some farewell advice to higher education. First, beware of "relevancy"—a year in the inner city does not guarantee sensitivity or sophistication; it may produce "narrow, bigoted zealots" and "romantic revolutionaries." The new "urban studies," he warned in *Educational Record*, are probably doomed before they start, if they are merely a response to guilt feelings, to a vague sense that one must "do something."[41] Watch out, he added, for the "T-Group temptation," which says "the college must 'swing'; it must 'turn on'; it must be 'hip,' " and which leads one into "encounter groups, marathon groups, sensitivity groups, affinity groups, white and black caucuses, and could even embrace astrology, witchcraft, divination, contemplation, drugs, rock music, and the whole psychedelic bag." The new enemies were the "devotees of feeling" among the student body, the "faculty barbarians" who ape the students, and the "losers" who "expect the demise of American higher education by no later than the second quarter of next year."[42]

Greeley was backing off now from the notion of education that developed the total personality (that had been prostituted by "relevancy" and "group therapy") and was asking again for an emphasis on the intellect. He told me several years later, "I thought with the Hazen report I'd made some contribution to the beginning of higher educational reform, and I was appalled by some of the things that were claiming to be higher education." The advocates of feeling had taken over; *cognition* was on the run. Greeley still included the noncognitive in his outlines of the ideal educational experience, but (as he wrote in the *Journal of Higher Education*) he no longer wished to give "aid and comfort to the pop psychological kooks who currently abound in the land."[43] Though higher education was in a critical period, he wrote in the conclusion of *Recent Alumni and Higher Education*, the barbarians and losers could still be defeated.

The barbarians and losers could be defeated: a sad, sour note to end enormous amounts of work—committees, books, reports, articles too numerous to mention. Greeley had invested heavily in higher education, and now the market had crashed. There was nothing to do but quit and lose touch with the schools, such as Immaculate Heart College, that had so inspired him. In 1974 Greeley's only connection with higher education was his presence on a reconstituted Hazen committee—that and nothing more. As he looks back on a time of hard, hard work that never paid off, he can only say, "I was glad to get out of it."

If the picture in higher education had become bleak, so had that in the Catholic elementary and secondary school system. What *The Education of Catholic Americans* confidently predicted would never happen *did* happen; five million students attended 13,000 parochial schools in 1967, but only four million attended 11,000 such schools in 1973. Between 1963 and 1974 the percentage of Catholic children in parochial elementary and secondary schools dropped from 44 to 29, most of the decline occurring at the elementary level. The Greeley-Rossi report was correct in its assessment of *demand* for the schools—the decline was not due to parents' removing children from the schools—but it failed to foresee that few schools would be built to accommodate a Catholic population moving to the suburbs. Costs were soaring; there was an acute vocation shortage among teaching nuns. Catholic administrators, asking themselves whether parochial schools were the answer, were not about to take a chance on new construction.

Greeley's thoughts on the about-face of parochial schools were contained in a book on which he collaborated with a Milwaukee lawyer by the name of William Brown. The book was about the size of Mary Ryan's and, like hers, it asked a simple question: *Can*

Catholic Schools Survive? (1970). Principal author Brown said yes, they can and should—and without public assistance. To Catholic parents he said, calculate the cash difference between voluntary contributions to Catholic schools and the involuntary tax increases sure to come if Catholic schools close down, and you will quickly discover that the price of having one's own schools, and being able to do what one wishes in them, is small indeed.

Brown's figures were preceded by Greeley's analysis of the decline of parochial schools. Lack of demand was not the cause—70 percent of Catholic parents have steadily expressed a preference for Catholic schools. Nor was a hostile culture out to do in the schools. No, the problem lay with Catholic educators themselves, they and the journalists who criticized old models but failed to provide new ones. On the brink of success, everybody lost their nerve. They lost confidence, faith, morale, enthusiasm. They suffered the self-hate characteristic of any immigrant group in the later stages of acculturation. The shift from the mentality of the Counter-Reformation to that of the Ecumenical Age, from immigrant slum to professional suburb—both of them peaking in 1960—was too much. There was no new vision, no new theory, to replace the rigid certainties that had propped up Catholic education in the past. And so the fight for the schools was given up even before it began.

Cemented in Greeley's thinking now was a distinction between a Catholic *population* (as he knew it from opinion polling and from life in the parish) and a Catholic *liberal elite* overpowered, as he put it, by a death wish. Catholics in the neighborhoods were enthusiastic about the schools. They wanted them in 1963, and they wanted them when surveyed again in 1974. But liberals in Catholic education and in the media could not hear the voices from the neighborhoods. Should the schools fail to survive, said Greeley, historians will say "not that Catholic education was crushed by a hostile non-Catholic society, nor that it was abandoned by an uninterested Catholic population, but rather that it committed suicide."[44]

5 The Wake of Vatican II

One morning in the summer of 1964, when the analysis of the parochial school data was in a particularly acute stage, Father Greeley received a phone call. "You've been transferred," the voice said.

"Oh?" replied Greeley. Immediately he called the rectory at Christ the King and found that a certain letter *had* come in the mail. He asked to have it read to him. It was true; he had been transferred to St. Thomas the Apostle parish, just across Fifty-fifth Street from the University of Chicago. No more than that—the letter contained no explanation, no mention of the future of his work at NORC.

Greeley hastened to St. Thomas for a talk with the pastor there. He knew the man well, for he had been a curate at St. Angela's during Greeley's seminary years and toastmaster at the banquet following Greeley's first Mass. Greeley asked about his work at the university. His new pastor hesitated; then he pointed out that the parish had three hospitals to take care of, that it wouldn't be fair to the other priests, that he couldn't make an exception for Greeley. The university work would have to go.

"I spent twenty-four pretty bleak hours," Greeley recalls. It seemed he had no choice but to comply, but then he thought of Archbishop (by then Cardinal) Meyer, the man who, after all, had sent him to graduate school and encouraged him to stay on at NORC He called Meyer's office.

The cardinal was not available, but a short time later Cletus O'Donnell, chancellor of the archdiocese, returned Greeley's call. "You're not upset about the change, are you?" he began.

"Well, yes I am. I've got these commitments . . ."

"Oh, we want you to keep those up. We moved you to the university parish so you would be closer. We just wanted to make it more convenient for you. Everybody knows we want you to continue at the university."

"Oh yes? My pastor doesn't."

"Well, we'll straighten that out."

The matter was taken care of quickly and in the fall of 1964 Greeley left Christ the King (a parish which, for all his ambivalence, he hated to leave) and moved to St. Thomas. Another curate at Christ the King, Father John Hotchkin, was leaving too—to do graduate work in theology. "Father H" had arrived in 1960, fresh from the North American College in Rome. "He taught me theology," Greeley says, and it's true. The books of letters to John and Nancy are full of references to the theological ideas of John Hotchkin. The two of them had great times during their years together and, with all their enthusiasm for projects, gave their pastor a run for his money; but it seems that by 1964 the pastor had had enough. He wanted a full-time curate, not one who spent most of his hours at the university or writing in his room. "The pastor got rid of us," Greeley recollects. "I'm sure he did."

Life at St. Thomas quickly became unbearable. Greeley was tied down to the rectory by a hospital call system and had to dash off at all hours on a moment's notice; the pastor resented the fact that Cardinal Meyer's office had "straightened out" the matter of Greeley's university work; the payoffs in friendships with parishioners were no longer present. In March 1965, just six months after he moved to St. Thomas, Greeley wrote the cardinal asking to be released from parish work. I cannot do both, he explained, either the parish work or the university work has to go. The problem was especially difficult because Greeley was about to embark on his national tour of Catholic colleges—a plan devised to help extricate him from St. Thomas.

Meyer granted Greeley's request—and then he died. His reply to Greeley's letter, it turned out, was his last official act.

The loss of the cardinal was staggering. Here was a man who actually encouraged Greeley to write, to develop his skills in graduate school, to continue on as a research scholar after graduation. If Greeley had a problem putting together the roles of parish priest and NORC researcher, the cardinal's door was open for consultation and support.

In the summer of 1965, after Greeley left St. Thomas for a room in the rectory of St. Dorothy's parish, Chicago received a new archbishop, John Cody. Greeley phoned for an appointment to report on his work and arrived one day with the galley sheets for *The Education of Catholic Americans*. When Cody came into the office, Greeley remembers (bitterness coming into his voice) he began to criticize. You write too much—everybody says so. What kind of arrangements do you have for censorship? You're drifting away from parish work, you know. I'm not going to leave you at the university for very long. "By the way, how much do they pay you?"

"Not very much," Greeley replied. But he wouldn't specify the figure.

Their conversation soon reached an impasse. "So there I was with the galley sheets of *The Education of Catholic Americans*. I brought them in under my arm. I walked out with them under my arm. And that was the end of me and the archdiocese of Chicago. I've been an un-person ever since."

It had all happened suddenly, dramatically—from Christ the King to nothing, from a supportive archbishop who said "write more" to a hostile one who said "you write too much." To this day Greeley's anger has not abated. Greeley never asked to leave Christ the King, never wanted to be a priest without a parish, never imagined a superior like John Cody. But suddenly, as total surprises, these were *faits accomplis*. "I got out one step ahead of the sheriff. If Meyer hadn't released me from parish work just before he died, I would have been defenseless. Even then, if Cody had moved on me, he could have gotten away with it." By 1966 it was too late. *The Education of Catholic Americans*, the first survey ever of the American Catholic population, had made Greeley a national figure.

More was happening to make the summer of 1965 a "horrendously hellish" one. Some of the young people Greeley had known at Christ the King kept coming to see him, first at St. Thomas and then at his new home at St. Dorothy's. Their relationship was different now—he was a friend, not a man of authority. Barriers came down, and Greeley saw and heard for the first time things that shook him to the core. "I was appalled to see how much some of these people were suffering. I can't talk about young people today, but at that stage of the game there was just an immense amount of self-hatred and self-loathing. I guess later on in the decade they were able to take it out by being angry at society but these kids weren't able to do that. All kinds of people were dangerously close to suicide."

These were the children "spoiled" by their parents (that was what he was told a decade ago)—children, Greeley realized now, who had been given everything but love. Now the feeling began to drown them. *I*—not just my products or my accomplishments—am worthless; *I* am no good. Greeley finds words difficult as he thinks back, but notes, "I sent an awful lot of people off to therapists that summer."

Just before that fatal season hit, in May 1965, Greeley published "The Temptation of the New Breed" in *America*.[1] A year had passed since his original article, and one could sense the discomfort that would soon explode. The New Breed, he complained, is increasingly handicapped by a lack of ideology. They have *no* specific goals, can make *no* critical social analyses, are capable of *no* systematic commitment to work. Talented, yes, but disdainful of the grubby, day-to-day work of building an organization—or even working within an organization.

> We ask the New Breed what they want of us, or what they want of society, and they say: "We want you to love us, we want you to permit us to make something of the world where you have failed." But then if we ask: "How have we failed, and how do you want us to love you?" their words become vague. They tell us simply that we have failed because there is not enough love or freedom in the world.[2]

Freedom and love are not enough, Greeley argued. The New Breed "must abandon the cheap cliches and slogans of the books of existentialist philosophy and become hard-nosed and practical. . . . The basic problem is that the very best young people we have are not sure *who* they are, *where* they are going, or *what* they want out of life." He had soured on the New Breed.

> I cannot help feeling that, for all their rejection of "phoniness," the New Breed's emotionalism has just a bit of phony about it, too. The problems they have can be solved with intelligent effort; it is possible for the New Breed to take counsel, to put their life in

order. What I find almost inexcusable is the tendency of so many of them to drift. It seems to me that in their lives there are, indeed, just too many "great big hairy deals."[3]

A year later the lesson of the summer of 1965 had sunk in; they were crying for *love*, no more, no less. In June 1966, two years after he baptized the movement, Greeley wrote "A Farewell to the New Breed." He was wrong, he said; the young do not need an ideology and a practical program as much as they need encouragement and love—come to think of it, just what they were asking for. "They do not have enough faith in their own goodness, their own dignity, their own value, their own promise." They despair, not of reforming society, but of their own value. Greeley himself failed to encourage them, he added. "I admit in all honesty that it will be a long, long time before I am able to excuse myself for this failure." And he asked anyone who was listening to "love them with a love that does not require them to fit into his patterns or do what he wants them to do, to progress along the path he has chosen for them or adopt the values he thinks they ought to adopt."[4]

Greeley tried to follow his own advice with the New Breed, tried to put together lives that had shattered almost overnight. He did it by forming a parish (in view of his difficulties with the cardinal, something *he* needed, too) of twenty-five or thirty New Breeders. It was a floating, experimental, "underground" community that began to come together at a summer home he had acquired on the eastern shore of Lake Michigan. Greeley purchased the house, located in the community of Grand Beach, in the fall of 1965. He was to discover that many of the South Side Irish (including the mayor of Chicago) had second homes there. To Greeley, the house at Grand Beach came to be what Twin Lakes was when he was a boy. To fellow priests, it became to focal point of envy and resentment, a visible sign of a substantial, independent source of income.

Greeley's new parish found Grand Beach an ideal place to gather—the lake, the sand, the wind, the friendship, the unity in belief, all of it an hour from Chicago. Greeley was on his tour of American Catholic colleges when he purchased his new home, and often he would fly into Chicago and head directly for Grand Beach for a weekend with his young parishioners, returning on Sunday to his basement room at St. Dorothy's. As the community developed, it had days of recollection and discussion intertwined with the liturgy—often, in the beginning, very moving and very exciting experiences.

The community prospered and Greeley wrote about it and about other underground churches that were developing along with it. He wrote with the same combination of hope and practical advice that had ushered in the New Breed just two years before. The New Community, he said, is a term for "nothing more than groups of friends periodically meeting to discuss their life, their work, their faith." Members of communities like his simply do not find what they need in their urban parishes, even in the most dynamic of them. At home they participate in a madhouse of parochial activities and remain committed to their parishes, but they are on the trail of something else, something closer, something more meaningful: "a place where a person is able to be himself because he loves and is loved, . . . where he is able to speak his mind because it is safe to do so, . . . where he does not have to impress others with his brilliance, or his wit, or his success, . . . where he need not be afraid to speak of his hopes and his fears, or of his joys and his failures."[5] The New Community was a response to the anguish of the New Breed.

The New Community was also part of something more extensive than Christ the King parish or even the American Catholic Church. Rural communes were being formed almost daily in remote parts of the western United States; "educational villages," composed of tightly knit groups of younger faculty and students, were appearing on university campuses; the cursillo and pentecostal movements were creating small, intense religious communes; Orthodox Jews had banded together on the fringes of Harvard. And there were Zen monasteries, Meher Baba groups, intimate fellowships of believers in astrology or the *I Ching*. Quasisacred attempts at intense interpersonal fellowship were sprouting all over the landscape.

One could sense Greeley's hope for these ventures—and especially for his own community—in his litanies of advice. *Do* require hard work, he said; *do* tolerate diversity; *do* be patient with each other as you gradually unmask yourselves. *Don't* force honesty, openness, love. These grow slowly, organically, and cannot be sped along by gimmickry. Let no one become the amateur psychologist of the group; it would be better to have a professional one, even an out-sider. Though it is not especially easy, try "to steer a middle path be-tween pressure, manipulations, and covert aggression on the one hand and distrust, fear, and insecurity on the other."[6] Above all, have no newsletter, no national secretariat, no national con-ventions, no national chaplain, no national program committees. That, after all, is what we are trying to avoid.

At the beginning, Greeley thought the New Community to be terribly important:

> It may well become a revolutionary development of the Church. It may represent a major step forward in the Christian life com-parable to the appearances of the communities of hermits in the fourth century, the monastic communities of the sixth century, the friars in the twelfth and thirteenth centuries, and the congrega-tions in the seventeenth and eighteenth centuries.

The young of Christ the King, a few of them already priests and nuns, others coming together and thinking of marriage, were being *healed.* Perhaps parishes like his actually did "mark the beginning of an entirely new era in the history of Christianity."[7]

But then, slowly at first, and almost inevitably (it seems in retro-spect), the community began to teeter, and Greeley's new hope, like so many previous ones, began to disintegrate.

Memories of the downfall of his parish are most painful to Greeley (this is, perhaps, the hardest topic for him to talk about). He was their priest, he recalls, not because he wanted to be, but because he was older, the center, in a way the reason for its existence. They began to define him in ways he could not accept. "You're trying to dominate my life," they said, and for a while he believed them. Those that he had sent to therapy began to consider *him* the source of their problems. "I became conscious of being an object of trans-ference." He became uncertain, hesitant—so many of them were saying it that they might be right. Perhaps the problem *was* psycho-logical, perhaps it *did* lie with a need of his to dominate, to have dis-ciples (rather than with a mission to preach, to be loyal to, a de-manding gospel), perhaps he *was* creating a mold for them (rather than simply challenging them), perhaps the problem *was*, after all, interpersonal (rather than religious). It was another difficult period for Andrew Greeley. After he had an opportunity to sort things out, he said no.

No—he was not engaging in some kind of countertransference. No—he was not trying to dominate their lives. No—he did not have an insatiable craving for disciples. No—the problem was not psychological. "At least at that stage in their lives," Greeley looks back now, "they were either unable or unwilling to make the kind of religious commitment I was challenging them to make. To pretend that we had a common faith was a mistake, and to sustain the pretense for a year or two years after was causing needless anguish—for me in any case." The problem was *religious*, he insists. "At some stage you say, 'Either you are going to respond to this or you don't need me as a priest. I m here to preach the gospel.' *That* broke the community—that challenge."

The community ground to an end slowly, perhaps because of Greeley's own stubbornness in wanting to make it work. "My big mistake was in not quitting earlier," he says. Many of the experimental churches ended the way his did, only more abruptly. As his New Community broke up, the pain sparing no one, he sorted out his feelings in "The Risks of Community," an article that appeared in the July–August 1970 issue of the *Critic*. It had been four years since his speculation that the Church might be witnessing a revolutionary development in lifestyle and six years since his landmark description of the New Breed.

Now he was a psychoanalyst performing an autopsy. What had happened? Without anyone's realizing it, a group of close friends who immensely enjoyed each other began to recreate their familial pasts. Every one became a caricature of the weakest dimension of his personality, analyzing and reanalyzing who was responsible for what, who said what injurious things to whom, needing to blame someone for what was happening, directing the blame to the parent figure in the group. The only way out of the mess would have been to acknowledge it for what it was—a regression to familial patterns of behavior. No one, however, wanted to make the admission. No one dared make the suggestion that some (those who could not see what was happening) ought to leave the group. There was nothing left but self-destruction.

This time the destruction was so great that the New Breed could not be put together. Adolescents who seemed so open and malleable, as Greeley phrased it, were closed off to him by the whole burden of their family experience. By 1971 the community was completely disbanded. In 1974 only two of the original group remained close to Father Greeley. One was Nancy Gallagher of *Letters to Nancy*, and the other was her husband Bill McCready, a close associate of Greeley's at NORC. The vast majority—among them, John of *And Young Men Shall See Visions*—simply vanished. The New Community, it turned out, was not the salvation of the New Breed but a stopping-off place on its exodus from the Church.

And the man who had hoped so much at the outset of his public life, whose career intersected American Catholicism as it seemed on the verge of enormous success, sustained another loss. The reaction of the liberal elite to his "optimistic" data was one thing, but the abandonment of these young people was of a different order altogether. "The pain of separation is not diminished by the observation of one psychiatrist who has spent a considerable amount of time studying such patterns: 'When will they forgive you? Some of them may perhaps be reconciled with you on their deathbed—some not even then.' "[8]

And what of the Catholic Church at large, following in the wake of a pope and a council that were, in their own way, just as much of a new breed? All through the sixties Greeley wrote about institutional Catholicism, beginning in 1964 with "We are but one step away from greatness; and before the rest of the world knows it, we are going to take that step,"[9] ending in 1969 with "For the first time in my life, I am profoundly worried about American Catholicism."[10] He produced furiously during this time, dictating most of his material, writing one weekly column for the *National Catholic Reporter* and another for local Catholic papers, creating articles of diagnosis and prescription and exhortation for the *Critic, Sign, Commonweal, America, Overview,* and *Homiletic and Pastoral Review*. The titles of his books expressed his ambivalence: *The Hesitant Pilgrim* (1966), *The Crucible of Change* (1968), *A Future to Hope In* (1969), *Life for a Wanderer* (1969), *Come Blow Your Mind with Me* (1971). Early in the game he indicated the basis of his hopes:

I am optimistic enough to expect, *in the long run*, an increase in
religious and priestly vocations. I think the quality of books published by Catholic firms will notably improve. I foresee a much
greater reliance on social science and planning in ecclesiastical decision-making. I see the collegial principle becoming operative in
the Church once again, with bishops acting in much more intimate cooperation with their presbyterate, and priests in much
more intimate cooperation with their *laos*. The fraternal use of
authority will gradually replace the paternalistic, and even the
curate will cease to be the "nonperson" he so often is.[11]

He was realistic enough to identify problems—the mass of
Catholics were apathetic, a theoretical perspective on the American
Catholic phenomenon was lacking, lay intellectuals were becoming
alienated from the main body of Church structure, educational institutions needed reform, power had to be decentralized—but he felt
these did not threaten the existence of the Church, and he felt they
could be overcome. Besides, *American* Catholicism had a special
genius to see it to success.

For one thing, said Greeley, the American Church was imbedded in "virtually the only industrial country in the Western
world where the vast majority of the population maintains a formal
religious affiliation and goes to church with some frequency." Nor
had the working class left the American Church as it had, say, the
French. "American Catholicism has never been identified with an
Old Regime which stood in the way of social progress; on the contrary, it has to a considerable extent succeeded in identifying itself
with the aspirations of the immigrants to gain acceptance in American society." The clergy has always been similar in background to
the laity, so much so that, twenty years ago, Cardinal Cushing could
remark with pride that no bishop in the country had come from a
family in which a parent had gone to college. Consequently, there
has been little anticlericalism (so he said in 1966)—or its equally
pernicious opposite, clericalism—in the American Church. Because
the church has been independent of state support, the laity has had
to pay for churches and schools, developing a keen sense of participation by doing so. Independence has meant that the Church has
been free to experiment. Experimentation has produced excesses, of
course, but "if unfounded enthusiasms are a price that must be paid
for a relatively open Church, then I think we will be ready to cheer-

fully pay the price." Finally, and perhaps most important, America and American Catholicism have believed in freedom. A man like John Courtney Murray spent a lifetime advocating freedom for the universal Church, and he lived to see his life's work justified in the final session of the Vatican Council. Indeed, in many ways it seems that the entire Church is finally catching up with values that have been part of the American experience—"openness, flexibility, organizational efficiency, freedom, ecumenism, cooperation between clergy and laity, public opinion, incarnationalism, technical progress."[12] There *are* things wrong with the American Church, Greeley said, but its principal weakness is no more than a fear of living up to the best in its own experience.

If America had its own genius, so too did the Midwest. "Catholicism Midwest Style," Greeley wrote in 1966, meant openness, flexibility, and creativity—more of these were to be found in Chicago than on the red plains of Oklahoma, on the banks of the Mississippi, or in the towers of Manhattan Island. The midwestern Church "has been much less threatened by American society than has the Church in other regions. It could afford to relax, experiment, innovate; there was no one to make fun of its mistakes."[13] When Catholics arrived on the eastern seaboard, they found themselves threatened by a well-established WASP aristocracy not particularly eager to have them as neighbors. In Chicago, St. Paul, and St. Louis, however, Catholics were on the scene in large numbers from the very beginning. It was *their* society as much as anyone else's. Everyone was an immigrant, and there was little discrimination against Catholics *qua* Catholics. Catholic colleges did not have a Harvard or a Yale hanging over their heads. The midwestern Church was provincial, unsophisticated, inarticulate, true enough; Greeley was chagrined to admit it was "willing to let its reflecting be done by journals of opinion from the East." But still, he felt, there was confidence and vitality in the nation's heartland. "You can become alienated in the midwest if you want to, but, by damn, it's harder."[14]

In *The Catholic Experience* (1967) Greeley elaborated on the genius of the American Church with a "sociological interpretation" of its history. The book sketched the lives of great "Americanizers" and "anti-Americanizers" in the Catholic Church, the former rejoicing in American culture, seeing opportunity rather than danger in her democracy, going so far as to believe that the American experience had much relevance for universal Church, the latter worried about anti-Catholic bigotry, wary of materialism; secularism, and paganism, fearful that becoming thoroughly American meant becoming less Catholic. There was no doubt in 1967 where the author's sympathies lay. As the Americanizers performed on his pages he marveled at their brilliance and applauded loudly. And when the anti-Americanizers took over, he buried his head in his hands.

First to take the stage were the Carrolls, Charles and John— Charles, a signer of the Declaration of Independence, a distinguished ally of George Washington throughout the Revolutionary War, a member of the United States Congress; John, a cousin of Charles and the first bishop of the United States. The Carroll clan belonged to the Maryland aristocracy, and were active participants in the social, economic, and political life of the colony, proof to anyone with an open mind that Roman Catholics in the emerging United States were patriotic, and evidence, centuries later, that the liberal Americanizing tradition in American Catholicism was truly the first born.

John Carroll, like many of the brave figures of *The Catholic Experience*, was ahead of his time—indeed, ahead of our time. He insisted that the Church organize itself in a manner suited to the American environment. When it seemed certain, as the eighteenth century came to a close, that Rome would make him America's first bishop, he demanded that the American clergy *elect* their bishop and that Rome be limited to confirming that election. Rome agreed, and Carroll was thus chosen by the vote of his fellow clergy. Carroll also supported the system whereby Church property was owned by boards of lay trustees elected by members of the parish—a system that worked well in many places but still was subject to abuse. And he called for a vernacular liturgy, asking, "Can there be anything more preposterous than an unknown tongue" which insured that "the great part of our congregations must be utterly ignorant of the meaning and sense of the publick office of the Church."[15]

No one could have been more American in his dealings with the government than Bishop John Carroll. "He would congratulate public officials when they were elected, he would offer prayers for them, and he was friendly with them on a personal basis . . . . He was a patriot and would support the War of 1812 even though his Federalist background certainly must have made him less than sympathetic with it."[16] In his communications with Rome he backed the American position on the relationship between church and state—a position almost inconceivable on the other side of the Atlantic.

To judge from *The Catholic Experience*, John and his cousin Charles were earlier incarnations of those talented presidents of Catholic colleges whom Greeley was meeting face-to-face. They were "calm, confident, competent men who took leadership positions for granted and whose self-assurance was so immense that no one dared question it." John might have been a more ancient manifestation of that Spencer Tracy of college presidents, Michael Walsh. A young man who knew him wrote of his spirit and cheer, of his dignity, of the respect he commanded: "The Archbishop in fact was a thoroughbred, and a polished gentleman who put everybody at their ease in his company while delighting them with his conversation."[17]

The likes of John's cousin Charles would not appear again until John Kennedy. Charles may not have been a devout Catholic, "but he in fact was the one who persuaded his fellow Americans that it was possible to be a sincere practicing Catholic and at the same time an unquestioned patriot."[18] By their influence, the Carroll cousins set the tiny American Church (only one percent of a population of three million) on a carefully charted, confident course between loyalty to Rome and a fiercely independent American spirit.

The problems of Bishop John England, the next figure to take the spotlight in *The Catholic Experience*, were more complex than those of the Carrolls. He arrived in Charleston, South Carolina, on December 28, 1820, with twenty-two years of life ahead of him, "twenty-two years in which he would shake the American church as it had never been shaken before and has not been shaken since."[19] America at the time of England's arrival was being swamped by waves of immigrants, most of them Irish like himself. When John Carroll died in 1815, the Catholic population in the United States was 90,000. When John England died in 1842—only twenty-seven years later—the figure was moving rapidly toward two million.

Would the mass of immigrants, and the religion they brought with them, become insecure, defensive, rigid, and parochial, or would they become open-minded and generous? History would say the former, but John England still stands as testimony that it could have been the other way.

> John England was a man bigger than life; indeed, there were oc-casions when he seemed twice as big as life . . . . His performance in the first year in Charleston was sufficient indication of what was to come. Two weeks after his arrival, having issued a lengthy and eloquent pastoral on the nature of the bishop's office, England set out on a visitation of his huge diocese. During the winter and spring as he traveled at breakneck speed around the southland, he also found time to make plans for the construction of a cathedral, to found a Catholic book society, write a lenten pastoral, publish an English catechism, put the skids permanently under the rebel-lious trustees in Charleston, preach in Episcopalian and Presby-terian churches, write a letter to Maréchal suggesting a national council, prepare for publication and translation of a missal with an introduction and explanation of 120 pages that he himself had penned, make plans for a new translation of the Bible into English, and begin to lay the groundwork for a weekly Catholic newspaper and for a constitutional convention in his diocese.[20]

England continued at the same pace for the rest of his life (and even delivered a stirring oration on his deathbed). He published a constitution, subscribed to by clergy and laity, by which his diocese would be ruled, founded a national newspaper, the *United States Catholic Miscellany*, established a seminary with a revolutionary educational scheme, battled for collegial government in the Ameri-can Church. His respect for the United States was "passionate." He was indeed, in the chapter's title, the "Super-American from County Cork."

England failed to leave his mark on the American Church be-cause, although he succeeded in his relationships with non-Catho-lics, he could not gain the support of his fellow bishops. His enemies in the hierarchy blocked the appointment of men he named as successors in the Charleston diocese, and Rome sent instead a man to "clean up the mess" that England had left behind him.

The heroic England was followed in *The Catholic Experience* by a villain, John Hughes, archbishop of New York, a "fearsome man." At precisely the time when the crises of the immigration experience were most severe," Greeley wrote, "Hughes's influence can only be considered a major disaster."[21]

In retrospect, it was easy for Carroll, presiding over a small native American church, and England, whose Charleston diocese was not terribly affected by immigration, to adopt a stance of Americanization. However, "for John Hughes in New York two decades before the Civil War, the Americanization of the immigrant, at least as it was described by the native Americans of New York City, seemed more frequently to mean that the immigrants must become Anglo-Saxon Protestants or they would not be welcomed in this country. John Hughes was not prepared to let this happen."[22]

It was not without reason that native Americans were troubled, and even terrified, by Catholic immigrants. The immigrants were uneducated and often unruly. They lived in slums and worked for lower wages than did native Americans. Their votes could be captured by a corrupt political machine. Their political and religious leaders were often demagogues. They threatened to undercut the existing social and economic structure of the city. It was even said that they were of racially inferior stock.

It is also understandable that immigrants would become defensive in a culture growing more hostile by the day. The Know Nothing Party had come into existence; churches were being burned; inflammatory literature was being circulated; convents were being stormed. But John Hughes, argued Greeley, was not the man for this time. He served only to make a bad situation worse.

Possessed of a fierce temper, the man thrived on controversy. He saw himself as the protector of a flock not able to take care of itself, surrounded by ravenous wolves. He read every newspaper he could get his hands on and let no attack on the Church (or on John Hughes) go unanswered. He was devastating, had amazing powers of ridicule, and could win arguments, but he could not compromise and gain friends. Hughes managed to destroy New York's Public School Society and railed against the double tax Catholics had to pay for the education of their children. When nativists burned Catholic churches in Philadelphia in 1844, Hughes told the government of New York that if the same thing happened there "the city would become a Moscow." He was prepared to have armed forces of

Catholics in New York's churches ready to take lives in defense of their property. The churches, it turned out, were never burned.

John Hughes was an ineffective administrator and a poor financial planner. He was, simply, a warrior—one, unfortunately, who reinforced the prejudices of the nativists against immigrant Catholics and helped set the Church on a course of anti-Americanization that lasted until the end of the nineteenth century.

The Americanizing trend returned to reach its peak in the 1890s. In the previous decade immigration had reached close to its all-time high, the Catholic population doubling from six to twelve million. The mood in the country was one of optimism: the Civil War was becoming a distant memory, industry and commerce were expanding at a fantastic rate, the United States was becoming a great power. The nation's optimism rubbed off on Church leaders like John Ireland, John Keane, John Lancaster Spalding, and James Gibbons. For the leaders by this time knew that the church could survive in America, knew that it could handle immigration and expansion, knew indeed that it was on the brink of spectacular success.

Said Ireland: "I can truly say that my Catholic heart and my American heart are one, and I am delighted to say that the free air of America has cheered the soul of Leo XIII, and that he has not been without guidance from our institutions. When the question is asked, 'Do you put Church before country or country before Church?' I say that one is not to be put before the other. They are in different spheres altogether."[23]

Said Keane: "During the past few years, my duty has compelled me to cross the ocean four times, and I have never visited the old countries abroad that I haven't come back thanking God that I am an American."[24]

Said Spalding: "We have shown that respect for law is compatible with civil and religious liberty; that a free people can become prosperous and strong . . . ; that the State and the Church can move in separate orbits and still cooperate for the common welfare; that men of different races and beliefs may live together in peace."[25]

Said Gibbons (in Rome): "For myself, as a citizen of the United States, without closing my eyes to our defects as a nation, I proclaim, with a deep sense of pride and gratitude, and in this great capital of Christendom, that I belong to a country where the civil government holds over us the aegis of its protection without interfering in the legitimate exercise of our sublime mission as ministers of the Gospel of Jesus Christ."[26]

These were men of radically differing temperaments, but men with much in common—incurable optimism (with the exception of Spalding in his moody moments), confidence, expansiveness, belief in democracy and the separation of church and state, social consciousness, eagerness for friendship with non-Catholics, pride in the American Church, concern for education, an active rather than a contemplative orientation, loyalty to Rome. They were cultural assimilationists, too. That fact hardly detracted from Greeley's enthusiasm for them when he wrote *The Catholic Experience*, though it would make a considerable difference in just a few years.

The enthusiasm of the Americanists of the 1890s came to an abrupt end. Pope Leo XIII issued an encyclical, *Testem Benevolentiae*, in which he condemned the "Americanism heresy"—a heresy, it seemed, that existed more in the preface of a French translation of the life of Isaac Hecker (another of the heroes of *The Catholic Experience*) than it did in America. While the encyclical did not name names, while it did not even affirm that certain condemned doctrines were in fact held in the United States, it took the élan from the 1890s. "Gibbons, Ireland, and Keane, even though they argued with some conviction that they had not been condemned, were deeply hurt by the letter, and some of the joy and verve went out of their lives."[27] The encyclical alone did not undermine the development of more men like Ireland, Keane, and Gibbons in the United States. The establishment there of an apostolic delegation (the Curia's man could now keep a watchful eye on the Americans), the training of future bishops at the American college in Rome (where they could be socialized into the appropriate ways of thinking), and the Modernist controversy all played a part as well. But it is eminently clear to the author of *The Catholic Experience* that bishops like these have not appeared in America since.

There were others heroes and villains in *The Catholic Experience*, Americanizers like Orestes Brownson in the nineteenth century, bigots like Father Charles Coughlin, the "radio priest" of the

postdepression years. The last man to capture Greeley's imagination, however, was John Fitzgerald Kennedy; and, writing in
1967, the author had a unique proposal in his regard:

> Canonize John Kennedy? At first such a suggestion surely seems
> facetious, and unquestionably would bring laughter to the lips of
> the aloof, witty, ironic man who was the first Catholic President of
> the United States. Yet in another age, when the manner and pur-
> pose of canonization were different, John Kennedy would cer-
> tainly be hailed as a saint. In the early years of Christianity, canon-
> ization was . . . the popular acclaim which the Christian
> community gave to someone who had become a hero. Great politi-
> cal leaders, especially those who died in the service of their country,
> were quite apt to become such heroes and be hailed as saints. Eng-
> land has its Edward, France has its Louis, Hungary has its
> Stephen. John Kennedy would certainly fit the qualifications be-
> cause one wonders if any man who has ever lived has ever been so
> much of a hero to so many people in so many different nations of
> the world.[28]

If we cannot make him a saint, Greeley continued, "perhaps the
most appropriate title would be 'doctor of the universal Church.' "
When Kennedy spoke as a candidate for the presidency before the
ministerial association in Houston, Texas, "for the first time in the
history of the American Church, a Catholic preaching the Church's
doctrine on the relationship between religion and society was believed, believed at least enough to be elected President of the United
States."[29] Anti-Catholic nativism did not die easily in 1960 (Kennedy's religion is estimated to have cost him five million votes) but it
was, albeit by the skimpiest of margins, defeated. For his role, for his
ability to make Catholic doctrine clear and credible, Greeley offered
Kennedy the unofficial title of "doctor of the Church."

On Inauguration Day 1961, American Catholicism, in the person of John Kennedy, had come full circle. For the first time since
Charles Carroll the most powerful American Catholic was not a
member of the hierarchy. The Catholic Church, having survived the
immigration trauma, was once again a legitimately native American Church; and within it the liberalizing tradition was victorious.

The triumph of the 1960s, however, would last no longer than
that of the 1890s. In the spring and summer of 1968 the nation's

emotions were grated by a series of shocks and surprises. The bombing of North Vietnam, and Lyndon Johnson, were on—then off. Martin Luther King, Jr. and Robert Kennedy, bearers of hope, were gunned down. In Europe the Russians took possession of Czechoslovakia, and in Chicago police and people battled in the streets as Democrats attempted to nominate a presidential candidate. Few people noticed when Paul VI issued "The Credo of the People of God" on June 30, but many were genuinely stunned a month later when he promulgated *Humanae Vitae*, the encyclical forbidding the use of "artificial" contraception.

Greeley's response to the document was to advise "cooling it." Data indicated that many Catholics were ignoring the pope's directives anyway—if not practicing even *more* birth control. Don't confront the issue, he said; the best strategy was "staying away from crisis wherever feasible and working out compromise solutions,"[30] all the time, of course, protecting one's own conscience.

But even that advice seemed like a band-aid to cover a ravenous cancer. In January, 1969 *Time* passed on to its readers predictions Greeley had made in *Overview*, a monthly newsletter of Chicago's Thomas More Association. Priests and nuns were going to abandon their vocations in increasing numbers, and new recruits were going to become scarce; more laymen and priests would refuse to accept the Church as authoritative teacher, especially in matters sexual; tensions between priests and bishops would grow; the Catholic educational system was in deep trouble because of a collapse in the morale of educators and, consequently, more and more schools would close. "Many of the auxiliary institutions of American Catholicism will suffer. Diocesan papers, publishing houses, book stores, and magazines, will be hard hit, and many will disappear from the scene."[31] Five years before, a "golden era" had been on its way.

Precise documentation of the American Church's abrupt setback did not come until 1974, when NORC replicated its 1963 study of parochial education. In the elevan years between the two surveys, weekly Mass attendance by adult Catholics dropped from 71 to 50 percent. In 1963, 70 percent thought it "certainly true" that Jesus handed over the leadership of the Church to Peter and the popes, but in 1974 only 42 percent believed likewise (and only 32 percent subscribed fully to the doctrine of papal infallibility). This decline in

Church authority was particularly evident in the matter of sex. In 1963, 45 percent approved artificial contraception; in 1974, despite *Humanae Vitae*, 83 percent did. Remarriage after divorce was accepted by 52 percent in 1963 and 73 percent in the new survey, sexual relations between an engaged couple by 12 percent in 1963 and 43 percent in 1974. In 1974, 36 percent felt that legal abortions should be available for married women who did not want more children (27 percent would consider one for themselves in such circumstances).

Later data were more chilling. Between 1965 and 1975 the number of seminarians decreased from 50,000 to 18,000. Religious sisters dropped from 180,000 to 135,000 religious brothers from 12,000 to 8,6000. Among the general population of Catholics, apostasy rates doubled from 7 to 14 percent. And all of this in the aftermath of such promise.

When Greeley was invited to More House, the Catholic Center at Yale University, to present a series of lectures in March, 1970, he attempted to set the dizzying sixties in perspective. Why the sudden disaster? Greeley began with a portrait of the 1950s, the years in which he was ordained a priest and was exhilarated by the enthusiasm of Christ the King parishioners. "Organizationally the church of the 1950s was prospering," he said. "It represented the finest flourishing of immigrant Catholicism, and in some ways was extraordinarily impressive. The immigrants and their children had built the most extensive and elaborate religious institutional structure in the world. It was John Courtney Murray who remarked, 'Good, very good, but not good enough.' "[32]

In 1960 two wheels that had been turning in the Catholic Church—slowly, independently, each at its own pace—happened to strike the twelfth hour simultaneously. In America the immigrant era ended, and the Church of cap-and-sweater people like the parishioners at St. Angela's was now the Church of suburbanites like those at Christ the King. And in the universal Church the era of the Counter-Reformation came to a close as Pope John ushered in the Ecumenical Age. Two defensive postures that had reinforced each other were being abandoned. "The lid was about to blow off."[33]

Within an all-too-brief period the reversals predicted in *Time* were facts of life. There would have been turmoil even without the Vatican Council, but when Pope John opened his little window, pent-up forces blew into the Church and were legitimized. There was an opportunity for a rapid reform of Church structure, and renewal seemed on its way—at least until John died and Church leaders lost their nerve and tried to put on the brakes. Most important, however, all those Catholics who had learned to question and criticize the old Church, who dismantled it with abandon, gave not a moment's thought to constructing something to replace it.

There were four major areas of destruction, and the first of them was the schools. As the 1960s opened, Catholic education could look back on the two most impressive decades in its history, but ten years later schools were closing and enrollment declining. The schools' *clients* had not done an about-face, but a handful of educators who read a few tiny books questioning the protectionist rationale of Catholic education lost confidence in what they were doing. They suffered from self-hate, too: "The grandson of the immigrant has to be out of the ghetto for a while before he does not have to feel defensive about his origins and is freed from the necessity of validating himself in the eyes of the outside world by attacking that from which he came."[34]

Ecclesiastical authority was in even more trouble than the schools by the end of the 1960s. Its legitimacy and credibility were under direct, even contemptuous, attack—something unheard of a decade before. Eighty percent of the Catholic population did not take seriously the Church's teaching on birth control, and substantial proportions of elite groups did not believe any of its teachings on other matters. Greeley explained the sudden shift with his "Meat on Friday" hypothesis: fiddle with even the smallest part of an ossified symbol system—repeal the ban against meat on Friday—and the entire apparatus is likely to fall apart. *That* was the weakness of the 1950s: beliefs and organizational patterns so rigid that even the slightest change, the barest breath of fresh air, could not be accommodated. All the structure could do was come down.

The decline of the clergy—the third disaster area— was more surprising than that of the schools or of ecclesiastical authority, for most of it occurred after 1965. The crashing of expectations that soared after the Vatican Council along with increasing uncertainty about their role created "a near-panic among the younger clergy and religious." The value system of the old Church specified that the priest was the leader and protector of the immigrant population, but with that clear delineation gone, what was the priest to do? Younger clergy "are disillusioned about renewal; they do not believe their leaders; they lack a sense of participation in decision making; they do not know what to do with the new freedom they have found; and they are very much afraid of the future."[35]

Sexuality was a fourth area in which the old had deteriorated without something new to take its place. "Sex is certainly the most corrosive issue facing Roman Catholicism at the present time . . . , the only subject on which the mass of the population is as disaffected as the elites." The Church's stance on birth control was questioned in private even in the fifties, but in the sixties younger clergy were willing not only to express their doubts publicly, but to act on them in the confessional. Again, the finger was pulled out of the dike. "If the birth-control theory can be questioned, then there seems to be no reason—at least in the minds of many—why the Church's position on divorce and, indeed, premarital and extramarital sexuality, and even homosexuality, cannot also be called into question."[36]

The story of the sixties, then, was the destruction of the old Church. A new one could have been built as the old came down, but "American Catholicism failed to respond to the challenge in the 1960s because neither the hierarchy nor the clergy nor the intellectuals were able to respond."[37]

There was no concealing Greeley's depression at the fate of an American Church that had ripped itself apart while he stood powerless on the fringes. His enthusiasm for John Kennedy would diminish in the years to come, and so would his support for the Americanizers on the issue of ethnic enclaves. In 1970 he was unwilling to say that *Humanae Vitae* was the *cause* of the turnabout in the fortunes of the Church (as *Testem Benevolentiae* had been in the 1890s), but data collected in 1974 would leave him no choice.

Those data were released in *Catholic Schools in a Declining Church* (1976). Not only did they alter Greeley's earlier "Meat on Friday" theory, they also proved false the claim of right-wingers that American Catholics were "turned off" by changes initiated by the Vatican Council. The Vatican Council, first of all, alienated only a minority of American Catholics: 19 percent thought that "changes in the Church" were for the worse; 14 percent were indifferent to them; and a full 67 percent thought they were for the better. Nor did the decline begin when Catholics were allowed to eat meat on Fridays. No, practically all the blame for the deterioration in American Catholic religiousness—the kind of religiousness sociologists can measure, at any rate—could be placed squarely on the doorstep of *Humanae Vitae*. The encyclical on birth control was far more important than Greeley had thought earlier.

According to Gallup data, Catholic Mass attendance dropped only two percentage points between the end of the Council in 1965 and the publication of *Humanae Vitae* in 1968, but it declined eight percentage points in the three years following the encyclical. Apostasy rates, which had remained at 7 percent from 1953 to 1967, doubled after the encyclical (no change was observed in the same period in the Protestant rate of 9 percent); the same thing happened with rates of resignation from the priesthood and religious orders. The young were particularly susceptible. Between 1967 and 1974 approximately a quarter of college-educated Catholics under 30 left the Church. In the decade bracketed by the two NORC surveys financial contributions to the Church from Catholic families declined by 31 percent, and three-fourths of the loss (which totaled $1.7 billion in 1974) was directly attributable to a negative reaction to the birth control directive. On practically every measure of religious devotion and loyalty to the Church, the largest chunk of variance was related to subjects' acceptance or rejection of *Humanae Vitae*.

In the words of Greeley, "The Vatican Council appears to have been one of the great religious successes in human history. Many of the fundamental practices and structures of the Catholic Church, unchanged for over 1,500 years, were transformed in the space of a few years, months, or even on a single Sunday morning."[38] American Catholics were uplifted by the changes and seemed eager for more. Then came July 29, 1968.

We know now that by that date, most Catholics had already made a decision about the morality of the Pill. They were *for* it, and when Pope Paul denounced it (let it be said, against the advice of a commission appointed to study the matter), Catholics discredited him and the institution he represented. If he could be so patently wrong on such a critical issue, one affecting what goes on in the beds

of married people three times a week, he could be wrong about anything. Catholic people felt disillusioned, betrayed— is *this* what the
council and the "changes" were all about? Most did not leave the
Church, and Pill-users continued to receive communion as often as
other Catholics. But the damage to institutional Catholicism was
profound, and all that Vatican II might have become was prema-
turely aborted. "I have no doubt," Greeley said, "that historians of
the future will judge *Humanae Vitae* to be one of the worst mistakes in the history of Catholic Christianity."[39]

As the 1960s came to a close, the waves of Greeley's dream were
striking with fury. A leader of an intimate community that was
tearing itself to pieces, Greeley saw similar self-destruction throughout the American Church. His investments, like those of his father,
were disappearing in a great spiritual crash. At the time Greeley told
a group of friends:

> The things I wanted to accomplish have all been failures. I think
> I'm realistic enough to know that I am not responsible for the
> failures, but failures they were just the same. I dreamed of training
> a new Catholic lay elite in Christ the King and this did not happen.
> I hoped my decade of research on Catholic education would make a
> contribution to the rejuvenation of this battered but important
> institution, but it did not. I wanted to be a sociologist to help plan
> the future of the Chicago Archdiocese and I shall never do this. I
> hoped that the post-Conciliar renewal would lead to the emer-
> gence of a stronger American church, simultaneously Catholic and
> American, and to this effort devoted much of my writing for many
> years; and it is now clear that the post-Conciliar renewal has
> turned from a rout into a disaster. I had high hopes for the Asso-
> ciation of Chicago Priests and wrote most of the draft which led to
> the personnel board; I now know that the ACP is a failure. I was
> deeply involved in the higher educational reform movement, parti-
> cularly by authoring the Hazen Report which is now considered a
> landmark in higher education literature; but this reform is now as
> dead as the students at Kent State. I thought that community of
> young people with whom I associated might become a center for a
> new style of religious dedication and I now have little expectation
> that it will ever get much beyond a pleasant study group.[40]

"I despair," he told them, "about the future of American Catholicism. I think that very little of it will be saved." And of himself: "I
conclude that I am not a man for this season."

Despair in Father Greeley, however, always manages to evoke its opposite. Even as the disastrous sixties reached their denouement, a leprechaun, down but not out, found its way to the tip of his pen. Greeley reported on the first papal press conference ever held in the English language. The pontiff was an Irish-Italian raised in Brooklyn and a graduate of the Harvard School of Business:

(Kevin Cardinal Orsini was elected Pope by "inspiration" on the forty-third day of the conclave; ninety-six-year-old Cardinal Antonelli leaped from his throne in the Sistine Chapel and shouted in his feeble voice, "Orsini Papa!" With varying degrees of weariness, surprise, dismay, and joy, all the other cardinals echoed the shout: "Orsini Papa!" It was then pointed out by several of those present that this was indeed a legitimate and definitive way of selecting a pope, even though it was one that apparently had not been used in the history of the Papacy. Almost without realizing it, the cardinals had selected their youngest member, the forty-six-year-old Orsini, as the new Pope. There were some, later on, who claimed that Antonelli had been sound asleep, and in his sleep had had a nightmare of Orsini becoming Pope. His cry of "Orsini Papa!" it was alleged, was not an inspiration from the Holy Spirit, but the result of a bad dream. In any case, Orsini's supporters had seized the opportunity to proclaim their man the victor, and after forty-three days of a conclave in which nine cardinals had already died, no one was prepared to dispute his claim to the Papacy.)

Kevin I, attired in a gray Savile Row suit, light blue shirt, and Paisley tie, finally arrived at the Monte Mario for his press conference, a transcript of which appeared the following day in the New York *Times*:

Q. (*Times* of London) Your Holiness, the whole world is wondering—
A. Please don't call me Your Holiness. I don't know that I'm all that holy, and it's sort of an old-fashioned name. You can call me Pope or Mr. Pope, but please don't call me Your Holiness.
Q. Well, yes, sir. The whole world is wondering what your position will be on the birth-control issue.
A. I think it's a very complex issue and one that I certainly wouldn't want to address myself to in any specific detail this morning. We have really messed up this sex business in the Church for a long time and I don't think we're going to be able to make any coherent Christian statement on family planning until we do a lot of thinking and talking about the whole question of sexual personalism. . . .

Q. (St. Louis *Post-Dispatch*) There has been considerable talk of restoring the practice of popular election of bishops to the Catholic Church. Would you care to comment on this possibility?

A. Oh, I'd be happy to comment. Two of my predecessors of happy memory—I can't quite remember what their names were, but they were back in the sixth century—said that it was sinful to choose a bishop by any other methods besides popular election. Being at heart a very conservative fellow, I agree with them. . . .

Q. (St. Louis *Post-Dispatch*) Then, am I to understand, sir, that you are in favor of limited terms for bishops and perhaps even for the Pope?

A. Well, if you think I'm going to stay in this office until I die in it, you're sadly mistaken. This may be a fine job for five or ten years, but after that I'm going to want to retire someplace where it's peaceful and quiet. . . .

Q. (*Wall Street Journal*) Are we to take it, sir, that you are going to make public the financial status of the Vatican?

A. Well, I'm going to try and do it as soon as I can figure out what the financial status is. As far as I can understand, nobody but God exactly understands the finances of the Vatican, and unfortunately he's not about to make a private revelation on the subject.

Q. (*Triumph*) Most Holy Father—

A. I'm not Holy, and I'm certainly not Most Holy, and I'm also certainly not your father or anybody else's, so call me Pope, or Mr. Pope, or Bishop, and drop the rest of that nonsense.

Q. (*Triumph*, again) You will, of course, maintain the papal diplomatic service?

A. I will most certainly do no such thing. . . .

Q. (Manchester *Guardian*) What do you intend to do about *Osservatore Romano*?

A. I wish to heaven I knew what to do about it—would you like to be editor of it?

Q. No, sir, I wouldn't.

A. Yeah, that's what they all say. Next question, please. . . .

Q. (Frankfurter *Zeitung*) Do you expect there to be any heresy trials in your administration?

A. Good God, no! . . .

Q. (Frankfurter *Zeitung*) But what do you think of the case of Reverend Dr. Hans Küng?

A. You mean do I think Hans is a heretic? Why, don't be silly. Hans is basically a conservative. I never could understand why people thought he was dangerous or a radical. How in the world can anybody who owns an Alfa-Romeo be a radical?

Q. (*Il Messaggero*) What, your Holiness—I mean, Pope—what is your opinion on the forthcoming Italian elections?

A. I hope everybody votes in them.

Q. (*Il Messaggero*) But what party are you supporting?

A. We've got a secret ballot in this country just like most other countries, and who I vote for is my secret.

Q. (*Il Messaggero*) But are you going to take a stand in Italian politics?

A. What's the matter? Do you think I'm crazy? . . .

Q. (Milwaukee *Sentinel*) Do you intend, sir, to continue the practice of censorship of books that are written by Catholics?

A. I think it would be a good idea to take every imprimatur in the world and throw it in the furnace, and we ought to throw half of the book censors in the furnace, too. The basic thing to say about censorship is that it didn't work, it doesn't work, and it's never going to work, and the quicker we forget about it, the better off we're all going to be.

Q. (Washington *Post*) From all you've said so far, sir, it would seem that you are really anticipating a very notable decline in papal authority. I wonder if you could tell us whether you think that this is a drastic change in Church doctrine?

A. Well, I don't know where you got that idea; I must say, as a matter of fact, I think what I'm talking about is a rather notable increase in papal authority. . . .

Q. (*Seventeen*) Do you have anything to say for young people?

A. Well, I'd say to the young to be patient with us older people because we're going to try and learn how to listen to you, and that we'll try, in our turn, to be patient with you while you try to learn how to listen to us. I don't think there's much wrong with young people that a little bit of experience won't cure—and there's not much wrong with older people that sharing the enthusiasm of the young won't cure.

Q. (New York *Times*) Thank you, Mr. Pope.

A. You're quite welcome, Scotty.[41]

I once asked Father Greeley about the muse who created that piece: "What *is* a leprechaun?"

His face brightened. "A fun spirit—the Holy Spirit when he goes to Ireland. He's always serious, but so serious that he's a playful, laughing spirit. He wheels and deals and whirls and swirls and dives and dances and claps his hands." A bubbling yet hardened old sprite, bouncing on the surface, yet knowing the depths, knowing, in fact, something that we do not about life and death, about sustaining loss. Greeley smiled and hit upon the spirit's essence: "He plays tricks."

"You mean he pokes fun?"

"No. Plays tricks."

I knew from his tone that "plays tricks" said it all and said it perfectly. Somehow, some part of Andrew Greeley was able to view all that had happened to him in the 1960s as a leprechaun-like spirit having fun with him, surprising him, making jokes at his expense. Some Holy Spirit, though, I thought later. He whispers in Greeley's ear to *challenge* the young, knowing full well that *love* is what they need. He tells him the good news about future Catholic intellectuals and chuckles as he fails to add that good news is bad news. He gets Greeley wildly enthusiastic over a new church and a new school but doesn't mention the cracks in the basement. And, as a matter of fact, he steers him right to the top of the roof (where he can take in the broad view of a sociologist) so he'll be sitting in just the right spot as the buildings come crashing down.

That's like calling someone over for a look at the dike and then pulling your finger out of the wall.

Or inviting him to a wedding and then throwing a wake.

6   **And Then God Died**

When Harvey Cox published *The Secular City* in 1965, it did not take long for Andrew Greeley to ignite a crackling debate over the very premise of that widely acclaimed book. To Cox, "secularization" meant "the loosing of the world from religious and quasi-religious understandings of itself, the dispelling of all closed world-views, the breaking of all supernatural myths and sacred symbols." It meant, simply, the aging and eventual passing away of religion, a peaceful end, to be sure, but a death nevertheless. Secularization, he argued, was the by-product of urbanization, a structure of common life increasingly characteristic of rural villages as well as cities, in which impersonality, tolerance of diversity, and anonymity have replaced traditional moral sanctions and long-term acquaintanceships. "The urban center is the place of human control, of rational planning, of bureaucratic organization—and the urban center is not just in Washington, London, New York, and Peking. It is everywhere."[1] When man moved from tribe to town, he changed his gods, and as he now migrates from town to technopolis, he alters his deities once again, this time finding them no longer necessary.

Do not attempt to stem the tide of secularization, preached Cox—a Baptist theologian—in *The Secular City*, for you will be sure to lose. Let us, rather, welcome the new metropolis, celebrate its arrival, and discover the spiritual possibilities within it.

> Secularization rolls on, and if we are to understand and communicate with our present age we must learn to love it in its unremitting secularity. We must learn, as [Dietrich] Bonhoeffer said, to speak of God in a secular fashion and find a nonreligious interpretation of biblical concepts. It will do no good to cling to our

religious and metaphysical versions of Christianity in the hope
that one day religion or metaphysics will once again be back. They
are disappearing forever and that means we can now let go and
immerse ourselves in the new world of the secular city.[2]

We are liberated, he declared, from the religious and metaphysical
tutelage of the past; we can now turn from a preoccupation with
other worlds to the salvation of this one, we have at last—praise the
(secular) lord—"come of age."

In stepped Andrew Greeley. Was religion itself (not just the
American Catholic Church) in a state of decay? Greeley thought not
and said so in a *Commonweal* symposium edited by Daniel
Callahan.

The trouble, Greeley said bluntly, is that Cox's secular city just
does not exist. "The question at issue is not whether the unsecular
city is better than the secular one, but whether the secular city actually exists and whether secular man is very common." What proof
does Cox offer for his theory of faceless modern man? "Cox quotes
T. S. Eliot, Sören Kierkegaard, Ortega y Gasset, [Rainer Maria]
Rilke, Franz Kafka, and Ferdinand Tönnies; and this, my friends,
is the sociological dimension in contemporary theology. We argue
to an anonymous, mobile, secularist society on the grounds that
everyone knows it exists (including sophomores) and that theologians, philosophers and the literati know it more than anyone
else."[3]

Greeley acknowledged that Tönnies did describe a shift in
lifestyle from peasant society to industrial society, from *Gemeinschaft* ("community") to *Gesellschaft* ("association"). And Greeley
found the distinction illuminating: *Gemeinschaft* man living a life
that was traditional, intimate, family-centered, static, having relationships that were few in number but face-to-face and of lifelong
duration; *Gesellschaft* man, on the other hand, mobile, anonymous, unhampered by roots, relating to others in impersonal,
rational, contractual ways; *Gemeinschaft* man constrained by the
very closeness of his ties to tradition and to others; *Gesellschaft* man
"liberated" (or so Cox claimed) by the anonymity of his urban life,
"liberated" enough to divest himself of God.

Greeley had no quarrel with Cox's claim that *Gesellschaft* had
made its appearance, but he adamantly refused to concede that it had

replaced its opposite. Secular man exists, all right, but side by side with unsecular man and, if the evidence is to be believed, in far smaller numbers than unsecular man. *Gemeinschaft* communities still flourish amidst the anomie of urban life; indeed, in some strange way, they crop up in the most bureaucratized segments of the city. The metropolis, Greeley argued, is not anomic, but symbiotic, "made up not of atomized individuals, but of hundreds of tightly organized and competing local neighborhood communities," often defined along religious and ethnic lines. Real-estate men planning developments know as much. So do politicians drawing up tickets. So do journalists, community organizers, and civil rights leaders. So does the Chicago Commission on Human Relations. So does the federal government. So does everyone, it seems, except those "at the upper levels of university life" (that was for Cox) "or in the mass media" (that was for Daniel Callahan and *Commonweal*).[4]

Cox was given a chance to reply to Greeley's remarks, and reply he did. He did not, he answered, say that unsecular, *Gemeinschaft* man has disappeared from the city. "Even today," he had written in *The Secular City*, "we find residents of New York City with a tribal mentality"—but perhaps Father Greeley forgot to read that page.[5] The real differences between Greeley and himself, Cox went on, concern the future. How can Father Greeley, pledged to the most sophisticated kind of sociological analysis, be so sure about what is coming? Greeley's position belies "an unarticulated but operative theory of social stasis," an assumption that things will basically remain the same. This orientation is common in contemporary sociology, but is not without its critics. Even the patriarchal Max Weber assumed that society's change was linear and directional, not cyclic or homeostatic.

When Callahan gathered the arguments together in *The Secular City Debate* (1966), he wanted to leave out Greeley's reply-to-the-reply, but Greeley raised "blue bloody hell" and so he— Greeley—was given the last word. The last word consisted of respect for Cox ("In a world where it is difficult to find anyone who will engage in an honest argument, Mr. Cox is only too willing to argue, and for this I salute him") but none for Callahan ("Mr. Callahan clearly does not want to argue and so I will not argue with him").[6] He then pinpointed the essence of his quarrel with Cox. If we agree, he said, that the city is both secular and unsecular, we must be arguing about the future—will the secular prevail? And the burden of proof, said Greeley, is on Harvey Cox (the reverse, of course, of what Cox had told Greeley). Greeley would believe it when he saw it. Nor, said Greeley, did he espouse a static theory of society; he believed that society is changing, but the change is one of "differentiation" and not "secularization."

"Differentiation," Greeley later told readers of *The Hesitant Pilgrim*, is a concept of Talcott Parsons, who sees society moving toward greater and greater complexity. As it does, multipurpose institutions of the past abandon some of their functions to newly emerging institutions. Religion and society, in Parsons's view, were at one time practically identical; but now many of the functions performed by religious organizations—such as medical care, education, and social welfare—have been taken over by secular ones. This does not mean that religion has become less important, but rather that its function has become more focused—to provide meaning and a sense of belonging. An analogy is the family; once the seat of such activities as manufacturing, education, and entertainment that have progressively become removed from it. Their removal, however, has not diminished the importance of the family. It still provides a center of intimacy in a society becoming more impersonal by the day. In a similar way, said Greeley, religion has *retreated* from society's institutional life—and Cox is correct in this sense—but the retreat is a manifestation not of secularization, but of differentiation. The religious dimension of man's life is as important as it ever was.

So the debate came down to predictions about the future. Would secularization and *Gesellschaft* come to dominate man's manner of association, or would they follow the pattern of differentiation, falling into coexistence with religion and *Gemeinschaft* bonding? In 1966 the argument took a bizarre turn when theologians Thomas Altizer and William Hamilton tossed into the fray the proclamation that God had died. "We must realize that the death of God is an historical event, that God has died in our cosmos, in our history, in our *existenz*,"[7] they wrote in *Radical Theology and the Death of God* (1966); and in no time at all the American public was being informed of, and even propagandized about, their theological "breakthrough." When *Catholic Digest* asked Greeley to comment on data collected for them by the Gallup organization in 1965, he saw his chance to cut down this "mad offspring" of the secularization hypothesis. The Gallup data were replies of a national sample of adults to questions concerning religious beliefs and practices—questions identical to ones asked of another national sample in 1952 by Ben Gaffin and Associates. Despite the fact that the 1952 data cards had been lost, one could still make broad comparisons between 1952 and 1965—a rare opportunity, at that time, in sociological research. In *What Do We Believe?* (1968) the 1952–1965 differences were analyzed by Protestant historian-theologian Martin Marty (who saw an erosion of distinctive theological positions among Protestants, but no evidence of secularization), Jewish rabbi-scholar Stuart Rosenberg (who complained about the small number of Jewish respondents and insisted the questionnaire was inappropriate to the Jewish experience), and Catholic priest-sociologist Andrew Greeley.

Greeley began by commenting on "the God who would not stay dead." The God-is-dead outburst, he charged, is nothing more than a "public relations gimmick," touching "what apparently is an important aspect of the American personality, the willingness, even eagerness, to believe that everything is rapidly going to hell." Well, everything is not going to hell, he said, nor does God "even seem to be appreciably ill."[8] In 1952, 99 percent of America's adult population believed in God and was at least "quite sure" about that belief. In 1965, the percentage was 96—an insignificant change. The only noticeable decline in belief was among the small number of Jewish respondents, from 97 percent in 1952 to 75 percent in 1965. Figures for Protestants were 99 percent in 1952 and 98 percent in 1965; for Catholics, 100 percent in 1952 and 100 percent in 1965. Even 75 percent of those who professed no religion or a religion other than the major three—they were 7 percent of the total sample—were "quite sure" of God's existence in 1965 (this compared with 83 percent in 1952). None of the data gave the slightest hint that a religionless society was on its way.

Other variables in the survey told the same story. Belief in the divinity of Christ, in the Trinity, in life after death showed only negligible changes from 1952 to 1965; nor was there any difference in the number of respondents who said they prayed or considered themselves active members of a church. The only question that yielded results in any way compatible with the secularization hypothesis was "How important would you say religion is in your own life?" In 1952, 75 percent said "very important"; by 1965, the percentage had dropped to 70. But this was only the most meager support—especially in view of the fact that in the same period church and synagogue attendance had actually taken an upswing.

And what of young people—those whose beliefs and behaviors were likely to give an indication of what was coming in the years ahead? "The Future of God," Greeley reported (cautioning that the young were a dubious basis for prediction), looks about the same among those between 18 and 25 years of age as it does among those over 25. Catholic youth in 1965 were as likely as older Catholics to believe in God and more likely to believe in life after death. Protestant youth were somewhat less likely to pray and to believe in life after death than were Protestants over 25, though more of the younger generation (100 percent, in fact) said they believed in God. (The comparison could not be made for Jews because of the small numbers of respondents.) Greeley concluded that "young American Protestants and Catholics are, if anything, more likely to believe that God is not dead than are their parents."[9]

Religion had not declined appreciably in the United States between 1952 and 1965. That conclusion was consistent with the best data available on the subject, data that were admittedly tenuous. It was hardly a spectacular finding. As the authors wrote, "The reality which we are describing, alas, in this volume tends to be very gray, very complicated, and relatively dull."[10]

The year 1969, however, was not so dull. Pentecostalism and the Jesus movement gained strength. Harvey Cox, the high priest of secular theology, joined the ranks of renascent supernaturalists in *The Feast of Fools*. And more, wrote Greeley:

> During a recent unpleasantness between the University of Chicago and its SDS, the normal, decorous quiet of the Social Science building was rent one fine afternoon by ear-piercing shrieks. Secretaries, research assistants, and even a few faculty members dashed to their office doors to discover who was being murdered. Three young women dressed in shabby and tattered garments were stand-

ing in front of the Sociology Department office shrieking curses: "Fie on thee, Morris Janowitz! A hex on thy strategy!"

WITCH (Women's International Terrorist Conspiracy from Hell) had come to put a curse on the Sociology Department.

So far, nothing seems to have happened to Professor Janowitz or the Sociology Department. But if it does, there are going to be an awful lot of frightened people along the Midway. (I offered as a matter of professional courtesy to sprinkle holy water on the departmental office, but, while social science is ready for witch-craft, it is not yet ready for exorcism.)[11]

WITCH was just the tip of the iceberg. Across the land, Greeley told readers of the *New York Times Magazine* in June 1969, "There's a New Time Religion on Campus." Asian philosophy, meditation, yoga, Zen, the *Bardo Thodol*, tantra, the kundalini, the chakras, the *I Ching*, karate, aikido, the yang-yin, macrobiotic diets, Gurdjieff, Meher Baba, astrology, astral bodies, auras, UFOs, tarot cards, parapsychology, mysticism, sorcery, spiritualism, magic— and, of course, psychedelic drugs—all had appeared on campus. A Catholic university had a coven of warlocks. On the West Coast, semimonastic cults subsisted on vegetarian diets and spent long hours in contemplation. "What (you should excuse the expression) the hell is going on?"[12]

What was going on, Greeley answered his own question, was something funny yet quite serious, a put-on that was not a put-on, a strange admixture that in days long past was called *liturgy*—or sacred play. "To put a hex on the Sociology Department is comic, but it is also a tentative assertion that there are powers in Heaven and on Earth that may transcend sociology departments." Though the bizarre return of the sacred is limited to a minority of students, it is curious that the resurgence is taking place among elite groups at the best universities—at precisely those places, in other words, where secularization ought to be the most effective and the most complete. "One repeats the question: What the hell is going on? God is dead, but the devil lives?"[13]

What was going on? When Greeley asked students in his Sociology of Religion class, they began to talk immediately about the failure of science. "Let's face it," one graduate student said, "science is

dead. While the newspapers and magazines were giving all the attention to the death of God, science was really the one that was dying."
The science he was speaking of was rational, positivistic, empirical
science—precisely the kind at which Greeley was spending a career.
"Imperialistic" science had not ended war or injustice, had not
responded to men's needs. Nor did the "rational" faculty and
administration at the university live up to their own scientific principles. "One may disagree with such an indictment of science,"
Greeley commented, "and yet when Berger, the hero of *Hair*, says,
'Screw your science, screw your rationality,' he speaks for many of
his generation."[14]

Religion at least recognizes that man is more than reason; so the
students explained their feelings to Greeley. Religion does something about a sinking sense of alienation and unimportance. Why
use the *I Ching* when the IBM 360 is available? Because, one student
said, "The *I Ching* says that there are powers that stand beyond and
are more powerful than the 360, powers with which in some way
you can enter into a meaningful relationship when you can't do it
with the 360." And the cults are something to which their members
can *belong*: "If you get into a group like that, you at least know that
somebody will notice the difference if you're murdered. Around the
university, you could be dead in your room for days and nobody
would even know the difference." Religion offers *meaning*, too, the
beginnings of an interpretive scheme. In the words of a young
woman, "The sacred is even better than drugs because when you're
on drugs the world looks beautiful to you only if you're on a trip
and ugly when you're not on a trip. But religion has persuaded some
people that the world is beautiful most of the time, despite the ugli-
ness we see."[15]

It would not be fair to say that these neo-sacralists "believe in
God"—at least in the one they left in their parish congregations—
but, in Greeley's judgment, they are experimenting with the
"experience of the sacred" and are authentically religious.
"Personal efficacy, meaning, community, encounter with the ecstatic and the transcendental, and the refusal to believe that mere
reason can explain either life or personhood—all of these have traditionally been considered religious postures."[16] God might have died

down the street in the faculty lounge of the divinity school, but He had just popped up among students at the heart of a "secular" campus.

The year 1969 also saw another Greeley assault on the secularization hypothesis. Is religion on the wane? he asked in *Religion in the Year 2000*. If we cannot answer that question with good longitudinal data (and that contained in *What Do We Believe?* was far from the best), we can at least make use of comparative data. How, for example, would the vitality of religion compare with that of the American political system?

> ITEM: Approximately 60 percent of the American electorate votes in national elections. Approximately 68 percent of the adult population attends religious services in any given four-week period.

> ITEM: 27 percent of the electorate reports it discussed politics with others prior to an election; 90 percent of the people in the Detroit area, the only geographic source of data on this point, reports discussing religion with others during the month just past.

> ITEM: Approximately five families in every 100 made a financial contribution to a political party or candidate in 1956. At least 40 in every 100 made a financial contribution to a religious body; three in every 100 tithe.

> ITEM: Only 7 percent of all respondents says it has no strong feelings about its religious beliefs. . . . the proportion of the electorate that declares itself indifferent to political positions and issues is always greater than 7 percent.[17]

The comparisons could be multiplied at great length, according to Greeley's source, Guy A. Swanson, but there would be little point in going on. If we juxtapose data on religion with data on contemporary politics, we must be cautious indeed—and that's putting it mildly—with assertions of the present irrelevance of religion.

In *Religion in the Year 2000* Greeley for the first time presented sociological evidence in opposition to his own—presented it, that is, so that he could proceed to demolish it. Sociologists Charles Glock and Rodney Stark, for example, had discovered (especially in liberal

Protestant denominations) that substantial numbers of respondents to their questionnaires said that the existence of God was only "probably"—not "certainly"—true. And, when asked to describe how they thought of God, surprisingly high percentages failed to say He was a person—a concept at the heart of their Christian tradition. Glock and Stark concluded that there were large numbers of doubters, and large numbers of unorthodox believers, within the boundaries of the traditional religious denominations.

Greeley rebutted by saying that a response of "probably" true to the question of God's existence did not indicate doubt but a high degree of religious and theological sophistication. Respondents were aware that the existence of God could not be demonstrated with the certainty of a mathematical theorem; yet they still remained religiously committed. The same could be said of their concept of God. Ambiguity did not reflect doubt but an appreciation of the complexity of the question of God.

Another argument advanced in support of the secularization hypothesis was that America's degree of religious participation was an exception to the norm for nations in the industrial West. "One need only visit European countries"—so the argument ran—"or look at the European survey data to realize that Church membership and Church attendance are very low in these countries and that in some of them, such as England, comparative figures from the preceding century indicate the extent of the decline in religious practices."[18]

This was an impressive argument, Greeley conceded, yet he had answers. First of all, belief in God was not at all that low in Europe. Surveys in Scandinavia, Italy, the Low Countries, Czechoslovakia, and Great Britain showed that between 80 and 85 percent of adults believed in God. And surveys were ambivalent as well. In one West German poll, only 68 percent of the respondents said they were certain of God's existence, but 86 percent admitted to praying! Furthermore, a lack of overt practice need not mean that religion has disappeared from the personal lives of people. David Martin looked at apparently religionless individuals in Great Britain and noted:

> Of the doubters and agnostics and atheists, over a quarter say they pray on occasion to the God whose existence they doubt; one in twelve went to church within the past six months. . . . Over half

the nonbelievers consider that there should be religious education
in the schools. . . . Nearly a quarter tend to think that Christ was
something more than a man.[19]

Greeley's interpretation of these and other of Martin's data was
that "Church membership and Church affiliation in England may
be less striking than in the United States" (perhaps because England's working class can only view the Anglican parson as a squire
from the seventeenth century) "but basic religious convictions still
seem to persist in great masses of the population."[20]
    Why, then, does the secularization hypothesis prevail?

It seems to me that there are any number of reasons for this; all
kinds of people—journalists (particularly those writing for religious journals), religious leaders, professional viewers-with-alarm,
and other insecure types—have a considerable amount of emotion
invested in the proposition that the world is going to hell in the
proverbial hand basket. Secondly, theologians feeling very much
in the backwaters of the university world are frequently almost
pathetically eager to prove that they are as enlightened as are their
colleagues in the "real" sciences, who apparently are the people
they have in mind when they speak of modern man. . . .[21]

    The most important reason for the current strength of the
secularization hypothesis, however, is the belief in many sectors of
academia that religion and science are incompatible. Often religion
"is dismissed with the facile agnostic answer that one can neither
prove nor disprove the existence of God or of the Transcendent"—a
dismissal more likely to occur in social science and humanities
departments than in the physical or biological sciences. "Perhaps
the physical scientists and the biologists are less likely to be so
certain about incompatibility because they realize what a chancy,
uncertain, unpredictable thing the scientific quest really is."[22]
Instead of predicting the demise of religion, however, it would be far
more useful to sort out the complex relationship between religion
and science—a relationship which has not produced unbearable ten-
sion for the overwhelming majority of people.
    If religion is not going to fade away, what will be its shape in
the year 2000? Greeley's forecast was not at all startling: religious
denominations would not yield to the ecumenical movement;

doctrinal orthodoxy would remain; people would still worship in local congregations; the religious masses would not abandon the churches (nor, on the other hand, would they cease to be passive); despite an increase in part-time or limited-term clergy, full-time clergy would continue as the majority of religious functionaries; the Low-Church liturgy of the underground would not replace other forms of worship. Against this backdrop of revolutions that would never come to pass, Greeley saw "a number of very dramatic changes in North Atlantic and American religion." Religion and social science were about to enter into a dialogue from which both would profit immensely. Religion, in particular, would come to appreciate the essential link between religious development and personality development, to understand the central role of sexuality in the entire developmental process. There would be more tolerance of diversity within and between the various religious traditions, and there would be democratic structures capable of managing that diversity. Individual responsibility would continue to be stressed, and greater concern would be shown for small, intimate, fellowship congregations. By the end of the century clergymen would clearly understand that their role was to be that of an expressive and affectionate leader. Finally, there would be a continued decline in Puritanism and substantially more emphasis on the nonrational, "both the ecstatic and Dionysian nonrational and also the reflective and the contemplative and mystical nonrational."[23]

Above all, religion in the year 2000 would still *be*.

"Death-of-God" theology burned itself out as quickly as it had been ignited. By 1970 the media were discovering a religious revival in America, and sociologists and theologians were describing it as "counter-secularization." Ridiculous, said Father Greeley in an issue of *Social Research*. "Society was never really 'de-sacralized' in the first place."[24] The secular city was born in Selma and died in Watts, and (he added in the *New York Times*) "the only place God might really have been dead was in the divinity schools and I have a hunch that all he actually did was to go on a sabbatical."[25]

Greeley was less concerned now with the *statistics* of belief in God, more inclined to search for an *explanation* of the reasons for the persistence of religion. He was under greater pressure to "utter theory" and cut down those critics from sociology who dismissed him as nothing but an empiricist out to destroy the conventional wisdom. His emerging views on religion would show the influence of many social scientists (and he would quote them all at great length), but none was as important as Clifford Geertz, a colleague at the University of Chicago and a former student of Talcott Parsons. Greeley and Geertz often had lunch together at Chicago and frequently attended each other's seminars. Greeley would never tire of acknowledging his debt to Geertz, describing it in one book as "immense," saying in another that Geertz was "the most distinguished social scientist of religion currently practicing."[26]

The seeds of Greeley's sociology of religion were sown in *What Do We Believe?* when he pinpointed two functions of religion—to provide senses of belonging and meaning. In 1972 a book was devoted to each of these. The first was *The Denominational Society*, a textbook in the sociology of religion, not "very high-level theorizing" to be sure, but "an attempt to use the theories of other men to understand the complexities of American religious phenomena."[27] The second, *Unsecular Man*, went to the heart of Andrew Greeley's understanding of religion.

The Denominational Society contended that the United States was one of only four societies in the western world (the others were Canada, Holland, and Switzerland) in which there was neither a single established church nor a variety of protesting sects, but denominations, a unique organizational adjustment to the fact of religious pluralism. Why did religion in America take on denominational characteristics? For one reason, the religious pluralism of the original colonies inhibited the development of an established church. For another, the "belonging vacuum" created by immigration from Europe to America, by the transition from peasant village to industrial metropolis, insured that religion in this country would provide not only meaning but also a sense of social location and social identity.

It was Emile Durkheim who emphasized the integrative function of religion in society; indeed, for him, the collective and the religious were practically coterminous. Anthropologist Bronislaw Malinowski took objection to Durkheim's identification of society and religion, yet he agreed that religion was "the very cement of social fabric. . . . Its function is to hold society together in face of the stress and strains brought to it by disasters and threats that are both internal and external."[28] Since Malinowski's time social theorists have argued that religion can fractionate society as well as unify it—and their arguments are cogent indeed. Nevertheless, it remains true that religion, in the variety of its manifestations across the globe, has proved capable of bringing the people of a given society together.

In America it brought together wave after wave of immigrants landing on a strange and alien shore. Religion in this country has always been an ethnic phenomenon. In *Protestant, Catholic, Jew,* Will Herberg described how immigrants *became* ethnics—Poles and Russians and Slovaks and Greeks—*after* arriving in this country, and he noted how integral to the process were the various churches. By providing places where they could meet and be with their own kind, churches helped bewildered immigrants sort out who they were in a complex and confusing society. The religious institutions that emerged were not churches in the European sense, for none aspired to become *the* national ecclesiastical institution; nor were they sects because they were socially established, normative, nuclear to the society.

Denominationalism explains the unusually high level of religious observance in America. In Europe there was simply no "belonging vacuum" of the magnitude that the immigration experience created here, no need for people to search for a place where *their* language was spoken and *their* customs carried on.

One thing more: it would be a mistake to make the facile assumption that America's pluralistic political structure set the stage for the pluralism of its religious denominations. An equally strong case could be made for the reverse of that proposition, that the multidenominational nature of the original colonies was a *fait accompli* that the framers of the Constitution had to deal with. Delegates to the Constitutional Convention came as representatives of denominational states, as Congregationalists, Friends, Presbyterians, Anglicans. Their milieu was one of pluralism, and the document they created outlined a political structure able to deal with pluralism, able to absorb the variety of immigrants who came in later years.

Unsecular Man, the hub of a constellation of other Greeley volumes, opened with characteristic bluntness. "Let us be clear at the beginning: this is a volume of dissent. It rejects most of the conventional wisdom about the contemporary religious situation"—wisdom perpetrated by popular journals, divinity schools, self-defined "relevant" clerics and laymen, pop sociological-religious analysts, sociologists who do not specialize in religion but feel free to pronounce upon its state. Greeley not only saw to it that his enemies knew who they were; he also made sure that he himself was standing out in the open, that his position would not be misinterpreted: "the basic human religious needs and the basic religious functions have not changed very notably since the late Ice Age."[29]

Greeley ticked off the list of opposing views. Religion is *not* in a state of collapse, he said, contrary to the declaration of Eugene Fontinell in his book, *Toward a Reconstruction of Religion*. In opposition to Martin Marty in *The Modern Schism*, Greeley argued that liberalism, evolutionism, socialism, and historicism have been extremely unsuccessful rivals of religion. John Cogley stated in *Religion in a Secular Age* that modernity and religion are antonyms for millions in the West, but Greeley contended that vastly more millions are able to harmonize religion and modernity. Ramon Echarren argued in an issue of *Concilium* that mankind is changing profoundly; Greeley said it is not. In *A Rumor of Angels* Peter Berger expressed the belief that the supernatural is today more remote from the lives of people than at any time in the past; Greeley countered that primitive societies, too, had their equivalents of atheists and agnostics and that enthusiastic religious commitment is no more unfashionable today than it was among neolithic man.

After displaying the data contained in *Religion in the Year 2000* to show that the supernatural is very much with us, Greeley turned to the most elementary assumption of the "conventional wisdom," that of organic social evolution. The assertions of Bonhoeffer and Cox that secular man had "come of age" were "rooted in the faith—and here I use the word advisedly—that secular man and technological man are the inevitable result of an evolutionary process which cannot be resisted."[30] But the version of mankind moving forward in a single direction through crisis and change is precisely that—a vision, something in the eye of the beholder, not in social events themselves.

In *Social Change in History* and *The Social Bond*, Robert Nis-

bet put together a devastating case against the evolutionary perspective. "Change," he wrote, "cannot be deduced or empirically derived
from the elements of social structure." Though we may prefer to
believe otherwise, fixity is the true characteristic of human institutions. Nisbet analyzed a number of them: the family (where mono-
gamous marriage has remained the norm despite the continued presence of deviations and evasions); the calendar (it took the Protestant
world several centuries to adopt the vastly superior Gregorian
calendar); science (which, according to Nisbet, "can suffer from the
kind of conventionalism of the old and hostility to the new that we
are more accustomed to thinking of in areas of politics, religion, or
life styles"); and literature (the supposed haven of the creative,
change-inducing mind; in actuality the abode of "routinization,
conventionalism, and downright conservatism").[31] Even the university, that place where, given its commitment to openness and curiosity, one would expect the most dramatic changes—even the university is characterized by the persistence of basic structures. The norms
of academic consensus, the criteria for faculty and student advancement, for example, are much the same today as they were at the
University of Bologna in the thirteenth century.

Change *does* occur (Greeley concurred with Nisbet), but rarely
in the basic structures of society—and certainly not in the basic
human needs to which religion responds. Mankind—Greeley meant
most men at many times in their lives—has needed and will continue to need some sort of ultimate explanation, some sort of
meaning; and religion is a symbol system that provides just such a
meaning.

According to Clifford Geertz, religion is one of several systems
by which men order and interpret their lives. Religion differs from
common sense (another of the cultural systems that provide understanding) because it goes deeper. Common sense is "a simple acceptance of the world, its objects and its processes, as being just what
they seem to be."[32] Common sense, however, does not answer all
man's questions. It did not explain, for example, why a large toadstool grew up in the house of a Javanese carpenter in the space of a
few days. It does not explain why the just suffer and the unjust prosper. Common sense, as a Javanese image has it, is like a water
buffalo listening to an orchestra.

Science penetrates more deeply than common sense. Science could have told the carpenter why the toadstool made its sudden appearance in his living quarters. But science is not religion, for its attitude toward underlying realities is one of rational, detached, questioning impartiality. Religion, on the other hand, seeks to produce commitment to the underlying reality, to encounter and become involved with it, not simply to analyze it. Religion tells its adherents what the structure of the real is *and* how one is to live in harmony with that structure.

Neither is religion *art* (for the artist attempts to dwell on appearances and to disengage himself from the question of factuality, while religion attempts to go behind surfaces and create an aura of utter actuality), nor is it *ideology* (which is an attempt to explain—and produce commitment to—political reality alone). The symbols of religion are unique; they tell truths about phenomena beyond man's analytic capacity, about moral evil, about human suffering. And they tell them not in abstract schematic propositions but in concrete, often poetic, stories that invite the hearer to become emotionally involved and committed. The religious myth "is a comprehensive view of reality; it explains it, interprets it, provides the ritual by which man may maintain his contact with it, and even conveys certain very concrete notions about how reality is to be used to facilitate mankind's life and comfort."[33]

When we moderns wish to explain why a drought breaks and rain comes, we describe certain changes in atmospheric conditions; not so the ancient Babylonians, as Henri Frankfort points out in *Before Philosophy*. The same facts were experienced by them as the gigantic bird Imdugud coming to their rescue. "It covered the sky with the black storm clouds of its wings and devoured the Bull of Heaven, whose hot breath had scorched the crops."[34]

Childish fantasy? Or contact of the *entire* person with an existential reality? The Babylonians wished to understand a natural phenomenon, to be sure, but they were after more: Why should there be powers in the world hostile to us, and why should there be powers on our side? And why should the thunderstorm save us in the nick of time by ending the drought? These were questions that involved the Babylonians at the core of their existence, sources of bafflement to be grappled with. The myth of Imdugud was not mere fantasy—not legend, saga, fable, fairy tale. It was true myth, and true myth, Frankfort tells us, "presents its images and its imaginary actors, not with the playfulness of fantasy, but with a compelling authority. It perpetuates the revelation of a 'Thou.' "[35]

Is modern man, who can give a scientific explanation for drought and rain, beyond religious myth? No, Greeley replied, for there is no less mystery today than in years past:

> We understand thunder, lightning, storms, the movement of heavenly bodies, but a case could be made that even in physical science a good deal of bafflement remains. . . . and as Monsieur Piccard remarked after his submarine journey in the Gulf Stream, "The more we learn about the mysteries of nature, the more unfathomable these mysteries seem to be; because the more we understand, the clearer it is to us how much we have yet to understand and how much we probably never will be able to understand."[36]

Besides, human relationships have expanded in number and kind, and their increasing complexity has rendered them more puzzling. And even though we understand more about the depths of human experience, what we have discovered has served only to raise more difficult questions.

> For archaic man, the dimensions of human existence were relatively limited, the complexities of his life relatively few, and the mysteries of his relationships relatively uncomplex. He may have been baffled by the signs in the heavens, but he was less baffled by himself and his fellow man. We may understand more than he did about the heavens, but the mystery of man is far more convoluted for us than it was for him.[37]

The question of ultimate meaning is further intensified for modern man because, as Thomas Luckmann points out in *The Invisible Religion*, he inherits no *single* meaning system from his society. There exists, rather, a supermarket of such systems, and modern man, that "consumer of interpretive schemes," must shop for and select the components of the meaning system according to which he wishes to live. He has the freedom of choice (though in actuality he may not exercise it), but along with that freedom comes the burden, and the pain, of responsibility. Delivered from the constraints of community, he is also deprived of the support of community. Thus, "modern man is *more* religious than his predecessors precisely because now he must interpret and choose and his predecessors did not have to do either."[38]

Unsecular Man, a book that sold out twice in the hard-cover edition and is now available in Dutch, German, Italian, and Spanish, was far removed from the battles of the late sixties over the death of God. With it Greeley identified his understanding of human religious needs and wrote a preface for many books to come, among them *The Jesus Myth; The Sinai Myth; The Devil, You Say!; The Mary Myth; Sexual Intimacy;* and *Love and Play*. Greeley argued in *Unsecular Man* that theology must reinterpret myths "broken" by the criticism of modern science. Myths are "broken" when science—as it should—questions their description of what literally happened in the past. Far from demythologizing religion because of science's review, however, we should use science, as well as our own mythopoetic instincts, to penetrate to the heart of religious myths. "The relevant point is that the myth-makers were far more interested in conveying an interpretive scheme about the nature of ultimate reality than they were in telling a story that would measure up to the strict scientific canons devised only centuries in the future." Thus, what matters about the Sinai myth is not how many days Moses spent on the mountain, but rather "that the Sinai story conveys to those who heard it a world view, an ethical system, a sense of mission and hope rooted in the conviction that God has entered into a covenant with the Israelite people." And the basic issue in the Jesus myth is not the literal fact of His resurrection—the truth of that will never be known with certainty— "but the existential truth conveyed in the Resurrection story: through Jesus mankind triumphed over sin and death."[39] Greeley insisted—and near the end of *Unsecular Man* he preached—that the organized Church has to engage in this kind of creative interpretation of mythological traditions if it is to meet the religious needs of technological man.

It is late at night. A man has driven many miles to a house on the shore of a lake. He parks his car, walks down the steps to a pier jutting out into the water. On this moonless night the man looks up toward the great black umbrella of stars over his head and a feeling of unspeakable peace comes over him. In the next instant of awareness it is morning; he has no idea what happened to all the hours in between.

A young woman has just made love with her husband. They have snatched an interlude together in the middle of the afternoon. It was the best sex they ever had, and she lies exhausted in his arms. Suddenly, a new and very different kind of pleasure takes possession of her. She smiles first and then laughs; her entire body takes on a peculiarly delightful glow. This new pleasure makes intercourse seem mild in comparison. The whole of the universe has somehow flooded her being.[40]

So began another Greeley effort in the sociology of religion, this time a primer on mysticism. *Ecstasy: A Way of Knowing* (1974) was originally written for the Catholic readership of the Thomas More Association but was eventually published by Prentice-Hall. Why mysticism? Surely nothing in the spiritual life of the author steered him in that direction.

I am scarcely a mystic myself in any ordinary sense of the word; indeed I am not even very meditative or contemplative. I don't disapprove of either; on the contrary, I respect and admire those qualities. The lack of them in my own personality and character I account as a failing. But for reasons of nature and nurture I am a hard-nosed rational empiricist skeptic. By temperament and training I am one of the least mystical persons I know, and while my preconscious intellect may occasionally take over when I am writing a prose essay, most of my life is marked by strong vigorous control of the "reality principle," which means that for me deautomatization is virtually impossible. Again let me insist that I am not saying this is necessarily a good way to be; it is simply the way I am.[41]

No, what turned Father Greeley on to ecstatic experience (as much as a "rational empiricist skeptic" could be "turned on") was his reading of the poetry of John of the Cross and Gerard Manley Hopkins. These were men who articulated in a compelling way those things that Greeley believed; and more, they were men who "clearly had had direct and immediate contact with a reality Out There whose existence I accepted as a matter of abstract intellectual principle."[42] Mysticism, too, was part of the religious revival that greeted death-of-God theology; it was a kind of knowledge that stood in stark contrast to the positivistic science under attack from Greeley's students. And Greeley had met some "natural" mystics—or, in some cases, had discovered them among people he already knew. None of the mystics were prigs, or madmen, or misanthropes, as he had been led to believe by social science research and his own "dreadfully academic" seminary training in mystical theology. On the contrary, they were some of the most attractive people he knew. Some, simply assuming that everyone had experiences like their own, did not realize they were mystics. Others, like Nancy Gallagher McCready, wrote of their experiences, and their poetry made its way into Father Greeley's book:

> *Start with my toes,*
> *you old Ghost*
> *Spirit the soles of my shoes*
> *and teach me a Pentecostal*
> *Boogaloo*
> *Sprain my ankles with dancing*
> *Sandal around my feet,*
> *to roam with me in the rain*
> *and feel at home in my footprints.*
>
> *Oh! look at me spinning,*
> *Sprinkling, tonguing teaching*
> *Winsoming wondrous steps*
> *lift me, how!?*
> *We'd better quit now,*
> *too all dizzy down giggly*
> *Stop—you're tickling*
> *(my funnybone's fickle for you)*
> *Stop—I'll drop.*
> *I'm dying, I'm flying*
> *with your winding my feet and*
> *legs and waist*
> *Lassoed*
> *Stop chasing fool—I'm racing from you*
> *Don't catch me*
> *Do!*
> *I'll drown!*
> *Oh, drown me—most*
> *For I love you so,*
> *You Old Ghost!*[43]

Ecstasy contained what was now a familiar sight in Greeley's books—long quotations from writers in the field, in this case from mystics like St. Augustine, the Sufi poet Jami, Simone Weil, Teresa of Avila, Teilhard de Chardin, from the few psychologists and sociologists who had bothered to study mysticism. William James's description of the mystical state appeared early in the book, and it was followed by Marghanita Laski's brief empirical confirmation of James's observations and the list of "triggers" of ecstatic episodes—nature, sexual love, childbirth, exercise—which were reported by her subjects (mostly friends and acquaintances). The heart of *Ecstasy*, however, was the realization that there are large numbers of "natural," everyday mystics, people who do not consider themselves such, people leading otherwise normal, unextraordinary lives. It was *their* experience—that of a young man on a pier losing track of time, that of a woman overwhelmed by a presence after making love, that of a young man relieved of worry by the Ode to Joy—that introduced and set the tone for the entire book.

Mystics may well know what we do not. Though Greeley did not feel he had to postulate some special intervention by the divinity to explain a mystical interlude, he wished to take very seriously the mystic's claim—one documented as well in Abraham Maslow's study of "peak-experiences"—that in ecstatic experience one sees things *the way they are.* According to the mystic,

> . . . the experience is more one of knowing than of feeling. If anything is heightened in the ecstatic interlude, it is the cognitive faculties of the mystic: he knows something others do not know and that he did not know before. He *sees*, he *understands*, he *perceives*, he *comprehends.* The occasional mystic who has perused the psychological and psychiatric literature becomes impatient with the insensitivity of the writers: "They really haven't been listening" is the most common criticism. They don't realize that, above all, the mystic *knows* cognition is at the core of his experience.[44]

Thus, mystics are to be taken seriously—not uncritically, of course, but with the admission that "there is both a confidence and authenticity about their description that is persuasive."[45] Ecstasy, in the words of the book's subtitle, is a legitimate and valid *way of knowing.*

If Greeley could not join the ranks of the ecstatics, could not *know* the way they knew, at least, good sociologist that he was, he could *count* them. How many mystics were there in America? How did they get to be the way they were? Were they psychological misfits or were they well adjusted? Greeley would write later, "There may be a certain madness—or at least unmitigated gall—in using survey instruments, computer analysis, and log linear models to deal with what is the ultimate, if not The Ultimate, in human experience,"[46] but when the Henry Luce Foundation agreed late in 1971 to commit $150,000 to a NORC survey of the "Fundamental Belief Systems of the American Population," he and Bill McCready threw caution to the winds and included in their questionnaire items dealing with mystical—as well as psychic—experiences.

What proportion of America's adult population had had some kind of extraordinary inner experience? In 1973, 59 percent said they had experienced the *deja vu* phenomenon at least once in their lives; 58 percent had felt a sense of contact with someone even though that person was far away; 27 percent had felt in touch with someone who had died; and 24 percent said that they had "seen events that happened at a great distance as they were happening." On the item concerning mystical experience ("Have you ever felt as though you were very close to a powerful, spiritual force that seemed to lift you out of yourself?") 18 percent said "once or twice"; 12 percent said "several times"; and 5 percent said "often." At least a third of America's adult population, then, had had some experience of the ecstatic—and perhaps as many as ten million had had such experiences frequently. When asked to describe what the mystical interlude was like, most of those who had had one checked "a feeling of deep and profound peace." Listening to music and prayer were the most common "triggers" of ecstatic episodes, and their most frequent duration was "a few minutes or less" (though a surprising number of respondents said "a day or more").

Who were the mystics? There were as many in their late teens and twenties as there were in their sixties and seventies, but slightly more in the forty-to-sixty age bracket. A higher percentage of blacks than whites, of males than females, of college-educated than non-college-educated, of Protestants than Catholics reported having mystical experiences. Mystics were more optimistic and much more likely to believe in personal survival after death. They were, in general, more satisfied with their lives and "happier" than the population at large (the .40 correlation between frequent mystical experience and "balance affect" on the Bradburn Psychological Well-Being Scale was the highest NORC had ever seen in connection with that scale, and the correlation reached .60 for mystics of the "classic" type). White mystics were less racist than whites who reported no ecstatic episodes in their lives. The picture of the mystic as a frustrated, rigid, maladjusted, unhappy freak could not have been more thoroughly discredited by the replies of the nearly 1,500 participants in the study.

And how did mystics get to be the way they were? Greeley and McCready identified distinct patterns in the backgrounds of blacks and whites. White mystics tended to come from families in which mother and father were close to each other and joyous in their religion (the attitudes of the father were more decisive than those of the mother), while the dominant childhood experience of black mystics was closeness to the mother in a family where father and mother were not very close. (Black mystics, incidentally, were not disproportionately poor members of fundamentalist congregations, which one might hypothesize if he believed mysticism to be a response to deprivation.) The Greeley-McCready data were written up for the *Journal of Social Research* and the *New York Times Magazine*, where they drew an enormous response. They also appeared in monographs entitled *Reconnaissance into the Sociology of the Paranormal* (1975) and *The Ultimate Values of the American Population* (1976).

Mystics would hardly be impressed with these findings, the authors concluded. "Neither of us is mystical, and those we know who are find our efforts diverting but hardly profound."[47] But at least mysticism could no longer be written off as deviant behavior, as something "like" schizophrenia or "like" a regression to infantile relationships with reality. No, hard as it might be for psychologists to accept, the evidence indicated that mysticism was good for you.

Andrew Greeley's work in the sociology of religion, then, has moved from skirmishes over the death of God and secular theology to a theoretical analysis of the functions of religion and, finally, to an empirical investigation of extraordinary religious experiences. If he was on the winning side in the debate over secularization—and the years since the "death of God" show that he was—his victory won him no friends among his colleagues in the sociology of religion. In March 1974 the *Journal for the Scientific Study of Religion* took up his life work—supposedly, everything he had written—and subjected it to the review of four critics—Jeffrey Hadden, Patrick McNamara, Martin Marty, and Samuel Mueller. Greeley described their treatment as "absolutely vicious."

Mixed with the comment that Greeley was "both interesting and important to our discipline" were references to him as "the Howard Cosell of the Catholic Church" and "the man we all love to hate." Hadden said Greeley provided "more raw data than any living sociologist," yet his work was clouded by value presuppositions. McNamara praised Greeley's work on the Protestant ethic hypothesis and said *The Hesitant Pilgrim* and *The Crucible of Change* were "among the finest contemporary examples of applied sociology"—but why didn't he take on a *serious* theoretical analysis of the Roman Catholic Church? Martin Marty, a friend, thought Greeley's sense of history "routine and lifeless" and found in *What Do We Believe?* and *Religion in the Year 2000* "a kind of nostalgia for a static universe." And Samuel Mueller warned of misspellings in Greeley's work, straightened out some of his "sloppy" data analysis, and said Greeley simply produced too much.[48]

No one, individually or collectively, came to grips with the Greeley *corpus*. McNamara apparently had not read Greeley's analysis of American Catholicism presented at Yale in 1970, nor was he aware that that theoretical endeavor was being expanded into a book. Marty must have passed by the historical drama of *The Catholic Experience*. And Mueller—no doubt about it—missed the forest for the trees: his rectifying of Greeley's "sloppiness" only made Greeley's data more convincing. Hadden, at least, was aware of the problem of dealing with the sheer amount of information that Greeley had processed, the sheer quantity of his output. "Encountering the products of Greeley's' pen, typewriter, and dictaphone," he wrote, "is something like encountering New York City for the first time. One stands awed, inspired, and overwhelmed."[49]

In the next issue of the *Journal* Greeley came out swinging:

There is, of course, no escaping the assumption that quantity precludes quality, an assumption which all four of the commentators seem to share. So be it, although it is a judgment that is a little hard on Agatha Christie, Mozart, and G. K. Chesterton. Yet I must confess I find the suggestion that my work can't be careful because there is so much of it a little graceless when it comes from writers whose own work seems marked by neither quantity nor quality. . . . And let me rub it in a bit more, fellows: I've got three more articles coming out in the AJS and the ASR this summer and fall. I will take seriously the criticisms of those who are able to match that measure of professional competence.[50]

Greeley was angry. He included in his reply to the critics not a word of the positive things they had to say. Hadden was "patronizing." Marty engaged in "an ever so small omission that makes me look like a naive and innocent clerical Pollyanna." McNamara stacked the deck so Greeley couldn't win. Mueller was "snide," "dreary," "small-minded," and represented "the worst kind of mean, vicious, academic pettiness."

But I guess it is all my fault. There must be something wrong with me if I have led four such honorable scholars to depart from the narrow ways of truthful discourse. I am sure that if I wrote less and less broadly, if I were less of a loudmouth Irish priest (to use Professor Janowitz's endearing phrase), they would not find in me so much cause for anger.

Maybe I ought to reform my life, change my ways, settle down and concentrate on one thing, stop being an obnoxious Irishman and become respectable, stuffy, and dull. Maybe I ought to become sober and serious, and listen to papers at professional meetings.

Maybe I ought to marry and work out my problems in bed instead of at a typewriter.

Don't anyone hold his breath.[51]

7   **Sacerdos**

Early in my conversations with Andrew Greeley there came a quiet moment of surprise. I realized (or was it that for the first time I noticed?) that at the center of all those Greeleys I had been in contact with—beneath the puckishness, the despair, the hatred, the joy, the ambition—there was a simple, integrating self, so straightforward and so obvious that, like the air around me, I had easily overlooked it. This self, I learned later, was the one that raised its hand in the second grade when a teacher asked how many of her students were going to be priests. It was a natural act, raising one's hand, full of ease, a reflex set in motion without a moment's hesitation. As simply and readily as that, Andrew Greeley slipped into his life's work and expressed the basic stance toward reality that he would carry, unchanged, into his adult life.

Sacerdos, a priest: no memorable religious experience beckoned Andrew Greeley into the priesthood, nor have any extraordinary inner events cemented a decision to remain a part of it. Father Greeley has never doubted that the priesthood is his calling, has never struggled through a "vocational" or a "celibacy" crisis, either before or after ordination. He will tell you that his understanding of the priesthood has matured but not changed radically. The same can be said of his fundamental world view, of his understanding of the way things are. He has always believed in God and talked to God— no more, no less. "I don't exactly climb up Mt. Carmel, but neither do I descend into the dark night of the soul." His idea of God has evolved, but not with the terror of loss and the joy of rediscovery, the incredible depths and the dizzying heights, of souls troubled—and stimulated—by periodic revolutions. There has been an overwhelming sense of organizational chaos, of uncertainty, of conflict in his *public* life, but nothing like a *personal* crisis that shook his being to the core (the closest to that, he said, was the disintegration of his New Community). Much anxiety has occurred over *what he should do next* but none over *who he is* or *what he believes.*

I sense now that the presence of this self—set and secure in its location in the cosmos—explains the remarkable capacity of this man to sustain the anxiety, the nastiness, the hatred, the *evil* (he would use the word, for this is what he sees) swirling in and about him. His personal identity clear, his energies focus on the battle to be won, the enemy to be destroyed. He always has something left, something *they* cannot take away, when the inevitable results of building risk upon risk, having stalked him down, finally come to rip away his investments. Rooted, he has strength. Peripheral selves whip about in the wind, never fearing the change, because they are certain of contact with the earth.

If this simple inconspicuous self, this priestly self, helps one understand Greeley's capacity for conflict, it also lifts some of the mystery from his role in the secularization debate. Persistence, fixity, continuity, evenness, sameness, basic religious functions that "have not changed very notably since the late Ice Age"[1]—these were the themes at which he hammered with his statistics and his polemic, these the targets that drew fire from critics like Cox and Marty. Mankind's conditions of living may have changed, Greeley held, but not his fundamental orientation toward the universe; there have been no crises in the latter, no revolutions, but the same eternal needs for meaning and belonging. *At its core, the world has not changed*— nor, at his core, has the man who insisted time and again on the truth of that very proposition. Greeley's "feel" for a personal God at the base of the universe has been a constant in the midst of extraordinary upheavals on the periphery of his being. One needs certain eyes (and certain *I*'s) to see certain phenomena, personal crisis to see mankind in revolution, personal constancy, in the case of Father Greeley, to see the evenness of mankind's development.

From as far back as one thinks of such things, then, Andrew Greeley has thought of himself as a priest; and all through the sixties, all through that decade of hope ushering in despair, he wrote about the priesthood: a long pamphlet entitled *Priests for Today and Tomorrow* (1964), articles brought together in *The Hesitant*

Pilgrim (1966), retreats for priests written up as *Uncertain Trumpet* (1968) and *New Horizons for the Priesthood* (1970). Greeley's memories of life in the seminary and the rectory were not always pleasant—they honed the scalpel he used to dissect the structure of priestly life.

First to come under diagnosis was the seminary, a virtual breeding ground of immaturity. "Those who supervised us both in the seminary and after ordination feared strong men, men who knew who they were and what their priesthood was and who would not permit, under any circumstances, their basic human dignity to be violated." Hence seminary training was geared to keep the students (and "I shall include myself near the top of the list") docile and obedient. No program could have been more successful. "We had to suppress so much, pretend so often, simulate so frequently, that deep down inside, most of us, I fear, had every reason to suspect that we were phonies." Nor could the seminary students relate authentically to one another. "Because the seminary authorities did not trust us, they created situations in which we were really unable to trust our fellows; hence, we all built defense mechanisms which kept a hostile and suspicious world at bay."[2] The seminarians were warned that human affection was dangerous, that their goal was to become as detached as possible from the people with whom they worked, that "particular friendships" (that meant homosexuality, but the men didn't know it then) were to be scrupulously avoided:

> We were, of course, to be friendly, equally friendly, to everyone (though less friendly to women, of course), but deeply friendly to no one, deeply involved with no one, deeply attached to no one . . . . The result was not some superhuman who towered above the mundane relationships of ordinary men; the result was rather a non-human or zombie who was incapable of entering into any meaningful relationship with anyone.[3]

After ordination, the distrust, suspicion, and fostering of immaturity continued in the rectory. More than that, one would have to say that the relationship between pastor and curate was very often *evil*. It may have been "the greatest single obstacle to the spread of the people of God in the United States"[4] and was "surely one of the most depressive and degrading relationships that has survived from the feudal ages . . . . Even if it were not a violation of Christian charity, it would still have to be abandoned because of its consummate inefficiency."[5]

Analyze the roles of pastor and curate. The one has unlimited power; the other is completely expendable. The one becomes isolated because of his power (and, as Lord Acton noted, corrupt because of his isolation); the other puts as much distance as possible between himself and his pastor, ingratiates himself with the people of the parish, and becomes the middleman between them and his superior. The pastor, in turn, becomes jealous of his curate's popularity and reasserts his authority, causing the curate to lose more initiative and withdraw even further. The initial positing of roles could only lead in this direction, could only spiral a difficult relationship into an abyss. And while there is conflict in abundance between pastor and curate, it usually remains latent. The curate continues on as nice guy, a "mouse in training to be a rat."[6]

The immaturity engendered in the seminary and rectory was no more painfully and embarrassingly evident than in priests' relationships with women. It took a layman at a group discussion retreat to raise the issue for Andrew Greeley, and once raised, neither he nor the other priests present could turn to another topic for the duration of the conference.

> Most women find that our approach of supermasculinity makes us awkward, rude, boorish, and ill-mannered. We are frightened by them and have exploitative, domineering attitudes toward them . . . [We] leave most sensitive women wondering at the end of their conversations with us whether we will now go back to the rectory and, like other late adolescent males, reassure ourselves of our masculinity by reading the latest issue of *Playboy*.[7]

Whence this fearful yet exploitative attitude toward women? From family backgrounds with inflexible, Jansenistic attitudes toward sex, from fathers afraid of their sons' mothers, from high school and seminary experiences that objectified women, making them either lofty, unattainable idols or lowly objects of pleasure. "The fact that we got close neither to the goddess nor the prostitute merely reinforced our semiconscious fantasies." Would not marriage for the clergy be an answer, then? Absolutely not, Greeley countered, were one to judge from the behavior of the typical American male, married or single—he is as domineering in his attitudes toward women as is the celibate. Frankly, "I am not altogether sure that for many of us the problem is even soluble."[8]

Not that Greeley was opposed to relaxing the celibacy regulation for priests. Ideally, he argued, celibacy should be optional; nothing else would be consonant with the demands of human freedom. But sex is not a panacea for immaturity nor a guarantee of fulfillment:

> Human beings are closed up within themselves in fear and loneliness, not because they are not loved by a member of the opposite sex, but because they are not loved by themselves. Self-rejection, self-loathing, self-hatred will be solved neither by sex nor by marriage, but only by an understanding of what the factors were in our emotional background which make it impossible for us to accept our own goodness and virtues.[9]

Besides, because of the woeful state of theory about sexuality and celibacy in the western Catholic Church, optional celibacy would lead in no time to compulsory marriage. A modern rationale for celibacy simply has not evolved because the regulation has been taken for granted for so long. In the absence of such a rationale, subtle but strong pressures would deprive priests of the freedom to be celibate; and that loss would be tragic, not because celibacy is a good thing in itself but because it frees a man to build up the people of God. For himself, Greeley said, "celibacy seems to leave me freer to worry more intensively about more people, to put myself in the loving service of a far greater number of people—and in a far more intense way than I would be able to if I had a family of my own."[10] Not that priests, and Greeley included himself, have taken advantage of the freedom celibacy offers—their lives offer no more love than anyone else's, but that is their fault, not that of the celibacy regulation.

Greeley dealt with other problems, too, in these books: "the persistence of anti-intellectualism," which he spoke about with his colleagues at home while holding up the class of 1961 to the gaze of outsiders; that "familiar black book with the red-edged pages," read daily out of a sense of duty but contributing in no way to an attitude of prayerful contemplation; uneasiness over the meaning of poverty in an era of affluence; the lack of professional standards.

Worst of all were "friendly" priests in the recreation room, good-natured and charitable on the surface, jealous and resentful down below, their whole being geared to holding you down, keeping you in your place, asking "Who do you think you are?" "Passive aggression," Greeley called this attitude scornfully; it was no less devastating for being hidden behind the smile of "the good Father."

In these books Greeley never hesitated to *prescribe*. Perhaps his most important advice was the simplest: delegate power. Do so in the seminary to create the opportunity for responsible decision-making and risk-taking. Do so in the rectory: curates are not to be regarded as servants but as professional colleagues; they should refuse to be expendable; they must communicate to their pastor that they are as concerned about *their* parish as he is.

Power must also be delegated in the diocese as a whole. As he made the point, Greeley reassured the reader time and again that he was not out to destroy order and authority in the Church but only to make them more effective. He was, he said, arguing for collegial authority, an essential part of Church tradition, to replace paternalism. The Church needed senates made up of clergy and laity elected by their parish and supplemented by a selection of professional people, whose role would be to provide upward communication to the bishop. It needed semipermanent research organs within the diocese to provide a reliable information base for the bishop. These bodies would not engage in decision-making—that was the bishop's prerogative—but they would provide the advice on which sound decisions could be made.

Characteristically, Greeley reduced all the problems in the priesthood to *theory*, to a set of assumptions about the nature of men and organizations, to a set of models outlining goals and exemplifying how the goals were to be reached. And the marketplace was well stocked with theories of the priesthood. There was the apostolate-of-kindness theory (in which the priest is basically a nice guy) and the temporal-order theory (in which the priest is excluded from doing anything a layman could do just as well). There was the liturgical-functionary theory (here the priest presides over the Eucharist and then is free to do what any other human being would do) and the builder-of-community theory (in which the priest's goal is to mold the people of his parish into a community of worshipers).

Discarding each, Greeley opted—as he continues to—for the "old notion of the priest as a leader of his people." It was the theory, after all, that was most compatible with the spirit of the Vatican Council. The priest does preside over the Eucharist each morning, but then he moves on to "serving the people of God, whether it be in the parish, in community organizations, in social protest, in academic work, in editing newspapers, in administering ecclesiastical institutions, in educating the young."[11] This model is like that of priest-as-liturgical-functionary, except that work beyond the liturgy also is seen as appropriate to the priestly role. The priest-as-leader is much like a senior colleague in a research collegium. He "influences the minds and hearts of men by permitting their minds and hearts to influence him." His function is not to give orders but to obtain commitment and consent. He does "everything in his power to encourage the charisma of the various members of the community. Indeed, it is primarily by serving his people in such a way that they are encouraged to develop their own talents and charisms that the priest contributes to the upbuilding of the Christian community."[12]

Throughout all his commentary on the priesthood Greeley showed an overwhelming concern for the practical. Theory was important because, in the final analysis, there was nothing as practical as good theory and nothing as damaging as bad (which usually meant unexamined) theory. And when basic theory was not essential to an issue being discussed, practical diagnoses and practical prescriptions peppered the text like so much buckshot. All the copy written in the mid-sixties was replete with examples, illustrations, and how-to's, with judgments about anything and everything, from Florida vacations (they may be all right) to tape recorders (not so good because we don't use the ones we buy). To an audience long accustomed to look for the practical, Greeley's work was cast in the right form.

To readers who agreed with him, his diagnoses and prescriptions were welcome; "incisive," · "clear," "down-to-earth," "refreshing," "responsible," "candid," "stimulating" were the words they used. By others—and I have spoken with them—they were deeply resented. What priest would like to be told that he was a zombie, "an amorphous blob of behavioral variables rocked about on a current of confusion and uncertainty,"[13] or that he was immature, afraid of women, exploitative, manipulative, superficial—a mouse? What member of the new breed of priests would care to be denounced for showing up at a party clad in a sweater instead of a Roman collar ("ashamed of the collar," said the author), for frequenting bars ("he thinks it is part of the humanism of the priesthood"), or for trying to make it with his parishioners as a teenybopper? And what authority, his critical readers ask, does this man have to *pontificate*—a kind, fair-minded Carmelite used that word—on the problems of the priesthood? Who appointed him spokesman? Who gave him the right to make such caustic and sweeping generalizations? And what makes his experience—and while we are at it, what makes that national whatever-it-is research organization at Chicago—so important that he is offered as an exemplar for all of America's priests? Does he *do* parish work or just hide behind his pen in his Lake Michigan home attacking those in the "secure Catholic ghetto" who do? Such questions were spoken or merely hinted at, but all were indicative of resentment. Prophet or not, many priests in his own archdiocese, in his own country, did not welcome him.

It was not until March 1969 that Greeley rolled in the heavy machinery of empirical sociology for a look at the American Catholic priesthood. On the first of that month NORC received a contract from the National Conference of Catholic Bishops to execute a national survey of active and resigned priests. The country's hierarchy, headed by John Cardinal Dearden of Detroit, was aware of trouble in the priesthood. Resignations were increasing; the cry for optional celibacy was becoming more strident; the media were devoting more time and space to disgruntled priests. Deciding that serious study was needed, NCCB committed $500,000 to investigations of priestly life from theological, historical, psychological, and sociological perspectives. Of the money, $300,000 found its way to NORC. During his negotiations with NCCB, Greeley had pressed for a study of the laity, too, for they were the priests' clients and the ones who ultimately paid the bills. But NCCB said no; their half million dollars was to be spent entirely on the priesthood.

What would the priesthood look like at a time when organized American Catholicism was in a state of chaos? During the year and a half following the start of their contract, NORC worked hard on the answer: 7,500 questionnaires, each 46 pages long, were mailed to carefully prepared samples of America's diocesan and religious priests and bishops; 1,500 of them were accompanied by the Personal Orientation Inventory, a measure of personal maturity. By the end of September 1970, 79 percent of the priests sampled had responded, 71 percent providing usable data. Curiously, only 59 percent of the country's 276 bishops—the persons who had authorized the study—returned their questionnaires.

A preliminary report on the findings was delivered in October of 1970 to the Ad Hoc Committee for Study of Priestly Life and Ministry, the NCCB unit (chaired by Cardinal John Krol of Philadelphia) with which Greeley's NORC team was in direct contact. It was a gathering that seemed harmless enough in advance. The relationship between the Krol committee and Father Greeley's staff had been entirely cooperative, and there was no reason to anticipate a change. And when it convened at Chicago's O'Hare airport, the meeting got off to a beautiful start, as well it might have. To the relief of those present, America's priests showed up in the data as psychologically well off, even above college-educated males of the same age in their morale. Greeley, in fact, had been surprised by the good shape the priesthood seemed to be in. Priests, by and large, were not accurately represented by the frustrated malcontents parading in the media. Nor were they any less mature or "self-actualized"—at least insofar as these traits could be measured—than comparable population groups. They were reasonably satisfied with their jobs and with the quality of their relationships with superiors, colleagues, subordinates, and lay associates. Furthermore, the overwhelming majority were still committed to the priesthood and interested in continuing their education. They accepted the fundamental doctrines of Christianity and acknowledged the need for papal and episcopal authority in the Church. There was restlessness, to be sure, and serious problems that could be clearly defined, but the clergy were not out to demolish the organizational structures of the Church or to rebel against the bishops.

And then the data on birth control were passed around the table. The participants took a look at the findings—and the air turned frigid. There could be no mistaking the meaning of those columns of figures. Only 40 percent of America's priests (and only 13 percent of those 35 and under) assented to the official teaching of the Church as outlined in *Humanae Vitae*. This compared with 83 percent of the bishops—a mammoth, unheard of difference. If that were not enough to stagger the committee, the tables also showed that Pope Paul's encyclical of July 1968 had actually boomeranged and driven priests even further from the official teaching of the Church. The handful of bishops present could only be stunned; these were *their* priests disregarding papal pronouncements—and disregarding *their* pronouncements, too, for the vast majority of bishops had lined up publicly in support of the papal position.

Greeley remembers well the reaction of those present. "The response was deafening silence. After the presentation one Cardinal left the room and did not return. When the presentation was complete, not a single question was asked, not a single word said. All the faces around the table were grim and stony."[14]

The findings on birth control were not the only ones to shock the bishops. Only 40 percent of the priests (and only 19 percent of those 35 and under) were willing to exclude all possibility of divorce for Catholic couples. Only 29 percent (and 8 percent of those 35 and under) felt that deliberate masturbation was a mortal sin. Despite a number of pronouncements from the hierarchy that there would be no change in celibacy regulations, priests still thought one was on the way: 65 percent (88 percent of those 35 and under), compared with only 18 percent of the bishops, expected a change. Priests did not uniformly reject the Church's stance on matters sexual—for the most part, they supported Church teaching on premarital sex and abortion—but they showed enough discrepancy to indicate that the power of the hierarchy to gain the assent of its priests to Church doctrine had disappeared, and that it had done so, seemingly, overnight.

Later analysis would reveal subtler, but equally profound, differences between priests and bishops. There was the matter of their contrasting spiritual orientations. While many priests agreed with formulations of orthodox doctrine, their values emphasized, as Greeley put it, "process rather than substance, existence rather than essence, open-endedness rather than immutability."[15] Did faith mean essentially "belief in the doctrines of the Catholic Church?"

Only 45 percent of the priests (but 69 percent of the bishops) thought so. Or was faith "primarily an encounter with God and Christ Jesus rather than an assent to a coherent set of defined truths?" Such a definition was preferred by a majority of priests (69 percent) but not of bishops (46 percent). So-called modern values (for example, "For me, God is found principally in my relationships with people") were more manifest in priests than in bishops, and the difference could not be explained solely by age. In their descriptions of the spiritual life, bishops were simply more "conservative" and less "modern" than priests of comparable years (although, curiously enough, they were more "liberal" regarding ecumenism and several social issues).

Most revealing, and lying at the core of other differences, was the split between hierarchy and clergy in their feelings about authority and the distribution of power in the Church. Both groups saw the *actual* distribution of power in the same way—bishops were the single most influential force in the diocese, and chancery officials were next in line. And both agreed that this is the way a diocese ought to operate in the *ideal*. Other groups such as priests and laity should have more power, granted, but the bishop still should be the single person with the most authority. When the survey questions narrowed down to the specifics of who ought to have decision-making power in concrete situations, however, glaring differences appeared in the replies of bishops and priests. Two-thirds of the bishops said *they* should determine where a priest is assigned, but only 41 percent of the priests agreed. Nearly three-quarters of the bishops felt it was up to them to decide where a priest has his living quarters—just 36 percent of their priests felt likewise. Over half the bishops said it was their prerogative to authorize Mass in homes or apartments—only 29 percent of the priests agreed. In short, priests wanted a considerable decentralization of power in practical matters and bishops did not.

But such decentralization was not occurring, and the resultant behavior of priests must have been disconcerting, if not outright galling, to the bishops gathered to hear the NORC data. Nearly one-third of America's priests, according to those data, never said the breviary. Over two-fifths had modified the rubrics of the Mass to fit certain occasions; one-third had said Mass without the proper

vestments; one-fifth had given Communion to non-Catholics; a
sixth had given sacraments to those who were divorced and re-
married—all this despite clear injunctions to the contrary. And the
future did not look promising; more priests wanted these preroga-
tives, and it was the youngest of them who were going ahead and
simply acting on their own. Indeed, it was the youngest priests who
were most at odds with the position of bishops throughout the entire study.

As he drove home from that ill-fated O'Hare meeting Greeley
had the uncanny feeling that the entire priesthood study had dead-
ended even before any of its findings had been made public. "From
that moment on, I am convinced that some of the members of the
committee were determined to put as much distance as possible between them and our report. I could have done two things. One was
just sit back and let them destroy the study. Or I could have chosen
to fight them—which I did. In either case they were through with
me."[16]

Events passed quickly after the meeting. At NORC Greeley was
"dazed" by staff dissension that had been building up over the
months. It had never happened before, but then never before had his
staff been made up of graduate students who were priests like himself. He had been stunned a month before when Father Richard
Schoenherr, the man responsible for the day-to-day direction of the
project, announced his decision to leave the priesthood. Worried
that the report might be read as a justification of that personal decision, Greeley took over control of the project. Then the president of
the National Federation of Priests' Councils asked Greeley for data
tapes so the results could be analyzed from the priests' viewpoint—
not from that of the bishops, as Greeley was sure to do. Greeley refused. In the meantime, Cardinal Krol decided to get an outside professional evaluation of the study. He asked Greeley if he objected,
and Greeley said no. Later Krol informed him of the names of the review panel—sociologists Everett Hughes, Sally Cassidy, and John
Donovan. Then Greeley protested. Hughes was all right, but Cassidy and Donovan were "enemies" sure to tear the report apart. His
complaints, however, were wasted on the cardinal, and the evaluation team remained intact.

Greeley had no idea what conclusions the evaluators were
reaching until he opened a copy of the *New York Times* one day in

July 1971. Then he learned that their report, hostile to the NORC survey, was being secretly distributed to the nation's bishops. Greeley had not merely been denied a chance to read the evaluation of his work, but it had also been leaked to the press without the opportunity for him to comment. He wrote NCCB protesting this treatment and asked for a copy of the evaluation. He was never sent one. When he finally obtained a copy through a friendly bishop, his worst suspicions were confirmed. The criticisms of Hughes, Donovan, and Cassidy concentrated not on the results reported by Greeley but on questions he failed to ask, approaches he neglected to pursue, avenues of analysis he passed by. *They* would have done it differently. "Vicious, dishonest, unfair," is the only way he can describe their review.

Feelings became more intense. Greeley complained directly to Cardinal Dearden, insisting now that the evaluation not be released in the same volume as the NORC report. It would serve only to discredit the study. Why not have a neutral party, skilled in survey research, evaluate the comments of the evaluators? Why should the evaluators exempt themselves from the forums provided for criticism by the sociological profession? And why were outside evaluations not commissioned for the theological, historical, and psychological investigations of the priesthood? "What is the reason for the NCCB having less confidence in our professional competence than in the competence of other scholars?" he wrote Dearden. In October 1971, the cardinal, attending a Synod of Bishops in Rome, replied: Take up the matter with Cardinal Krol. "Dearden let us down," Greeley said. A friend and a confidant in the beginning, he vanished when the going got tough. "I'd never trust him again."

In December Greeley protested again, this time to the entire Krol committee. Not only was the evaluation to be bound in with the NORC report without any reply from Greeley, but Greeley would not even be allowed to make revisions or check the galley proofs before publication. His protest did little good, although he was subsequently permitted to make a statement at the forthcoming meeting of the Ad Hoc Committee on the Implementation of the Priesthood Study, a five-bishop body that had replaced the Krol committee.

For all too long it had been painfully obvious what was going on. The $300,000 of bishops' money, invested in "objective" scientific research, had told them exactly what they did not want to hear, what they *could* not hear. You are operating in a vacuum, the data said. While your priests are not rebelling against you, they are ignoring you, dismissing you, "cheating" on you. If you do not believe, look at their scientifically assessed attitudes on birth control. And the responses of the bishops, in such circumstances, was inevitable: Shoot the messenger (scientist or not), discount and discredit the message he brings.

But at the February 1972 meeting of the Implementation Committee Greeley decided not only to duck but to shoot back. "I have no desire to be directly involved with the U.S. Catholic Conference at the present time, because as that body is now constituted, it is impossible for a scholar to work with it and maintain any standards of professional self-respect . . . . Honesty compels me to say that I believe the present leadership of the church to be morally, intellectually, and religiously bankrupt."[17] To the surprise of Archbishop Philip Hannan of New Orleans, chairman of the committee, Greeley released his comments to the press, and soon the entire text of his remarks was in the *National Catholic Reporter*. They revolved around his assertion that the fundamental crisis in the Church derived from a mistaken theory of leadership.

What does leadership mean—especially in the United States of America, 1972—if not the ability to gain the confidence of one's people, to establish one's credibility with them, to build, however slowly, a consensus among them? Whatever may have been the case in the past, said Greeley, real authority no longer comes automatically with an office, by some divine right; it must be earned. "All the reassertion of the authority in the world will not by itself recapture confidence, credibility or consensus."[18] The only answer is representative governance. John Carroll, America's first bishop, saw that. Why not today's hierarchy?

Why not? Again, because of a theory, because of a particular way of viewing their role in the church that justifies for the bishops the concentration of decision-making power in their own hands. Greeley had spelled it out in *America*: "As humble as they may be about their own personal inadequacies, they are confident that the charism of their office provides them with special inspiration from the Holy Spirit"[19]—an inspiration, by the way, not granted to priests and lay people. Bishops find themselves in a lonely, difficult position. Being "successors to the apostles," they, like the pope, inherit authority of divine origin, and if the authority is God's, how can they give it away, delegate it, share it? Much as they might *like* to do so, the power is simply not theirs to give. They feel their role is to remain true to the tradition of the Church and loyal to the promptings of the Spirit. Credibility? Consent of the governed? The concepts are meaningless according to the theory by which the bishops govern.

The dilemma confronting the organizational Church, and particularly its priesthood, said Greeley, is that one cannot have it both ways. If the bishops continue to operate under *their* theory—and most of them will—they will continue to lead in a vacuum. And priests in increasing numbers will continue to disregard them. In many dioceses,

it must be said in all honesty, the only power the bishop has left is the power of the pursestrings, and unless the present erosion of authority is arrested, it is no apocalyptic prediction to say that by 1980, there will be no such thing as ecclesiastical authority in the American Church (except over the checkbook) save in those dioceses where bishops have been able to overcome the skepticism, not to say cynicism, of their priests by their own efforts.[20]

On the other hand, should bishops become aware that authority rests on the consent of the governed, that one leads by building confidence, credibility, and consensus, then their theory of divine governance will have to go. That would be nobody's loss, Greeley wrote later, for much of it is

absolute nonsense theologically, historically, psychologically, and sociologically. Father Raymond Brown has pointed out in his book, *Priest and Bishop*, that bishops are not really the successors of the apostles in the way most of them would like to imagine, and whatever the theological explanation of "infallibility" may be, such infallibility has not prevented the papacy from all kinds of disastrous mistakes both in the past and in the present.[21]

Greeley had recommendations aplenty for Archbishop Hannan's Implementation Committee; but the most important, fusing his anger with the inescapable meaning of the data, was for representative governance in the Church, and in particular for the democratic nomination of bishops. Nothing else was tolerable in the United States of America in 1972. Nothing else would recapture for the bishops the confidence, the credibility, the consensus—the power—they had lost.

Though Greeley refused to believe his analysis would have any impact on the hierarchy, he did achieve two minor victories. First, he published his own commentary on the priesthood study, *Priests in the United States: Reflections on a Survey* (1972), even before the appearance of the official report he had authored for NCCB, *The Catholic Priest in the United States: Sociological Investigations* (1972). Second, the administrative board of the NCCB decided at the last minute to publish its report without the discrediting evaluation. "They had to go to the bindery and separate it out," says Greeley with obvious relish.

Both of these volumes tried to unravel the perplexing question of attrition from the priesthood. Though no reliable data existed prior to 1966, it did appear that the resignation rate was on the upswing. From 1966 to 1969, nearly 5 percent of the diocesan clergy in the United States resigned, and that rate grew from 0.4 percent in 1966 to 2 percent in 1969. Three percent of the NORC sample—or approximately 2,000 diocesan priests—said they "probably" or "definitely" would leave. Another 10 percent were "uncertain" about their future. While these rates of actual and planned resignation were probably low compared to that of Protestant denominations, the increase was alarming. Why were men leaving the priesthood?

Greeley was able to study that question from two perspectives, that of priests thinking about resigning and that of priests who already had done so. The major NORC sample provided data on the former, and a special sample of resigned priests, interviewed from July to December 1970, supplied answers for the latter. Priests *planning* to leave did so for a variety of reasons; and Greeley, using the recently developed technique of path analysis, summarized the interplay of explanatory variables. The desire to marry was itself a cause of resignation, but even more, it was a channel through which other causes—principally, frustration with the structure of priestly life—expressed themselves. The implication was clear: no one was to take the easy way out and think that modifying the celibacy regulation would magically revitalize the priesthood.

The view from the other side of the fence was essentially the same. The most common explanation for leaving given by ex-priests was the desire to marry, but almost as important was the feeling that they could not live within the institutional structure of the Church. Eighty percent of the resigned priests, incidentally, were married, four-fifths of them to Catholic wives, and an astounding 43 percent to former members of religious communities. These men seemed to be on a "binge of health" following their agonizing decision. They scored higher than active priests on measures of self-actualization, and those recently married had marital adjustment scores *higher* than those of college-educated males (but these scores diminished with each added year since resignation). Two-fifths of the resigned priests considered themselves active Catholics and attended Church weekly; another two-fifths identified themselves as Catholics who were not a part of the official Church; and one-fifth said they were no longer a part of the Church. Forty percent were interested in a return to the active ministry, but only 10 percent wished to do so on a full-time basis.

Greeley had a strong personal reaction to the question of resignation from the priesthood. He insisted, first of all, that the resignation process be modified to ease the burden on the man who wishes to leave. "I think former priests should be treated with dignity and respect, and that options ought to be open to them to serve the Church either as priests or as laymen." When a friend of *his* leaves the priesthood, Greeley feels a sense of abandonment, loss, and tragedy—for the man who leaves, for himself, for the priesthood, for the Church. Yet if a man's only option is to resign, then "as the Irish politicians would say, 'Do what you have to do.' "[22]

But why, for all that, do the media and "some liberal Catholic lay people" make folk heroes of priests who leave, and why do they do so to the detriment of those who stay? Greeley deeply resented the implication "that the best priests are leaving or that the normal and healthy males are leaving the priesthood . . . . I am particularly angered at those resigned priests who argue (as James Kavenaugh has) that it is only sexual immaturity that keeps us in the priesthood. If I am expected to respect the decision of a man to leave, then

I expect him and all his friends to respect the decision of the overwhelming majority of us who elect to stay."[23]

Further, the argument that one reforms an institution by
leaving it is "politically absurd. The folk heroes of the present time
ought not to be those who quit—however good their reasons for
quitting—but those who stay to fight. In the words of John L.
McKenzie, 'Why quit? Stay and bother them.' And in the words of
Hans Küng, 'Why should I quit? Let the pope quit.' "[24]

Actually, Greeley argued, the concern shown for the problem of
resignation is misdirected. Attention—more than that, serious research—is desperately needed at the other end of the manpower con-
tinuum: *in 1972 there were only half the number of seminarians
there had been five years earlier.* (Between 1965 and 1975 the number dropped by nearly two-thirds.) Perhaps the most important, yet
most overlooked, finding in the entire NORC report had to do with
vocational recruiting. Sixty-four percent of America's priests in 1965
said that they actively encouraged boys to enter the seminary, but
only 33 percent said they did so in 1970—a drop of over 30 percent.
This decline in enthusiasm for recruiting, Greeley said, "could be
the most chilling finding in our entire report."[25]

Like the majority of priests in the 1970 survey, Greeley has always felt that celibacy should be a matter of personal choice for
priests; yet, like the majority, he anticipates he would not marry
were the choice his. He has always believed that women should have
the same access to Holy Orders as men. "Why *not* ordain women?"
he explains his position simply, noting in the same breath that the
majority of American Catholic laity are opposed to the idea. But to
him optional celibacy and the ordination of women are peripheral
issues. He wrote in 1972, "If I were a bishop interested in preserving
my power, I would cheerfully support birth control and marriage
for the clergy, hoping that such concessions would take priests'
minds off the fact that the Church is governed by a small, self-per-
petuating power elite."[26]

To talk face-to-face with Andrew Greeley about the priesthood
is to sense the disillusionment and the anger brought on by his
dealings with the American hierarchy. One hears of seminaries that
have become psychological machines, of priests' organizations that

have become selfish. Of the NORC study he says, "I would never touch the project again, or anything like it, because I was caught between the militants in the priests' organizations on the one hand, rather hostile priests on the staff on the other, and the bishops on the third. The bishops figured if an objective professional study was done it would confirm what they thought was true. And then it turned out that it didn't. And so they concluded that we weren't objective after all."

Greeley's crisis was part of the larger collapse of American Catholicism—one, he insists, that was not inevitable. "The tragedy of the American Church, I would argue, is that it didn't have to be that way. There was a wealth of talent and dedication and organizational skill that got sold down the river, fundamentally by its leadership. If Cardinal Meyer had lived, it would have been a different story. If John Cody hadn't come to Chicago, it would have been a different story. If Paul VI hadn't been elected pope, it would have been a different story. If we had just a few more intellectuals, solidly trained intellectuals, who weren't trying to work out their family aggressions against the Church, against God, if there were a few more priests who could have stood for a model of priestly commitment when all the resignations were going on . . ."

His voice trailed off and he paused. "The collapse of American Catholicism was not something that was written in the cards. We were very unlucky."

Never once, though, did I hear Greeley's disillusionment affect in the slightest his feeling of commitment to the priestly life. In fact, in my very first interview with him—on a Friday evening in the summer of 1973—it took less than half an hour for him to offer, "My core identity is that of parish priest." He said it as if it were the one thing that could never be taken away from him. All the research, all the books, all his "achievements" were so much irrelevant excess created by some momentum outside himself. When we spoke the following morning about his career, I rattled off, at one point, a summary of the past several hours. We had covered the beginnings at the University of Chicago, had mentioned Ford, Rockefeller, the National Institute of Mental Health, and the National Science Foundation, had referred to Sheed and Ward, Doubleday, and the *New York Times*, had compared the reception of his work in Europe and in the United States, and had looked ahead to his then-planned move to Loyola University. We had discussed the politics of the priesthood study. I reminded him of his statement of the night before: "You still say you are just a parish priest?"

"Yes," he replied without hesitation.

"Sure," said Father Paul Asciolla, who was listening in on our conversation, "and Sam Ervin is just a country lawyer." His remark brought a grin from Greeley, but not a retraction.

Well, Sam Ervin *is* a country lawyer. He is more than that, to be sure, but the character of his roots was plainly evident to the millions of viewers watching an intricate Watergate investigation that same summer.

And Andrew Greeley *is* a parish priest. In his summer of 1973, when it appeared that he had been stripped of support from every conceivable side, when he was, in the words of his friend, "all alone," it was that identity which remained. It was that to which he returned, finding in it the meaning of *his* existence, *his* reason for being.

8   The White Ethnics

Amazement comes quickly to the face of Father Greeley when the thought occurs that the 1961 NORC survey of college graduates—his first involvement in survey research—did not contain a single question concerning the ethnic identity of respondents. He was astonished *then*, too, when he first saw the questionnaire, because just outside the building where it was composed were clearly defined ethnic turfs. Blacks surrounded the university; Lithuanians and Poles lived in Marquette Park; Jews in South Shore; Irish in Englewood, South Shore, and farther out in Beverly Hills. Chinatown was a short distance to the north. Yet the climate in the United States was such that most social scientists thought ethnicity was no longer an important feature of American social life—not the kind of thing, surely, that one would bother about with a question in a national survey.

Peter Rossi was one who thought otherwise. One of his first questions to Greeley upon the latter's arrival at NORC was "What are you?"

Greeley recounts the incident. "What do you mean? I'm a Democrat."

"No, no. I didn't mean that. You're a Democrat, and a Catholic, and a priest. But like I'm Italian and Feldman's Jewish. What are you?"

"Oh. I'm Irish."

"Oh, OK."

Greeley was surely Irish, but before his arrival at the university he was not self-consciously Irish. He had always lived in Irish Catholic environments—in St. Angela's parish, in the seminary, in Christ the King—and consequently had never given much thought to his own national background. But now it was different, and, like countless immigrants who took on national identities only after their arrival in the United States, "I became an Irish Catholic ethnic at the University of Chicago."

In 1962, thanks to the efforts of Greeley and Rossi, the second NORC survey of the June 1961 college graduates did contain an ethnic question, and Greeley used the results it yielded to demonstrate a slower acculturation process in the United States among Italians and Eastern Europeans than among Irish, Germans and British. During the ensuing years, too, Greeley fought to have a question on ethnic identity included in every NORC survey, but he was successful only half the time. By 1971, however, no one at NORC could ignore ethnicity, and no one, surely, had to ask Andrew Greeley about his ethnic background.

The reasons go back to 1969 and a meeting of Protestants, Catholics, and Jews in upstate New York to reflect on growing polarization in the United States. Asked to suggest speakers for the conference, which was sponsored by the Ford Foundation, Cardinal Terrence Cooke of New York happened to name Andrew Greeley. Greeley delivered a paper, and Mitchell Sviridoff, a Ford vice-president (and, in Greeley's words, "a precinct, neighborhood kind of guy who knew what I was talking about") happened to like it. Greeley goes on. "So one day they called me and they said, 'Hey, where's your proposal?' I said, 'What proposal?' And they said, 'To set up an ethnic center.' "

In the midst of bad times, the call was manna from heaven. Ford's interest in ethnicity "fit with my disillusionment with higher education and my profound disillusionment with being a social scientist for the Church. And I figured, and it turned out to be the case, that by studying ethnicity one could study American Catholic life and say the hell with the hierarchy." Greeley added later, "I can do nothing but speak praise for McGeorge Bundy, Mike Sviridoff, Basil Whiting, and the whole Ford bureaucracy. They have been very good to us. I'd hell of a lot sooner work for them than for John Krol."

With "megabucks" from Ford, then, the Center for the Study of American Pluralism—Andrew M. Greeley, Director—was launched as a unit within NORC in January 1971. Greeley's output on ethnicity accelerated sharply. First was an article for the *Antioch Review*—a few days to produce 10,000 words on request—that analyzed and championed "The Rediscovery of Diversity" in the United States. The article began where the secularization debate left off, with a discussion of the return of *Gemeinschaft* to overthrow rational, scientific, anonymous *Gesellschaft.* "Men were promised affluence and dignity if they yielded their old primordial ties. They now suspect that the promise was an empty one and are returning to those primordial ties with a vengeance."[1]

In 1971, America heard of pluralism once again because of blacks:

> The mainline American society may have endorsed pluralism in theory, but in fact its basic tendencies were always assimilationist. It has now, however, become official: it is all right for blacks to have their own heritage, their own tradition, their own culture. If it is all right for the blacks, then it ought to be all right for everyone else.[2]

For those who still thought ethnicity to be of little moment, Greeley assembled a grim collage. Men do not often become violent, he said, over rational differences in ideology—such as that between capitalism and socialism—but over primitive, tribal differences of "color, language, religious faith, height, food habits, and facial configuration." Millions may have died over purported ideological struggles in Korea and Vietnam, but many more—perhaps as many as twenty million—have died in conflicts having nothing to do with ideology:

> One need only think of the Hindus and Moslems at the time of the partition of India, of Sudanese blacks and Arabs, of Tutsi and Hutu in Burundi, of Kurds in Iraq, of Nagas in India, of Karens and Kachins in Burma, of Chinese in Indonesia and Malaysia, of Khambas in Tibet, of Somalis in Kenya and Ethiopia, of Arabs in Zanzibar, of Berbers in Morocco and Algeria, of East Indians and blacks in Guiana, of Ibos in Nigeria, and, more recently of Bengalis in East Pakistan to realize how pervasive is what might be broadly called "ethnic" conflict and how incredible the numbers of people who have died in such "irrational" battles. Two million died in India, five hundred thousand have perished in the "unknown war" in the Sudan, and two hundred thousand more in

the equally unknown war in Burundi. The numbers may have been over a million in Biafra and over a half million in Malaysia and Indonesia, and as high as one hundred thousand in Burma and Iraq.

The ethnic conflicts have not been so bloody in other parts of the world, but tens of thousands have died in the seemingly endless battle between those two very Semitic people, the Jews and the Arabs. The English and the French glare hostilely at each other in Quebec; Christian and Moslem have renewed their ancient conflicts on the island of Mindanao; Turk and Greek nervously grip their guns in Cyprus; and Celt and Saxon in Ulster have begun imprisoning and killing one another with all the cumulative passion of a thousand years' hostility.[3]

Ties of blood were strong, all right, demanding often that blood be shed. And perhaps such ties were deeper and more pervasive than the ties of urbanized *Gesellschaft* man. But was not the diversity they created a prelude to destruction—not at all something to be celebrated? Even if Cox overestimated the dispersal of *Gesellschaft* man, was he at least correct to take hope from his arrival? More bluntly, was not ethnic diversification evil?

One might think so until he considers the alternative—"rational, liberal, scientific, democratic homogenization"—which has failed all over the world and in fact set the stage for the resurgence of interest in tribe and clan. We simply have to face the fact that, like it or not, diversification is structured into human experience. As Noam Chomsky and Claude Levi-Strauss have suggested, "man has no other way to cope with the reality in which he finds himself, including the reality of his own relationship network, than by differentiating it. . . . Diversity may lead to hellish miseries in the world, but without the power to diversify—and to locate himself somewhere in the midst of the diversity—man may not be able to cope with the world at all."[4] Besides, there are many indications (even in grubby NORC data) that diversification leads just as often to integration—indeed, is an unavoidable precondition for integration.

America has waxed and waned on the subject of diversity, Greeley went on to say in the *Antioch Review*. Individuals are torn between pride and the sense of belonging they derive from their own ethnic groups and a feeling of resentment at being trapped by that group. "We praise the melting pot out of one side of our mouths and honor cultural pluralism out of the other."[5] It is precisely this ambivalence that explains the lack of serious research in the past quarter century on the topic of ethnicity. And what an oversight this was. Englishmen, Scotsmen, Welshmen, Irishmen, Germans, Italians, Poles, Africans, Indians (from both Asia and America), Frenchmen, Spaniards, Finns, Swedes, Lebanese, Danes, Armenians, Croations, Slovenians, Greeks, Luxembourgers, Chinese, Japanese, Filipinos, and Puerto Ricans come together and form a nation that not only survives, but works, and works reasonably well—only for years no one bothers to notice.

In *Why Can't They Be Like Us?* (1971) Greeley charged that the white ethnics in particular had been systematically ignored. Some Americans said that to speak of *differences* was destructive and immoral (though they "granted" blacks, Chicanos, and American Indians the right to their own ethnic consciousness). Others went further. *Harper's* magazine, for example, printed a cover with the stereotype of Stanley Kowalski slumping, half naked, over a bar in Gary, Indiana. It was prejudice that Greeley was talking about—and prejudice among the nation's elites. "The intellectual who 'loves' blacks and the 'poor' but has contempt for the Irish or the Italians or the 'middle class' is in the final analysis every bit as much a bigot as the blue-collar worker who 'hates niggers,' for both are asking, 'Why Can't They Be Like Us?' "[6]

So the enemy was not just a liberal elite within Catholicism but its corresponding coterie outside the Church. Intellectuals, said Greeley, constitute an ethnic group as parochial and full of hate as the white ethnics they love to parody. When he dropped that charge in the *New York Times Magazine* in the summer of 1970, he was not simply being facetious or striking an analogy. To be sure, the analogy was there. Like an ethnic group intellectuals had (1) presumed consciousness of kind, (2) territorial concentration (enclaves in New York, Washington, Boston, San Francisco, and Chicago's Hyde Park), (3) shared ideals and values, (4) strong moralistic fervor and a sense of persecution, (5) distrust of outsiders, and (6) a tendency to see themselves as the whole of reality. But Greeley's analogy was only a means to an end. Ultimately it herded a diffuse enemy together so as to make them a better target. *They*—the intellectuals—were absolutely convinced of the superiority of mind (which is to say, of their own superiority), felt that those who could articulate ideas ought to run society, and conjured up dark, sinister forces bent on the destruction of the programs of social reform they had devised (which is to say, bent on *their* destruction).[7]

The intellectual ethnic group was not paranoid, really, said Greeley. Their fears were simply the logical outcome of arrogant assumptions. They were moralistic, too, their moralism rooted in a Protestant Puritan or a Jewish messianic past and reinforced by the threat posed by the rest of society. And their behavior was full of contradictions. Theodore Roszak railed against the "technological establishment" and rhapsodized about a "nontechnological counterculture" in a book mass-produced by a very technological printing press and mass-marketed by a very establishment publishing house. And Noam Chomsky denounced American society as imperialistic and demoralized while continuing to pocket an income from an institution as much a part of the American establishment as any institution could be. Oh, they were compassionate, all right, the assault continued, but how sincere was compassion "for the poor and the black," "for drug addicts, terrorists, arsonists, rioters, Russians, Chinese, Arabs, and the Vietcong"[5] if it stopped short of the middle-class and working-class citizen, especially if he were white and over thirty? No, the white ethnic existed in the subconscious of the intelligentsia only as the hard-hat draped over the bar in Gary, Indiana—droll, quaint, boorish, and fascist. He did not even feel guilty when intellectuals thought he ought to feel guilty. Every ethnic group had a scapegoat; the white ethnic was that of the intelligentsia, and they had made him into an object worthy of condescension.

Well, what could one say about white ethnic groups—particularly from the inside? First, one could say that, to them, people like Rennie Davis, Irving Howe, Arthur Schlesinger, and Joseph Alsop were practically look-alikes. They had more in common with each other than with anyone else who was not a member of the intellectual ethnic group. And if that seemed astonishing to intellectuals, what did intellectuals know about the differences between the Polish National Alliance and the Polish Roman Catholic Union? More important than the white ethnics' lumping together—and distrusting—intellectuals was the basic fact of their existence: They were still very close to the immigrant experience and even now insecure about their acceptance. (In the 1960s half the adult Catholics in the country were either immigrants or the children of immigrants.) Scar tissue from the depression was still evident in their thinking. Well fed and well housed, they nevertheless resented the amount of their tax dollars (which were considerable) that was earmarked for welfare programs to subsidize other social groups. After all, they argued, no such subsidies ever were offered them. And they were afraid—afraid of violence, of higher taxes, of black militants and student protesters, of experts and professors, of liberal do-gooders and planners, of religious and moral corruption. They were profoundly committed to family, home, and neighborhood and feared that these were under attack, especially by black in-migration. For all their fears, however, ethnics were fundamentally hopeful. "The assumption prevalent among the elites that the ethnics are 'alienated' is not confirmed by the available data."[9]

Ethnics believed in the freedom and dignity of the individual person, were offended by social injustice, and carried a profound respect for America's tolerance of diversity.

> There is one last component that must be mentioned, and that may be offensive to some. The ethnics *like* the United States of America. The flag, the Star Spangled Banner, the Constitution, the Declaration of Independence, the Capitol, the office of the Presidency—all these are admired symbols which together sum up the gratitude the ethnic feels for what the United States has made possible for him: freedom, dignity, comfort, security—things which his ancestors in the countries from which they fled or were driven would not have dreamt possible. The ethnic is a patriot because he is grateful for what the United States has done for him. He is not, at least not anymore, a superpatriot. He was less likely than his fellow Americans to favor the Vietnam war, and his opposition to communism did not lead him to object to rapprochement with China or the Soviet Union. It was not an ethnic who said, "My country, right or wrong."[10]

Why, Greeley asked, don't we *listen* to the ethnics instead of dismissing their views as "racist" or "fascist"? As matters stand now, they are left out, isolated even from their own political leadership.

They need tax relief, alternatives in education, safe neighbor-hoods—why should law-and-order be a cry solely of the political right? And they need to be *known*, known through the medium of careful, systematic research. There was simply no demographic, socioeconomic, or sociopsychological data on the later stages of the acculturation process of American ethnic groups. "The ethnics are not angels or saints, folk heroes or a new messianic people. They are human beings like the rest of us, and they deserve to be understood in their full complexity of good and bad, positive and negative, open and closed just as much as anyone else."[11]

Greeley expressed all these feelings in a variety of circum-stances. Asked by the American Jewish Committee in 1969 to pre-sent a paper at Fordham University, he responded with the few data he had. His talk appeared as a small volume, *Why Can't They Be Like Us?*, which Greeley later substantially enlarged for publication by E. P. Dutton and Company in 1971. In the fall of 1970, just after his piece in the *New York Times Magazine*, the higher education journal *Change* published "Malice in Wonderland: Misperceptions of the Academic Elite," another attack on myopic academics and intellectuals bent on remaking the rest of the world (whether it wanted to be remade or not), unaware of what motivated the human beings who were to be the objects of their missionary zeal.[12] Renas-cent interest in the neighborhood was acknowledged in "The Urban Church," a chapter in Daniel Patrick Moynihan's *Urban America* (1970). And a speech at Southeastern Baptist Seminary on the ethnic's "civil religion" was later published in the February 1973 edition of *Worldview*.

All the while Greeley's Center staff was sifting existing data for whatever they contained in the way of ethnic information. The 1963 survey of adult American Catholics (published as *The Education of Catholic Americans*), for example, contained an ethnic question, and there were enough subjects in five of the response categories— Irish, German, Italian, Polish, and French—to allow analysis. A dozen dependent variables were chosen, and one of Greeley's first inventories of ethnic traits was begun. It showed that the Irish, first of the five groups to arrive in America, were the most successful of the Catholic immigrant groups (and the most similar to Jews) in terms of amount of education, income, and job prestige. They also were the most pious (but the least given to religious extremism), the happiest (or at least they said they were), the most open-minded, the least racist, and the least anti-Semitic.

German Catholics were almost as successful as Irish Catholics in occupational status, only slightly less devout (and slightly more given to religious extremism), somewhat less happy, and somewhat less open-minded. Italians and Poles, more recent Catholic immigrants, were not nearly as well off educationally, occupationally, or financially as the Irish and Germans. They scored lower than these groups on happiness and open-mindedness and higher on racism. Italians were the least pious of the five groups, the most likely to live in the same neighborhood as their parents, the least likely to belong to the Democratic party. Poles were nearly as devout as the Irish and had the highest percentage of Democrats in their midst. The French—which meant, for the most part, French-Canadians in New England—were distinguished by low scores on the index of piety and high scores on religious extremism and anti-Semitism. Based on their self-reports, the French were also among the happier of the immigrant groups.

Then there was the class of 1961, interviewed for the fifth time in 1968. They provided more recent data on ethnicity, data not limited to Catholic groups, and data containing a built-in control for level of education. Would ethnic differences be apparent among young Americans "melted down" seven years before by the common experience of a college education? The answer was yes. While college education did have a leveling effect—softening Polish attitudes toward blacks, for example—differences of 20 and 30 percentage points between ethnic groups were not uncommon on many measures of attitude and behavior. To name one: 84 percent of the blacks in the class of 1961 agreed in 1968 with the Kerner Commission that "white racism is the cause of Negro riots in the city." Among white groups, 54 percent of the German Jews and 51 percent of the Irish Catholics agreed—but only 34 percent of the German Catholics and 28 percent of the Irish and German Protestants did likewise.

More comprehensive than these initial sketches was "Making it in America: Ethnic Groups and Social Status," published in the September–October 1973 issue of *Social Policy.* How were the various religious-ethnic groups dispersed in the structure of American society? What were their typical occupations and levels of education and income? U.S. Census materials and data from *Current Population Surveys* were solid on black and Spanish-speaking groups, but they were of little use in estimating the demographic distribution of other religious-ethnic groups, simply because census-takers were not allowed to ask questions about religion—and, for some, religion was an essential part of ethnic self-definition. The best source of demographic and socioeconomic information was a composite of seven surveys done by NORC between 1963 and 1972 and a composite of 20 undertaken by the University of Michigan's Survey Research Center in the 1950s and 1960s. Even these data had to be described as "shaky" and the conclusions drawn from them "tentative and speculative" because subsamples of some groups, even in a survey of ten to fifteen thousand respondents, were quite small. Nevertheless, data that allowed comparisons did check out against *Current Population Surveys*, and they left certain overriding impressions. "American society had bestowed economic, occupational, and educational success on its Jewish, British-Protestant, and Irish-Catholic populations. German and Scandinavian groups have done moderately well. The southern and eastern European Catholic groups have done less well, and the Blacks and the Spanish-speaking, quite badly." The relative positions of Irish Protestants and "Other" Protestants—groups that had been in America from the beginning, but ones that lacked a self-conscious ethnic identity—had declined over the past two decades. "Precisely because they do not identify themselves as a group and are not so identified by others, their deteriorating position is not obvious to the rest of society and perhaps not even obvious to many of them."[13]

Through all the analyses one impression became clear. When viewed from the perspective of ethnic and religious background, America was alive with diversity. Americans had not washed together into a dull grey but remained a patchwork of color. "Even when social class is held constant there are differences among ethnic groups in personal orientations, occupational values, expectations toward spouse and children, and quantity and quality of intimacy in family relationships."[14] Ethnicity *was* predictive of differences. And as for the conflict this country was experiencing, it seemed to fall into intelligible patterns when one did not shy away from mini-categories such as German Jew, Polish Catholic, Italian Catholic, English Protestant, first-arrival, second-arrival, and so on.

Journals as diverse as the *Public Opinion Quarterly, Dissent, Scientific American, Sociology of Education,* the *New Republic, Worldview, Social Studies: Irish Journal of Sociology, Eire— Ireland,* and *International Migration Review,* as well as Lee Rainwater's book *Social Problems and Public Policy,* passed these findings on to the public. *Ethnicity in the United States: A Preliminary Reconnaissance* (1974), a volume authored by Greeley and published by Wiley-Interscience, brought much of the data together and contained a statement of the theoretical outlook guiding the Center's research.

The theory began with a definition of "ethnic group," one Greeley borrowed from Richard Schermerhorn: "a collectivity within a larger society having real or putative common ancestry, memories of a shared historical past, and a cultural focus on one or more symbolic elements defined as the epitome of their peoplehood."[15] The critical observation, Greeley said, is one that Nathan Glazer made in 1954. When immigrants come to a new country, said Glazer, they do not already constitute a group or a community; rather, ethnic groups *come into existence* after immigrants arrive in a new land. When Eastern European peoples, speaking the various dialects of their villages, came together in the cities of America, they had to create a common language—and so the first newspaper in the Lithuanian language was published, not in Lithuania, but in America. Similarly, noted Glazer, the Erse revival began in Boston, and the nation of Czechoslovakia was launched at a meeting in Pittsburgh.

And recently, Greeley added, we have witnessed attempts as deliberate and self-conscious as these earlier ones to create ethnic groups. The black power movement may be seen in this light, as can the emergence of American Indian groups. Spanish-speaking persons are attempting to create an ethnic group in the Northeast, as are Appalachian whites in Chicago. Ethnic symbols, too, change in a fashion that the acculturation model of ethnicity can in no way accommodate. "One of our colleagues observed that when she was growing up in Florida she thought of herself as an American; when she went to Washington, D.C., she discovered that she was Cuban;

and when she came to Chicago, she was told that she was 'Spanish-speaking.'" The tricolor bumper stickers now proudly displayed on the cars of Americans from southern Italy and Sicily were once, in Italy, the hated symbol of the "foreign" domination of the Piedmontese. "The Sicilians came to the United States and discovered that they were Italian-Americans. Now they have discovered that they are Italian, a process exactly the reverse of that suggested by using only the acculturation picture."[16]

Something, then, about the nature of American society (or any society) brings about a need for *ethnogenesis,* the creation of an ethnic identity, among immigrants—even second, third, and fourth generation immigrants. Greeley's perspective had two major consequences. First, the American experience—not the European—came to be seen as the principal contributor to an immigrant culture. "America's ethnic groups," Greeley wrote, "are rooted only very partially in the European preimmigrant experience, and have been shaped to a very great extent, however differentially for different groups, by the American experience."[17] As a result, American Italians are very different from Italian Italians, American Irish from Irish Irish, American Poles from Polish Poles, and so on.

Second, if it is *America* that is the source of the creation and manipulation of ethnic symbols, then ethnic differentiation can be expected to continue—albeit alongside ethnic homogenization—as long as America continues. We are not headed for a melting pot, as the very powerful assimilationist mythology would have us believe. Yes, American Italians will continue to be different from Italian Italians, but this does not mean that they will become indistinguishable from American Poles or American Irishmen. Put another way, "The Kennedy administration was, one supposes, quite different from the administration of Prime Minister Sean Lynch in Dublin, but it was also very different from a WASP administration in this country, or the kind of administration we will have when finally Americans get around to electing a Jewish president."[18]

New models invariably produce new questions, and in the case of the ethnogenesis paradigm, the basic question became *why?* Why did ethnic collectivities come into being, and why, after that, were they transformed and transmuted? Greeley's answer: because the benefits of ethnogenesis outweighed the costs. Soon after their arrival in the United States, immigrants discovered that they had already been placed by the rest of society in a category based on their national origin. They also found that to succeed at the American political game one had to be part of a collectivity—why not their national collectivity? The raising of ethnic consciousness provided a number of advantages:

> The ethnic group became one of the avenues to political power for immigrants. It provided a special market in which the emerging business and professional class within the immigrant community could build its own economic base. It offered a social mobility pyramid which the more ambitious immigrants could ascend; and if the social pyramid of the host culture was inaccessible, they could at least move to the social apex within their own collectivity. And psychologically, it provided continuity between the Old World and the New and made possible the preservation of a minimum of family values that were thought to be essential.[19]

Ethnic identity was a way of stepping *into* American society, not a symptom of withdrawal from it. It was "a way for the immigrant population to look at its present and future in America rather than its past in the Old World." Polish-Americans and Czech-Americans supported nationalist movements in their own countries only *after* the United States entered World War I—a sign that their support was more an exercise in American patriotism than in Polish or Czech nationalism. And the nineteenth- and early twentieth-century Irish-Americans who favored freedom for Ireland argued that only when Ireland was a free and independent nation would Irish-Americans be accepted by native Americans as full-fledged citizens. "The hyphen in the hyphenate American was a symbol of equality, not of inequality. In an urban environment where virtually everyone—including the native American—was something else besides 'American,' one had to be an ethnic to find one's place on the map."[20]

As part of the process of ethnogenesis, personality traits were selectively reinforced as being part of one's ethnic identity, and they were therefore transmitted from one generation to the next—provided the trait proved useful:

> Did hard work and intellectual ambition prove extremely helpful in American society? Such work and ambition could be reinforced by telling children that it was an especially Jewish trait, and to be good Jews they must develop it. Did a certain kind of informal

political skill open up avenues to power and prestige? Then such
political skills could be legitimated and reinforced on the grounds
that they were Irish.[21]

Immigrants stood to gain enormously, then, from the officially
sanctioned structure of differentiation in America. There were costs,
to be sure. Jews were excluded from certain clubs and buildings and
companies, and there were similar, if more subtle, biases against
Catholics, especially those from southern and eastern Europe. And
differentiation did lead to conflict, but somehow the conflict rarely
became violent. "The immigrants never saw their claim to be
hyphenated Americans as involving any danger of tearing apart the
new society, which on the whole was relatively benign to them."[22]
By and large—if you were white—creating and maintaining an
ethnic identity provided benefits that far outweighed the costs.

Furthermore, it was required by the political and social structure in America that membership in an ethnic collectivity be
optional. One was an ethnic in America only if he wanted to be—
there was no coercion. And ethnic boundaries were permeable,
especially if one were making a good deal of money. Thus, ethnic
identification became a "limited liability"; one could call upon it
when it was useful and dispose of it when it became a burden. All of
this, at least, was the way it was *supposed* to be. It was not the way it
was for blacks (Greeley admitted that his theory "becomes a
dilemma on the subject of non-white groups"[23]), and it certainly was
not always true for whites. But the structure of permeability was at
least officially sanctioned, and that is why ethnic differentiation in
the United States has been, on the whole, rather successful. The
interesting question, of course—and one that research had yet to
answer—was: Who used an ethnic map of the world, and when, and
to what advantage? And who still does?

The emerging perspective of Greeley's Center, then, conceived
as an extension of the many forms of assimilation and acculturation theory, was on the origin and natural history of ethnic
groups—groups that were formed from amorphous collections of
European immigrants. In *Ethnicity in the United States* Greeley
listed the questions raised by such a perspective. What was the interplay between ethnic *origin* (one's actual ancestry), ethnic *identification* (whether or not—and where—one placed oneself on an ethnic

chart), ethnic *heritage* (the conscious recollection one had of his ethnic history), and ethnic *culture* (attitudes, personality styles, and behaviors associated with particular ethnic groups)? For example, the American Irish (that denotes ethnic origin) apparently had a rather weak ethnic identification and almost no consciousness of an ethnic heritage but displayed a good deal of distinctively ethnic culture—overchoosing law as a profession, for example. What of other groups? And what happened to one's ethnic identification when one's ethnic origins were mixed? Did he *choose* an identification, as one of Greeley's colleagues did between his French, Dutch, Scotch, Irish, and Sioux Indian ancestry? (He chose—what else?—to be Irish.) And did the choice affect behavior—making Greeley's colleague more politically active, for example, because it was the Irish thing to do? Finally was it true (and Greeley thought it was) that the most durable part of an ethnic culture was the expectations one had of the behavior of intimate others, of brothers and sisters, of spouses, of children, of parents?

In January 1973 the Ford Foundation extended for two and one-half years its support of the Center for the Study of American Pluralism, and it has continued its sponsorship down to the present. During the Center's life, the Henry Luce Foundation, the National Institute of Mental Health, the Markle Foundation, the Twentieth Century Fund, the National Institutes for Alcohol Abuse and Alcoholism, and the National Endowment for the Humanities have financed projects on the political socialization of children, the transmission of religious and achievement values across generational lines, the political activities of ethnic women and their attitudes toward feminism, the activities of ethnic journalists, the political participation of ethnics, and the correlation between ethnicity and drinking behavior. Sage Press published a series of monographs on religion and ethnicity, and in April 1974 Academic Press initiated an interdisciplinary quarterly entitled *Ethnicity* and edited by Greeley.

In one of his reports to the Ford Foundation, Greeley noted an improving climate for research on ethnicity. "It is now moving toward the top of the list of priorities of many Idea Merchants and Idea Consumers," he wrote.[24] So fashionable had the idea become, in fact, that in 1974 Greeley tried to put together a consortium of grants totaling five or six million dollars for a mammoth investigation of the country's diversity on the occasion of its bicentennial. Greeley's "megastudy" would have used instruments powerful enough to bring into focus smaller groups that appeared only as blurs in the typical national sample—Serbs, Slovaks, Greeks, Armenians, Orientals, Czechs, even Sephardic Jews, Kalmulks, Crimean Tartars, and Russian Germans. The project met the approval of Ford's trustees, but it was killed when the foundation suffered severe setbacks in the stock market.

Though he lost his megastudy, Greeley was at least able to use data from NORC's 1974 survey of American Catholics to update the social and economic position of Catholic immigrant groups. In *Ethnicity, Denomination, Inequality* (1976) and *The American Catholic: A Social Portrait* (1977), he published results that astonished even him. Though Catholic ethnics *felt* insecure economically (immigration and the depression were still that close), they were nevertheless making a great deal of money. By the mid-seventies Irish Catholics had progressed to the point where they were the richest and best educated white gentile group in the country. At the same time, German Catholics (early immigrants like the Irish) stood at the national average in educational attainment but far above it in family income. Southern and Eastern European Catholics, objects of bigoted immigration laws a half century before, were climbing beyond anyone's expectations. Italians and Poles far surpassed the national norm financially and were rising rapidly in their level of education (though they were still below average); Slavs had passed the norm financially but remained below it educationally. French Catholics, low in educational attainment, were only a bit above average in income. On the whole, Catholic ethnic groups (not counting the Spanish-speaking) were dead center educationally and dead center in occupational prestige. But they were second only to Jews—and moving faster than Jews—in the amount of money they made.

There was an interesting pattern in these, the most recent of the Center's data. Save for the Irish, Catholic ethnics had jobs that were financially rewarding but not prestigious. Either income was more important than prestige to those with the immigrant memory or—Greeley was becoming adamant about this—there was discrimina-

tion that excluded Catholics from the upper levels of professional
and corporate success.

In the midst of it all there was time for fun, for a whole volume
of honesty-compels-me-to-say's (when you hear that phrase, duck)
directed at the American Irish. Parts of *That Most Distressful
Nation: The Taming of the American Irish* (1972) had previously
amused, perplexed, and irritated readers of the *New York Times
Mazazine* (St. Patrick's Day week, 1971), the *Critic*, the *New Republic*, and *Dissent*. The book itself was a compendium of Andrew
Greeley in all his personal pluralism—opinion, conjecture, advice,
NORC data, secondary source history and anthropology, poetry (by
Nancy McCready), autobiography. It covered safe, noncontroversial
topics like religion, sex, politics, race, alcohol, and raising children. Parts were lucid and witty; parts were disjointed and hard to
follow. There was haste and repetition (Greeley must have relished
an anecdote about an Irish monk proving his virtue by sleeping
between two maidens with pointed breasts—he told it twice within
twenty-five pages). But it was all there—that is, *he* was all there,
every part of him, "stubborn, perverse, wrongheaded, and paradoxical"[25]; and he spoke not from the computer terminal but from
the pub.

The theme of *That Most Distressful Nation* was captured by
Daniel Patrick Moynihan's opener in the foreword: "Would it be
fair to say of American Irish history, as Oscar Wilde said of Niagara
Falls, that it would be more impressive if it flowed the other way?"
The past was one of heroic struggle—sheer stubbornness, at least—
in the face of unspeakable oppression. Greeley's people endured
"the most savage, the most repressive legislation that the modern
world has ever seen." The penal laws reached their peak in the early
1700s. All priests in Ireland were required by the British to register
their names, and those who failed to do so were to be castrated;
bishops were banished under penalty of being hanged, drawn, and
quartered; Catholics were forbidden to marry Protestants, with
death the penalty for any priest performing such a marriage;
Catholics were excluded from the legal profession; they could not
acquire land from Protestants, own a horse worth more than five
pounds, manufacture or sell books or newspapers, or grant mort-

gages; Catholic orphans were to be brought up as Protestants; their homes, in the words of an observer of the times, were "the most miserable hovels that can well be conceived."[26]

Add to that the horror, a century later, of the potato famine, "one of the great disasters of modern Western Europe," in which 1 to 1.5 million Irish Catholics died in the space of three years, "while the British Government barely lifted a finger to save them." Indeed, the head of the British Treasury saw the famine as the solution of an "all-wise Providence" to the Irish problem of overpopulation, and the London *Times* rejoiced that the Irishman would soon be "as rare on the banks of the Liffey as a red man on the banks of Manhattan."[27]

The only escape was emigration, much of it to the New World. They came, abysmally poor, unskilled, on "coffin ships" like the *Elizabeth and Sarah*. It completed the crossing in eight weeks; 42 of the original 276 passengers died en route. Similarly, the *Agnes* arrived near Detroit with 427 passengers, but only 150 remained after the fifteen-day quarantine. Of 100,000 emigrants who left for Canada, 17,000 died on the way and another 50,000 upon arrival. "Was England guilty of genocide in the 1840s?" Greeley asked. Not the way Adolf Hitler was, he said, but at least those who lived through Hitler's extermination camps "were hailed as heroes and encouraged by a world that acknowledged the inhumanity of what had happened to them."[28] No such solace met the Irish survivors who came to this country unwelcome, unwanted, and despised.

Through it all they never caved in. From the time of the Celts to the Easter Rising of 1916, the Irish never stopped rebelling. They paid for the millenium of revolt, strife, and depression with the emptiness of their cultural, scientific, and intellectual development; but the wonder was not that they failed to produce an impressive intellectual community, but that they were able to produce anything at all. A political style emerged to insure their survival. It was not unlike the *modus operandi* of the Chicago Irish politician. "Personal loyalty, informal arrangements, tight family structures, ridicule, boycott, and great love of legal learning combined frequently with little concern for the enforcement of the letter of the law, a fondness for legal contention and argument, suspicion of formal governmental regulations, indirect and circuitous ways of accomplishing one's purposes."[29]

And the Celtic poets developed characteristics not unlike those of Andrew Greeley. They were proud, sensitive, religious, bitter, and witty men; their comics were savage—no fate was worse than being a victim of the poets. "The poets loved to play with words, to deliver neat and witty epigrams, to engage in wild flights of fantasy; but they were testy, easily angered men, and when they turned their fury on you, you were in great trouble indeed."[30]

When it came to the Irish family, there were few positive things that Greeley could say about it. Drawing on the anthropological literature that existed, adding hearsay and impression, Greeley concluded that the Irish were cold, repressed, inflexible, and incapable of intimacy or tenderness. A County Mayo psychiatrist named David Dunne described the problems of his patients: "greed, envy, bitterness, frustration, sexual and otherwise, guilt, hatred, anger, a general feeling of a lack of love, often associated with a fear of love, a fear of loss, indeed a very high expectancy of and apparent resignation to loss, with consequent fear and avoidance of tenderness and intimacy." Added Greeley, "I had the uncanny feeling in reading Dunne's article that he knew my family all too well."[31]

In the countryside of Ireland the father was the unquestioned ruler of the house, but his power waned in the city; and the mother's role, already of great importance, became all powerful. In the United States Irish mothers tended to be like their counterparts in the cities of Ireland. There were even subspecies of the Irish matriarch. The Woman of Property bought and sold two-flats, moving her family from one to the next if it appeared she could clear $1,000 in the deal. Her husband was not very ambitious (which was probably why she married him), and her family looked happy (though the Irish were remarkable at concealing pain). The more common Pious Woman was usually in bad health but nevertheless worked tirelessly for her husband and children, engaged in a multitude of religious devotions, and was frequently heard to utter "I really can't complain" (though in fact she complained as much as she prayed.) Her children were devoted to her and to her Church, and many of them received "vocations" to the religious life. The Respectable Woman, by far the most common of the matriarchs, was the one who produced most of the hardworking, achievement-oriented American Irish. Her entire life, and necessarily that of her family, was governed by the simple question, "What will people say?" Her children went to college, got married, and became professionals—so they could tell themselves people were saying nice things about them.

Sex in Ireland was never discussed in the home. Girls were rarely given advice at all ("after marriage nature would take its course"), and boys learned what they had to learn from older boys and men and from watching animals. It was hard to say what sex in marriage was like, because so few would talk about it. It appeared, nevertheless, that the husband usually initiated sexual activity, employed the male superior position (without removing his or his wife's underclothing), achieved orgasm rapidly, and then fell asleep. The woman was assumed to be uninterested in sexual pleasure. Nudity was abhorred as something sexual (as was physiological evacuation), and sex itself was considered dangerous, a cause of insanity.

What about Irish sex in America? Save for the fact that children were conceived, there wasn't any. The Irish male was awkward, tongue-tied, clumsy, and rough in his attempts at intimacy. His wife's most positive contribution was to "do her duty" and never refuse her husband.

But things were changing—or were they? Actually very few data existed to substantiate or prove Greeley's "hunches, impressions, and stereotypes" of the American Irish. Indeed, survey data on Irish-American males only added to the confusion. Irish males were, in Chesterton's phrase, "the men that God made mad"; their psyches showed more contradictions than appeared in any other ethnic groups studied. Were the Irish inner-directed? Very much so—but also very outer-directed. Fatalistic? To be sure—but also very trusting. Was their heritage one of rigid, inflexible, harsh, cold family relationships? It seemed so—but in the 1960s Irish males provided their children with more physical affection than any other white ethnic group. One had to throw his hands up at the data and wait for more to come in.

There was ample data, however, to show that the Irish made it big in America. The descendants of those Celtic heroes hit it just right—the economy was expanding rapidly when they arrived, and they were a large pool of laborers who knew the language—and now, even though their progress had been slowed by the Great Depression, they were second only to Jews in economic prosperity. One hundred and ten years after the potato famine John Kennedy was president of the United States—and the immigrant era was over. Yes, the Irish were successful, but at what price? Suburban Irish communities were "terribly insecure and threatened places." And the past, save for "the creature" and memories of the crash in 1929, was lost.

Indeed, Irish propensity for drink—for "the creature"—said it all. In Ireland, 11 percent of personal income in a recent year was spent on alcohol, and the American Irish were just as addicted to drinking as their European counterparts. In the 1940s the Irish rate of admission to New York hospitals for alcoholism was three times that of any other ethnic group, and NORC data collected in the middle sixties testified that the American Irish were still number one in their fondness for "the jar." Part of the Irish heritage survived—regrettably—after all. " 'The Creature' is at first a help in the struggle for success, then an excuse for not making it, and finally a solace for failure."[32]

As for the next generation, they were Studs Lonigan all over again—a different veneer, maybe, but the same self-loathing, the same capacity for self-destruction:

> Dubious about his masculinity, harassed by his mother, nagged by his sisters, lacking a confident father to imitate, and paralyzed by guilt, Studs was already bent on self-destruction when he graduated from St. Anselm's in 1916. His deep prejudices against "smokes" and "kikes," his noisy bravado, his violence with women, and, above all, his passion for John Barleycorn all served to protect a small and insecure sense of self. Studs Lonigan loathed himself, and his whole life was a systematic effort to punish himself for his own worthlessness. . . .

> None of this has changed. The site has moved from Fifty-eighth and Indiana to Beverly, but the self-loathing and self-destruction continues. South Side Irish—a marvelously gifted and creative

people—have been bent on destroying themselves for three-quarters of a century. It looks as though they are beginning to succeed.[33]

And yet, there were some—one, at least—who had broken through, who were no longer tentative in the face of life, who had the nerve to put their despair, their hope (their Irish selves) on paper. Greeley concluded with poetry written by Nancy McCready for a toddler named Liam:

I shall not give to you, my son, a heritage of
*   splintered dreams*
that slushed down the sink with stale beer and
*   squeezed out tears of pain*
for all the years that might have been if I had
*   lived*
instead of killing dead my heart and ours, bit by
*   bit,*
with breaking rage and chunks of sorrow,
passion which guilt turned sour and then, misunderstanding
took my soul and crashed it in the night.
I shall not go desperate dying into life.
The enemy that dare to take the sea's surge from our eyes
I shall defy and drag to hell and back and shake the
*   skull of suicide*
which says the gift will be ungiven and the hope denied.
No, for we shall sing, my son, and eat the sweets of
*   victory.*
Lie peaceful down your head
This hunger will not be quieted, nor ever fully fed
Not before we hold the stars and until then,
we'll go a'brawling and wooing life
There're fights to be fought and battles won
But never in the name of life direct our own undoing
Nor allow while we breathe that Life should be undone![34]

When I first approached Father Greeley about writing this book in March 1973, he was in the midst of an intense struggle at the University of Chicago, fighting with every political instinct he possessed for a tenured position in its School of Social Service Administration. It was the eighth time he was being considered for full faculty status in one of the schools or departments of the university—all of them distinct from NORC. As he saw it then, his chances for a favorable decision were "about 50.1 to 49.9." In view of his secure position at NORC, I wondered what was the attraction of the university itself. "Why do you want in?" I asked.

He said he was tired of living by his wits—meaning, I took it, that he was tired of the demands of hustling grants to keep his Center afloat, even though he was very successful at grantsmanship. A joint appointment with tenure would relieve some of the financial drain on his NORC projects. But his *first* reaction to my question was less calculating. It was sheer instinct. "Because they want me out."

"Why do they want you out?"

He reached immediately into a desk drawer, pulled out a Roman collar, and held it up.

A short time later, despite a recommendation for his appointment from Social Service Administration, Greeley was once again turned down by the University of Chicago.

According to Andrew Segal and Don Rose of the *Hyde Park-Kenwood Voices,* several members of the Department of Sociology had not only vetoed Greeley's appointment in their own department but had also, through the years, blocked proposals for his tenure at other schools and departments in the university—and had even intervened to smother a recent offer from Northwestern University's Center for Urban Affairs. Despite a list of scholarly publications as long as, if not longer than, that of any tenured member in the department, despite the respect with which his skills were regarded by funding agencies (wrote Segal and Rose), Greeley's opposition, led by Edward Shils and Morris Janowitz, considered him "undistinguished" and "lacking in depth."[35] Some even questioned his ethnic studies as a rationalization for racial hostilities. Supporters of Greeley attributed his rejection to the traditional friction between survey researchers and academic sociologists, to NORC's marginality vis-a-vis the university proper, to Greeley's propensity for stepping on toes, to jealousy—and to sheer anticlerical prejudice. He was a victim of exposure, said others; he had published too much; he had said too many things too loudly. Greeley later opined that some of his trouble stemmed from his article on intellectuals in the *New York Times Magazine.* But he

remained convinced that the basic reason for eight successive rejec-
tions by the university was his Irish Catholic priesthood. Peter
Rossi, who had tried to secure an appointment in sociology for
Greeley when he first came to NORC, agreed. "Everyone will admit
anticlericalism is going on," said Rossi, "but nobody wants to go on
the record. One high-ranking member of the Sociology Department
told me years ago, 'I am opposed to the appointment of a Catholic
priest just as I would be opposed to a Communist; both are so in the
thralls of their party lines that they couldn't be objective.' "[36]

A year after the incident a bitter Greeley told me of a conversation with Rossi. "I remember saying to Pete Rossi a year or two ago,
'Pete, you know all these guys that now hate my guts were friendly
when I came.' And I said, 'How come?' And he said, 'Well, they
thought you were going to be a convert.' And I said, 'You mean
leave the priesthood and the Church?' He said, 'Well, maybe that.
They would have liked to have had that, but even short of that, they
thought you'd start seeing the world through their viewpoint; and
what they discovered is that you didn't and wouldn't, that you'd
insist on being your own obnoxious Irish self.' "

Nothing will erase the scars of Greeley's dealings with the university. Though he did not come to Chicago seeking an academic
career, though he has never needed the financial security that tenure
brings, his anger was aroused in 1967 when the unanimous recommendation of the Department of Education for his appointment as
professor was killed at upper levels of the university's administration. Wrote Greeley to the *Hyde Park-Kenwood Voices:*

> It was only after that appointment was denied me—after five
> months of being assured that there would be no problem—that I
> began to want what had been offered and then snatched away.
> Similarly, I had settled down once again to the NORC role two and
> a half years ago when the new dean, Robert Adams, summoned me
> to his office, read a memo from his secret file (which he implied
> Mr. Shils had written) calling me a stereotypical New Leftist, told
> me an injustice had been done, and that he would see that the
> wrong was righted.[37]

The wrong was never righted, and now, having battled the
forces across the Midway for the last time, a pervasive motivation of
Greeley's is "showing those S.O.B.'s, getting even with them." An

offer from a prestigious university would show them (though Greeley would probably refuse it—as he did one from Duke University—because he "belongs" in Chicago). The largest grant ever conferred to a sociologist would surely show them. (Greeley was after it when he proposed his bicentennial megastudy to the Ford Foundation.) Greeley's voice toughens as he reflects on the entire affair. "I have learned about evil—implacable enemies who make me an inkblot, friends you cannot count on."

Because NORC did not give him the support he felt he deserved in the crisis, because, too, he had been passed over for the NORC directorship in 1971 (Greeley attributes this to anticlericalism on the part of NORC trustees and university officials), Greeley prepared in the spring of 1973 to pull up stakes and move his Center for the Study of American Pluralism to Loyola University. In July, Richard Matre, vice-president and dean of the faculties at Loyola, announced that Father Greeley would become a professor there and that Greeley's Center would be housed on Loyola's Lewis Towers campus. But in the middle of August a letter reached Greeley at Grand Beach indicating that Loyola could not implement the agreement they had negotiated—Greeley's research efforts would have to take a back seat to his teaching duties. Greeley went out to water ski, returned, and then called NORC director Jim Davis. "Jim, I think I know where I can sell you a full-fledged research program, if you're interested in buying."

Davis was very interested. "I can't criticize someone for changing his mind," he told Greeley. By 3:30 that same day Greeley had driven to Chicago and was in Davis's office proposing a deal. The two came to terms quickly. Greeley would get a ten-year contract at the same salary offered by Duke University, promotions and raises for his colleagues, and an agreement to take two months of his salary from NORC overhead rather than from his projects. Greeley walked down to Bill McCready's office and said, "Bill, unpack. We're staying."

The wounds from NORC's lack of support healed quickly (Greeley has never considered NORC part of the "university"). But not so Greeley's outrage at the University of Chicago. Of late, he has been quick to cry prejudice—against Catholics, against priests, against the Irish—wherever he sees it. In February 1973, *School*

Review published his charge that state aid was not going to Catholic schools—the only system capable of breaking up the soft, inept monopoly that is public education—because of powerful elements of anti-Catholic nativism. In March, on the occasion of another demonstration in the *American Journal of Sociology* that Catholic intellectuals from the class of 1961 were on schedule in the development of their academic careers, he proposed a study of anti-Catholic feelings at elite schools, pointing out that social scientists argue (as some did at a conference in 1971) "that the Catholic absence from academia in the past was the result of intellectual inferiority but that the absence of women and blacks was a result of discrimination."[38] A year later he charged in the *Critic* that "the sign 'No Irish Need Apply' . . . still hangs at the entrance to most intellectual literary circles and at the backs of most senior chairs in the country's major universities."[39] He said more in *The Communal Catholic* (1976) and *An Ugly Little Secret* (1977):

> ITEM: The stereotypical white ethnic—meaning racist, hard hat, ignorant, hawk, slob—is a euphemism for Catholic. You can denounce white ethnics and still feel virtuous that you are not anti-Catholic, even though all white ethnics seem to be Catholic. And of course you need not be deterred by the data that show that ethnic Catholics are less likely to be racist and more likely to have been against the Vietnam war from the beginning. . . . Catholics are conservative and that is that . . .

> ITEM: The Institute of Urban Life in Chicago finds that Poles and Italians are almost totally absent from the boards of large corporations. The various keepers of the nation's conscience, like the National Council of Churches, would have worked themselves into paroxysms of guilt if the finding concerned blacks; yet they remained completely silent . . .

> ITEM: The anti-abortion issue, led by four pathetic cardinals presenting their views before Congress, is described as a Catholic ploy to impose its moral views on Society. . . . Actually, . . . while the overwhelming majority of Catholics and Protestants support abortion if the mother's life is in danger or if there is risk of delivering a defective child, the majority of both groups are against abortion if the woman simply does not want any more children. Thus, by opposing abortion on demand, the Catholic hierarchy is speaking for the conscience of the majority—however crude and inept it may be as a spokesman. Don't hold your breath to read that in *The New York Times*.

ITEM: A Jewish leader chided me because Catholics were not vigorous enough in their support of Israel. It was not, he told me, high enough on our agenda. I asked him how high Ulster was on his. He told me that was different. How different? Well, the killing in Ulster was senseless violence, and the Irish had never been victims of genocide. I asked him if he had ever heard of Cromwell, and he asked me what that had to do with it.[40]

He was angry in the aftermath of his final defeat by the Department of Sociology, but there were other feelings too. A man who had set out in 1960 as a commuter between Christ the King and the University of Chicago, who had begun to bridge the worlds these institutions represented, now found himself an outsider to both. "I have been disowned by both my parish and my university. I have been blacklisted in both my diocese and my profession," he wrote in "Confessions of a Loud-Mouthed Irish Priest." "What's more, I have managed to achieve all these things in less than a dozen years and, to tell the truth, without even seriously trying."[41]

He had been forced to leave Christ the King a decade ago, but it had never been clearer that the parish was where he belonged—spiritually if in no other way. "I don't live in the neighborhood just now, and when I show up there some of the inhabitants reach for their squirrel rifles, but just the same, I am at ease in the neighborhood, understand its people from the inside, and can be both critical of them and sympathetic toward them without having to fall back on bathos or nostalgia." Yes, for all its faults, Christ the King had it all over the University of Chicago, *Gemeinschaft* over *Gesellschaft*, the neighborhood of the ethnics over the Big World of the intellectuals. A priest he was, but a *parish'* priest, a neighborhood priest. An ethnic too, unalienated, his roots still intact; in view of the Big World, "that's about as bad as you can be."[42]

He explained: in the neighborhood, friends come first, ideas second, but in the university it is ideas first and friends second—if at all. The neighborhood is a place where trust, fidelity, counting on people are a necessity; without them, homes are overrun by terror. But loyalty is counterproductive in the Big World of the intellectuals. There, contract, short-term commitment, an intelleuctalized code of moral principles are the order of the day; the emphasis is on mobility and career success; one is committed to his friends only if it is "rational" and conducive to one's self-interest. The Big World runs on ideas, true; but, "as a young Irish lawyer in Chicago puts it, 'Someone who won't be loyal to a friend will never be loyal to an idea.' "[53]

Greeley may never make it back from the university to the parish, but he will remain convinced that the neighborhood is right about what it takes to make society work and that the Big World is wrong. And those in the Big World who make and implement social policy had better begin to believe that "the people in the neighborhood may know something about human life that we have forgotten."[44] Greeley will continue to be a scholar in the cosmopolitan world of university, foundation, and government, but only as a "spy from the neighborhood," only to convey the wisdom and strength of *his* people.

"I am, damn it, still capable of standing by my own kind, come what may, and I wouldn't trade that for anything—not even for a membership in the National Academy of Science."[45]

9   Politics:
Conscience or
Coalition

On May 17, 1968, Philip and Daniel Berrigan, two Irish Catholic priests, one of them an early friend of Andrew Greeley, invaded the offices of Local Board 33 in Catonsville, Maryland, stashed 300 draft files into wire baskets, took the baskets to the parking lot outside, and (TV cameras recording it all) burned them with home-made napalm. In August of that year, the nation's television viewers saw the Irish Catholic mayor of Chicago, Richard J. Daley, shout obscenities at a man trying to address the Democratic National Convention, and they watched his police brutalize angry demonstrators outside the convention walls. Nothing could have intensified the conflict between Andrew Greeley and the liberal intelligentsia more; nothing could have been better calculated to widen the chasm between them; and nothing, surely, could have revealed more dramatically the political soul of the neighborhood—than Greeley's denunciation of the Berrigans and their "prophetic act" and his espousal of the Chicago-style politics of Mayor Daley.

The mayor of Chicago—what else was he but a bad joke, inarticulate, lower-class, profane, a tyrant sitting on top of a machine? This man was preferable to a pair of nonviolent clerics putting themselves on the line, expressing their country's moral revulsion at the Vietnamese war? Preferable, later on, to George McGovern, who identified with the best impulses of his time, who had the courage to state in clear terms that the war was immoral and that America should "come home" to her true values?

In January 1971 the *Holy Cross Quarterly* took up the Berrigan flag and devoted an entire issue to the consequences of their raid in Cantonsville. It was appropriate that the *Quarterly* do so. Daniel

Berrigan, like the priests who teach at Holy Cross, was a Jesuit, and Philip Berrigan graduated from Holy Cross in 1950 before becoming a Josephite priest. When the *Quarterly* came out that January, both brothers were in prison for destroying draft records, and Philip was under indictment for plotting to kidnap Henry Kissinger and blow up the heating system of some federal buildings in Washington. (Daniel was named a co-conspirator in the case; both were cleared when it later came to trial.) William Van Etten Casey entitled the issue's editorial "Thank you, Dan and Phil," wrote of the Berrigan case as a "collision of conscience with the state," and added, "I believe they are the living extension of one of the roles that Christ took upon himself—a harsh, demanding, unpopular, and, at times, a necessary role."[1]

The *Quarterly* was not alone. *Commonweal* said the Berrigans were calling for a moral revolution based on the personal conversion of individuals."[2] Francine du Plessix Gray celebrated their Catholic radicalism in the *New Yorker* and later in a book entitled *Divine Disobedience,* and Gary Wills lauded their resistance for *Playboy.*[3] Others spoke of the Berrigans as a challenge, a burden, "prophetic," if not models then at least signs. Noam Chomsky argued that it was the actions of persons like Philip and Daniel Berrigan that brought the war before an otherwise apathetic and ignorant American public. Opinion polls, like those showing that antiwar demonstrations boomeranged (they increased, rather than decreased, public support for the president) were, to Chomsky, "meaningless."[4]

In the midst of all the adulation, Father Greeley, not at all of the opinion that the polls were meaningless, let fly a vicious attack. In a syndicated column reprinted in the *Quarterly,* Greeley acknowledged that Daniel Berrigan was nonviolent, all right, but beware—the logic in his thinking led inevitably to violence. "Make no mistake about it. The self-righteous moralism displayed in the Berrigan interviews will not tolerate the immorality of those who dare to disagree with him. If Daniel Berrigan was in power, I would be in jail—and not for destroying government property either, but because I was immoral."[5]

"Turning Off the People" is how Greeley had described radical protest like that of the Berrigans in the June 27, 1970, issue of the *New Republic.* Between 60 and 90 percent of the American people, he asserted, had been alienated by such protest. Many of them were the white ethnics to whom he was close. Revisionist history notwithstanding, these people were anti-Communist; they knew from first-hand experience of Hungary, the Berlin Wall, Czechoslovakia, the "Communist menace" in Europe. And they were deeply patriotic to a country that had given them financial success and personal freedom. How could the student protesters, the children of the well-to-do, knock America? they asked. "I don't know the exact cost to the peace movement of burning the American or waving the Vietcong flag, but my impression is that these incidents have been of extraordinary symbolic importance." Indeed, to the ethnic, protesters and Wall Street bankers were cut from the same cloth:

> From the perspective of the Polish TV watcher on Milwaukee Avenue on the northwest side of Chicago, the long-haired militants are every bit as much part of the Establishment as are the presidents of corporations, Wall Street investment bankers, and other Anglo-Saxon and Jewish members of the power elite. In their frame of reference, Richard Nixon to some extent, and Spiro Agnew, to a very considerable extent, are *anti*-Establishment figures, and someone like David Dellinger with his Yale degree is an Establishment personage. They see the protesters and the militants as sons and daughters of the well-to-do, who have attended elite colleges and are supported financially by their parents through all their radical activity. A Harvard graduate is, after all, a Harvard graduate whether in a picket line or in a board room of a large corporation.[6]

If the goal of the protesters was to demonstrate the immorality of the United States in Vietnam—or simply to demonstrate the immorality of the United States—and then to use rational discussion to convert others to their point of view, they could not have been more unsuccessful. Not only was their initial premise arrogant, said Greeley, but their style often dripped with contempt for the people they wished to win over—like the Milwaukee Avenue TV viewer. Their demonstrations were to convert him to their cause? There wasn't a chance in a million, Greeley insisted, that they would succeed.

Not that it was impossible to win the white ethnic population to the cause of peace. Ethnics, and along with them the majority of Americans, were *confused* by the war; that is what Greeley heard in the neighborhoods, what he determined from the polls. People complained of American involvement in Vietnam (their sons, after all, were fighting the war and dying in it), but in the same breath they condemned the Berrigans and "all those hippies who burn the flag." They said, let's get in and get it over with or let's get out. Were they hawks or doves? Moral or immoral?

Actually, what data did exist—piecemeal indicators from Gallup, Harris, and NORC—revealed that ethnics were at least as dovish, and probably more so, than the typical American. In 1967 only Catholics from Eastern Europe—perhaps because of the proximity of their homeland to Communism—were more hawkish than native or Western European Protestant Americans. In February 1970 blue collar workers were *above* the national average in favoring withdrawal from Vietnam (and Catholics were more in favor than Protestants). Further, the more involved an ethnic was in his community (the greater his "ethnic identification"), the more likely he was to be a dove on the Vietnam war (and, incidentally, the more likely he was to be in favor of racial integration). In the face of such evidence, Greeley asked a meeting of political scientists in the fall of 1971, why does the stereotype of the racist-hawk white ethnic persist among so many liberals?[7]

Would it not be better, he went on in the *New Republic,* to avoid condescending labels and try to converse with the white ethnics, with "middle America"? If one wished to gain support from the American population for withdrawal from Vietnam, he would, first of all, separate "peace" from the "peace movement," and particularly from its radical fringes. He would also root appeals to the cause of peace in American patriotism rather than in the "hate America" rhetoric of the radicals. He would ask the ethnic why we were under obligation to defend a country that did not want to defend itself (that was a line of reasoning the ethnic understood). And, finally, he would search the ambiguities of the war for instances, no matter how vague, in which American objectives seemed to have been achieved. To describe the war as a total waste was simply counterproductive.

Counterproductive—Greeley's critics seized upon that word. What, after all, did opinion polls have to do with conscience? Did one take a moral stand only if the majority of Americans agreed with it? Noam Chomsky could only dismiss Greeley's views as "outlandish," "fantastic," and "weird," asserting that the audiences *he*, Chomsky, had spoken to were genuinely moved by witnesses like the Berrigans.[8]

So the argument penetrated to instincts deeper than philosophies. Was one to bear witness to the impulses of conscience, as the Berrigans did, even when the testimony might have unknown, and possibly detrimental, effects? Or was one to leave those impulses aside and determine, coolly and pragmatically, what it would take for the cause to succeed? And if one did bear witness, and if he paid the ·consequences for doing so, would he be at all able—psychologically—to accept the evidence (should it arise) that his action was in vain, or worse, self-defeating? And how did the pragmatist, "doing what he had to do," avoid dishonesty, avoid telling the people one thing while believing another, avoid telling one group *X* and another *Y*, all in the cause of building support for victory?

In the middle of the fury Greeley countered with his answer: Richard J. Daley. The mayor of the "despised Second City" was many things in Greeley's hands, a weapon first of all, something to brandish in the face of all those New York liberals. It was their sophistication versus Daley's malapropisms; their moral purity versus his machine's corruption; their appeals to conscience versus his political deals. All Daley did, Greeley said, was win. All he did in the last election was run against a Jewish candidate and get 65 percent of the Jewish vote. "He is neither smooth nor handsome, articulate or witty. . . . And though Daley is not nearly as pretty as John Lindsay, he just wins by almost twice as much."[9]

Why was Daley successful? The fundamental problem of urban government, Greeley argued, was not corruption (though there was corruption aplenty) but powerlessness. The federal government refused to give the cities real power; the taxation powers of the cities were meager at best, and most of their affluent citizens left for the suburbs on evenings and weekends. In addition, the mayor of

Chicago had very little statutory power, certainly less, say, than the mayor of New York. The task of a mayor, then, and especially the mayor of Chicago, was to amass enough personal power to get decisions made and implemented, to get the city to "work." The alternative to collecting power was anarchy, the sheer inability to govern at all.

How, then, did Richard Daley amass power? Dispensing jobs was one way. As head of the Cook County Central Committee, he retained the capacity to provide large numbers of people with employment. (The organization, one black radical remarked, saw to the employment of a higher proportion of blacks than any other corporate bureaucracy in the Chicago area. The reason was neither "affirmative action" nor a love of blacks. The mayor simply could not survive without the black population in his coalition.) A second way of gaining power was to offer to the loyal wards such services as prompt street repair, snow shoveling, and garbage removal (ideologues hated to bother with these "trivia"), and to delay them in the wards headed up by mavericks like Bill Singer. Especially important was the mayor's ability to dispense wealth (in the form of insurance business, for example)—or at least his willingness to let others accumulate wealth. "Dick has made a deal," one of Daley's supporters told Greeley. "He has let them get rich and they in turn have given him political power."[10]

Strong mayors of Chicago—and only Anton Cermak and Richard Daley have been strong mayors—were also masters at the art of power brokerage. Daley took it as a given that the city was composed of a diversity of national, racial, economic, and religious groups, and he saw his role in that mix as "arranging and rearranging power and resources in such a way as to prevent one group from becoming so unhappy with the balance that they will leave the system."[11] He knew that the balanced ticket was essential to victory in this power brokerage game and that to exclude a group from its place on the ticket was to insult and offend it. Any group that could deliver votes was heard from and responded to, not all the time, but at the *right* time—when the majority would not reject the response, when the leader of a constituency simply *had* to have a concession to retain his credibility with his people. As one leader put it, "The mayor doesn't give us everything we want, but he knows what we have to have, and that he gets for us."[12]

Mayor Daley also derived power from bestowing recognition on the various ethnic communities in the city. The communities called it "respecting" them. He expressed a sense of pride in the city as a whole, calling a Picasso sculpture "a great honor for the city of Chicago" even though personally he thought it horrendous, mediating a strike by the Chicago symphony orchestra so Chicago might continue to have "the world's finest orchestra—a real champion." Ludicrous as his simple-minded pride might appear to Hyde Park intellectuals, it struck others in the city as a genuine concern for their place of residence.

Clout in Springfield and Washington was the final source of the mayor's power. If he had influence with the state and federal governments (because he delivered Chicago for the winning gubernatorial or presidential candidate), he could use it to bring resources to Chicago. And that was a strength he could use to build up his own position in the government of the city.

Votes were the essential currency of the machine system. If Daley had power in Springfield and Washington, it was because he could deliver Chicago. If a ward committeeman had power with Daley, it was because the committeeman could deliver his ward. And if precinct captains had any clout with their ward committeeman, it was because they could get out the Democratic vote in their precincts. Finally, there was the citizen. He had a vote, something *they* wanted, and he found his precinct captain to be marvelously responsive to his requests when the captain knew that there were two, perhaps as many as four or five, solid Democratic votes under that citizen's roof. The citizen, in this system, had far more power than when he stood helpless before a government bureaucrat.

What, then, of the Daley organization? Too much corruption? There was no doubt about it. Was it on its last legs? It would survive as long as Richard Daley survived, but because of its inability to attract young, enthusiastic Democrats and keep them in the fold, it might not outlive him by many years. Not only that (Greeley listed the machine's faults), the "Chicago system" neglected groups in the city that were unorganized, inarticulate, and powerless; and it overlooked the presence of small but potentially explosive cadres. Nor did it know how to communicate with intellectuals, because its concrete and instinctual style was "not likely to be swayed by the moralism, the dogmatism, and the perfectionism of the academic."[13]

"Those experts," the mayor is supposed to have said, "they don't know nothin'." *That* was a loss, because the intellectual was better able to spot long-range trends and anticipate problems than was the politician whose primary concern was staying afloat in the present.

The response to Greeley's articles on Mayor Daley was hardly warm. A *New Republic* piece, in fact, was a direct hit on a hornet's nest. As Greeley explained later in the *Bulletin of the Atomic Scientists:*

> The article was not a defense of the Cook County organization; I know its weaknesses better than most Americans. But it was not the usual ritualistic condemnation of the Daley machine that is *de rigueur* for most American liberals, and I found myself being clobbered from all sides. The *Chicago Journalism Review* published a series of vitriolic articles which were personal attacks on me and the mayor without any attempt to respond to the contents of my article. Professor Harold Isaacs of the Massachusetts Institute of Technology described the article as a "love letter to Mayor Daley" (which it most assuredly was not). The editor of *The Maroon*, University of Chicago student newspaper, called me on the phone to ask whether I was in favor of "political corruption." One of the members of the sociology department denounced me as a racist, and another opined—with unintended flattery—that I was nothing but a loud-mouthed Irish priest. Studs Terkel had a nasty comment to make in his review of Mike Royko's *Boss* in *The New York Times Book Review.* . . . The word went around the Hyde Park community that I was the "house intellectual" of the Daley organization.[14]

Greeley was hardly Daley's house intellectual. "I have never met the mayor and have never spoken with him on the phone," he wrote.[15] But he had chosen Daley—not without qualification—and rejected the Fathers Berrigan—again, not without qualification. He said it was because Daley knew how to win and because the Berrigans were morally arrogant and sure to lose. But there was more to his choice than that, for it fit into the ongoing momentum of his disaffection with "those university-and-media-based liberals and intellectuals" (many of whom lived in Hyde Park) who did not know Chicago from the inside, who did not know its mayor from the inside, who did not know the Irish, the Italians, and the Poles from the inside, who did not know Andrew Greeley from the inside. Richard Daley was all that they were not and all that they despised;

he was that part of Andrew Greeley that they were not and that they despised. And so he was flung in their faces. There were important political messages in these articles, to be sure, the beginnings, in fact, of a "Catholic politics" cemented in the neighborhood experience of Catholic people; but the raw skin, the sensitivity leaning toward paranoia, the cries "I am I" and "my kind of people are to be respected" were as much a part of these articles on politics as were the analyses of a loyal liberal Democrat who, above all, wanted to win.

Greeley had some unsolicited advice for the National Democratic Party, too, but early in 1972 publishers were not interested in passing it on. So Greeley waited until the crushing defeat of George McGovern, revised the manuscript, and had it published by New Viewpoints as *Building Coalitions* (1974). His goal now (he told *Time* magazine) was to tell the party "how to put itself back together." His targets were the images of America in the minds of the liberal leadership in 1972, for it was those pictures, he argued, more than stands on specific issues or mistakes in campaign strategy, that brought about the Democratic presidential disaster.

The McGovernites, alas, were possessed of a *religious* (there was no better word for it) picture of American society. To them, said Greeley, America was sick, or worse than that, evil and corrupt. Its people were guilty of racism, either by active discrimination or passive acquiescence; they were apathetic about their country's imperialistic war of aggression; they were unconcerned about the coming environmental crisis. These same people, however, possessed profound spiritual resources, and they were capable of repentance, of reform, of "coming home" to their true values. Already there were signs of hope: oppressed blacks, Spanish-speaking persons, women, and youth were aligning themselves with enlightened members of the professoriate and with progressive strains within the Democratic Party to form a New Coalition. The coalition was *for* the forces of liberation, *for* abortion, *for* amnesty, *for* legalized marijuana, *for* the emancipation of homosexuals. The New Politicians knew that the coalition would alienate many regular Democrats, but their calculations showed that the attrition of these would be more than offset by the "great legions" of young voters—twenty-five million of them—who would be lured into the fold. One could do without the corrupt bosses of the old politics. One could, in fact, do without corruption—if people were penitent and "came home." There was an inevitability to the movement, Greeley noted; the New Politicians saw themselves on the crest of the wave of history, and one either rode it to the shores of the Promised Land or fell off and drowned in its wake.

Granted, Greeley commented, this was a lofty, noble vision. But it belonged in a church and not in the political arena. It was the *cleric* who urged his people to a maximum of generosity and moral concern. The *politician* was satisfied with whatever generosity he could get from the voter *and still win.* "Winning isn't everything perhaps, but, as Charlie Brown has observed, losing isn't anything." Winners, not losers, shaped the direction a country took. And if the Ph.D.'s weren't advising their politician employees of that basic reality, they ought to be fired. "Better they be unemployed," Greeley told the politicians, "than you."[16]

The analysis went on. One avoided being the loser by getting enough votes—an obvious truth, so obvious that only someone like the mayor of Chicago could see it. And one got enough votes by understanding the voter. The picture in the minds of the McGovernites (as well as pundits like Eric Sevareid, David Brinkley, James Reston, and TRB) was that 1972 presented the voter a "clear choice." One was either "liberal"—and bought the entire liberal package on peace, inflation, poverty, abortion, marijuana, amnesty, busing, military spending, and racial quotas—or one was "conservative" and rejected the entire package. But what, Greeley asked, was the essential connection between the "liberal" stands on all these issues?

> An Irish lawyer is against the war and against abortion, for a family assistance program and against the legalization—or even against the decriminalization—of marijuana. He thinks his positions are consistent: war and abortion are murder, family assistance and drug control are both necessary for an orderly society. Is he a "conservative" or a "liberal"?

> A Detroit housewife, who is vigorously opposed to busing even though her son is in an integrated high school and she strongly supports integrated schools, thinks of herself as consistent, be-

cause, in her judgment, both stands come from a concern over quality education. Is she a "conservative" or a "liberal"?

The black man who dislikes the militant leaders (and slightly more blacks dislike the militants than like them), is opposed to busing (as are about 45 percent of the blacks in the country), and is bitterly opposed to the legalization of marijuana (as are about 66 percent of the blacks in the country); but, nevertheless, he enthusiastically supported George McGovern as a friend of the black people. Is he inconsistent? Is he a "liberal" or a "conservative"?

The Polish physician who is against the war but also against the decrease in military spending on the grounds that both weaken America's international position—is he inconsistent? Is he a "liberal" or a "conservative"?[17]

The smart politician, Greeley contended, avoided the one-dimensional thinking that lumped all of these people into the "center." He knew that forcing "clear choices" on complex individuals meant losing elections. He understood that one man's consistency was not another's, that the logic separating "law and order" from "peace in Vietnam" in one man's thinking held them together in another's. An astute campaigner in 1972 would have separated issues of substance—like peace, race, poverty, and pollution—from issues one did not commit political suicide over—like amnesty, abortion, and marijuana. He would have realized that three-fifths of the American population was willing to support liberal postures on the former but that a majority was against amnesty, quotas, and busing. Skillful strategy would not have soured the pot by mixing the "liberal" positions on the latter with the "liberal" positions on issues of greater substance.

The reform Democrats of 1972 were aware (rightly so, Greeley advised) that the public admired a man who was firm and unswerving in his commitment to truth, who was willing to sacrifice his political future because of commitment to principle. Compromise and the manipulation of truth by a politician were seen by outsiders as signs of personal weakness and corruption. And while the New Coalition's image of the voter was correct in this regard (they nominated a man who was "right from the start"), the image was incomplete because it was not pluralistic enough. For if a political leader *did* take a firm, vigorous stand on what seemed to be truth to *one* group of the electorate, he would be rejected by countless other groups who did not see truth in the same way. "For what seems Truth to one is Big Lie to another, and what is morally imperative action to one is down the road to hell to another."[18]

Make no mistake about it; "telling the truth, the whole truth, and nothing but the truth, as seen by each person in political oratory would increase viciousness and hatred throughout society."[19] In a pluralistic society there were as few truths clear to everyone as there were choices clear to everyone. The politician, then, was in a bind from which only a few could escape (or even turn to their advantage). He had to be the honest, uncompromising leader the public wanted and still make the compromises essential to the maintenance of the political process. Like the ancient Israelites, he had to build bricks without straw:

> The political leader, then, is forced by the nature of the circumstances in which he finds himself to evade and avoid, to sugarcoat and to mislead more than the rest of us. He does so not because he is dishonest (thought he may be), not because he likes to manipulate people (though it is very possible that he does), but because his role is essentially one of "conflict management." The conflict manager must be extremely careful of what he says and how he says it.[20]

In the last fifty years, said Greeley, only Franklin Roosevelt and John Kennedy had managed conflict with skill and grace. Relying on the analysis of Andrew McFarland, Greeley categorized Taft, Wilson, Harding, Coolidge, Hoover, and Eisenhower as having a low tolerance for conflict. Truman, he judged, was good at the political game and seemed to enjoy it, but he had occasional fits of temper. Lyndon Johnson was a skilled practitioner of conflict management in the Senate, was flexible as President in matters of domestic policy, but lost his cool and refused to accept the criticism of subordinates in the cross-pressures generated by Vietnam. The background of one president made it impossible for him to become a hot-tempered isolate: "One cannot imagine that cool and aloof Boston politician, John Kennedy, cutting himself off from dissenting opinion or losing his cool because, as a Catholic, he was an outsider."[21]

In Greeley's view, the best of the political leaders was not a mere juggler of pressure groups, trying to give each the concessions it wanted when it had to have them. He also educated the public (white America's change in racial attitudes over the past twenty years was to a large extent due to political leadership) and moved them—carefully, it was true, because he could not move too far beyond the coalition that was supporting him. A national political leader had to be particularly adept to handle the problems of the seventies:

> A national political leader in the 1970s will have to possess extraordinary skills of bargaining and coalition formation. He must liquidate much foreign military involvement and still prevent the resurgence of isolationism. He must respond to legitimate demands of the militants and at the same time persuade other Americans that the demands are indeed legitimate. He must persuade 'middle Americans that the fundamental principles on which the society rests are not being destroyed but are rather growing and developing. He must restore confidence in the integrity and honesty of public officials. He must begin to find solutions to the technical problems of pollution, waste, and conservation of resources in an exceedingly complex and advanced industrial society. Even though he probably will not be able to convince some of the young, he still must realize that he has on his hands a whole generation that has every reason to be cynical about politics and politicians. Finally, he must find some way to end the peculiar economic situation where depression and inflation coexist and reinforce one another.[22]

In a chapter entitled "Facts in Black and White," Greeley set about to alter another picture in the minds of the Democratic leadership, that of the state of race relations in America. In the 1972 strategy of the New Politicians, Greeley saw an assumption that blacks and working-class whites could not be brought together in sufficient numbers to win an election. Hence the working-class white had to be dismissed (how else, after all, was one to deal with racism, bigotry, and "backlash"?) and his absence made up for by the more tolerant legions of the young. The strategy, of course, failed.

None of those, Greeley asserted, who designed the 1972 Democratic campaign were aware of the fact that "white backlash" simply did not exist in the proportions the media led us to expect. Indeed, if survey data (such as the data Greeley had been monitoring at NORC) had been studied carefully, it would have been evident that "white backlash" did not exist at all. Despite all the turbulence of the late sixties, despite prime-time coverage of riots in Watts and Detroit, despite newspaper accounts of blacks arming for guerilla warfare, despite the emergence of Stokely Carmichael, H. Rap Brown, Eldridge Cleaver, and Bobby Seale as national personalities, whites over the past ten years had continued to show greater and greater acceptance of racial integration. Greeley had said it before in *Scientific American* and *Public Opinion Quarterly*. In 1972, 86 percent of a probability sample of white Americans agreed that whites and blacks should go to integrated schools—that was 23 percent more than in 1963, and 56 percent more than in 1942. A similar increase in acceptance was evident on questionnaire items dealing with residential, social, and marital integration, and all indications were that the trend would continue. Even if one took the *minimal* position—that these replies represented changes only in what whites thought they *ought* to say—the shift was nevertheless dramatic. There was no evidence at all of the white backlash "discovered" by less representative samplings of the climate in America.[23]

But wasn't opposition to busing as intense as it appeared in the media? To this, the NORC data said yes. In 1972 only 6 percent of whites in the South and only 15 percent of whites outside the South were in favor of busing black and white school children from one district to another. (The figures for blacks in favor of busing were 52 percent in the South and 55 percent outside the South.) The majority of whites, then, who endorsed school integration in principle were against integration as achieved by busing. Were they hypocrites? Were they covert racists? Or were they afraid of danger? Committed to the principle of neighborhood schools? Dubious of the effectiveness of busing in improving the quality of education? Whatever the case (the data were not refined enough to say), it would have been most inaccurate to write off their feelings about busing as so much bigotry—especially in view of the fact that a substantial minority of blacks agreed with them. Indeed, all the other evidence indicated that white America's attitudes toward racial integration had been consistently moving to the left. For politicians the message was clear; a style that adapted itself to "white backlash" was responding to something that wasn't there, whereas an assumption that persons in the center could be led even further to the left in the matter of racial integration was in tune with the thinking of the American population.

Responses of black Americans to survey questions were also essential to the political strategist of the seventies. Greeley fused his own reading of black political leadership and the results of opinion polling in the late sixties: "black political leadership is becoming much better organized, much more sophisticated, and much more insistent . . . blacks do not want to withdraw from American society . . . now they want to be involved on their own terms, which is to say they want the rest of society to accept their right to dignity and to respect while maintaining a cultural heritage of their own."[24] To sample the data: in 1966, 80 percent of American blacks said they preferred to live in an integrated neighborhood; 63 percent would choose an integrated club rather than an all-black club; 38 percent already belonged to an integrated church. In 1968 less than 20 percent of blacks interviewed in fifteen major cities gave separatist responses to each of ten questions dealing with various aspects of integration. At the same time, however, the majority of blacks endorsed cautious militancy (in 1966, for example, 77 percent thought the federal government would do little about civil rights were it not for demonstrations, but only 15 percent said in 1968 that blacks should be ready to use violence to gain rights). Blacks also strongly supported black pride and black solidarity. In 1968, 96 percent said "Negroes should take more pride in Negro history," and 70 percent agreed that "Negroes should shop in Negro-owned stores whenever possible." Data just in from a 1972 survey did not alter the basic picture. Blacks combined strong endorsements of racial integration with equally strong feelings that one must insist on solidarity among one's own people. An emphasis on black culture was not equivalent to a desire for separation.

Other data showed that it was erroneous to assume that black political objectives always conflicted with those of whites. In 1968 a CBS survey found that blacks endorsed goals of better jobs, better education, better housing and police protection, and more government effort to help blacks solve problems. Most American whites did not object to such goals, which were at the top of the black agenda (only 16 percent of whites, for example, were opposed to govern-

ment job training programs—which 89 percent of blacks wanted).
Busing, forced integration of white neighborhoods, and a guaran-
teed family income were the three practical issues on which a consensus between black and white did *not* exist. While there were some
issues dividing blacks and whites, then, there were considerable
areas of agreement—areas upon which Greeley said wise political
leadership ought to capitalize.

In *Building Coalitions* Greeley had few solutions to the "racial
problem"—nor, incidentally, has he ever offered many. He is highly
impressed by the changes in white attitudes monitored by NORC
and says that they "have been so great that you could say that ours is
probably the least racially prejudiced of any large multiethnic
society in the world." He insists that nothing is solved by having
"experts" take from the middle-class white—take in the form of unfair taxation, decreased property values, closed doors on neighborhood schools—and give to the poor black. America *wants* racial
justice and peace. Survey data show that the majority would even accept a 10 percent tax surcharge to achieve them (provided the surcharge were accompanied by a removal of inequalities in the tax
structure). And half the racial "problem" would disappear if "solutions" did not exact such a price from the white population. Instead
of compulsory busing, for example, why not guarantee to school
districts within a metropolitan area a subsidy of three times the per-
pupil cost for every minority child they enrolled—up to a limit, say,
of 15 percent of enrollment (or whatever the percentage of minority
children in that area)? No child, white or black, would be *forced* into
busing, yet high-quality suburban education (and buses to get to it)
would be available to inner city students on terms the suburban districts would find financially irresistible. How much panic selling of
white homes would there be in neighborhoods faced with racial
integration if we had property value insurance? "I'm absolutely convinced that half of our racial problem in the city would be solved
. . . if you knew that a black face showing up down the block wasn't
going to plummet your investment by $20,000." Why not, in addi-
tion, grant a $1,000 income tax deduction for every immediate
neighbor one had of a different race? Greeley's outlook is straightforward; you cannot change confirmed bigots, but you can take the
financial loss out of racial integration—and even, in some cases, put
profit into it.

In *Building Coalitions* Greeley insisted that blacks were an absolutely indispensable part of the liberal Democratic coalition—so indispensable, in fact, that in 1976 "a black vice-presidential candidate on a 'national unity' ticket could well represent one of the most brilliant political ploys of the century."[25] (Greeley had advocated the 1972 nomination of Andrew Young along with Edmund Muskie.[26]) In a tantalizing footnote the reader is informed that more Americans are now saying they would be willing to vote for a qualified black presidential candidate than were saying they would have voted for a qualified Catholic in 1960. Will the Democrats read the times correctly and be brave enough to nominate a black for the vice-presidency? "Doubtful," Greeley prognosticated. "Very doubtful."

And where did all the Catholics go in 1972? And where would they be in 1976? (The question is practically the same as "Where did all the ethnics go?") In 1972 the media were saying that Catholics were deserting the Democratic Party, and to some extent the media were correct: 48 percent of the Catholic voters chose George McGovern—more than the Protestants who voted for McGovern but fewer than the Catholics who usually voted for the Democratic presidential candidate. (Since 1928 the only Republican to garner a majority of the Catholic vote was Eisenhower in 1956.) The McGovernites said the reason for the Catholic defection was the behavior of President Nixon. He courted Cardinal Krol, promised support for parochial schools, and expressed his opposition to abortion. But Greeley argued that such an analysis was superficial. Catholic attitudes on abortion at the time of the election, for example, were nearly indistinguishable from those of Protestants. Besides, the analysis overlooked more profound sociological events: (1) Catholics were "making it" into the upper middle class and were feeling the political cross-pressures of their religious and ethnic heritage, which inclined them to be Democrats, and their new-found social class, which steered them toward the Republican Party; (2) at the same time, Catholics who remained in the working and lower classes were being hard pressed by the new black militancy and felt, as a result, that their own interests were being overlooked by the party that traditionally stood up for them. Most important, that party, for all intents and purposes, kicked them out of the coalition in 1972 when it insisted that they be ideologically pure and buy the entire platform prefabricated by the New Politicians.

When NORC surveyed America's Catholics in 1974, Greeley discovered that pressures to abandon the Democratic party had not taken a serious toll. Catholics were as Democratic in the seventies as they were in the fifties—just to the left of center—even though their religious affiliation was clearly more tenuous. What was the presidential ticket for them in 1976? Greeley's choices were Morris Udall and Jerry Brown. "Of course, it will never happen, but they'd win going away."

Throughout *Building Coalitions* Greeley argued for congruence between political style and the basic structure of the American political system. There were no analyses of the economics of political power, no tales of Big Money secretly finding its way into campaign coffers, no uncovering of power elites or an Establishment controlling American society. To the contrary, the political realities that Greeley saw were spelled out quite explicitly in James Madison's Federalist Papers and in the Constitution itself, and they were quite simple—to gain power one must gain the support of the people; one gains the support of the people by representing their interests; to increase one's power, one bargains and negotiates with other representatives, trading off support in one area for support in another. The trick, if one wishes to effect change, is not to spread power out but to concentrate it. Madison was not an eighteenth-century prophet trying to provide a structure for pluralism in some distant future; he was, rather, trying to cope with the extraordinary pluralism all about him. His political experiment has produced a structure and a culture of marvelous flexibility for absorbing new groups and for undergoing rapid social change without collapse. "I happen to think it is the most noble work of polity that human ingenuity has ever devised."[27]

On the heels of *Building Coalitions* came a syndicated column, Greeley's first in the secular press. It began in July 1974, appearing twice a week in twenty newspapers across the nation (that number has more than doubled)—among them the *Chicago Tribune*, the *Detroit News*, the *New York Daily News*, the *San Francisco Chronicle*, and the *Denver Post*. It was Greeley's chance to speak—to shout, if necessary—on behalf of Middle America.

> Most of us—God forgive us for it— are "Middle Americans." We are not poor or nonwhite. We are heterosexuals and if we are

women our consciousness has not been raised. We are not part of the "third world."

On the other hand, we don't have Ph.D.s or live on the East Side of Manhattan or Cambridge or Chevy Chase or Berkeley. We don't teach at the great universities or write for the important intellectual journals or work for the "national media." Some of us are even in the most unhappy of categories—white Protestant males over 60: the kind of people Ms. Clare Randall, the new general secretary of the National Council of Churches, is busy cleaning out of that organization.

We are, in other words, the bad guys.[28]

Or *are* we—90 percent of America's population—the bad guys? *We* wanted to get out of the war long before the government did—even though the "peace" movement drove some of us into the government camp. *Our* racial attitudes and behavior have changed remarkably in the past twenty years. We have been ahead of our government on pollution and gun control. Labeled militant anti-Communists, we accepted the detente with Russia and the rapprochement with China with amazing ease and good grace. When meat prices go up, we stop buying meat—despite Earl Butz. When big cars become uneconomical, we stop buying big cars. Beset by an oil shortage, we reduce consumption by 8 percent (and we are smart enough to blame the shortage on the government and the oil companies—not on the Israelis or the Arabs or the Russians). "Mind you," Greeley set the tone in his very first column, "the American people, like all people, have faults. But from my part of the bench they look like the most generous, most sophisticated, most resilient population that humankind has ever known."[29]

In his ensuing columns Greeley overlooked nothing:

Nixon: "What offends me most about him is not that he is a crook but that he is a dumb crook. Dishonesty in a President of the United States is neither unusual nor particularly offensive, but stupidity is intolerable."

Nixon's resignation: "Richard Nixon was driven from the Presidency by a massive coalition representing most of the mainstream of our society. He was thrown out by the American people."

Gerald Ford: "He is exactly what he always was: a small town, Middle Western, conservative Republican who almost never reads a book. . . . On his record he is the enemy of the poor, the black, the workers."

Ford's pardon of Nixon: "The fix was in. I'll make you Vice President, Jerry, and you pardon me. Explicit? It didn't have to be. Ford stands revealed as the political hack he always was. . . . Nixon gets amnesty without an indictment, without a plea, without a trial, without a verdict. The young men who would not fight in Viet Nam have to work their way back."

Food: "The American food-producing system works. The socialist food-producing system that is to be found in countries like China and Russia does not work."

Oil: "The oil countries have done evil things to the rest of the world—not merely, not even mainly, to the West. Much of the suffering in South Asia this winter will have been caused by a fertilizer shortage produced by the high price of oil."

Amnesty: "It should be amnesty for everyone—the draft resisters and the little Watergate fish as well as the big ones."

The economy: "I can tell you one group that won't be called upon to sacrifice: those corporate administrators whose monopolistic control enables them to fix prices in many major industries."

The sexual revolution: "I wish these sexual revolutionaries appeared a little more joyous and happy and a little less somber and earnest when they appear on the late TV talk shows to preach their gospel of liberation. It doesn't look like they are having much fun."

Racism: "I am completely committed to eliminating not only the last vestige of racial prejudice from American society but also the residual effects of the prejudice and injustice of the past. I believe in this—as do most Americans—because no other course of action is appropriate for those who buy the vision of American democracy. Still I gotta feel guilty? Well, sorry about that, but I won't."

WASPs: "The English Protestants started this country. They set up its political structures and its political philosophy. They let the rest of us in; they were, in other words, true to their own principles, though at times it must have been against their better judgment."

The IRA: "If it were from any other country in the world, our fashionable liberals would hail its members as revolutionary heroes."

Marlon Brando: "He should give land to the Italians. He never exploited Indians, but he sure exploited Italians."

Mike Royko: "He is crude enough to fit the stereotype of the Chicago Slav and liberal enough to appeal to the contempt civilized Americans have for Chicago and 'da Mare.' "

Abortion: "I can't figure out why abortion supporters don't come right out and say it's moral to kill babies under some circumstances."

The fall of Saigon: "We 'lost' in Viet Nam not because the enemy were better fighters or better human beings, but because the American people quite properly decided that we were going to lose, and through their Congress forbade any further involvement."

Patty Hearst: "If you think you are without sin, then fire the first machine gun."

John Kennedy (once proposed as a doctor of the Church): "What a President does in the Oval Office is what counts and not what he does in bed at night—or in the afternoon, or any other time."[30]

Over the months Greeley turned out to be *for* Peter Rodino, Otto Kerner, Edward Levi, Pat Moynihan, "da mare" (as in, "da mare looks good, don't he?"), pluralistic integration, illegal aliens, New York City, clout (but not reform, thank you), the Chicago Bears, Columbus Day, Lent, haunted houses, and front porches. And he was decidedly *against* psychohistory, "Libthink," Clayton Fritchey, clerical black, *Nashville,* socialism, the *Christian Century,* the Minnesota Vikings, the Detroit Lions, the Green Bay Packers— and the end of summer. Once he reflected on himself as a liberal:

> I am a liberal [without quotation marks] and always have been and confidently expect to be so always. There was a time when American liberalism was flexible, pragmatic, experimental, when it could make common cause with working men and women, with "ethnics," with those who did not go to graduate school.
>
> There are many liberals of this variety still in the country, but un- fortunately, the name "liberal" has been appropriated by a nar- row, doctrinaire clique that is about as tolerant of dissent as the Congregation of the Inquisition used to be. I don't know how this clique ever came to monopolize the word "liberal"; maybe the rest of us are to blame for letting them do it.[31]

"John Cogley first pointed out to me that Greeley has, prob- ably, the greatest natural vein of journalistic talent of any American

Catholic; he is a natural-born pamphleteer, a polemicist who writes quickly, crisply, colorfully. Francis X. Murphy recently likened him to Belloc and Chesterton."[32] Michael Novak wrote these words in *Commonweal,* but not everyone shares Novak's opinion. To Mike Royko, formerly of the now defunct *Chicago Daily News,* Greeley is "an intellectual priest who dabbles in journalism," who preaches how lucky we are to have "lardy little pocket-stuffers guiding our city."[33] And Greeley's reaction to readers who are put off by his columns? "If you're going to write a column," he told me, "it has to be a column that challenges people to think. Otherwise they are not going to read it. People will say (oh, it strikes me as the most mindless thing anybody could say), I don't always agree with your column. Well, of course, you stupid so-and-so, you don't always agree. If you did you wouldn't read it."

Still, there is the matter raised by the Berrigan brothers. I asked Father Greeley what had been his position on Vietnam, and he replied, "I was against it from the beginning on the purely pragmatic grounds (and I'd still be against it on pragmatic grounds) that the United States has no business getting involved in a land war in Asia—just no business. Now if there is a local administration capable of maintaining itself, then I can see us sustaining them. We learned in Korea that over the long haul (and the long haul is reasonably short) the American people will not support a massive military involvement not on our continent. The same thing could be said, I think, of the First and Second World Wars.

"I remember saying in 1965, when the secret escalation was going on, that Lyndon Johnson was the smartest politician in the United States and that he was not going to have a major army in Vietnam when the 1966 congressional elections came along. It was just unthinkable that he would. But he did."

"And weren't the radical protesters the first to cry out against the war?" I noted.

No, he replied, David Riesman was, and he later turned against the radicals. "It is surely the case that the perennial dissidents in the society were the first ones to *militantly* cry out against it. They would have cried out against anything in the United States, just on principle. They happened to be right on that one."

Then I went after the nub. "Where does morality enter into politics?"

"Oh boy, that's a tough one." Greeley was silent. "First of all, I don't believe you can derive a political program from a moral code. That is to say, there is no such thing as a moral environmental policy that one can induce *a priori* from one's moral convictions. There is no such thing as a single policy to deal with any problem that has a monopoly on morality." Another pause, and he continued. "Morality in politics involves the exercise of the classic virtue of prudence. He who is imprudent in politics is immoral. Now, what's imprudence? Well, in American society, imprudence, first of all, is doing anything that drives a major component out of the coalition which is the society or the coalition which is your party. Immorality is excluding any American from the rights that all Americans have by law or by Constitution. Is busing moral or immoral? I don't know, and I don't know how anybody else does. Stealing from the public fisc is immoral. Lying to the public is immoral. Tolerating injustice about which you can do something is immoral."

"Is Watergate—what Nixon did—moral or immoral?"

"Well, it's terribly dumb. Yeah, sure it's immoral. It's immoral to deprive people of their rights to privacy and enter somebody's office. That's wrong. Obstructing justice is immoral. Violating an oath of office to uphold the Constitution is immoral."

"Is the corruption in Chicago politics immoral?"

"You better believe it is."

"And Daley letting the men around him get rich—is that immoral?"

Greeley was more hesitant. "Hard to tell. Hard to tell."

"You don't know the facts."

"Oh no, I know the facts. What I don't know is how accurate his judgment is that much of that has to be tolerated if you're going to govern the city. I just don't know. I mean, I guess any political system has to tolerate a certain amount of corruption. Does he have to tolerate as much as he does? I don't know."

"Do you distinguish between politicians who are more and less moral?"

"Well, the first thing I look for is competency. I mean, is the man capable of putting together a coalition that can win an election and govern a country? If he's not competent, he can be a saint, and I don't care. . . . Well, ok, suppose he's competent and he's a crook. Well, if he's a competent crook running against an incompetent saint, I think I'd probably take the competent crook."

Greeley has always insisted on the complexity, the amorphousness of human life. "There's more to reality than moral dicta," he will say, speaking of Catholicism in the same breath with politics. Or "I am opposed to preprogramed moral systems." Or "I don't know of any problem that faces the United States today for which there is a clear moral solution." We need moral codes, ethical systems, to be sure, he says, but "you can't fit everything that happens in human life into the neat categories of an ethical system." Moral principles are clear and unambiguous, but moral practice is chancy and uncertain and obscure. "When you make a moral decision, when you apply your principles to the circumstances in which you find yourself, the best you can hope for is that you haven't made too much of a mess of things. You have tried to act sincerely and honestly, to do what is best, to live your principles in the crazy, foggy, confusing world of daily life." Reflecting on Vietnam in a column, he added, "It took moral courage to resist the war, but it also took moral courage to fight in it. . . . I am outraged by the rigidity of those who think their moral decision is the only decision that men and women of good faith and intelligence could possibly make."[34]

So Andrew Greeley, in his own words, is nonideological, pragmatic, flexible, "a religious believer but a political agnostic." He cites Geno Baroni: ideology doesn't get the sidewalks fixed. Most things don't work, and so you keep trying new things. If you are bound to a policy because it's morally correct, you lack the capacity to change should it fail. Who is the ideal politician? Greeley feels that David Martin, writing in *Dissent*, came closest to identifying him:

> Consider the following proposition: that the highest moral responsibility could conceivably reside in a civil servant or a politician at the ministry of defense, who uses the coolest rational calculation to tread that narrow edge which is marginally closer to survival than all the alternatives. . . .

His highest achievement will be a tiny victory, his normal achievement just to survive. This he will never be able just to explain, and may have to accept the mortification of having to claim that a tiny victory was a great one. He may even acquire a reputation among the cognoscenti for naive reasoning and dishonest appeals, simply because the public neither wishes to know his actual reasons nor would be willing to face the stark alternative involved in that reasoning. It may even be that he is a man of the highest intelligence who must accept the contempt of an intelligentsia which has never tried to understand why he must appear stupid in public and appear ignorant of what he may know better than anyone. Perhaps such a man has some claim to his humanity and ours.[35]

"Are you a politician?" I asked Andrew Greeley.

"No."

"An adviser to politicians?"

"No." He did tell me, however, that since his articles on Chicago politics, he has made one good "organization" contact and that since *Building Coalitions* he has been talking to several well-known political figures.

If not a politician, then, or an adviser to politicians, Greeley identifies with certain types of political social scientists—his close friend Pat Moynihan, for example. Greeley met Moynihan in 1962, just after he received his Ph.D:

Pete Rossi dragged me off at the ASA meetings in Washington to a Trotskyite reunion in a room in the Shoreham hotel. The whole crowd that went to Townshend Harris High School, CCNY, and then Columbia after the war were assembled there—Bell, Glazer, Lipset, etc. There was one face that clearly didn't belong. The face looked at my collar and said, "What are you doing here?" I looked at the face and said, "I might ask the same of you." The then Assistant Secretary and now Ambassador Moynihan and I knew we had each encountered one of our own kind.[36]

Greeley later wrote of Moynihan, for whom he has immense respect: "To say that he is Irish is to say that he is a realist in an age of romantics, a pragmatist in an age of ideologues, and a sentimentalist in an age of sophisticated cynics. There was too much pressure in the history of Ireland for the mick to afford romanticism. Those who survived were too shrewd to be caught in the trap of ideology, and they suffered too much to remain cynical for very long." Moynihan was formed "in the world beyond the university where the dogmas, the rituals, and the conventions of academia do not carry much weight."[37]

Greeley hinted there about the source of his own political instincts: an Ireland that needed to survive, immigrants from Ireland who had to adapt to a new country. Greeley's father was a nonideological, liberal Democrat, a loyal member of the Cook County Organization, "an uncompromising believer in all the principles of the New Deal." So subtly are these instincts passed from one generation to the next. When young Andy was four years old, he stood by a railroad station, holding his mother's hand, looking at a poster of Franklin Roosevelt. It was 1932. He asked his mother who the man in the picture was. She said, "That's Roosevelt; he's running for president." "I remember," Greeley says of the incident, "her absolute confidence that he would win." In 1932, it hadn't been so clear that he would.

10   Intimacy

Intimacy is a game.

When Greeley says this, when he introduces his books on inter-personal contact with such titles as *The Friendship Game* (1970) and *Love and Play* (1975), he is not expressing his despair at the sham and the phoniness of human relationships, not trying to expose the myriad ways in which we subtly manipulate each other, not think-ing of people who are, as we say, "just playing games." His views are not a reaction to Eric Berne's *Games People Play* (New York: Grove, 1964), even though they stand in stark contrast to Berne's. To Berne, the best of social intercourse is game-free; autonomy, spon-taneity, awareness, and especially intimacy begin where game-playing leaves off. To Greeley, the problem in interpersonal rela-tionships is not that people *play* but that they have lost the capacity to play *well*. With fun and enjoyment gone, "playing games" comes to mean deceit and mutual exploitation.

The difference between Berne and Greeley, of course, has to do with an interpretation of play. "The 'play' crowd has long since forgotten what a game is," says Greeley.[1] In a game, in the very best game, the players artfully combine rigorous discipline with grace, ease, and spontaneity. Indeed, it is the long hours of arduous prac-tice, the work of getting to know the playmate's moves (and the playmate may be a spouse, a dancing partner, or a wide receiver), that enable two people to abandon themselves to play. True play— play as children play with their best friends, with their favorite toys—involves respect for the playmate and respect for the toy. It brings on a change in consciousness; one is transported from the profane world of work into a world whose moods are so trusting, whose sounds are so gentle, that one hears in them the rumors of an

Absolute. *Paradisos*, after all, is the Greek word, not for "heaven," but for "park."

Play is a word about which we are profoundly ambivalent. It rings pure, clear, and innocent; but there are murky undertones—as when one is said to "play around" or to have a little "plaything." We praise the play of children but feel guilty if we play ourselves. Play, too, is an experience about which Father Greeley admits a personal ambivalence. "I enjoy it," he told me. "I like nothing more than goofing off, but I have a very strong work ethic, and it has taken some effort to play." His father lost his leprechaun after the Great Depression, and Andrew was "trained in nice Protestant virtues: diligence, responsibility, honesty." Andrew nearly lost his leprechaun, too, in his personal "crashes" of the late sixties and early seventies; but he has, he thinks, coaxed him back to life—and none too soon. "I have strong playful strains in my personality, but it takes effort to let those strains out."

The paradox of *working* at play: I saw it in action during a break in our interviewing when Father Greeley, with grim, almost compulsive determination, took his guests water-skiing. Hardly a smile crossed his face—reviewing one's life is no easy task—as he piloted his boat up and down the Indiana-Michigan shoreline and then took his turn plunging into the icy waters of the lake, rising up on his skis, and skittering back and forth across the wake we left. Later he told me that Grand Beach was a place to *work*—at least it was that way in the beginning. Only slowly, laboriously, has it become a place to play as well.

In the late 1960s, out of experience, out of need, out of curiosity, Father Greeley began to write about the cycle of work and play. A new "theology of play" was appearing on the heels of the "death of God" (Harvey Cox's *The Feast of Fools* was the unlikely sequel to *The Secular City*), and its tenets spoke to Greeley's growing realization that he, like many of Beverly Hills's upper-middle-class Irish, was simply working too hard. Robert Neale's *In Praise of Play* helped him articulate his position. "The worker is a mundane man, a man so tied to the monotony of everyday life that he cannot pull himself out of his worldly concerns to engage in the sacred play that is religion. The worker must use the world, manipulate it, bend it to his will. The player accepts the world and delights in it."[2]

A Future to Hope In, following the Dutch scholar Johan Huizinga, saw play as the basis of ritual, poetry, music, dancing, philosophy, even the rules of warfare. "Civilization is, in its earliest phases, play. It does not come *from* play, like a baby catching itself from the womb. It arises *in and as* play and never leaves it."[3] Mankind has used technology to master the world, said Greeley, but in the process has lost touch with the world and corrupted it. If he were not so serious, if he thought of the world as a playground, if he treated his playground the way children treat their favorite corner of the park, he might recover his respect for nature and his sense of unity with it, might recapture what is at the core of his civilization.

Besides, work has become so sophisticated—much of it is no longer "servile" but "liberal"—that unless man is playful he will not be very good at it. Persons who overcommit themselves to work, who pride themselves on seventy- and eighty-hour work weeks, are actually counterproductive. "The professional (man or woman) who has confidence in himself, stable friendships, skills in the art of playfulness, and a happy marriage will be able to do more in a twenty-four-hour work week than his opposite member would be able to do in a seventy-two-hour week."[4] The person who overworks cannot permit himself to "let up" for fear that if he does his basic lack of talent will become manifest. He has swallowed the assumption of modern industrial capitalism that what we *do* is synonymous with what we *are.* But try to tell Professional Man—Greeley was pointing the finger at himself too—that he can afford to relax. He'll only say you're kidding. Tell him his career will profit more from reading a sonnet or painting with water colors, and he'll reply that you don't know how hard things are at the office. "Tell him that the key positions in society must be manned by playful, speculative men who understand that wisdom comes only with the ability to be detached and relaxed, and he says that maybe when the kids get to college he will have time to visit museums."[5]

It is not easy to play.

The sheer fun of play was hardly the motif of Greeley's first complete volume on intimacy, *The Friendship Game.* That book, written in the aftermath of the collapse of his New Community, emphasized the difficulty, the terror, the pain, the convolutions and distortions of close relationships. It began, "Man is essentially a lonely creature" who would like to be free of others and, like Alan Ladd in *Shane*, "ride off toward the mountains leaving human intimacy behind." And it ended with nothing more than, "like it or not, all of us have to learn to love one another."[6] Between beginning and end there was little in the way of fun.

What did Andrew Greeley, "trained to believe that friendship was something that he was not to be permitted,"[7] then realizing that friendship was at the core of the Christian message—what did he learn about this most difficult, demanding, exhausting of games?

He learned, first of all, about the experience of fear, of terror as primordial, and of the same type, as the infant's fear of falling. If we leave ourselves open to others, they may kill us, mutilate us, either physically or emotionally. We know the trepidation others instill in us, but we are shocked to discover that *we* terrify *them*. "Frequently, the terror flashes through the eyes of someone whom we would have thought immune from fear, and surely from fear of us." One sees "in his eyes the look of the haunted animal awaiting death." He is afraid of us and we of him, said Greeley; the mutual terror forms a bond that makes demands of its own. It is only through an invitation to friendship, a call to put aside the terror, that the chains of fear can be broken. The invitation says, "I will actually let you see me be afraid of you if you will let me see you being afraid of me."[8] The words contain a foretaste of pleasure and joy, but they demand just as surely a risky leap into an abyss.

And friendships fail, and people fall into the abyss. Why does it happen? Again we sense Greeley's understanding of the young of Beverly Hills. Friendship fails because of shame, because of the feeling that one is inadequate. To offer friendship, one must believe that he has something worth revealing to a friend, that he has intrinsic value that others will find attractive. The dancer, in other words, must have some initial confidence in his ability to dance. When someone engages in the slow, steady process of self-display (not crude, indiscriminate exhibitionism, which is actually a cover), he must assume that he is attractive. And the truth is that we are all attractive, though we *choose* inadequacy and shame because they excuse us from breaking out of the barriers that surround us. "Shame justifies our frigidity; frigidity in turn reinforces our shame. We are not good enough to be friends; we will not try to be a friend to anyone; we will strongly resist attempts at friendship from anyone else. Furthermore, as we become more practiced in our frigidity, we develop methods of blaming it on others. We offer ourselves to others in such a way as to guarantee that they will reject us."[9]

People lose at friendship, then, because they want to lose. They are psychologically frigid because, in the final analysis, they choose to be. Why is it so important to be a loser? What are the payoffs in self-defeat? For one thing, said Greeley, the loser has the power to punish all those who have invested in him and expect something from him. His failure hurts them—and he wants to hurt them. For another, he is able to maintain a solid defense against anxiety. If success is not really possible, then there is nothing to be anxious about. And his attitude can be veneered with the pride and self-respect of a perfectionist. "If he only had more time he would have done it perfectly but, as it is, the unfair time limitation imposed by a hostile world forces him to produce something that is so far beneath his own high standards that he can disavow all responsibilities for it."[10]

Greeley had often seen self-defeaters and self-haters in his life. That is how he described the Catholic left, Catholic educators, the Berrigan brothers, the reform Democrats, the New Breed turned New Community. Of the latter he said, "Sometimes, as a matter of fact, I am convinced that I have dealt with a whole generation of losers. Most of the young people with whom I have worked in my life are not risk-takers. They differ only in the degree to which they seem committed to imposing defeat after defeat upon themselves."[11]

Greeley had said it elsewhere: People become losers because of their familial past; and if one invites a loser to friendship, he can count on that crippling past's coming to the surface. In a sentence that might have been taken from Berne, Greeley commented, "we can expend all the energies of the relationship on fighting with surrogate parents and really ignore each other."[12] Psychoanalysts call the phenomenon transference (and, unlike Greeley, they see it as an instrument of cure). Because of transference we selectively perceive the other, seeking out the weak links in his personality; we distort; we construct a tightly interlocking network of hurts, injuries, and angers. We force each other to respond with the neurotic in him, not with the healthy; with the worst, not with the best. Gradually there builds an unconscious emotional investment in maintaining the inauthenticity that has stolen into the relationship.

The way out—the way beyond the terror and into the delight—is to admit what is happening and to refuse to enter the quagmire. One must be his best, most integral self in a relationship. He must remain true to his most authentic insights and instincts. If a friend demands that we abandon our privacy, our freedom, our selfhood, if he insists that we belong so totally to him that we become less than human, we must adamantly refuse. It is extremely difficult, it requires a vigorous sense of self, to reject the neurotic demand without rejecting the friend, but it must be done.

If we must offer the other, our most confident self, we must also elicit the best in him. "A man, for example, may be terribly insecure about his masculinity, and yet with the slightest show of encouragement from his wife rapidly grow in confidence about his maleness; his wife, in her turn, may be deeply troubled about her adequacy as a woman, and yet be on the verge of breaking out of those troubles with the slightest reinforcement from her husband."[13] Friends are firm, yet warm. They confront, yet support. They make demands, yet offer tenderness. They *challenge* the other—do so relentlessly—insisting that they be who and what they really are *without ever implying in the challenge a withdrawal of affection*. Demands are not to be a condition of love, but something that flows from love that is sure of itself.

There is, in other words, commitment in friendship. Friends recognize freedom, said Greeley, including the radical freedom to withdraw from the relationship, but there seems to be a turning point in a select number of relationships beyond which commitment to the relationship is no longer optional. That turning point (and most friends think they have reached it before they really have) is a trap, "a trap that we have freely chosen, a trap that oddly enough liberates us more and more."[14] Freedom is admirable, but it is most admirable when it is focused and disciplined. Radical commitment to each other enables friends to explore each other freely, without fear; it enables them to make demands—with skill, of course, and with patience and sensitivity and an appropriate sense of timing. It also allows them to accept, for the moment at least, the incompleteness and imperfection of their relationship.

The wonderful thing about the friendship game, said Greeley, is that, if both sides play well, both sides win. And we must win some of the time, for there is no other way to be a human being. "Friendship is the only way that we can come to see the riches of our own possibilities, when the admiration for those possibilities is so powerfully reflected in the face of our friend that we can no more escape it than we can the glare of the rising sun." With friends we are more relaxed, more sensitive, more creative; we are more excited and at the same time more serene; more energetic, yet more casual; more confident, but also more vulnerable. With friends we breathe purer air, hear sharper sounds, see more dramatic colors. "Friendship, indeed, seduces us into being ourself."[15]

And writing about friendship seduced Greeley into revealing himself, "perhaps more than I would want." He tells us that it is hard for him to resist irrational demands without losing his temper; that he is an expert at sulking; that he should get out of frustrating relationships sooner than he does. He speaks of an inability to combine tenderness with firmness. "Curiously enough, or perhaps not so curiously considering the chemistry of sexuality, I am much better at challenging women than men, for with women I can be gentle and tender and supportive while at the same time being insistent and demanding, but I have no idea how to be gentle and tender with other men."[16]

He has been torn by doubts as to whether the challenges he makes to friends are valid ones. And he has learned of the special problems of the person with talent:

> The gifted person does not have to have friends as gifted as he. What he needs, rather, are friends who are strong enough to enjoy his gifts without being threatened by them. Strong enough to have loved him for what he is without having to try to cut him down to size, gentle enough to heal his wounds when his enemies yap at his heels, tender enough to caress him out of his moods when he is depressed and discouraged by the animosity of others which, try as he might, he simply cannot understand, and resourceful enough to persuade him that he is indeed lovable, not merely despite his gifts but, in fact, because of them. The giant on the mountaintop looks so mighty and powerful that one would conclude that he does not need friends. In fact, he needs them more than others, or the mountaintop will turn into a wall and he will become humpty-

dumpty, and the king's horses with the king's men will arrive to
support him just a little bit too late.[17]

In an interview he reiterated that point. "I can have really close
relationships only with people who aren't threatened. Otherwise,
just forget it." He has learned, he says, that he is most effective and
most attractive when he is vigorous and forceful, that no purpose is
ever served in human relationships by being less than one's most
direct and authentic self.

The style of *The Friendship Game* is that of the "spirituality"
columns Father Greeley was writing at this time for the *National
Catholic Reporter*. The words are *spoken*, some of them actually
dictated, others verbalized as they are typed. "When I type, I talk
aloud. This sounds corny, or odd, but I *hear* it. I write what I hear. I
know what I am going to say, and it flows," he told me. "When I
have a clear and powerful insight, and I am writing with attention
to it, the words fairly dance on the page before me. I say things I am
not conscious of ever having thought before, in ways that surprise
me."[18]

Greeley says he writes as a social scientist, but in books of this
type the social scientific content varies. In *The Friendship Game*,
there is no empirical research on friendship or self-disclosure,
though there is ample, and sometimes indiscriminate, use of psychoanalysis. To borrow terms from cognitive psychology, Greeley
writes as a *sharpener*, not a *leveler*. He accentuates detail, highlights
differences in opinion, does not plow hills into valleys to even the
horizon. Or, to use a dichotomy I have developed elsewhere (*Fantasy as Mirror*, New York: Jason Aronson, in press), he is a *projector*
rather than a *reflector*. Concerned with the vigorous expression of
himself, he necessarily fails to mirror empathically the ideas of
others. Sharpening ideas and projecting oneself, it seems to me,
clarify issues; they also heighten the emotional content in communication, move the focus from *what* is said to *who* is saying it, and
increase the potential both for warm, enthusiastic support and
bitter, hateful denunciation. The stakes are high when a sharpener,
a projector, writes.

There is another pair of words, too, that helps depict this man
when he writes about intimacy. In *The Duality of Human Existence*
(Boston: Beacon, 1966), David Bakan used the word *agency* to

subsume those human motives whose goal is self-protection, self-assertion, conquest, mastery—motives that create separation. Its opposite is *communion*, a word that summarizes desires for openness, for contact, for being at one with other organisms. Greeley's approach to intimacy—communion—is, paradoxically, agentic. Union is not the given; separation is. And separation is not overcome by *being with* the other; rather, one *builds* an edifice, a bridge—slowly, painfully, skillfully—and hopes it will support him as he dares the odds and crosses the chasm to reach the other. Friendship is a "challenging and demanding game"; with "practice," the right "tactics," the right "strategy," one can win at it, master it. Friendship is not letting the other, or the self, *be*; it is making extraordinary demands on both partners in the relationship. The self is not water, but rock. The relationship does not grow on its own terms; one controls and directs it. Friendship is not trusting and adapting to whatever emerges; it is "choice, . . . a long series of decisions, . . . a determination to push on in the face of obstacles that strongly suggest we should not push on."[19]

Even Greeley's way of knowing is agentic. He approaches the dynamics of interpersonal relationships with the rational, mechanistic descriptions of psychoanalysis. He attempts to order what is disordered, find logic in the illogical, control what is uncontrolled, bring intellect to the depths of emotion. Mystery is not allowed to *be*. The human psyche is a cave, and Greeley explores it with a searchlight that reveals the formation of stalagmites and stalactites, that shows where a stream turns a corner or disappears under a wall, that lights up the twisting, deceptive routes of tunnels wide and narrow. He learns of the depths—agentically—by mastering them. He does not know the cavern—and the human person—communally, dousing the light, experiencing the essential blackness of the place, feeling the coolness in the air, sensing the current of the stream around his legs. He does something to the cave rather than, mystic-like, allowing the cave to do something to him.

Why is friendship so *hard*? Why is play something to *master*? I think of Father Greeley's upbringing in a nondemonstrative Irish family where intimacy was avoided—and of his seminary training, which taught that intimacy was to be shunned. I recall the experiences of a precocious child, whose talent set him apart from his grade-school chums, made friendship with them difficult; and I remind myself that this pattern repeated itself in Greeley's priest-hood years. He is a celibate, too; he has never *felt* sexual union, which he says is the prototype of all human friendship. But these ex-periences and these freely chosen circumstances, in Greeley's view, were not crucial in shaping his thoughts on friendship. "Intimacy is hard for everybody. It's not any harder for me than for most people." *The Friendship Game* was written amidst the pain of a broken community, and that explains some of the emphasis on the difficul-ties of interpersonal relationships. But Greeley also wished to counter the preaching of "pop psychology," which said one could attain intimacy in a weekend; and he knew of couples in their middle years who had given up on their relationship because inti-macy just wasn't supposed to be *that* hard.

There is more, too. My thoughts go back to Andrew's father, a man of "immense integrity," who lived, psychologically, at some distance from his son. Not only was he a model of hard work, striv-ing, and loyalty; not only did his fate in the depression make his son anxious to guard against a crash; but the very fact of his distance made him something to reach for, in his son's words, "a figure to stir up all kinds of ambitions." Father Greeley is the kind of man who strives, reaches, places strenuous demands—upon himself, upon others, upon relationships. Intimacy is another arena in which to achieve—not collect trophies, but simply do extraordinarily well. Greeley does not expect to have a lot of friendships in his life, but "Do I have high expectations of it when it exists? Yes, it turns out I do. I wouldn't have thought I did, but people tell me I do."

When I asked Father Greeley, a celibate, what his sources were for books like *Sexual Intimacy* (1973) and *Love and Play* (1975), he quipped, "That's my affair." He never did answer the question directly, saying only that anyone who is a parish priest and has eyes and is sensitive to human relationships knows what he knows. "I can walk into a situation where there is a man and a woman present and in a very brief period of time intuit what is going on between them. It's not hard. It's a burden, because maybe you wouldn't want to know."

Whatever their sources (Greeley occasionally named a research report but always shielded the identities of friends with whom he had conversed), these books were destined to arouse, and in many cases shock, their intended readership. For the Catholic Organization Man and his wife whose life together had grown drab, routine, and lifeless, Greeley fused religion and sexuality, not so the former oppressed the latter, acting as a superego to an id, but so the two met, liberating and reinforcing each other. The books were not how-to-do-it sex manuals, though the practical Greeley could not avoid chapters like "How to Be Sexy"; nor, on the other hand, were they codes of morality. They were, rather, theological reflections, exercises in interpretation, direct outgrowths of *Unsecular Man*. Men and women understand their mating experience in terms of the symbols their cultures provide. It was Greeley's hope that such symbols, especially the ones of the Judeo-Christian religious tradition, would underwrite—not frustrate, as they have in the past—the quest for genital intimacy.

Why *this* effort at this point in time? Because someone asked him to write a pamphlet, Greeley offers. But there is more—a statement made at the More Lectures at Yale in 1970: "Sex is certainly the most corrosive issue facing Roman Catholicism at the present time, an issue that, for the Catholic Church, is something analogous to what the Vietnam war is for the American republic. It is . . . the only subject on which the mass of the population is as disaffected as the elites."[20]

A Catholic writing about sex in the early 1970s ought to touch upon birth control, abortion, homosexuality, premarital and extramarital intercourse, divorce, celibacy—any topic that invites moral comment. But Greeley argued that religion is not a moral code and that religious interpretation of human behavior has little to do with specific prohibitions or permissions. Issues of indissolubility, reproduction, the importance of human life, respect for the body are *secondary* considerations for a theology of sexuality. Before looking at these, one should ask, simply and bluntly, what resources do religious symbols (in this case, those of the Judeo-Christian system) make available to facilitate and promote intimacy, to heighten the ecstasy of lovers writhing in genital union?

A chapter of another Greeley book, *The New Agenda* (1973), recalled the sexual doctrine of "apologetic" Catholicism. One could not enjoy "voluntary" sexual pleasure outside of marital intercourse, and "involuntary" sexual feelings outside that context were not "seriously" sinful if one did not take pleasure in them. Of course, no "artificial impediment" was to stand in the way of conception. Greeley found nothing in the New Testament to justify such an approach and identified other forces in the West—Platonism, chronic underpopulation, Puritanism, eighteenth-century casuistry—as sources of the rigid, juridical, sin-obsessed approach to sex that led ultimately to the disastrous *Humanae Vitae*. New Testament symbols have nothing of that. On the contrary, "It is surely no misinterpretation of the intent of the twenty-fifth chapter of St. Matthew to say that the Christian believes what Jesus has told him, 'Whatever you do to your spouse, you do to me.'" The New Testament forces us to ask, "When a man patiently, gently but demandingly, brings his prudish and frightened woman to orgasm and teaches her how to be an enchantress, is he doing something to God? And when a woman pursues her husband so effectively that he simply cannot avoid her sexual entanglements and is persuaded that she wants him even more than he wants her, is she doing something to God?"[21]

Not only does the New Testament ask these questions, Greeley asserted, it answers them clearly in the affirmative. That affirmation has to be placed in the context of enormous changes in sexuality in the past century and a half. "In our era the problem is not underpopulation but overpopulation; marriage is no longer an important institution for the transmission of property; infant mortality rates are low, life expectancies are long, and the amount of time a child is dependent on his parent has trebled over even a century ago."[22] With changes in the role of women, with the virtual perfection of methods of contraception, sexuality has evolved into a means of finding personal fulfillment and happiness.

Contemporary sexual standards allow anything. "Pre-marital, extra-marital (or in the slick euphemism of Eugene Fontinell, 'co-marital') intercourse, homosexuality, necking and petting, masturbation, and everything else short of bestiality (and in some cases I suspect even that is not excluded) become legitimate forms of human behavior, so long as they are 'growth-producing.' " Shallow, glib, prone to self-deception, the New Sexuality nevertheless has hit upon a central insight: sex is between persons and not between organs. "It is embarrassing to observe that Carl Rogers certainly perceives that and Paul VI apparently does not."[23]

What the New Sexuality misses, however, and what the story of Yahweh and his people, of Christ and his Church, celebrate, is that "the psychodynamics of intimacy are such that there is a strain toward permanency in any important intimate relationship," that "the kind of consideration, self-discipline, trust, tenderness, patience, strength, and affection that are necessary for genital intimacy to be growth-producing are much less likely to exist if one can obtain orgasms elsewhere whenever one feels like it or whenever one is able to persuade oneself that such orgasms are self-fulfilling."[24] Permanency and exclusiveness, however, cannot be *legislated* into a relationship. They are not a wall that the conscience builds out of a sense of ought. They are, rather, desires that arise instinctually if a relationship is maturing in intimacy.

In such an atmosphere of growing commitment, one wishes to be "sexy" for his or her partner. Being "sexy"—a chapter from *Sexual Intimacy* on this topic appeared in *Redbook* magazine— means creating an erotic atmosphere around oneself, inviting potential sexual partners, enjoying playfulness and variety in a genital relationship. "The sexy person says in effect, 'I am not merely a woman or a man. I am a playmate, a lover with whom you can have all kinds of fun. With me, even some of your wildest fantasies can be enjoyed in reality. I am not just an outlet like everyone else of my sex. I am a challenge and an opportunity."[25]

Father Greeley continued. We often are not sexy because we feel inadequate. "One is afraid to reveal one's sexual organs because they may not be good enough. Physical shame is intimately connected with human shame; fear to reveal sexual organs results from feelings of human inadequacy." Shame—over our bodies, over our selves— inhibits openness and playfulness, blocks the communication of sexual hunger, grays the revelation of sexual fantasies. Were we aware of our bodies as instruments of playfulness and delight—"the nerves and muscles of the human body, and particularly of the human sex organs, were made to be played with by a member of the opposite sex"[26]—were we struck forcibly by the attractiveness of that figure in the mirror, were we to work at and learn the skills of erotic self-display and seduction, we would be a mystery, a challenge, an opportunity to our spouse. We would be "sexy."

At the heart of sexiness is the element of *surprise*. Two lovers know at the beginning of the day that they will make love in the evening. Is their routine predictable, devoid of variety and wonder? Or are there questions on the margins of awareness that tease and puzzle each of them throughout the day?

> The husband, for example, may be asking, how will she respond? Will she be hungry and passionate, perhaps even more aggressive than I? Will she be shy and passive? Will she want me to take her directly and forcefully—perhaps even on the living room floor after the children are asleep, or shall I make it a long and involved seduction scene? Will I wait until we get into bed, or will I begin to undress her? What will she look like? What will she be wearing? Will she have on that transparent lingerie in which she looks so delicious? Will she let me take off her bra?

> And the woman will be semiconsciously dwelling on similar questions. When will he start? Will it begin even before supper or will he wait? Where will his hands and his mouth go first? Will he be in one of those moods when he wants to strip me leisurely? Shall I turn the tables on him tonight and strip him first, or will I surprise him with my plan to trap him at his work in the library when I approach him wearing only panties and a martini pitcher—or maybe only the martini pitcher? Will I kneel on top of him, forcing my body down on his?[27]

If surprise is at the heart of erotic invitation, it is also at the heart of God's invitation to his people. "God's intervention in our lives was a total and complete surprise. Yahweh on Sinai caught Israel flat-footed, and the resurrection of Jesus caught the apostles equally flat-footed. Yahweh proclaimed on Sinai, and Jesus renewed the proclamation, that life is wonderful and filled with surprises, the greatest of which is God's incredible love for us." The realities spoken of by the Judeo-Christian symbol system insure that the wife who catches her husband flat-footed in the library is acting in accordance with *the way things are*, for it ". . . is strict theological truth to say that the capacity to cause surprise and delight in others by erotic self-display is a continuation of Yahweh's work."[28] Religious symbols exist not to crush sexual intimacy but to facilitate it.

Sexual Intimacy went on to discuss the "insatiable female" and the "uncertain male." Research indicates that a woman can experience orgasmic satisfaction indefinitely, that "uninhibited by cultural and psychological barriers, a woman's sexuality appears to be both more intense and more demanding than that of a man."

Powerful cultural restraints that have long controlled female sexuality are currently being lifted, and that presents a dilemma for most women: orgasm has become obligatory. "Intense sexual pleasure is now all right, but how does one go about experiencing it?" Greeley's answer is that her lover must understand what it takes, physiologically, to arouse her ("he has his hands, his mouth, his penis—what does he think they are for?"[29]), and she must guide him, bluntly and explicitly, to the kind of refined knowledge he needs. It is not easy to begin communication. One does not break out of well-established patterns of shame, reticence, timidity, and fear without a good deal of pain. But there is no other way to grow.

The male, on the other hand, is afraid of failure and rejection—and his sexual failure is more obvious than that of the woman. He also finds it difficult to combine strength and tenderness, agency and communion, the instrumental with the expressive. Expected to be hard-driving, ruthless, and ambitious in the world of his career, he is supposed to be compassionate, tender, and sympathetic at home. The dilemma extends to his lovemaking. "The net result is a male who, in the genital encounter, is neither agentic enough nor communal enough. He does not know either when to be strong or when to be weak, or how to take, or how to permit himself to be taken, and you really cannot be virile unless you can combine the expressive with the instrumental. The 'stud' may 'ball' a woman but that's all he can do. The virile man, on the other hand, knows how to make love, knows how to combine aggressiveness with tenderness, demand with surrender." Further, though he may be reluctant to admit it, a man needs to be mothered. "To be 'mothered' means to be smothered with affection, to be covered with sensuous attention, to have every part of one's being, body, and spirit gently and passionately caressed, to experience a relationship which furnishes the psychological equivalent of a hot bath and a warm, dry robe after coming in out of a cold, damp rainstorm."[30] There is no limit to the amount of caressing—direct, physical, sensuous, "obscene" caressing—that a man can absorb. It may be easy for him to become aroused physiologically (and to get "laid"), but if arousal means more than the stimulation of erectile tissues, if it means the development of confidence in one's ability to combine strength and tenderness, agency and communion, then arousal is extremely difficult. Courage is needed for the man to admit and communicate a need to surrender, for the woman to break through his defenses and offer what he desperately needs.

And such courage can be underwritten only by an act of faith in oneself, in the other, and in reality. One has to believe that reality (and one can spell it with a small *r* or a capital *R*) is ultimately gracious, that things will be all right in the end. It is precisely such a conviction that Yahweh communicated to his people, that Jesus ratified with his death and resurrection. These religious symbols ought to persuade Christian lovers to take the risk of self-exposure. "If Yahweh can admit he 'needs' the affection of his beloved, then why should any man be afraid to admit the same thing?"[31] And if Jesus rose from the dead, why should husband and wife doubt that risk and pain and death in their relationship now will mean joy and resurrection later on?

Indeed, the most striking characteristic of the entire Judeo-Christian symbol system is the *fidelity* of God to his beloved people. In the book of Exodus Yahweh made it clear that no matter what we did as his people, he would remain our God. In the sexual imagery of Osee, Jeremiah, and Ezekiel, he emphasized that, though we whore with false gods, he will never turn his back on us and seek another people. So, too, should husband and wife be faithful to each other.

But Greeley's understanding of faithfulness in marriage was not the traditional one. "I am suggesting that marital fidelity ought to mean a commitment to improving without limitation the quality of one's total relationship with one's spouse, especially and particularly the quality of lovemaking. The unfaithful person, then, is not so much the one who has a playmate somewhere else, but rather, one who does not by seduction and facilitation keep his wife a playmate. Similarly, the unfaithful woman is not so much one who goes after another man as one who has stopped (or in fact never began) going after her husband."[32] One is either having more and more fun in bed or less and less. Fidelity is a commitment to seek more. Infidelity is giving up.

Fidelity provides lovers a safe arena in which to fight. "Lovers must fight. They can only love if they fight; it enhances the quality of their love. Love without conflict is tame, passionless, dull." Fighting says that lovers care about their relationship, that they are not afraid to reveal their anger, to show the raw edges of their personality. In a genital relationship one must demand from the other—as Yahweh demanded from his people—the best that he or she is capable of giving.

> The young man whose passive wife closes her eyes when he is doing to her the things a man should be doing to a woman ought to be possessed by outraged fury. He ought to shake her angrily until her eyes open wide and shout, "Damn you! Look at me when I play with you!" . . . Similarly, the young woman whose husband is a timid and disappointing lover is scarcely being very effective when she buys him a book. She should face him with withering scorn and demand, "Don't you know anything about how to seduce a woman?"[33]

Sexual Intimacy emphasized the need for practice, skill, determination, and work in a genital relationship. One of Greeley's favorite analogies, used already in *The Friendship Game*, was the tough but sophisticated professional quarterback—a Tittle, a Jurgensen, a Unitas, a Tarkenton—who had the guts, the instincts, the savvy to read the defense of the opposition, to call the right audible, to deliver the ball under pressure—to win the game. Critics, when they did not scoff at the idea of a priest writing about sex, said Greeley "romanticized" or "idealized" the marital relationship; but he was in fact setting high, almost impossible levels of performance, just as he had done in *The Friendship Game*. Greeley's Christians had to be the best at everything, and that included lovemaking. "The God of the Testaments, New and Old, is not a 'nice' God at all but a lover consumed with *eros*. It is disgraceful for his followers to mate with each other in any but the most fervent, erotic way."[34]

Greeley's sequel to *Sexual Intimacy*, a small volume entitled *Love and Play*, retained the agentic, striving motifs of its predecessor—lovers had to be strong, competitive, and demanding—but its mood was more authentically playful. Greeley wrote of suspense in play, of lovers who remained mysteries to each other—teasing, surprising, seducing enigmas—not only in their bed but in their entire life together. If you know all there is to know about your spouse, he said simply, the game is over. The truth of the matter is that human beings are extraordinarily complex; the mystery of the other is never exhausted; the more we discover, the more we realize there are heights and depths and breadths yet unknown. It all depends on how the relationship is defined. "Another human being is either a closed and uninteresting book or a constant and endless source of fascination. Whether he be interesting or not depends as much on our definition of and response to him as on any intrinsic quality of his own nature."[35]

To explore the mystery of another is extremely erotic—is, in fact, the most erotic thing a human being can do. "When that exploration is reinforced and facilitated by sexual lovemaking, the lovemaking becomes an episode in a grand adventure, taking on an intensity of pleasure that it would otherwise not have." The trouble is that exploration takes time and skill and patience; and being explored, well, it permits another to have a frightening amount of knowledge and power over one. All in all, "it is much, much easier to buy a copy of *Playboy* or advertise in one of the spouse-swapping journals."[36]

If play is suspenseful, said Greeley, it is also fantastic. It delivers itself to the ingenious, creative, energetic impulses of the imagination. The fantasy world of lovers is raw, primal, infantile, perverse. Incest and rape, homosexuality and sadomasochistic orgies exist in the same chaotic preconscious that is the source of our most beautiful religious symbols. Shall this uncontrollable wellspring of "dirty thoughts" be capped? Or shall lovers allow it to burst forth, even delight in its force and vigor? There is only one answer for the Christian who plays: Let the imp out of the bottle and listen to what he has to say. Couples will vary in the extent to which they share sexual fantasies, and Greeley advised that communication along these lines remain optional; but, by and large, the "slow, gradual, tasteful, witty sharing of daydreams is probably a sign of healthy development." A woman yearns in fantasy to caress and kiss the penis of a young lifeguard on the beach; indeed, if the truth be told, there are many, many penises she would like to kiss. She never will—but there are always her husband's organs to be kissed whenever she wishes. And her husband daydreams over a scotch in the golf course bar that tall, athletic women with large breasts take off all his clothes and tie him to a bench. They pinch him, tickle him, play with him, kiss him, make him suck on their breasts, then drag him off to the shower to cover him with soapsuds and embrace his wet, slippery body. "Chances are that his fantasy will not come true, but a warm, soapy, stimulating shower with his wife is another matter altogether. She may resist at first, but if he is afraid to ask, afraid to try, afraid to insist (as many men are), then an opportunity for playfulness that would creatively release some of his fantasy energy has been passed by."[37]

Play is suspenseful, fantastic—and festive. The ancients *celebrated* when a young animal was born, when the seeds were planted in the fields, when the first fruits were harvested—when life won a victory over death. In like manner should sexual play celebrate life, rejoicing in all the goodness and dignity and strength and growth that one has experienced. The organs of the other may simply be sensitive glands that one enjoys touching; or they may be revelations of grace, love, and elegance at the core of the universe. Christian lovers know—or at least they should know—that breasts, vaginas, and penises are more than organs. When they unite there is "a revelation, a sacrament, the Eucharist, a participation in the basic life forces of the universe."[38] Their union should bring to mind the festivals of the ancients, celebrations that fused religion and sex in sheer exuberance over the fact of life.

Sex and play, finally, are humorous. The naked human body (even a beautiful one) is funny, if only because we spend most of our time wearing clothes. And sexual arousal is even funnier; men and women of reason, sobriety, and control, aristocrats and paupers alike, are reduced to the same common denominator, thrashing about, uncontrolled, like the animals they are. Parents find children precious, important, beautiful— but also funny. The laughter of lovers at each other, expressed in a similar context of mutual affirmation, adds immeasurably to their relationship. It hints, too, at other things: all laughter is a laughing at death, according to Peter Berger's *A Rumor of Angels* (New York: Doubleday, 1968), a response of confidence to those fears and anxieties ultimately rooted in death. The private jokes of lovers are rumors of "a great Cosmic Joke in which life successfully puts down death."[39]

Suspense, fantasy, festivity, and laughter. They are woven into the fabric of a relationship strengthened by long years of discipline and practice. You have to work at play, said Andrew Greeley, until you get good enough at it to relax and rejoice in it. In discussing the dynamics of games, *Love and Play* was actually pressing for fidelity in a sexual relationship; its basic position was that true playfulness can only occur in an environment created by permanent commitment. Children do not play with strangers or casual acquaintances—they play with friends. How can lovers do otherwise? In the words of D. H. Lawrence, "Where there is real sex there is the underlying passion for fidelity."[40]

And so, Christian lovers, said Greeley, play with each other in defiance of death. Tease, surprise, seduce, sing, dance, clap your hands. Believe in the import of Scripture: "life, for all its tragedy, is still ultimately a comedy, indeed, a comic, playful dance with a passionately loving God."[41]

We have come to the heart of Andrew Greeley.

11   The Yahwistic Myths

And so we seek to understand the man. Enough of the survey research entrepreneur, the lay psychologist, the giver of advice, the caustic journalist. Enough, too, of selves closer to the core: Chicagoan, Irish-American, Democrat, man of the neighborhood, even Catholic priest. I have chosen in this book—and it is a choice—to see a man, to define his core, by listening to how he interprets reality, by asking what meaning he ascribes to the events of his life—to the victories and defeats, to the coming and going of friends and foes, to the fundamental births and deaths that these are. I am looking at a man's ego rather than his id, "explaining" him by describing his belief system rather than by speculating about the vicissitudes of his libidinal development, capturing his adult years rather than reacting to his first psychological steps. May I leave Father Greeley with some of the mystery that any human being possesses.

As far back as 1961—and, really, as far back as an unpublished master's thesis—Andrew Greeley was writing about the religious myth. To him, myth did not mean fable or fairy tale, but "a universal category of belief." To speak of "the soteriological myth," for example, did "not imply that redemption is a self-deception, but merely that there seems to be a universal tendency for man to believe in redemption and a redeemer."[1] A decade later, articles in *America* and *Concilium*[2] and books like *Come Blow Your Mind with Me* and *Unsecular Man* argued against the urgings of theologian Rudolph Bultmann and Bishop John A. T. Robinson that religious symbols be "demythologized." Greeley contended that the 1960s had witnessed a decline of confidence in rational enlightenment and a resurgence of interest in the intuitive, the mystical, the psychedelic. It was hardly the time to evict the mythological from religious traditions; on the contrary, one ought to make it feel more at home, understand it on its own terms, and, if necessary, translate it into propositional language. One had to ask what the *imagery* of the Judeo-Christian tradition provided in the way of answers to humankind's fundamental religious needs.

Clifford Geertz had written of religion that it presented a conviction about the inherent structure of reality and told man how to come in contact and be in harmony with that reality. That is what the Judeo-Christian—the Yahwistic—myths were all about: explaining, speaking to the whole person (the poetic as well as the cerebral sensitivities), communicating a conviction, and—a favorite word of Father Greeley—*underwriting*. To underwrite is to reassure, to back up, to guarantee safety in the face of risk, and so to say, go ahead and take a chance. In the face of the complexities, the pain, the signs of death in human life, Greeley believes that this—underwriting—is the function of the Yahwistic symbols. What, then, are the convictions they generate about human living and human dying? Divested of thousands of years of accretion, what are they saying about the structure of reality?

To hear Father Greeley answer these questions is to hear *him*.

Jesus.

Who was he? What does the Jesus symbol—stripped of the piety, the theological controversy, the ecclesiastical triumphalism that has encrusted it—what does it convey about the inner meaning of human life, about the structure of the universe? If the deposits of later centuries are scraped away, the "historical" Jesus stands forth "unique, original, and startling. It is small wonder that he frightened and shocked his contemporaries and that they would not accept what he said. It is also small wonder that we have done our best to obscure the shocking nature of the symbolism of Jesus ever since."[3] So Greeley wrote in *The Jesus Myth* (1971), a book that brought the approach of Clifford Geertz to the latest in New Testament scholarship.

It is—and was—hard to categorize Jesus. He dominated the crowds, was master of his band of disciples, yet always insisted he was the servant. He was familiar with publicans and sinners, yet the quality of his friendship was determined by him, not by the publicans and sinners. He was not a political revolutionary (and many Jews were estranged from him because he was not), yet he wept over the impending fate of Jerusalem and was executed as a political agitator. "In other words, Jesus went about providing answers to questions that no one was asking and refusing to answer the questions everyone thought important." The establishment Sadducees, corrupt heirs of the ancient church, would have nothing to do with him. The Pharisees, "liberal reformers filled with self-righteousness and zeal," were horrified by his disregard of the law and his condemnation of their moral arrogance. The Zealots, hoping for a drastic political reorganization that would right the injustices all around them, were disillusioned by his refusal to act as a political messiah. And the Essenes, who had withdrawn from a corrupt society to build a perfect world of their own, were no doubt appalled by his proclamation of a kingdom for all men. "One can imagine that a frequent question people asked about him was, 'But where does he really stand?' "[4]

To those who would ask such a question, Greeley continued, Jesus said simply: the kingdom of God is at hand. His words were not a threat (though many have turned them into precisely that) but a proclamation of incredibly good news and an invitation to a banquet. A new reign was about to begin and that was cause for celebration. Rejoice, Jesus said, because at the core of the universe is an incredibly generous and loving God. God is like the father of a son who has frittered away his inheritance. When the son crawls home to beg forgiveness, the father rushes out to embrace him, silences his carefully rehearsed statement of sorrow, clothes him in the finest of garments, and throws a party, complete with music and dancing, good food and good drink. God is a shepherd crazy enough to track down one lost sheep when ninety-nine are safely in the herd, an employer lunatic enough to give workers a full day's pay for only a single hour's work. "What is the universe all about?" Greeley asked. "The reality with which Jesus felt so intimate was passionate love, so passionate as to appear by human standards to be insane."[5]

If we listen to the parables of Jesus, said Greeley, we then discover that God is throwing a party and that we are all invited. It is up to us to accept the invitation, to say firmly and decisively that we will come. How foolish it would be to act like the invited guests in the parable of the Great Feast and say, I just bought a field and have to look after it; or, I must try out five new pairs of oxen; or, I just got

married, please excuse me. If we pass up this invitation we will not
get another. The host will go out to the streets and alleys, if
necessary, and ask others to come, saying to us, you will never again
taste of my dinners.

The invitation of Jesus was good news—fantastic news. "The
message responds to the most basic and agonizing question that
faces all who are part of the human condition: Is everything going to
be all right in the end? Jesus' response was quite literally to say,
'You bet your life it is.' "[6] Human beings hope against hope that life
is not capricious, that there is purpose behind it all, that death is not
the final answer. They do, as Freud said, *wish* for a God who assures
order and meaning and immortality. What Jesus said, in effect, was
that our wildest dreams, our loftiest hopes, our maddest fantasies,
our deepest wishes are true. And more: the heart of reality is even
more gracious and more beneficent than we could possibly imagine.

The good news was not cheap consolation, not "pie in the sky
when you die," said Greeley. Jesus did not deny the terrible realities
of injustice and suffering and death; he said merely that love will
triumph in the end. His message is not opium for the masses; on the
contrary, it will not tolerate the discouragement that causes so many
social movements to burn themselves out in a few years. It conveys a
fundamentally optimistic view of reality, a view that gives (or at
least ought to give) hope and confidence, qualities that underwrite
sustained commitment no matter how completely the sky clouds
over.

The challenge laid down by Jesus was ethical, but not primarily
so. The principal responsibility of the invited guest was to accept
the news of the kingdom and enter the feast *now*—without delay,
without hedging, without looking back. This "basic existential
leap" in which we "decisively commit ourselves to the notion that
the Really Real is in fact insanely generous love"[7] produces a *metanoia* (or total transformation of the person), and the ethics of the
kingdom *follow from* the *metanoia*. If one goes all the way in his
acceptance of the great assurance offered by Jesus, he will experience the love of God and naturally (though still not without pain
and difficulty) extend that love to others. He will feel the forgiveness of God and thus have the wherewithal to forgive others. The
Good Samaritan was not paying the price of admission to the kingdom when he stopped to help a man who should have been his

natural enemy; no, he had already entered the kingdom and could not do otherwise. Nor is the Sermon on the Mount strict moral imperative; it is nothing more than a description of the style of life of those feasting at the banquet given by the Lord.

As for the resurrection of Jesus, said Greeley, it is something that can never be confirmed by historical fact (the only fact of which we can be certain is that the early Christians had a profound experience of Jesus immediately after his death). What the Easter symbol *means* is far more important than the details of the resurrection. It means that the Really Real is love so powerful that even sin and death cannot contain it; it is love so resourceful that we too (in what manner we do not know) shall live. So the issue is not our belief in the way in which Jesus lives but our acceptance of the kingdom that his resurrection validates and our confidence in the belief that victory is ultimately assured, that everything will be all right in the end.

Why, then, do so many refuse to accept this incredibly good news? Not because what Jesus said was burdensome or threatening, Greeley answered, but because it was hopeful, spectacularly hopeful, *too* hopeful. Men have rejected this message not out of greed or ambition or fear, but out of cynicism, not because events in Jesus' life (and the existence of God) are impossible to verify, but because men "believe that evil triumphs over good, that life is absurd and is a tale told by an idiot, that the Really Real is malign, and that only a blind fool would believe that things will be all right in the end."[8]

Then too, accepting the invitation to the kingdom is not easy. It was not easy, Greeley wrote, for his New Community. Having discovered the possibility of leading a life of confidence, hope, love, and joy, they suddenly realized that these make demands. They understood "how much they would have to give up, how many of their foolish fears and defenses they would have to put away, how open their lives would be to ridicule and laughter, the many risks they would have to take."[9] It became clear—though no one would admit it—that the joys of the banquet were simply not worth the demands it made.

So, strangely enough, the Jesus symbol—the most important religious symbol in the West—stands for gaiety, not fear, for self-confidence, not self-deprecation, for invitation, not condemnation. And, even more strangely, it has been rejected (and distorted by

"Christians") precisely because of this, precisely because it is good
news, not bad.

Greeley wrote more about Jesus—a collection of meditations
entitled *Jesus Now* (1972), a piece in the *New York Times* that was
reprinted later in a number of other papers including the *Chicago
Daily News* (where it drew the ire of readers as a "contumelious
attack on the Divine Founder of Christianity"[10]). *The Jesus Myth*,
itself one of the few books written on Greeley's own initiative, was
his most popular work and is now available in five languages. "Why
was it so popular?" I asked. "Because it's about Jesus," he said—and
no more than that.

The Father, Yahweh.

The facts seem to be these. A group of Semitic slaves, a grab-bag
collection of tribes, really, escape from Egypt. Some of their number
have an experience near a sacred mountain in the desert; then all of
them come together and form a unity around a belief in one
common God.

Many questions of fact surround this remarkable social and
political event. What really happened on Mount Sinai? Was Moses
an actual historical personage? Did God personally engrave letters
on stone tablets? But these questions, failing to take the mythmaker
on his own terms, miss the point. What matters is that Israel chose
the symbol of the covenant (*berith*) to describe for itself the nature of
the Holy it encountered in the desert, and the question we should
ask, the *religious* question, is "What kind of relationship between
man and God does the covenant symbol describe?"

Greeley's development of an answer appeared in *Youth Asks,
Does God Still Speak?* (1970) and *What a Modern Catholic Believes
about God* (1971), but its most complete articulation was *The Sinai
Myth* (1972). The latter pushed his interpretation of the Judeo-
Christian symbol system back, beyond the Jesus myth, to its very
origins.

We err, Greeley said, if we think the Sinai experience recorded
in the book of Exodus was primarily ethical. Sinai was a religious
event, an encounter of man with God, and "the ethical code which
emerged from that encounter was simple, not especially original,
and rather of secondary importance."[11] The Ten Commandments

are part of a larger religious revelation; they do not enumerate the conditions for earning Yahweh's favor but the consequences and evidences of accepting it.

At the center of the religious experience of the Israelites was the feeling that God had offered a covenant—a promise, a treaty, a pact, an agreement—and that they had accepted it. The covenant, freely entered into by both sides, established a permanent relationship with responsibility for *Chesed*—love, loyalty, ready action—on both sides. The idea seems commonplace now, but at the time it was radical, perhaps "the most dramatic change in the whole history of human religions." In other religions God was identified either with nature or with society, "but for Israel the relationship with God was the result of positive action on the part of Yahweh himself. It was an action that demanded a positive response from Israel."[12] This Holy encountered in the desert was at the same time more powerful *and* more benign than that encountered in any religious experience before or since.

The fundamental insight contained in the symbol of God the Covenanter is that he is involved with his people, he is committed to them, he cares for them. At the time of the Sinai revelation it was an unbelievable perception, too good to be true. "Yahweh is not merely a God, not merely a Jewish God: he is a pushy Jewish God who refuses to leave his people alone."[13] The history of Israel subsequent to Sinai, said Greeley, is a record of a "jealous old peasant warrior sitting up on the top of Sinai and growing wrathful over the infidelity of his people."[14] He is angry not because the rules are broken time and again, but because he is jealous. And his jealousy is based on love.

We learn of the love in Osee and in parts of Jeremiah and Ezekiel. Here Yahweh is symbolized as husband and lover, indeed a "cuckolded husband who will not give up on his love."[15] Israel has been a harlot, a bride unfaithful to Yahweh, but still his passion for her cannot be cooled. Though sexual imagery pervades human religion, this image of God "hung up" on his people through all their whoring is so revolutionary as to be blasphemous. "Not only is the Really Real a Thou who cares for us and pursues us, it is now even a Thou of whom it can be said that he is sexually aroused in our presence: an idea which was shocking to the Jews, profoundly scandalous to their neighbors, and difficult enough for the Jansenists and the Puritans in modern Christianity to give much credence to."[16]

At the core of the universe there beats passionate love; that is what Old Testament myths *qua* myths mean to Andrew Greeley. It is the same meaning he found in the New Testament symbols of Jesus. Indeed, all that Jesus did was renew the theophany of Sinai. "It is not a new Yahweh that we encounter in Jesus but rather a more highly developed, more explicitly stated and more richly symbolized Yahweh."[17]

"God in your work gets more and more insanely generous," I commented to Father Greeley.

"Yep. Right. That's what he's like."

"Why?" A psychologist, I was thinking of "compensation" for the losses of the past few years, of "projecting" goodness *out there* to balance the evil he had seen. But no.

"Because I understand the Scriptures better. I think that's in the sources."

I pursued. "Is it that life is getting more vicious?"

"No, I don't think so. I've thought about that, but I don't think that's the case, because he operates at a totally different level of being than that. I think it's a cop-out to say, well I don't mind the bastards because God loves me. I do mind the bastards."

Whatever the origin of Greeley's position—and I am one to believe in congruence between the experiences of a man, like loss and loneliness, and what he seeks and finds (often because it's there) in Scripture—Greeley's Yahweh is indeed that pushy, demanding old warrior sitting on top of Sinai. He cares for you (so much that sometimes you wish he'd leave you alone), but you don't exactly mess with him, and you'd better tip your old sailor's cap when you mention his name—or else he might send some more big waves and remove the last smidgen of sand from under your house. You can, as "one of his creatures," write a book of *Complaints Against God* (1971) and gripe about the 747, April snowstorms, the necessity of sleep, and, well, that whole silly notion of his that he *wants* us. And, you know, you can even call him "The Boss" or its Irish equivalent, the "Ole Fella."

As a matter of fact, who ever had a conversation with the

Absolute, the Infinite, the Ground of Being, the Prime Mover, or *Ens a Se*? And who's interested (so Greeley wrote in his column) in "a punctilious, persnickety, tough deity who insists on being referred to piously as 'Almighty God. . . The only God worthy of believing in is one you can call 'The Boss.'" Blasphemy, maybe, but the Ole Fella himself told us to do it:

> On Sinai he announced that he had entered into an intimate, personal relationship with his people—uninvited and frequently not wanted. "I am Yahweh your God." Period, paragraph, end of revelation. All else since has been explication.
>
> Then someone came along and referred to God as "Abba, Father"—a term of familiar affection even more daring than "Boss." He added something about not calling us servants but friends. He also said that the Kingdom of Heaven was like a great banquet.
>
> Only a whimsical, crazy God could get so involved with his creatures. The creeps and squares have never been able to buy that and have tried to deceive the rest of us ever since.
>
> [Really told 'em off, didn't I, Boss? Let's have another party.][18]

The Spirit.

Scripture says little about this, the most ethereal of the Christian images of God. It refers to the Spirit as advocate, comforter, source of strength, wind, fire, and light. We are told that we are to be born again of the Spirit, that the Spirit will be with us until Jesus returns. There is little else.

If the Spirit makes only the briefest of appearances in the Bible, he is just as evasive in the works of Father Greeley. But he is there, darting up for acknowledgment in the titles of tiny volumes of reprinted columns like *The Life of the Spirit* (1970) and *The Touch of the Spirit* (1971), flitting into a paragraph or a chapter of a book about God. He is in Father Greeley, too, who will tell you quite seriously that he listens hard to what the Spirit—even though he is a mischievous prankster—is trying to tell him. "The Holy Spirit," he relates, "is that power in the cosmos which speaks to that which is most unique and most creative and most special in all of us."

The Spirit speaks to our spirit, St. Paul says, unlocking the fear and timidity that close us in, activating what is most visionary, most playful, most hopeful, most open within us. The Spirit is *wind*: "at times He whirls down the corridor of our house like a tornado; at other times He barely touches us as does a spring breeze."[19] The Spirit is *fire*, melting our frigidity, stirring us to passionate enthusiasm. The Spirit is *light*; it shines on our talents and refuses to let us cover with a bushel whatever makes us different from others. Do we know if the impulse we feel comes from the Spirit? If it leads us to risk ourselves and grow, if it elicits the best we are capable of (as it did the apostles on Pentecost), we should have no doubt as to its source.

The Spirit, blowing where he will, stands for improvisation, surprise, playing it by ear. "The Spirit simply will not be tied down, and when someone announces here the Spirit is, we have Him here, please come and see Him, they find that by the time they get us to the room where they claim to have Him, the nimble, agile Spirit will have flown the coop and will be somewhere else, perhaps laughing at our foolish notion that we could capture Him."[20] Never, never does He provide the simple, magical answer, says Greeley. God's appearance on Sinai was a surprise; the Good News of Jesus was a surprise; what the Spirit has in store for us will likewise be a surprise. Life for the Christian, in fact, should mean developing the capacity for surprise, the capacity to cope with the greatest uncertainty of all—death and what comes after.

Activating the unique in all of us, teaching us to relish the unique in others, surprising us, refusing to be captured, the leprechaun-like Spirit is the principle of diversity in the Judeo-Christian symbol system. Yahweh the Father stands for unity; without him there would be the chaos of the scattered tribes of Israel. Jesus the Son does too; he came, after all, to make us one. But the Spirit symbolizes and underwrites differentiation; without him we would have a religion of dullness. It is the Spirit who inspires us to experiment with alternatives in education, in Church structure, in priestly ministries; it is the Spirit who had dabbed the American landscape with ethnic variegation (and who zips in and out of the offices of the Center for the Study of American Pluralism); it is the Spirit who rejoices over a political structure that respects diversity; it is the Spirit who says Christian spouses must tease, surprise, and seduce each other and love with polymorphous perversity.

In another paper, Greeley continued. One could, he said, create a "theology of pluralism," a theology consonant with the stops and starts, the whirls and twirls, of this poltergeist Holy Spirit. Such a theology would be rooted in the American experience of unity amidst diversity and would resonate with the ancient philosophical and theological mystery of the One and the Many.

Why did God will that the Many be *so* diverse? Greeley asked. Wouldn't one language, one religion, one race have been enough— especially when one realizes that evil is deeply involved in diversity, that it is precisely over *differences*, differences as important or unimportant as skin color and facial configuration, that men fight and die? Perhaps the Scholastic theologians in the Middle Ages were right. They concluded from the tower of Babel myth that it was sin that introduced diversity into the world. On the other hand, were it not for the particularities of space and time that produced Shakespeare, Dante, Mozart, and Jesus—and Thai silks and Jewish humor and American black music and Irish whiskey—humankind would remain deprived of its storehouse of creative riches. Why would God tolerate such a paradox, good and evil stemming from the same fact of our differentiation?

There must have been a party, Greeley (now a mythmaker himself) mused, a splendid party where God got drunk and decided to show off for the angels. So he spewed out creation in reckless abandon, in senseless superabundance—all those galaxies, all those stars and planets, and on this earth such a mosaic of birds and reptiles, fishes and mammals and peoples in all those sizes and shapes and colors—and said, "There. Look at that! What a marvelous joke!" But, alas, we humans lacked a sense of humor and instead of delighting in the differences we thought it better to fight over them—thus Jesus was necessary to make us one again.

A homemade parable, explaining nothing but articulating completely Greeley's conviction, thought as well as felt, that human diversity is "a manifestation of the overwhelming, overflowing goodness and power of the divine love."[21] It is human sinfulness that refuses to revel in the diversity, that leads us to be frightened of those who are different from us, to strike out at them before they come to destroy us.

The Devil.
Satan, Lucifer, Prince of Darkness, call him what you will. To

the Buddhists, he was Mara; to the Assyrians, Pazuzu; to the Babylonians, Tiamat; to the Egyptians, Set. Among Algonquin Indians, he is Gluskap; in Siberia, Ngaa; among Teutons, Loki; among Celts and Slavs (one of the few things upon which they agree), Dis. He takes many forms. You may encounter him (or her, or it) as a snake, a crocodile, a pig, a billy goat, a coyote, or a crow. Or you may see a humanoid, male or female, with a hundred thousand serpents coiled about it, or a huge hook on its head, or a belt of skulls around its waist; you may even meet a strong, attractive young man—the fallen angel that Christians think of him as being. Father Greeley really wasn't very interested in this character until the *New York Times,* on the heels of *Rosemary's Baby* and *The Exorcist,* asked him for an article. It was then that "I began to reflect on why the devil myth had the powerful appeal it had, and . . . of course: because you can subsume under it a lot of data—the data of the evil that exists, and the struggle between good and evil, the struggle between life and death." Greeley gave the *Times* what they wanted and didn't stop until he had produced an entire book on the topic, *The Devil, You Say!* (1974).

What is the significance of the devil myth, one so pervasive that it unites in belief such diverse persons as Pope Paul VI and Charles Manson? Quite simply, it speaks to the mystery of evil (not the "problem" of evil, which is something college sophomores argue about). It is concerned with the nagging questions humans have always asked: Why does evil always seem to be overwhelming good? Why do we experience in ourselves the constant battle between love and hate, life and death, being and nonbeing? Why do we find ourselves doing the evil we wish to avoid and omitting the good we had hoped to accomplish? The story of the devil does not provide a solution to these problems, nor does it create syllogisms to explain them; rather, it expresses the response of the entire person toward a mystery for which he has the greatest respect.

Greeley's book on evil cast in the form of demons all those forces that had attacked *him.* He spoke of the Devil of Ressentiment, Envy Himself, as the most powerful of the spirits that torment human life (and, at the same time, as the one we are most secretive about). Envy says, in the words of social philosopher Max Scheler, "I can forgive everything, but not that you *are*—that you are *what* you are—that I am not what you are—indeed that I am not *you.*"[22] This devil operates as assassin, muckraker, second-rate scholar, inadequate athlete. These, like most of us, are fascinated by greatness but resent the fact that greatness is not theirs. So they must cut others down to their size. If the other is a gifted child, peers, teachers, and even parents ridicule him and remind him of his place—so he won't get a big head, they say. With adults the devil is more sophisticated, bringing into line talented novices in whatever profession—or, if they won't conform, condemning them to lives of lonely eminence. Greeley had seen it all and felt it, almost from the beginning of his life.

Envy is so utterly debilitating that its object may feel he is losing his mind. He attempts to be friendly and generous toward others, yet they are vicious to him. He does not understand—how can he, when he himself has never felt the emotion that is directed his way?

Envy's enemy is the Angel of Nobility, that force which gives us a sense of self-worth *prior to* comparisons, which eliminates the need for comparisons. Nobility—one need not be a public figure to feel it—comes from naive self-confidence, the self-confidence that belongs to one who believes, truly believes, that at the heart of things is graciousness and love more powerful than he can imagine.

A second source of evil, Greeley wrote, is Alienation, the devil who whispers in our ear that we can be free, fully human, and fully ourselves if only we break with our past. "Get out or they will destroy you just like they destroy everyone else." Alienation demands our liberation from the biases of neighborhood, ethnic community, town, and church. "Graduate schools, professional schools, and the institutions that train artists, musicians, and actors, as well as the colleges that feed their graduates into the elite universities, all assume that it is necessary to deracinate the young person as a prelude to making him an intellectual."[23] Alienation was hard at work in the sixties, insisting in the exuberance of Vatican II that immigrant Catholicism be *totally* destroyed, making it fashionable for Americans to hate their native land as they protested its policy in Vietnam.

The Demon of Alienation is, of course, a liar. You think you can leave home, but home comes with you, whether you admit it or not. The Angel of Loyalty is honest about the matter: "Take a good hard look at home. . . . Let there be no doubt in your mind that it may be narrow, inflexible, repressive, but also be clear that it offered goodness, richness, warmth, and support."[24] Loyalty, like that of Yahweh toward his people, is not blind. For all its devotion, it remains critical and demanding.

And there is the Gnostic Demon, agile on his feet, coaxing his victims to be "with it," tantalizing them with the Real Secret that will make them superior to everyone else. People with education are the targets; they are the ones in contact with the journals—like *The New York Review of Books*, the *Partisan Review*, the *New Yorker*, and *Commonweal*—which disseminate the latest fads and fashions. The Gnostic Demon is abetted by the Demon of Righteousness, who persuades us that we are right, "so right that our righteousness unites us with the basic cosmic forces,"[25] and his cousin the Ideological Demon, who preys on intellectuals looking for system, order, neatness, and precision as a way of coping with the messy complexities of life. "Label it," he says, "and you will understand it." The Do-Good Devil is another close relative, perhaps the craftiest of the clan. He poses as an exemplary Christian, as the Angel of Generosity, and tempts us to force virtue on others (and therefore to control them) whether they want our virtue or not. These demons are out in full force these days and having the best of it with their opposite forces, the Angels of Wisdom, Humility, Pragmatism, and Freedom.

What *evil* has Andrew Greeley seen in his life? Envy, alienation, gnosticism, self-righteousness, ideologism, do-goodism are the names he chose for the forces responsible for his losses, for his present isolation somewhere between church and university. And how strong are these forces? Strong enough for him to say, "I do not expect to see much of what I stand for vindicated in my own lifetime."

So the devil, that symbol for evil more cunning and more powerful than we can imagine, has prevented him and will continue to prevent him from the victories he seeks. But not—and this is how he locates evil in the Judeo-Christian symbol system—from Ultimate Victory. At the core of the universe, far deeper than evil can penetrate, is relentless, passionate love. Jesus assured us that we were already on the winning side, on the side of graciousness, that life for all its tragedy is ultimately a comedy. One must, therefore, out of religious conviction if not out of temperament, trust the Eros in himself, not the Thanatos, listen to the hopeful impulses, not those that urge despair, risk love rather than hide in hatred. The myths of the tradition that began with Yahweh have it that such an attitude is in strict accord with the way things are.

Greeley, then, like the Irish whose religion has always enabled them to bounce back, will never quit. As he told me, "I believe in the triumph of good over evil in the long run, of light over darkness, of love over hate, of life over death. Since I believe that, I keep working." And when evil stalks him down again—as it surely will—not as a pig, a crocodile, or a billy goat, surely, but maybe as Fear or Pride or Privatism, he is likely to take the attitude of St. Dunstan, Abbot of Glastonbury. One day that venerable man was busy making a chalice when the devil appeared to him. Without batting an eye, Dunstan removed his pliers from the hot fire and clamped them on the nose of Satan, who ran off with a howl and was never seen around those parts again.

Mary.

How is it that one whose description in the New Testament is so limited has called forth so much in the West? All the great Gothic cathedrals, all the paintings, all the poetry, all the sculpture—what is the power of *The Mary Myth* (1977)?

Now that the immigrant Church has collapsed, of course, the lady of Bethlehem sleeps in deep oblivion among the Catholic elite who write books. (Indeed, when the *New York Times* asked Greeley for an article on Mary—even after he had begun his book on her—Greeley's first response was, "Mary who?") In immigrant Catholicism Mary stood for defense of the faith, stern moral obligation, and, above all, purity. She meant that necklines were not to be too low or hemlines too high. To that end, Catholics engaged in processions, novenas, and May crownings; and everyone carried a rosary even though it was often broken into several discrete pieces. Small wonder that the elites today have nothing at all to do with her.

But if one views the Christian symbol of Mary against the history of world religions, Greeley wrote, he will begin to glimpse the source of its power and he will know that it cannot remain dormant for long. *Mary speaks to the universal intuition of God as androgynous, as feminine as well as masculine.* The fertility and vegetation deities of premodern humans were hermaphrodites, or at least female one year and male the next. From these androgynous deities developed a panoply of gods and goddesses, differentiated males and females—not a denial of the notion that the Ultimate was bisexual but a result of the difficulty humans experienced in dealing with a deity that was masculine and feminine at the same time. We moderns have chosen out of convenience to address God as male, though there is no reason why we could not do exactly the opposite. "We have gods and goddesses, and underlying the vast systems of ritual and cult we build to those deities there is still the notion that in whatever is *really* Ultimate, the two are combined."[26]

When Yahweh elbowed his way into the history of Israel, he warned his followers against the fertility cults—and the pagan goddesses that were part of their rituals. *He*, Yahweh, was the one God; any other deities, male or female, were inferior to him and not to be taken seriously. From now on *he* would be responsible for fertility. And so it happened that goddesses vanished from the scene, though sexual differentiation remained part of the religious imagery of Israel: Yahweh became the spouse, the passionate, jealous, sexually aroused lover, in pursuit of Israel his bride.

A female deity did not return to the Judeo-Christian tradition until the second century A.D. when Mary emerged (it is not clear how) as an object of devotion. As a symbol of the feminine aspects of God, she was to become a rich source of inspiration—painted, carved, written to, sung about, labored for. Of the many themes contained in the mythology surrounding Mary, Greeley chose to analyze four: Madonna, Virgo, Sponsa, and Pietà. Each speaks to a basic human dilemma, each carries a conviction about reality that underwrites a particular response to that dilemma.

Motherhood is the most elemental dimension of sexual differentiation, said Greeley, the one from which all other dimensions are derived. Women bear children and nurse them; men do not. So women have appeared in religions as the bearers and nourishers of life, as the Great Mother, as the rich, primal, undisciplined Chaos brought into order by the masculine principle. Isis, Demeter, Juno,

Ishtar, Artemis, Artargatis, Rati—the list is endless. As Madonna, Mother of God, Mary is like these, but different. She is not chaotic like the raw primal mass, nor is the life she offers potentially destructive. She is not identified with fertility but is the servant of Yahweh and the channel of his fertility. As such she reveals the life-bestowing, life-protecting (and sometimes fiercely protecting) aspect of whatever is at the center of the universe.

The Madonna, then, the tender, proud, and strong woman of Michelangelo's *Holy Family,* speaks to our anxiety and fear and despair. These are the portents of defeat and death. But encountering motherhood as a sacrament, "we become aware of the overwhelming power of life. . . . We perceive it as a gift, a given, as something wildly, madly, exuberantly gratuitous."[27] We restructure our perception; behind it all there is a Giver, utterly beneficent, of whom even the lovely-eyed Madonna is but a pale reflection. Despair? Hardly. One is reborn in hope.

As Virgo, the second theme analyzed by Greeley, Mary is *not* a symbol of repression and frigidity, *not* a negative sex goddess, though for all practical purposes today that is the meaning of her virginity. Greeley left untouched the debate over the physical virginity of Mary and pursued the meaning of *virgin* in its origins and in its most sublime traditions. Here "fresh," "renewed," "restored" are the connotations of the word. Mary, Semper Virgo, symbolizes how one can be transformed spiritually by woman (a hard saying in a *Playboy* culture that worships orgasm as the only meaningful sexual interchange). As Madonna she gives life, and as Virgo, she restores life to the freshness of its first moment, taking the role of goddesses like Sophia, Kwan-yin, Shakti, and Tara, assuming the power of the moon, the lotus, and the lily.

Our weariness in dying relationships, our despair of becoming anything but the routine, destructive selves we are, are rooted in the belief that "things" simply do not change for the better. To this existential fatigue the Mary of ·El Greco's *Assumption,* bathing the whole world beneath her in new light, says, "You are wrong." It *is* possible to be inspired, to be renewed, to begin again. The virgin stands for a second chance. Her flowing blue and red robes serve to protect us, to underwrite the risk that opting for newness brings with it. One can trust, be loyal, restore his commitments.

Sponsa is an image of Mary that deals with death. As seduc-
tress, Sponsa "deprives us of the individuality and the rationality of
life in the frenzy of orgasmic release." She is like the fertility goddesses, like Lillith and Astarte and Aphrodite and Venus, but she is
not a goddess of orgies. She is, rather, the counterpart of Yahweh,
and he was far from those "lusty, roustabout, horny gods of
antiquity." Yahweh lusted not after our bodies but after our whole
selves, body and soul, and he did so in the context of sustained
commitment. "God as the pursuing male is an image that is open
and explicit in the Christian religion; but God as the woman, attractive, charming, fascinating, is also strongly pictured in the Christian heritage through the Mary myth. Mary reveals to us God as al-
luring, tempting, charming, arousing, attracting."[28]

It is the experience of loneliness, constriction, and alienation to
which Mary responds as Sponsa, said Greeley. In the midst of our
isolation there are times when we encounter something or somebody that invades our personality, demands our interest, arouses us.
We need to abandon ourselves to it, to him, to her, and to do so passionately. The ability to say, with the strength and passion of
Botticelli's *Daughter of Zion*, "Be it done unto me according to Thy
word" frees us, removes our inhibitions, eliminates the separation.
We die to ourselves, we give ourselves over to the passionate goodness of the universe. And we are able to celebrate.

The final abandonment of ourselves to the universe is, of
course, death. We return to that from which we came, and the
Mother who once gave us life now receives us back. How will she
greet us? Like the Indian goddess Kali, sitting amidst flames,
adorned with our hacked-off hands and heads, consuming the
entrails from our open bellies? Like the Aztec Ilamatecuhtli, who
castrated her son and ripped out his heart? Or like the *Pietà* of
Michelangelo, who received the dead body of Jesus in loving arms
and pressed his head against her soft breasts? How do we reunite
with the raw, elementary forces that produced us?

We humans are ambivalent about life and death. The goddesses who bring one also bear the other. What is the attitude of
whatever is "out there" to our return? The answer of the Christian
symbol system is captured in the expression of Mary the Pietà. She is
sad, deeply sorrowful, yet resigned and serene, anticipating some-

how the resurrection of her son. She reassures us that our return to the great cosmic processes from which we sprang will be serene and blissful, and she holds out the promise of life after that. In response, we give up our panic and defensiveness in the face of death. We accept it and experience, paradoxically, the phenomenon of rebirth.

Giving life, freshening it, attracting it back, receiving it tenderly. Madonna, Virgo, Sponsa, Pietà. In the Ultimate there is both male and female, pursuit and seduction, fatherhood and motherhood. As a result, we can, with the greatest assurance, give ourselves over to the rhythms of androgyny in each of us. Even more, we can face life and death with hope, trust, abandonment, and serenity.

The power of the Mary myth needs no further explanation.

Greeley summed it all up in his book *The New Agenda:* "It is not merely that the Yahwistic symbol system is hopeful, not merely even that it is the most hopeful symbol system the world has ever known. It is an absurdly hopeful symbol system; it represents hopefulness beyond which man simply can't go"[29]—Jesus inviting us to a party; Yahweh pursuing us relentlessly; the Spirit calling forth our diversity; Evil, for all its power, overcome; Mary nourishing us in life and holding us in death. The promise of these myths is very real to Greeley, explaining, I am sure, his persistence in the face of defeat and isolation.

Make no mistake about it. Greeley was devastated by the past and is pessimistic about the future. "American Catholicism is going through a period of emotional exhaustion," he wrote in *The New Agenda.* "Powerful currents of excitement, hope, disappointment, anger, frustration, and bitterness have swept the Church. Now our energies are spent. . . . We say to hell with it and try to forget the last decade like it was a bad dream." Immigrant Catholicism died a tragic, unnecessary death, but that is over, so "let the dead bury their dead."[30] The trouble is that the future is no less bleak than the past. American Catholicism will continue to erode until it becomes indistinguishable from any other American denomination.

But still he *hoped.* It was only a flicker, but it was nevertheless hope. "During the pause that we are in now—and it is likely to be a fairly long pause—some people in the Church will be engaged in

forming the New Agenda; indeed, I have the impression that this
New Agenda is already beginning to emerge, though very slowly
and hesitantly."[31]

The fashioners of the New Agenda are young and few in
number. (Our thoughts return to his baptism of the New Breed.) But
they are sober, realistic Catholic intellectuals, disciplined, nuanced,
sophisticated, willing to develop in their own good time. They have
none of the headstrong—and potentially destructive—enthusiasm of
the New Breed. They are not asking the old questions or, like the
majority of their peers, trying to provide new answers to the old
questions. They are, rather, formulating a new set of questions and
with them a new set of goals for American Catholicism in the
seventies and eighties.

In his book Greeley outlined their (really *his)* agenda for the
future. The first task was to abandon the question of old apologetic
Catholicism, "Can you prove the existence of God?" and ask
instead, "Can you tell me, by revealing your religious myths, who
your God is?" The next was to eliminate "Is the soul immortal?" in
favor of "Is life absurd if man does not survive?" Instead of waiting
for the end of the world—as one did in the old Church—or for the
New Age of the secular ideologies—as many did in the new
Church—the architects of the New Agenda advocated confidence in
graciousness and work *now* to renew the social order. In the old
Church it was "What does it take to be a practicing Catholic?" but
on the New Agenda it was "How can a human find ecstasy of the
spirit?"

Finally Greeley tackled the issue of the uniqueness of Catholicism. The old question was "How was the Church different from the
world?" and the old answer was "Radically different"; the Church
had the truth and the world did not. The new answer was that
nothing in the Church should differentiate it from the world. But
the fashioners of the New Agenda were on an altogether different
tack. They asked, "What *unique contribution* can the Church make
to the world?"

The answer Greeley offered was that the Church can provide
confidence. For in one sense Christianity has added nothing new to
the human condition. "Many of the writers of the early Church
refused to think of Christianity as a new religion but saw it rather as
an integration of everything that was good and true and virtuous

already existing in the world." "Catholic" meant precisely that—universal, pluralistic, comprehensive. The novel element in Christianity, if there is one, "is not the human aspirations that it responds to but the confidence of the response." What Christianity does is confirm and validate "the most powerful and most hopeful insights that constitute the very structure of human existence."[32] It says what man has always hoped for can be—no, *is*—true.

Greeley's work in theology—he speaks of *The New Agenda* and his books on the Judeo-Christian myths as "theological reflections"—has been influenced by young men such as John Hotchkin, John Shea, and David Tracy. Greeley is also a close friend of Hans Küng (whom he describes as a "conservative") and was, from 1969 to 1977, the American sociologist on the editorial board of the international theological journal *Concilium*. Gregory Baum, a fellow editor of *Concilium*, has described Greeley's theology as "popular" and "pastoral." Baum wrote, "Because he deals with difficult and often ticklish theological issues in a manner not customary in professional theology, his thought has not been given adequate attention." It is regrettable, said Baum; Greeley's orientation as a social scientist and his emphasis on the experimental aspects of religion represents "the most fruitful trend in American theology today."[33]

Whatever the judgments of professional theologians upon his work, I find that *The New Agenda*—and later books like *May the Wind Be at Your Back* (1975), *Death and Beyond* (1976), *The Great Mysteries: An Essential Catechism* (1976)—speaks to one of the central mysteries of Greeley's person: the stark contrast between despair and hope. I have heard close friends say he is a pessimistic man, and I have seen utter dejection on his face. I have read, too, in *The Sinai Myth*, a book about hope, quite an admission:

> Whether my life is pervaded by trust, joy, hopefulness, and a "radiation of graciousness" is a question about whose answer I must remain extremely skeptical. I am one of those who spent his earliest years in the midst of the Great Depression, a time filled with both the general tragedy of those years and the special ones in my own family. When I see movies of the little boy I was before the disaster of the Depression, I am astonished at what a joyous, spontaneous little child he was. I have to go to the very depths of my own consciousness to find even a trace of that joy remaining.

Seriousness, diligence, responsibility (why else would someone
write so many books?), a sober, at times grim dedication to work—
these are the realities that have filled my life as long as I can
remember. What else does one do, after all, when one has unconsciously accepted responsibility for the Great Depression?[34]

Greeley's intellect, he said, tells him to hope but his "primal,
semi- and unconscious emotions say something quite different." He
added, "As long as I live, I will need to make a constant effort
against the morose and melancholy proclivities of my
personality."[35]

But I have also asked Father Greeley to describe the Spirit and I
have watched him think back to the summers, before the depression,
when his family trundled off to Twin Lakes, and I have seen him
become a new man, one as bright and witty and hard to capture as
the impish ghost that brought him forth—counterpoint to the
somber worker that is his father's son. The sudden change brings to
mind an expression of Freud's, "Mental life consists of contradictions and pairs of contraries." And one of Chesterton's, a favorite of
Greeley's, "Hope is only a virtue when the situation is hopeless."
Extend the melancholy in this man; you also stretch the joy. Deepen
the despair; you raise the level of the hope. Make him more alone;
the core of the universe becomes more intimate.

If the Yahwistic myths reveal Greeley as a man of hope despite a
fear of losing all, they also speak to his experience with American
Catholicism in the sixties and early seventies. The immigrant
Church fell apart, he said, because of a lack of confidence, a failure
in nerve, a sense of worthlessness—because of self-hate. Self-hate is
what he saw when Catholic liberals refused the news of a coming
Catholic intelligentsia and when they read *The Education of
Catholic Americans* as a confirmation of failure. Self-hate is what he
saw in the American Irish, in the talented young of Beverly Hills
who could not bring themselves to write. Self-hate is what he saw
when priests attacked their priesthood, Catholics attacked their
Church, and Americans attacked their country. Self-hate is what he
saw preventing friendship and foreclosing sexual intimacy. Self-
hate says, I am no good, that to which I belong is no good, I am
utterly worthless.

From his wrestling with Old and New Testament scholarship Greeley isolated the core of the Judeo-Christian symbol system. One could not imagine a God or a world view more suited to the spiritual and existential needs of the American Catholics of his experience. Incredible, but there it was in Scripture—at the center of everything, pursuing you relentlessly, believing in your worth, is infinitely gracious love. Jesus' message was not so much a command to love as an allaying of fear: "It's all right to love." *That*—the Great Assurance—is the ultimate meaning of things, *that* is what you hit at rock bottom, *that* is "what it's all about," and *that* is what Andrew Greeley hopes will carry American Catholicism on its New Agenda through the seventies and eighties.

Epilogue:
Grand Beach, Michigan,
1973-1977

Home to Father Greeley is a big white house atop a sand dune on the eastern shore of Lake Michigan. "Anyone who is interested in the atmosphere in which a writer works must, I think, know about Grand Beach if he is to know about me," he says. His sister says the place is Twin Lakes—and all that Twin Lakes stood for—reincarnate. I'm glad I visited him there in the summers of 1973, 1974, and 1977.

My first impulse as a guest in Greeley's home is to stand on the edge of the bluff and simply *be* in the vast presence of lake and sky. Straight ahead, where the two merge, is the source of things—of wind, of weather, of waves, of good and bad fortune for Grand Beach. On the horizon to the left, barely visible, are three tiny pegs, all that remain here of Chicago's largest skyscrapers, and, farther on, smoke from Gary's industry. In the course of a day at Grand Beach guests come and go, doing what they please in this great open house. The phone, carried out to the edge of the cliff, rings and is answered. Cabin cruisers move slowly down the shore; speedboats pull skiers; and sailboats nearly capsize. Inside is a huge banner quoting Hillaire Belloc:

> Where're the Catholic sun does shine
> There's music and laughter and good red wine
> At least I've always found it so
> Benedicamus Domino

In the evening the sun has moved to the west and faces you directly, the bright glare of daytime now a peaceful gold. As darkness threatens from the rear, the color intensifies and promises more. Then a path appears on the stilled waters, straight from the setting sun to you. You may move, or even turn your back and walk away,

but the shimmering trail follows. Even before you face the lake
again, you know it is there. You know as well that each of those who
are with you, diverse though they be, sees a path, his or her own,
across the same Endless Waters to the same Eternal Fire.

When I first spoke with Father Greeley in July 1973, it was the
coldest day of summer. Chill winds sent breakers headlong into the
sandy cliff on which we sat and talked (and sometimes shouted
above the wind and waves). The level of the lake was high, and
Greeley's home was in trouble. Two doors down, the house of a
neighbor was halfway over the edge of the eroding dune. Beneath us,
lining Greeley's part of the beach, was a thick concrete wall, brand
new; beyond it huge gray bags of cement, looking like the backs of
small whales, blunted the force of waves before they struck the wall.
All day trucks dumped sand over the cliff to replace what the lake
had washed away. Sometimes it was blown right back.

Andrew Greeley at that moment was at the nadir of his career.
Of his past achievements he said, "That and fifty cents will get you a
ride on the CTA. The things that really mattered to me, the things in
which I invested a good deal of my selfhood, have all failed." The
University of Chicago had made its final refusal of a tenured position. The Archdiocese of Chicago would have no part of his wish for
occasional parish work. His home, all he had left, gave every
promise of succumbing to the lake. The waves of his dream were
quite literally after him.

"When someone writes *The Catholic Experience* in the year
2000," I asked him at that time, "how would you like to be
remembered?"

"As one of the theorists of the new Church," he said, "as one
who bridged the gap between immigrant Catholicism and Vatican
III." Then, constructing a wall of his own, he added: as one who
wouldn't "buy shit" or "repeat cliches," as a stubborn, independent, troublemaker who challenged people. Later he said, "The
older I get, the more I see in myself the 'old fellow' (his father) when
he told off Anton Cermak (mayor of Chicago)."

"Did your father often tell people off?"

"Yes. Oh, yes. Telling people off—perhaps a more gentle word
for it is integrity, a more flattering word. Refusing to knuckle under
to Cody is just the same thing as his refusing to knuckle under to
Cermak. And, in both cases, at considerable cost."

Through the remainder of 1973 Greeley's wall held. When I returned in 1974, his reconstituted cliff still stood, impressive but far from beautiful. His home was safe at last, but it was still a house built on sand. One needed great conviction and hard work to keep it, to keep oneself, together. A little clout with the Ole Fella wouldn't hurt either.

So Greeley's conviction smothered his despair, and he worked on. In the *National Catholic Reporter* he staked out another alternative within the American Church, that of "communal Catholicism."[1] The term described a collectivity committed to Catholicism as a world view and as a community, unembittered by its parochial roots (even proud to be Catholic), self-conscious in its attempt to grasp the human and religious meaning of being a Catholic in the United States. Communal Catholics were *not* organized and were supremely indifferent to the institutional Church. They could not care less about what bishops did or failed to do (save with regard to parochial schools, of which they were staunch supporters). In the midst of charismatic renewal and Marriage Encounter and liberation theology—all of which Greeley continued to dismiss—an amorphous collection of ex-New Breeders caught his eye and captured his hope. His critics said Greeley's portrait was no more than a "sociology of his friends," that communal Catholics were irresponsible vis-a-vis the Church, that their children would never remain Catholic. Greeley, of course, thought them more powerful, though he conceded that their influence would be felt only in the long run.

Greeley extended his ideas in a book bearing the name *The Communal Catholic* and hinted there at a "Catholic alternative to capitalism and socialism." Between agribusiness and the collective farm there is another option, he said: the peasant and his family on their own plot of land—or, in another context, the experiments by Volvo in Sweden. The Catholic alternative begins with the recognition that *Gemeinschaft* has not caved in to *Gesellschaft*. Thus it values family, neighborhood, the local, the "particularistic"; it is upset by the way both capitalism and socialism have damaged these. It stresses loyalty—as diffuse, informal, and communal a virtue as one can find. It is optimistic about human nature and is willing to trust it; large bureaucracies, therefore, whatever their ideological trappings, are not needed to manipulate it. In the words of British

economist E. F. Schumacher, "Small is beautiful." Greeley's alternative was not uniquely Catholic (Gandhi, for one, expressed similar views), but it did represent a perspective to which Catholicism
had been historically committed, both in the high tradition of papal
encyclicals and in the low tradition of parish and precinct. It is to
these historical roots of a Catholic social ethic that Greeley has
devoted *No Bigger Than Necessary* (1977).

In the summer of 1977 Greeley's makeshift levee was stronger
than ever, and his sand dune had been terraced, landscaped, lined
with stairs, and outfitted with an attractive wooden deck. His
personal wall was holding, too, and his despair was likewise
landscaped with hope. Suddenly the Spirit was back, sowing
playfulness, joy, and unprecedented diversity: children's stories,
novels, short stories, science fiction, screenplays, poetry, and
photography—all to be published by Father Greeley in the years
ahead.

Greeley's attraction to fiction began on a Saturday morning
when he wrote a children's story, *Nora Maeva and Sebi* (1976), at the
request of a publisher. He enjoyed himself so much that a trilogy of
novels is now in the works. First to appear will be *The Magic Cup*, a
sixth-century Irish version of the quest for the Holy Grail. In it the
Irish Lancelot, one Cormac MacDermot, ends up with the cup and
the girl, both of which stand for God. Greeley contends that a happy
ending to the quest is truer to the original Celtic myth than the
Arthurian saga, which was heavily influenced by French Manichae-
ism. *The Magic Cup* will be followed by *The Final Planet*, a story of
the Irish of the future. A creaky old spaceship of monks and nuns
presided over by an Irish mother, the Abbess Deirdre Cardinal Fitzgerald, seeks a resting place among the galaxies. It comes across
Zylong and the Abbess sends poor Seamus O'Neill to explore it—just
as its communitarian culture is about to blow up. Greeley's plans for
a third novel on the Irish of the present are still vague because, he says,
they are harder to face. In the meantime he is finishing another
children's story, *Liam and the New Dog*.

Parts of Greeley's novels and nearly all his short stories deal
with women. A few of the stories may turn up in *Ellery Queen
Mystery Magazine*, but most will appear in a book of songs and tales
to be called *Women I've Met* (or, depending on his nerve, *Women*

I've Known). Greeley's heroines are strong, beautiful, and troubled. His heroes do not possess them physically, but, rather, penetrate them spiritually, examining their deepest feelings, seeing their distress, and healing them. In the process the men are transformed by the power of the women and give themselves over to intuition, compassion, and play.

As late as 1974 Greeley had ruled out the possibility of poetry because he had "no ear for it." But in 1977 his first poems were published in *The Mary Myth*, and more were scheduled for *Faces of Ireland* and *Women I've Met*. The transition came suddenly. "I was flying home from Ireland after a fantastic period and was reading a book on Mary. I just began to hear music and words. I pulled out a pencil and wrote a poem." Most of Greeley's poetry, like most of his fiction, is about women—about Madonnas and bitches, tomboys and nymphs, wives and nuns, little girls and grandmothers. Why women now? An editor's idea, he says, admitting however that "maybe at the present age in my life I have some need to articulate more clearly my relation as a celibate with women."

Greeley is also taking pictures these days, another sign that his mood is on the upswing. A set of Irish landscapes appeared in a book of meditations, *May the Wind Be at Your Back*, a volume of which he is "inordinately proud." A portfolio of brightly painted homes was published in the *Chicago Tribune*, and shots of kids, grownups, stores, houses, and ethnic festivals will be scattered throughout *Neighborhood* and *Faces of Ireland*. Greeley is experimenting with television, too. For several months he was a guest critic on Chicago's educational channel, and he has just completed his first television script. It is about a beautiful space commander named Cassie, whose inner pain is reached and healed by an Irishman straight out of *Star Wars*.

Some of the new genres have come easily to Greeley, but others, the fiction in particular, have been difficult to master. Greeley's new outburst has not dampened his interest in survey research, thanks to the timely arrival of another muse, the conversational computer. "It releases the flair and creativity of the researcher in a way it's never been released before." But Greeley is through with what he calls "Catholic writing." "With *The Great Mysteries* and *The Mary Myth* I just exhausted myself. My stomach knots up every time I think of writing for the Catholic marketplace. Most of the people in the Catholic marketplace are priests and nuns, and priests and nuns bother the hell out of me." The only Catholic book left in the hopper is *The Making of the Pope, 19—*, "one-third sociology, one-third journalism, and one-third espionage." Its final chapters await the actual election of a successor to Paul VI.

Other signs of rebirth have lit up Greeley's world: the doubling between 1963 and 1974 in the percentage of American Catholics who receive Communion weekly, the desire in 1977 of some in his devastated underground parish to meet again. These signs of life bring me back to my first interview with Father Greeley, the one that found him so depressed. I recall asking him what season of life he was in, expecting something around September. But my question was wide of the mark. He said his life was not as grand as the huge cycle of a single year, but rather a succession of springs following autumns, of births following deaths.

When my questions were done that day, Paul Asciolla and I slid down the steep sandpile to the lake and surveyed the damage along the shore. Then we climbed back up to the house for a sauna and shower. In the meantime Father Greeley straightened up a bit and did some dictating. After the six o'clock news he made his favorite Caesar salad and served us dinner. A young couple arrived—the niece of Cardinal Meyer and her husband (the night before I had learned their nationalities long before their names). We chatted briefly over a dessert of Michigan blueberries, in season now, and cream. Then I said good-bye to Paul and to the young couple. Father Greeley walked me to my car, invited me back to Grand Beach, and wished me a safe trip. I looked to the west as the sun slipped into the water, sure to rise on the next day.

Notes

In the following notes all books and articles are by Andrew Greeley unless otherwise indicated. For bibliographical data on books, see the following section, "Books by Andrew M. Greeley."

Preface

1. *Priests in the United States*, p. 178.
2. *Sexual Intimacy*, pp. 99–100.
3. *Complaints Against God*, p. 65.
4. *Building Coalitions*, p. 13.
5. *Come Blow Your Mind with Me*, p. 226.
6. Peter Steinfels, "Andrew Greeley, Divine Sociologist," *Commonweal*, June 12, 1970, p. 286.

Chapter 2

1. *What a Modern Catholic Believes about the Church*, p. 18.
2. Ibid., p. 19.
3. *The Church and the Suburbs*, p. 9.
4. Ibid., p. 188.
5. Ibid., pp. 122–123.
6. "The Vanishing Hero," *America*, December 12, 1959, p. 350.
7. "No More Radicals?" *America*, March 19, 1960, p. 733.
8. *Strangers in the House* (rev. ed.), pp. 37 and 52.
9. Ibid., pp. 155–156 and 167.
10. *And Young Men Shall See Visions*, pp. 3–14, passim.
11. Ibid., pp. 32–58, passim.
12. Ibid., pp. 9–10.
13. Ibid., pp. 96 and 153.
14. Ibid., pp. 175–176.
15. *Letters to Nancy*, passim.
16. Ibid., pp. 35–36.
17. Ibid., pp. 45–53, passim.

18. Ibid., pp. 84–106, passim.
19. Ibid., p. 182.
20. *And Young Men Shall See Visions*, p. viii.
21. *The Church and the Suburbs*, p. 84.
22. "Quadrigesimo Anno and 'New' Problems," *America*, December 13, 1958, p. 340.
23. "Sociology of Religion," *The Critic*, August–September 1962, p. 12.
24. *Letters to Nancy*, p. 8.
25. "A Farewell to the New Breed," *America*, May 4, 1966, p. 801.
26. "A New Breed," *America*, May 23, 1964, p. 706.
27. Ibid.
28. Ibid.
29. Ibid., p. 707.
30. Ibid., pp. 707–708.
31. Ibid., p. 709.
32. Ibid.

Chapter 3

1. Denis Brogan, *U.S.A.: An Outline of the Country, Its People and Institutions* (London: Oxford University Press, 1941), p. 65. Quoted in John Tracy Ellis, "American Catholics and the Intellectual Life," *Thought*, autumn, 1955, p. 353.
2. Ellis, "American Catholics," p. 386.
3. Thomas F. O'Dea, *American Catholic Dilemma* (New York: Sheed and Ward, 1958), p. 151. For a summary of the debate, see Frank L. Christ and Gerard E. Sherry, *American Catholicism and the Intellectual Ideal* (New York: Appleton-Century-Crofts, 1959).
4. Robert H. Knapp and H. B. Goodrich, *Origins of American Scientists* (Chicago: University of Chicago Press, 1952); and Robert H. Knapp and Joseph J. Greenbaum, *The Young American Scholar: His Collegiate Origins* (Chicago: University of Chicago Press, 1953).
5. Knapp and Greenbaum, *The Young American Scholar*, p. 48.
6. Gerhard Lenski, *The Religious Factor* (Garden City, N. Y.: Doubleday, 1961).
7. *Religion and Career*, p. 52.
8. "Entering the Mainstream," *Commonweal*, October 2, 1964, p. 33.
9. George Shuster, "New Statistics on an Old Problem," *Commonweal*, January 10, 1964, p. 436.
10. John Donovan, "Creating Anti-Intellectuals?" *Commonweal*, October 2, 1964, p. 39.
11. *The Changing Catholic College*, p. 50, and *From Backwater to Mainstream*, pp. 24 and 93.
12. Donovan, "Creating Anti-Intellectuals?" p. 39.
13. R. W. Mack, R. J. Murphy, and S. Yellin, "The Protestant Ethic, Level of Aspiration and Social Mobility," *American Sociological Review*, June 1956, p. 295.
14. "The Protestant Ethic: Time for a Moratorium," *Sociological Analysis*, spring 1964, pp. 20–33.
15. Joseph Veroff, Sheila Feld, and Gerald Gurin, "Achievement Motivation and Religious Background," *American Sociological Review*, April 1962, pp. 205–217.

16. "The Protestant Ethic: Time for a Moratorium," pp. 30-31, passim.
17. *Religion and Career*, p. 133.
18. "Sociology of Religion," *The Critic*, August–September 1962, p. 12.
19. "The Protestant Ethic: Time for a Moratorium," p. 33.
20. "Entering the Mainstream," p. 35.
21. *Religion and Career*, p. 18.
22. *Commonweal*, March 29, 1963, p. 17.
23. "The Catholic Message and the American Intellectual," *The Critic*, April–May 1964, pp. 34–40, passim.

Chapter 4

1. Mary Perkins Ryan, *Are Parochial Schools the Answer?* (New York: Holt, Rinehart, and Winston, 1964).
2. Ibid., pp. 161–173, passim.
3. John A. O'Connor, "The Modest Proposal of Mary Perkins Ryan," *The Catholic World*, July 1964, p. 220.
4. Andrew Greeley and Peter Rossi, "The Effects of Catholic Education, Part I," *The Critic*, December 1963–January 1964, pp. 34–38.
5. Andrew Greeley, Peter Rossi, and Leonard Pinto, "The Effects of Catholic Education, Part II," *The Critic*, October–November 1964, p. 49.
6. Andrew Greeley and Peter Rossi, *The Education of Catholic Americans* (Doubleday Anchor ed.), p. 91.
7. Ibid., pp. 91–92.
8. Ibid., pp. 76 and 117.
9. Ibid., p. 125.
10. Ibid., p. 185.
11. Ibid., p. 208.
12. Ibid., p. 239.
13. "Are Schools Worth It?" *America*, September 19, 1964, p. 286.
14. Quoted in "News and Views," *Commonweal*, August 19, 1966, p. 514.
15. Edward B. Fiske, "Study Evaluates Catholic Schools," *New York Times*, July 25, 1966.
16. "News and Views," *Commonweal*, August 19, 1966, p. 514.
17. "Degrees of Devotion," *Time*, July 29, 1966, p. 49.
18. "Parochial Benefits," *Newsweek*, August 1, 1966, p. 77.
19. Robert Cross, "The Greeley-Rossi Report," *Commonweal*, September 16, 1966, pp. 577–579.
20. Daniel Callahan, "Review of *The Education of Catholic Americans*," *Commentary*, January 1967, p. 83.
21. Mary Perkins Ryan, "Review of *The Education of Catholic Americans*," *The Critic*, December 1966–January 1967, pp. 77–78.
22. "The Catholic Campus," *The Critic*, October–November 1966, p. 84.
23. *The Changing Catholic College*, p. 59.
24. Ibid., p. 86.
25. "The Catholic Campus," p. 88.
26. *The Changing Catholic College*, pp. 176 and 185.

27. Ibid., p. 202.
28. Ibid.
29. Ibid., p. 203.
30. Ibid., p. 204.
31. *The Hesitant Pilgrim*, p. 10.
32. Doris Grumbach, "Review of *The Changing Catholic College*," *The National Catholic Reporter*, April 17, 1968, p. 13.
33. Daniel Callahan, "Academic Standards Are Secular," *The Saturday Review*, March 16, 1968, p. 77.
34. "Myths and Fads in Higher Education," *America*, November 11, 1967, p. 545.
35. *The Student in Higher Education*, p. 24.
36. Ibid., p. 9.
37. Ibid., p. 59.
38. *From Backwater to Mainstream*, pp. 147 and 149.
39. "Catholic Alumni: Seven Years After," *America*, January 25, 1969, pp. 96 and 100.
40. *Recent Alumni and Higher Education*, p. 172.
41. "The New Urban Studies—A Word of Caution," *Educational Record*, Summer 1970, pp. 232–236.
42. *Recent Alumni and Higher Education*, pp. 178–183, passim.
43. "Review of *Report on Higher Education*," *Journal of Higher Education*, October 1971, p. 613.
44. *Can Catholic Schools Survive?*, p. 26.

Chapter 5

1. "The Temptation of the New Breed," *America*, May 22, 1965, pp. 750–752.
2. Ibid., p. 750.
3. Ibid., p. 752.
4. "A Farewell to the New Breed," *America*, June 4, 1966, pp. 801–804, passim.
5. "The New Community," *The Critic*, June–July 1966, pp. 37 and 34.
6. Ibid., p. 36.
7. Ibid., p. 37.
8. *Come Blow Your Mind with Me*, pp. 93–94.
9. *The Hesitant Pilgrim*, p. 7.
10. Quoted by Peter Steinfels, "Andrew Greeley, Divine Sociologist," *Commonweal*, June 12, 1970, p. 286.
11. *The Hesitant Pilgrim*, p. 12.
12. Ibid., pp. 16–27, passim.
13. "Catholicism Midwest Style," *America*, February 12, 1966, p. 223.
14. *The Hesitant Pilgrim*, p. xvii.
15. *The Catholic Experience* (Image Books ed.), p. 49.
16. Ibid.
17. Ibid., pp. 46 and 62.
18. Ibid., p. 44.
19. Ibid., p. 63.

20. Ibid., pp. 74–76.
21. Ibid., p. 103.
22. Ibid., p. 104.
23. Ibid., p. 158.
24. Ibid., p. 163.
25. Ibid., p. 173.
26. Ibid., p. 180.
27. Ibid., p. 215.
28. Ibid., p. 280.
29. Ibid., p. 282.
30. "What Do the People Say?" *Commonweal*, October 11, 1968, p. 53.
31. "Roman Catholics: Clouded Future," *Time*, January 10, 1969, p. 63.
32. *Come Blow Your Mind with Me*, p. 122.
33. Ibid., p. 123.
34. Ibid., p. 129.
35. Ibid., pp. 132–133.
36. Ibid., pp. 134 and 133.
37. Ibid., p. 135.
38. Unpublished manuscript.
39. *Catholic Schools in a Declining Church*, p. 321.
40. Personal document.
41. Condensed from "The First Papal Press Conference—A Vision," *The Critic*, February–March 1969, pp. 14–19. Reprinted in *Come Blow Your Mind with Me*, pp. 222–233.

Chapter 6

1. Harvey Cox, *The Secular City* (New York: Macmillan, 1965), pp. 2 and 4.
2. Ibid., p. 4.
3. Daniel Callahan, ed., *The Secular City Debate* (New York: Macmillan, 1966) pp. 107 and 103.
4. Ibid., pp. 104 and 108.
5. Ibid., p. 115.
6. Ibid., pp. 124 and 126.
7. Thomas Altizer and William Hamilton, *Radical Theology and the Death of God* (Indianapolis: Bobbs-Merrill, 1966), p. 5.
8. Martin Marty, Stuart Rosenberg, and Andrew Greeley, *What Do We Believe?* pp. 117 and 123.
9. Ibid., p. 149.
10. Ibid., p. 153.
11. "There's a New-Time Religion on Campus," *New York Times Magazine*, June 1969. Reprinted in *Come Blow Your Mind with Me*, p. 26.
12. Ibid., p. 29.
13. Ibid., p. 30.
14. Ibid., pp. 31–32.
15. Ibid., pp. 33–35, passim.

16. Ibid., p. 35.

17. Guy A. Swanson, "Modern Secularity," in Donald Cutler (ed.), *The Religious Situation* (Boston: Beacon, 1968), pp. 811–813. Quoted in *Religion in the Year 2000*, pp. 32–34.

18. *Religion in the Year 2000*, p. 25.

19. David Martin, "Toward Eliminating the Concept of Secularization," in Julius Gould (Ed.), *Penguin Survey of the Social Sciences* (Baltimore, Md.: Penguin, 1965). Quoted in *Religion in the Year 2000*, p. 50.

20. *Religion in the Year 2000*, p. 51.

21. Ibid., pp. 68–69.

22. Ibid., p. 70.

23. Ibid., pp. 171 and 173.

24. "Superstition, Ecstasy, and Tribal Consciousness," *Social Research*, Summer 1970, p. 204.

25. "Religion Still Has Tenure," *The New York Times*, October 17, 1970.

26. *The Denominational Society*, p. iii, and *Unsecular Man*, p. 55.

27. *The Denominational Society*, p. 236.

28. Bronislaw Malinowski, "Magic, Science, and Religion, "in Joseph Needham (Ed.), *Science, Religion, and Reality* (New York: Macmillan, 1925), p. 82. Quoted in *The Denominational Society*, p. 36.

29. *Unsecular Man*, p. 1.

30. Ibid., p. 19.

31. Robert Nisbet, *The Social Bond* (New York: Knopf, 1970), pp. 303 and 308. Quoted in *Unsecular Man*, p. 23.

32. Clifford Geertz, "Religion as a Cultural System," in Donald Cutler (Ed.), *The Religious Situation*, (Boston: Beacon, 1968), p. 667. Quoted in *Unsecular man*, p. 58.

33. *Unsecular Man*, p. 93.

34. Henri Frankfort, *Before Philosophy* (Baltimore, Md.: Penguin, 1949), p. 15. Quoted in *Unsecular Man*, p. 89.

35. Ibid.

36. Piccard, quoted in *Unsecular Man*, pp. 74–75.

37. *Unsecular Man*, p. 75.

38. Ibid., p. 74.

39. *Unsecular Man*, pp. 248 and 247.

40. *Ecstasy*, pp. 1–2.

41. Ibid., pp. 121–122.

42. Ibid., p. 122.

43. Reprinted with permission of author.

44. *Ecstasy*, p. 4.

45. Ibid.

46. William C. McCready and Andrew M. Greeley, *The Ultimate Values of the American Population*, p. 156.

47. Ibid.

48. Jeffrey Hadden (Ed.), "Review Symposium: The Sociology of Religion of Andrew M. Greeley," *Journal for the Scientific Study of Religion*, March 1974, pp. 75–97, passim.

49. Ibid., p. 75.

50. "Andrew Greeley Replies to His Critics," *Journal for the Scientific Study of Religion*, June 1974, p. 230.
51. Ibid., p. 231.

Chapter 7

1. *Unsecular Man*, p. 1.
2. *Uncertain Trumpet*, pp. 25–55, passim.
3. *The Hesitant Pilgrim*, p. 241.
4. Ibid., p. 117.
5. *Uncertain Trumpet*, p. 36.
6. Ibid., p. 80.
7. Ibid., pp. 112–113.
8. Ibid., p. 114.
9. Ibid., p. 95.
10. Ibid., p. 101.
11. *The Hesitant Pilgrim*, p. 238.
12. *Uncertain Trumpet*, pp. 39 and 35.
13. Ibid., p. 23.
14. "Greeley on Greeley and Bishops," *National Catholic Reporter*, September 28, 1973, p. 15.
15. *Priests in the United States*, p. 90.
16. "Greeley on Greeley and Bishops," p. 15, and interview.
17. "The State of the Priesthood," *National Catholic Reporter*, February 18, 1972, p. 7.
18. Ibid., p. 15.
19. "After the Synod," *America*, November 20, 1971, p. 424.
20. "The State of the Priesthood," p. 10.
21. *Priests in the United States*, p. 107.
22. Ibid., pp. 196 and 198.
23. Ibid., p. 197.
24. Ibid., pp. 198–199.
25. Ibid., p. 204.
26. Ibid., p. 109.

Chapter 8

1. "The Rediscovery of Diversity," *The Antioch Review*, Fall 1971, p. 345.
2. Ibid., pp. 359–360.
3. Ibid., pp. 343–344.
4. Ibid., pp. 348–349.
5. Ibid., p. 350.
6. *Why Can't They Be Like Us?*, p. 19.
7. "Intellectuals as an Ethnic Group," *New York Times Magazine*, July 7, 1970.
8. Ibid.

9. "Civil Religion and Ethnic Americans," *Worldview*, February 1973, p. 24.

10. Ibid., p. 27.

11. Ibid., pp. 23–24.

12. "Malice in Wonderland: Misperceptions of the Academic 'Elite," *Change*, September–October 1970, pp. 32–39.

13. "Making It in America: Ethnic Groups and Social Status," *Social Policy*, September–October 1973, pp. 24 and 28.

14. "The New Ethnicity and Blue Collars," *Dissent*, Winter 1972, p. 276.

15. Richard Schermerhorn, *Comparative Ethnic Relations* (New York: Random House, 1969), p. 123. Quoted in *Ethnicity in the United States*, p. 291.

16. *Ethnicity in the United States*, pp. 315 and 297.

17. *Why Can't They Be Like Us?*, p. 33.

18. Ibid.

19. *Ethnicity in the United States*, p. 300.

20. Ibid., p. 296.

21. Ibid., p. 300–301.

22. Ibid., p. 300.

23. Ibid., p. 302.

24. "Report to the Ford Foundation, Second Year," *NORC Paper*, December 1972, pp. 4.

25. *That Most Distressful Nation*, p. xxvi.

26. Ibid., pp. vii and 29.

27. Ibid., pp. 34 and 36.

28. Ibid., p. 39.

29. Ibid., p. 48.

30. Ibid., p. 56.

31. Ibid., pp. 104–107, passim.

32. Ibid., p. 135.

33. Ibid., p. 249.

34. Reprinted with permission of the author.

35. In a communication to me Professors Shils and Janowitz confirmed that the Department of Sociology found Greeley's qualifications as a scholar "inadequate." They added that the *Voices* article was "hardly a responsible account."

36. Andrew Segal and Don Rose "Why No Protests over Andy Greeley?" *Hyde Park–Kenwood Voices*, July 1973.

37. Letter of July 18, 1973, addressed to the *Hyde Park–Kenwood Voices*.

38. "The 'Religious Factor' and Academic Careers: Another Communication," *American Journal of Sociology*, March 1973, p. 1253.

39. "Review of *Real Lace*," *The Critic*, March–April 1974, pp. 59–60.

40. *The Communal Catholic*, pp. 70 and 72.

41. "Confessions of a Loud-Mouthed Irish Priest," *Social Policy*, May–June 1974, p. 4.

42. Ibid., pp. 4 and 6.

43. Ibid., p. 7.

44. Ibid., p. 11.

45. Ibid.

Chapter 9

1. William Van Etten Casey, S.J., "Thank You, Dan and Phil," *Holy Cross Quarterly*, January 1971, p. 3.
2. *Commonweal*, quoted in David J. O'Brien, "The Berrigans and America," *Holy Cross Quarterly*, January 1971, p. 53.
3. Francine du Plessix Gray, "Acts of Witness," *The New Yorker*, March 14, 1970, pp. 44ff., and *Divine Disobedience* (New York: Knopf, 1970). Gary Wills, "A Revolution in the Church," *Playboy*, November 1971, pp. 159ff.
4. Noam Chomsky, "On the Limits of Civil Disobedience," *Holy Cross Quarterly*, January 1971, p. 27.
5. "The Berrigans: Phrenetic?," *Holy Cross Quarterly*, January 1971, p. 17.
6. "Turning Off the People," *The New Republic*, June 27, 1970, pp. 14–15.
7. American Political Science Association, September 10, 1971. See "Political Attitudes among American White Ethnics," *The Public Opinion Quarterly*, Summer 1972, pp. 213–220.
8. Noam Chomsky, "On the Limits of Civil Disobedience," *Holy Cross Quarterly*, January 1971, pp. 22–31.
9. "A Scrapyard for the Daley Organization?" *Bulletin of the Atomic Scientists*, February 1973, p. 12.
10. Ibid., p. 11.
11. "Take Heart from Heartland," *The New Republic*, December 12, 1970, p. 17.
12. "A Scrapyard for the Daley Organization?" p. 11.
13. "Take Heart from Heartland," p. 19.
14. "A Scrapyard for the Daley Organization?" p. 9.
15. Ibid.
16. *Building Coalitions*, pp. 24 and 25.
17. Ibid., pp. 88–90.
18. Ibid., p. 232.
19. Andrew S. McFarland, *Power and Leadership in Pluralist Systems* (Stanford, Calif.: Stanford University Press, 1969). Quoted in *Building Coalitions*, p. 229.
20. *Building Coalitions*, pp. 229–230.
21. Ibid., p. 235.
22. Ibid., pp. 247–248.
23. Andrew Greeley and Paul B. Sheatsley, "Attitudes Toward Racial Integration," *Scientific American*, December 1971, pp. 13–19; Andrew Greeley and Paul B. Sheatsley, "Changing Attitudes of Whites Toward Blacks," *The Public Opinion Quarterly*, fall 1972, pp. 432–433.
24. *Building Coalitions*, pp. 320–321.
25. Ibid., p. 321n.
26. "For a Black Vice-President," *New York Times Magazine*, September 19, 1971.
27. Ibid., p. 35.
28. Universal Press Syndicate, August 6, 1974.
29. Ibid., July 30, 1974.
30. Ibid., 1974–1976.
31. Ibid., October 29, 1974.

32. Michael Novak, "The Communal Catholic," *Commonweal*, January 17, 1975, p. 321.
33. Mike Royko, "All a Matter of Experience," *Chicago Daily News*, March 11, 1975.
34. Universal Press Syndicate, December 21, 1974.
35. David Martin, "R.D. Laing: Psychiatry and Apocalypse," *Dissent*, June 1971, pp. 250-251.
36. "Nothing But a Loud-Mouthed Irish Priest," in Gregory Baum (Ed.), *Journeys* (New York: Paulist Press, 1975), p. 196.
37. "Moynihan and Drucker—Demythologizers," *Educational Record*, summer 1969, pp. 319 and 325.

Chapter 10

1. *Love and Play*, p. 21.
2. *The Life of the Spirit*, pp. 27-28.
3. *A Future to Hope In*, p. 107.
4. Ibid., pp. 125-126.
5. *The Life of the Spirit*, p. 22.
6. *The Friendship Game*, pp. 25 and 159.
7. Ibid., p. 18.
8. Ibid., pp. 27-28.
9. Ibid., p. 53.
10. Ibid., p. 69.
11. Ibid., p. 74.
12. Ibid., p. 60.
13. Ibid., p. 61.
14. Ibid., p. 115.
15. Ibid., pp. 109-110.
16. Ibid., pp. 18 and 96.
17. Ibid., p. 129.
18. *Ecstasy*, p. 52.
19. *The Friendship Game*, p. 125.
20. *Come Blow Your Mind with Me*, p. 134.
21. *The New Agenda* (Doubleday Image Ed.), pp. 148-149.
22. Ibid., p. 124.
23. Ibid., pp. 125 and 127.
24. Ibid., p. 127.
25. *Sexual Intimacy*, p. 85.
26. Ibid., pp. 86 and 100.
27. Ibid., pp. 99-100.
28. Ibid., p. 101.
29. Ibid., pp. 104-108, passim.
30. Ibid., pp. 119 and 121.
31. Ibid., p. 126.
32. *The New Agenda*, p. 141.
33. *Sexual Intimacy*, pp. 150 and 191-192.

34. Ibid., p. 198.
35. *Love and Play*, p. 64.
36. Ibid., p. 66.
37. Ibid., pp. 131 and 134.
38. Ibid., p. 161.
39. Ibid., p. 181.
40. Ibid., p. 7.
41. Ibid., p. 30.

Chapter 11

1. "Myths, Symbols and Rituals in the Modern World," *The Critic,* December 1961–January 1962, p. 18.
2. "Myths, Meaning and Vatican III," *America,* December 19, 1970, pp. 538–542; "Religious Symbolism, Liturgy, and Community," *Concilium,* February 1971, pp. 59–69.
3. *The Jesus Myth*, p. 25.
4. Ibid., pp. 32–33.
5. "Would He Be Crucified?" *Chicago Daily News,* April 6–7, 1974.
6. *The Jesus Myth*, p. 44.
7. Ibid., p. 69.
8. Ibid., p. 52.
9. Ibid., p. 72.
10. "The Holy Week Biography: Our Readers Respond," *Chicago Daily News,* April 13–14, 1974.
11. *The Sinai Myth*, p. 12.
12. Ibid., p. 43.
13. Ibid., pp. 54–55.
14. *What a Modern Catholic Believes about God*, p. 57.
15. Ibid., p. 61.
16. *The Sinai Myth*, p. 62.
17. Ibid., p. 216.
18. Universal Press Syndicate, January 21, 1975.
19. *The Touch of the Spirit*, p. 30.
20. Ibid., pp. 22–23.
21. *The Communal Catholic*, p. 155.
22. *The Devil, You Say!*, p. 35.
23. Ibid., p. 49.
24. Ibid., p. 53.
25. Ibid., p. 78.
26. *The Mary Myth*, p. 55.
27. Ibid., p. 121.
28. Ibid., pp. 157, 161, and 163–64.
29. *The New Agenda*, p. 90.
30. Ibid., pp. 32 and 39.
31. Ibid., p. 34.

32. Ibid., p. 267
33. Gregory Baum, introduction to *The New Agenda*, pp. 11 and 19.
34. *The Sinai Myth*, p. 117.
35. Ibid., pp. 118 and 126–127.

Epilogue

1. "The Next Ten Years," *National Catholic Reporter*, November 1, 1974, pp. 9–12.

Books by Andrew M. Greeley

1959
The Church and the Suburbs. New York: Sheed and Ward.

1961
Strangers in the House. New York: Sheed and Ward.

1963
Religion and Career. New York: Sheed and Ward.

1964
And Young Men Shall See Visions. New York: Sheed and Ward.
Letters to Nancy. New York: Sheed and Ward.
Priests for Today and Tomorrow. Notre Dame, Ind.: Ave Maria Press.

1966
The Education of Catholic Americans (with Peter H. Rossi).
    Chicago: Aldine.
The Hesitant Pilgrim. New York: Sheed and Ward.

1967
The Catholic Experience. Garden City, N. Y.: Doubleday.
The Changing Catholic College. Chicago: Aldine.

1968
The Crucible of Change. New York: Sheed and Ward.
The Student in Higher Education. New Haven, Conn.:
    The Hazen Foundation.

Uncertain Trumpet. New York: Sheed and Ward.
What Do We Believe? (with Martin E. Marty and Stuart E.
    Rosenberg). New York: Meredith.

1969
From Backwater to Mainstream. New York: McGraw-Hill.
A Future to Hope In. Garden City, N. Y.: Doubleday.
Life for a Wanderer. Garden City, N. Y.: Doubleday.
Religion in the Year 2000. New York: Sheed and Ward.

1970
Can Catholic Schools Survive? (with William E. Brown).
    New York: Sheed and Ward.
The Friendship Game. Garden City, N. Y.: Doubleday.
The Life of the Spirit. Kansas City, Mo.: National Catholic
    Reporter.
New Horizons for the Priesthood. New York: Sheed and Ward.
Recent Alumni and Higher Education (with Joe L. Spaeth).
    New York: McGraw-Hill.
Youth Asks, Does God Still Speak? Camden, N. J.: T. Nelson.

1971
Come Blow Your Mind with Me. Garden City, N. Y.: Doubleday.
Complaints Against God. Chicago: Thomas More.
The Jesus Myth. Garden City, N. Y.: Doubleday.
The Touch of the Spirit. New York: Herder and Herder.
What a Modern Catholic Believes about God. Chicago: Thomas More.
Why Can't They Be Like Us? New York: E. P. Dutton.

1972
The Catholic Priest in the United States. Washington, D.C.:
    United States Catholic Conference.
The Denominational Society. Glenview, Ill.: Scott, Foresman.
Jesus Now. Chicago: Thomas More.
Priests in the United States. Garden City, N. Y.: Doubleday.
The Sinai Myth. Garden City, N. Y.: Doubleday.
That Most Distressful Nation. New York: Quadrangle.
Unsecular Man. New York: Schocken.
What a Modern Catholic Believes about the Church.
    Chicago: Thomas More.

1973
The New Agenda. Garden City, N. Y.: Doubleday.
Sexual Intimacy. Chicago: Thomas More.

1974
Building Coalitions. New York: New Viewpoints.
The Devil, You Say! Garden City, N. Y.: Doubleday.
Ecstasy. Englewood Cliffs, N. J.: Prentice-Hall.
Ethnicity in the United States. New York: Wiley-Interscience.

1975
Love and Play. Chicago: Thomas More.
May the Wind Be at Your Back. New York: Seabury.
Reconnaissance into the Sociology of the Paranormal (with William
    C. McCready). Beverly Hills, Calif.: Sage Publications.

1976
Catholic Schools in a Declining Church (with William C. McCready
    and Kathleen McCourt). Mission, Kans.: Sheed and Ward.
The Communal Catholic. New York: Seabury.
Death and Beyond. Chicago: Thomas More.
Ethnicity, Denomination, Inequality. Beverly Hills, Calif.:
    Sage Publications.
The Great Mysteries. New York: Seabury.
Nora Maeve and Sebi, New York: Paulist.
The Ultimate Values of the American Population (with William
    C. McCready). Beverly Hills, Calif.: Sage Publications.

1977
The American Catholic. New York: Basic.
Christ for All Seasons (with Nancy McCready). Chicago:
    Thomas More.
The Mary Myth. New York: Seabury.
Neighborhood. New York: Seabury.
No Bigger than Necessary. New York: New American Library.
An Ugly Little Secret. Mission, Kans.: Sheed, Andrews,
    and McMeel.

Index